Merge in the Mind-Bra

MW01010364

The main theme of this book is Merge, the basic operation of human language. The Merge operation has been assumed, at least from the mid-1990s, to be the fundamental core operation of human language syntax that is responsible for its Basic Property, i.e., that human language generates a pair of interpretations (sensorimotor, conceptual-intentional)—roughly, a "sound-meaning pair"—for each of infinitely many hierarchically structured expressions. Various complex grammatical devices that had been proposed in the literature to account for an intricate array of linguistic phenomena have been shown to be reducible to this simple formal operation, as it interacts with general computational principles. Accordingly, the precise understanding of Merge is of utmost importance for our theory of human language.

The present volume is a collection of nine articles that I wrote in the past several years (and, in most cases, have published in various places), all of which focus on the operation Merge, its nature, its interactions with other components of grammar, and its implementations in the brain. The papers are divided into two parts. The papers in Part I are investigations of Merge (and its related postulates) in theoretical syntax. The papers collected in Part II, on the other hand, are concerned with the neuroscience of Merge, i.e., they deal with how this fundamental operation is implemented in the brain. The book as a whole—though it's a collection of articles—offers a coherent and focused attempt at understanding the nature of Merge, from two distinct but related angles—theoretical syntax and the neurosciences.

Naoki Fukui received his Ph.D. in linguistics from MIT in 1986. Since then, he has been teaching at various places, both in the US and in Japan, including the University of Pennsylvania, the University of California, Irvine, Harvard University, and is currently teaching at Sophia University in Tokyo. He has published *Theoretical Comparative Syntax* in the Routledge Leading Linguists series as well as a number of other books and articles both in English and Japanese.

Routledge Leading Linguists

Edited by Carlos P. Otero, *University of California, Los Angeles, USA*

For a full list of titles in this series, please visit www.routledge.com

Merge in the Mind-Brain

Essays on Theoretical Linguistics and the Neuroscience of Language

Naoki Fukui

Routledge
Taylor & Francis Group

NEW YORK AND LONDON

First published 2017
by Routledge
711 Third Avenue, New York, NY 10017

and by Routledge
2 Park Square, Milton Park, Abingdon, Oxon OX14 4RN

Routledge is an imprint of the Taylor & Francis Group, an informa business

Library of Congress Cataloging-in-Publication Data
Names: Fukui, Naoki, author. | Fukui, Naoki, editor.
Title: Merge in the Mind-brain : essays on theoretical linguistics and the neuroscience of language / by Naoki Fukui.
Description: New York : Routledge, [2017] | Series: Routledge leading linguists; 23 | Includes bibliographical references and index.
Identifiers: LCCN 2016051226 | ISBN 9781138216143 (hardback : alk. paper)
Subjects: LCSH: Grammar, Comparative and general—Syntax. | Dependency grammar. | Brain—Psychophysiology. | Cognition and language. | Neurolinguistics.
Classification: LCC P291 .F76 2017 | DDC 410—dc23
LC record available at https://lccn.loc.gov/2016051226

ISBN: 978-1-138-21614-3 (hbk)
ISBN: 978-1-315-44280-8 (ebk)

Typeset in Sabon
by Apex CoVantage, LLC

Contents

PART II
Merge in the Brain   155

Original Publication Details

Chapter 1: Naoki Fukui. 2011. Merge and bare phrase structure. In C. Boeckx, ed., *The Oxford Handbook of Linguistic Minimalism*, pp. 73–95, Oxford University Press. Reprinted by permission from the Oxford University Press.

Chapter 2: Naoki Fukui and Hiroki Narita. 2012. Merge and (a)symmetry. An extended written-up version of the presentation at the Kyoto Conference on Biolinguistics (March, 2012). Appeared in this volume for the first time.

Chapter 3: Takaomi Kato, Masakazu Kuno, Mihoko Zushi, Hiroki Narita, and Naoki Fukui. 2013. Generalized search and cyclic derivation by phase: A preliminary study. *Sophia Linguistica* 61, pp. 203–222. Reprinted by permission from the Sophia Linguistic Institute for International Communication.

Chapter 4: Naoki Fukui and Hiroki Narita. 2014. Merge, labeling, and projection. In A. Carnie, D. Siddiqi, and Y. Sato, eds., *Routledge Handbook of Syntax*, pp. 3–23, Routledge. Reprinted by permission from Routledge.

Chapter 5: Naoki Fukui. 2015. A note on strong vs. weak generation in human language. In A.J. Gallego and D. Ott, eds., *50 Years Later: Reflections on Chomsky's Aspects*, pp. 125–131, MIT Working Papers in Linguistics. Reprinted by permission from MITWPL.

Chapter 6: Hiroki Narita, Hironobu Kasai, Takaomi Kato, Mihoko Zushi, and Naoki Fukui. 2016. 0-Search and 0-Merge. Appeared in this volume for the first time.

Chapter 7: Kazuki Iijima, Naoki Fukui, and Kuniyoshi L. Sakai. 2009. The cortical dynamics in building syntactic structures of sentences: An MEG study in a minimal-pair paradigm. *NeuroImage* 44, 1387–1396. Reprinted by permission from *NeuroImage*.

Chapter 8: Shinri Ohta, Naoki Fukui, and Kuniyoshi L. Sakai. 2013. Syntactic computation in the human brain: The degree of merger as a key factor. *PLoS ONE* 8(2): e56230. doi: 10.1381/journal.pone.0056230.

Chapter 9: Shinri Ohta, Naoki Fukui, and Kuniyoshi L. Sakai. 2013. Computational principles of syntax in the regions specialized for language: Integrating theoretical linguistics and functional neuroimaging. *Frontiers in Behavioral Neuroscience* 7: 1–13. doi: 10.3389/fnbeh. 2013.00204.

Introduction

Shortly after I moved from the University of California, Irvine, to Sophia University in Tokyo, I came to know Kuniyoshi Sakai of the University of Tokyo and started to work with him and his colleagues on the neuroscience of human language. Kuni—who has a strong background both in physics and biology—is one of the (very) few neuroscientists in Japan (or in any country, for that matter) who hold a deep respect for the field of generative linguistics as an emerging science, and, consequently, he has a very serious interest in what theoretical linguistics can offer for the neuroscience of human language. I enjoyed very much working with him, and our collaboration developed into a research project, with Kuni as the PI, supported by the Japan Science and Technology Agency (JST) in the category CREST (Core Research in Evolutionary Science and Technology)—which was in fact supported by the Japan Agency for Medical Research and Development (AMED) for its last year due to organizational reforms of the sponsoring institutions. The project lasted for five and a half years (from October 2010 to March 2016), during which I played a role in coordinating the project team's linguistic theory group and produced, in collaboration with other members of the team, various articles both in the areas of theoretical syntax and the neuroscience of language. The articles collected in this volume are mostly those that I wrote during the AMED-CREST period (with a few exceptions to be indicated next).

The main theme throughout the articles contained in the book is *Merge*, the basic operation of human language. The Merge operation has been assumed, at least from the mid-1990s, to be the fundamental core operation of human language syntax that is responsible for its Basic Principle—i.e., that human language generates a pair of interpretations (sensorimotor, conceptual-intentional)—roughly, a "sound-meaning pair"—for each of infinitely many hierarchically structured linguistic expressions. Various complex grammatical devices that had been proposed in the literature to account for an intricate array of linguistic phenomena have been shown to be reducible to this simple formal operation, as it interacts with general computational principles as well as with independently motivated extraneous conditions imposed by the two performance systems—i.e., the interface conditions on sensorimotor and conceptual-intentional interfaces. Accordingly, the precise understanding of Merge is of utmost importance for the theory of human language—particularly for the theory of its computational system.

The present volume is a collection of some of my recent papers on Merge—investigated from two related but distinct levels of abstraction. One is at the level of a theoretical model that explains various observations about Merge—its formal nature and its interactions with other principles of grammar. This is theoretical syntax. The other level, which has become increasingly important for the study of language, is neural implementations of the abstract syntactic operation—the neuroscience of human language. These two areas belong to human biology in principle, and any constructive approach to the study of human thought and its expression relies on this assumption. But unification of the sciences of the brain and higher mental faculties, the faculty of language among them, is a truly distant goal at present. Thus linguistics and neurosciences have been separated from each other for a long time, and linguistic research has been conducted quite independently of the findings in neurosciences and vice versa. The situation has been slowly changing over the past quarter century due in part to the development of imaging technologies and also because of the radical simplification of linguistic theory that has taken place in the past twenty years or so. Thus, in the past decade, theoretical linguists finally started to pay serious attention to experimental results in the neuroscience of language when they work on problems in, say, syntax. This book represents one of the first few works by a theoretical linguist that tries to combine insights from the two distinct, though fundamentally related, disciplines in an attempt to get a deeper understanding of the nature of Merge (and human language syntax in general).

The articles are divided into two parts. The papers in Part I: Merge in the Mind (Chapter 1–Chapter 6), are investigations of Merge (and its related postulates) in theoretical syntax. The works collected in Part II: Merge in the Brain (Chapter 7–Chapter 9), on the other hand, are concerned with the neuroscience of Merge—i.e., they deal with how this fundamental operation is implemented in the brain. The book as a whole is intended to offer a coherent and focused attempt at understanding the nature of Merge from two distinct but clearly related angles: theoretical syntax and the neuroscience of the human brain. Brief summaries of each chapter will follow.

Part I: Merge in the Mind

Chapter 1 ("Merge and Bare Phrase Structure") briefly explains how the theories of phrase structure and grammatical transformations have developed over time in such a way as to reduce complex rule systems to the simple operation of Merge and points out a certain set of generalizations—such as the one that Merge is driven by the search for symmetry—that seem to hold this operation as it interacts with other components of grammar, which forms a basis for further explorations of the nature of Merge that will be pursued in later chapters.

Chapter 2 ("Merge and (A)symmetry") is a revised and much-extended, written-up version of the presentation (under the same title) at the Kyoto Conference on Biolinguistics (March 2012). It puts forth the hypothesis that the need for constructing a predicate-argument relation imposed on human language by the conceptual-intentional (thought) interface, necessarily introduces a certain structural instability, which drives applications of subsequent linguistic computations, particularly, Internal Merge. It is then demonstrated that one of the generalizations discussed in Chapter 1—i.e., External Merge introduces structural asymmetries, whereas Internal Merge applies to the output of External Merge yielding symmetric structures, receives a rather natural interpretation. A new principle incorporating this insight is introduced, and it is further argued that this principle has novel consequences for comparative syntax.

In Chapter 3 ("Generalized Search and Cyclic Derivation by Phase: A Preliminary Study"), the relation between the central operation of Merge and other putative operations (sometimes implicitly) postulated in syntax is carefully examined. Merge builds syntactic objects, but Merge alone cannot capture the syntactic relations established between syntactic objects. These relations include Agree(ment), chain-formation, and binding. In order to capture them in a unified manner, this chapter proposes that syntax be equipped with a general search mechanism, which is called *Search*. Search is characterized here as an operation that establishes a relation between identical (complexes of) features. Then the question is addressed as to what might be the basic operations of syntax. In the course of investigating this question, some of the putative operations in syntax, such as feature-valuation, feature-inheritance, and Transfer, are closely scrutinized, and the conclusion is reached that they are unnecessary and therefore should be eliminated. Then, toward the end of the discussion, the chapter suggests the possibility that Search can, in fact, be reformulated in terms of Merge. This possibility is further explored in detail in Chapter 6.

Like Chapter 1, Chapter 4 ("Merge, Labeling, and Projection") discusses the development of the syntactic theory that has reached the concept of Merge. But this chapter tackles the history from a quite different angle than that of Chapter 1. That is, along the lines pursued in some of the recent literature, the "label-free" formulation of Merge is advanced in this chapter, and the history is analyzed from this point of view, offering a rather refreshingly new way of looking at the status of the present-day theory of phrase structure. The chapter also addresses a number of research questions for future investigations, offering a basic framework within which most of the theoretical proposals made in the other chapters (particularly, Chapters 2, 3, and 6) are couched.

Chapter 5 ("A Note on Weak vs. Strong Generation in Human Language") takes up the question of adequacy of weak generation for the study of human language. It is observed that not only the concept of weak generation *per se* but also the classical notions such as nested dependencies and cross-serial dependencies—those dependencies used in classical formal language theory in order to establish context-freeness, etc.—may, in fact, be irrelevant for the investigation of core structural properties of human language. It is then proposed that the notion of "Merge-generability" is perhaps the only relevant notion for processing syntactic structures. An experimental method for confirming the hypothesis is also suggested, which is currently underway.

Chapter 6 ("0-Search and 0-Merge") attempts to unify Merge and Search (and other putative miscellaneous operations), and literally reduce the linguistic operations to just two primitive proto-operations—0-Search and 0-Merge—a composite of which constitutes the complex operations that have hitherto been assumed to be primitive operations—i.e., Merge and Search. In accordance with the so-called "Merge-only" hypothesis advanced in the recent literature, this chapter tries to sharpen the conclusion of Chapter 3, which suggests that Search may, in fact, be reduced to Merge. The conclusion reached in this chapter, as stated earlier, is rather surprising: Merge as commonly formulated in the literature actually consists of more elementary operations, and, consequently, it is not really the most elementary syntactic operation. Thus Merge should be analyzed as a *composite* of the two most primitive operations—i.e., (i) the selection of n elements, $\alpha_1, \ldots, \alpha_n$, from a designated domain of computation, and (ii) the formation of an unordered set of these n elements, $\{\alpha_1, \ldots, \alpha_n\}$. It is then proposed in this chapter that Search, as Merge, should also be decomposed into the two primitive operations (i) and (ii). Decomposing Merge and Search in this way leads to a true unification of these two syntactic operations into a single composite operation, with their "difference" being only in the way they are composed. Numerous consequences follow from this analysis. For example, various locality constraints on Merge, labeling, chain-formation, binding, etc., are treated in a unified way under the proposed approach. Also, agreement can be characterized as a direct consequence of labeling, leading to the elimination of Agree(ment) as a syntactic operation.

Part II: Merge in the Brain

Chapter 7 ("The Cortical Dynamics in Building Syntactic Structures of Sentences: An MEG Study in a Minimal-Pair Paradigm") deals with complex interactions between hierarchical structures and other salient factors such as linear order and semantic information. The importance of hierarchical syntactic structures is well established in theoretical linguistics, whereas the linear order model for analyzing linguistic input is still very popular and widely assumed in neurosciences. This chapter examines these factors with magnetoencephalography (MEG) and measures cortical responses to a verb with either object-verb (OV) (first-Merged) or subject-verb (SV) (second-Merged) sentence structures, which are tested in a minimal-pair paradigm to compare syntactic and semantic decision tasks. The results of this and other related experiments reveal the dynamics of the multiple cortical regions that work in concert to analyze hierarchical syntactic structures and task-related information, further elucidating the syntactic processing that is crucial during online sentence processing.

The overall aim of Chapter 8 ("Syntactic Computation in the Human Brain: The Degree of Merger as a Key Factor") is to characterize the (possibly multiple) functions of language areas in most precise terms. Previous neuroimaging studies have reported that more complex sentences elicit larger activations in the left inferior frontal gyrus (L. F3op/F3t), although the most critical factor still remains to be identified. The experimental studies using functional magnetic resonance imaging (fMRI) reported in this chapter established many points, including (i) that the models based on Merge and the "Merge + Search" are the best to explain activations in the L. F3op/F3t and supramarginal gyrus (L. SMG), respectively; (ii) that the model with an inhibitory modulatory effect for the bottom-up connection from L. F3op/F3t to L. SMG was significantly positive; and (iii) that nonlinguistic order-related and error-related factors significantly activated the right (R.) lateral premotor cortex and R. F3op/F3t, respectively. These results indicate that the identified *network* of L. F3op/F3t and L. SMG subserves the calculation of Merge in recursively merged structures.

After reviewing briefly recent advances in theoretical linguistics and functional neuroimaging, Chapter 9 ("Computational Principles of Syntax in the Regions Specialized for Language: Integrating Theoretical Linguistics and Functional Neuroimaging") attempts to construct formal and abstract models that parametrically predict the activation modulations in the brain regions specialized for linguistic computations. Based on the two basic operations of human language syntax, Merge and Search, the chapter introduces and examines certain general hypotheses put forth in the authors' recent studies (see Chapter 7 and Chapter 8, for example). A promising direction is suggested for future research on the computational principles of syntax that should deepen our understanding of uniquely human mental faculties.

Many people—friends and colleagues—have immensely contributed to the research projects represented by the articles collected in this volume. I would first like to thank my co-authors for their invaluable contributions, and also for their kind permissions to reprint the co-authored articles: Kazuki Iijima, Hironobu Kasai, Takaomi Kato, Masakazu Kuno, Hiroki Narita, Shinri Ohta, Kuniyoshi Sakai, and Mihoko Zushi. Cedric Boeckx, Takuya Enomoto, Koji Fujita, Ako Imaoka, Terje Lohndal, Roger Martin, Tomoya Nakai, Masanobu Sorida, Juan Uriagereka, and the two anonymous reviewers of this book have contributed in one way or another to the research projects reported in this book, for which I am grateful. I also thank

Noam Chomsky—whose visit to Sophia University in March 2014 marked the highlight of the AMED-CREST project—for his intellectual as well as personal support over the years and, above all, for his creation of the entire scientific framework within which the research developed in the following pages is conducted. Finally, a special word of thanks goes to Carlos Otero for providing me with another great opportunity to publish a collection of my papers in the *Routledge Leading Linguists Series* that he is editing.

Naoki Fukui
Summer 2016

Part I
Merge in the Mind

1 Merge and Bare Phrase Structure*

1 Introduction

Since Aristotle, language has been taken as a system of associating sound—
or sign, as recent research has shown—and meaning over an infinite range.
One of the most important discoveries in linguistic sciences is that this association is actually not direct, but rather is mediated by "structure" whose
exact nature remains to be clarified by empirical investigations. Modern
linguistics has identified certain fundamental properties of the "structure"
of human language and the system that generates it. These properties can be
summarized as follows.

(1) a. hierarchical structure
     b. unboundedness/discrete infinity
     c. endocentricity/headedness
     d. the duality of semantics

There is a fair amount of consensus by now that these are the properties
that ought to be captured, in one way or another, in any linguistic theory
that aims to explain the nature of human language. The questions are: How
much mechanism is needed to account for these properties elegantly, and is
it possible to figure out what is behind these properties?

The rest of this chapter is organized as follows. In section 2, I briefly
review the history of modern linguistics (particularly generative linguistics), to see how these characteristics have been captured by various different components of grammar. In section 3, I focus on the operation Merge,
which is assumed in bare phrase structure theory to be the fundamental
operation in human language, and discuss its properties and problems. In
this section I also explore a few different interpretations of Merge and related operations (if such operations exist), and discuss some implications
for comparative syntax, particularly Japanese syntax. In the concluding section (4), I summarize the discussion, trying to figure out the current stage
of our understanding of the relevant issues, and speculate on future directions. Throughout the discussion, I confine myself to those issues directly
related to phrase structure theory, particularly bare phrase structure theory.

Accordingly, I cannot pay sufficient attention to various other important problems of minimalism that may in principle be related to the issues at hand. The reader is referred to introductory books such as Hornstein et al. (2005) for a more comprehensive discussion on minimalist syntax at large, in which the following discussion is couched.

2 A Brief History[1]

Let us consider (1a) "hierarchical structure" first. That linguistic expressions have abstract hierarchic structures, not merely sequences of words and formatives, is one of the fundamental discoveries of modern linguistics. This discovery goes back to pre-generative structural linguistics, particularly in the form of "Immediate Constituent (IC)" analysis (Wells 1947). IC analysis is couched in the "procedural" approach developed in (American) structural linguistics, and as such cannot be carried over to the theory of generative grammar, which explicitly denies the procedural approach (see, e.g., the introduction to Chomsky 1955/1975). However, the insights of IC analysis, along with important concepts drawn from historical phonology—the concept of "ordered rewriting rules" in particular—can be incorporated into the theory of phrase structure grammar. The theory of phrase structure grammar is developed on the basis of Post's combinatorial system (Post 1943), with an important modification regarding the notion of "vocabulary" (the terminal vs. non-terminal distinction), and is a set of rules (phrase structure rules) of the following form, where A is a single symbol and X, Y and Z are strings of symbols (Z non-null; X and Y possibly null):

(2) $XAY \rightarrow XZY$

Phrase structure rules express the basic structural facts of the language in the form of the "P(hrase)-markers" they generate, with terminal strings drawn from the lexicon. P-markers generated by phrase structure rules express three kinds of information about a linguistic expression:

(3) a. the hierarchical grouping of the "constituents" of the structure (Dominance);
    b. the "type" of each constituent (Labeling);
    c. the left-to-right order (linear order) of the constituents (Precedence).

Thus, the specific kind of hierarchical structure of a linguistic expression (i.e., the labeled hierarchic structure), along with how the elements are stringed (linear order), is explicitly expressed by phrase structure grammar generating a set of P-markers.

In (2), X and Y need to be non-null, when the environment in which A is to be rewritten as Z needs to be specified. This situation arises when a lexical item is inserted into a particular terminal position of a P-marker.

This type of "lexical insertion" is abolished in favor of the lexicon with subcategorization features (Chomsky 1965). The separation of the lexicon from the computational system—phrase structure grammar (PSG)—makes it possible to simplify the form of phrase structure rules for human language from the context-sensitive rule (2) to the context-free rule (4).

(4) A $\rightarrow$ Z

In (4), A is a single non-terminal symbol, and Z is either a non-null string of non-terminal symbols or the designated symbol "Δ" into which a lexical item is to be inserted in accordance with its subcategorization features (see Chomsky 1965 for details).

Thus, context-free phrase structure grammar (coupled with the lexicon) is responsible for expressing the properties of phrase structure of human language, particularly its labeled hierarchic structure with the designated left-to-right linear order. Property (1a) is thereby accounted for.

Let us skip properties (1b) and (1c) for the moment, and consider property (1d) next. This property, the duality of semantics, calls for a device other than phrase structure grammar. The duality of semantics refers to the fact (as has been noticed and studied from various points of view over the years) that generalized predicate-argument structure is realized in the neighborhood of the predicate (within the core part of a clause), whereas all other semantic properties, including discourse-related and scopal properties, involve an "edge" or a "peripheral" position of a linguistic expression (generally a sentence). This duality, particularly the latter fact, requires a device that relates two non-sister positions in the structural description of a sentence, i.e., a device that refers back to some earlier—not necessarily immediately preceding—step in the phrase structural derivation. However, a reference to constituent structure (i.e., to the past history of a phrase structural derivation) cannot be neatly expressed by context-free phrase structure grammar (see, e.g., Chomsky 1957). Thus, a new grammatical device has to be introduced to deal with the duality of semantics, and the notion of "grammatical transformation" is introduced for this and related purposes.[2]

Human language clearly exhibits the property of discrete infinity (1b), taken to be the most elementary property of the shared language capacity. Language is discrete, as opposed to dense or continuous, roughly in the sense that linguistic expressions are constructed on distinct and separate units (rather than continua), so that there are n word sentences and $n+1$ (or $n-1$) word sentences, but there are no $n.5$ (or $n.3$, etc.) word sentences (just like natural numbers). And language is infinite, since there is no n (in any human language) such that n is the number of words contained in the longest sentence (so that a sentence with $n+1$ words is a non-sentence). Most important cases of discrete infinity exhibited by human language are handled by special types of transformations—"generalized transformations"—in the early theory of transformational-generative grammar. These transformations are equipped with the function of embedding a structure (typically a sentence) into another structure of the same type (a sentence). With the abolishment of generalized transformations in the Standard Theory in the 1960s (Chomsky 1965), this function of (self-)embedding is transferred to phrase structure grammar with "recursive symbols" that appear both on the left-hand and right-hand sides of the phrase structure rules, allowing a kind of non-local recursion.

Toward the end of the 1960s, it became apparent that certain important generalizations about the phrase structure of human language, i.e., endocentricity/headedness (1c), cannot be stated in terms of phrase structure rules alone (nor in terms of transformations for that matter). Phrase structure in human language is generally "endocentric," in the sense that it is constructed based on a certain central element—called the "head" of a phrase—which determines the essential properties of the phrase, accompanied by other non-central elements, thus forming a larger structure.[3] This is the right intuition, but, as pointed out by Lyons (1968), the theory of phrase structure grammar cannot capture this. Phrase structure rules are too permissive as a theory of phrase structure in human language, in that they overgenerate phrase structures that are never actually permitted in human language, i.e., those structures that are not headed ("exocentric" structures). We thus need some other mechanism which correctly captures the endocentricity/headedness of phrase structure that appears to be a fundamental property of human language. X-bar theory is introduced mainly for this purpose.

The basic claims of X-bar theory, as it was introduced in Chomsky (1970), can be summarized as follows.

(5) a. Every phrase is headed, i.e., has an endocentric structure, with the head X "projecting" to larger phrases.
   b. Heads are not atomic elements; rather, they are feature complexes, consisting of primitive features.
   c. Universal Grammar (UG) provides the general X-bar schema of the following sort, which governs the mode of projection of a head:
      X' → X . . .
      X" → [Spec, X'] X'

The version of X-bar theory presented in Chomsky (1970) was in a preliminary form, and numerous refinements have been made since then. However, it is also true that all the crucial and fundamental insights of X-bar theory were presented in this study, and have been subjected to few substantive changes since. While claim (5c), the existence of universal X-bar schema, has been subjected to critical scrutiny in recent years, claims (5a) and (5b) have survived almost in their original forms throughout the ensuing development of grammatical theory, and are still assumed in the current framework (but see the following for a recent proposal to eliminate the notion of projection). In this way, property (1c), the headedness of phrases in the human language, is explicitly captured by X-bar theory.

As the principles-and-parameters (P&P) approach took shape around 1980, indicating the emergence of an explanatory theory of a radically different sort from the earlier traditional rule-based systems, "rules of grammar" virtually disappeared, replaced by the principles of various modules of UG (Case theory, X-bar theory, etc.). Accordingly, phrase structure rules disappear, for a substantial core system, which is, in fact, a rather natural move, since phrase structure rules are redundant to a significant extent, recapitulating information that must be stated in the lexicon. On the other hand, transformational rules are not redundant, and thus are ineliminable, although the exact form in which they should be expressed is open to question. It seems that complex transformational rules—which are specific to constructions in particular languages—need not be stipulated, and that over a large range, transformations can be reduced to the simple general schema Move-α (which says "Move anything anywhere"), given trace theory and the other principles of UG.

Thus, within the P&P framework, we are essentially left with X-bar theory (of some sort; see, e.g., Chomsky 1986) and Move-α. X-bar theory is responsible for properties (1a) (hierarchic structure), (1b) (discrete infinity),[4] and (1c) (endocentricity/headedness), while Move-α is mainly responsible for property (1d) (the duality of semantics). During the mid- to late 1980s, attempts were made to integrate the theory of phrase structure (X-bar theory) and the theory of movement (Move-α) by proposing that phrase structures are built "from the bottom up" by means of a formal operation very similar to adjunction (or substitution, depending on the structural property of the target)[5] employed in a transformational operation (Move-α). The basic claims of one such attempt, which are relevant to our present discussion, can be summarized as follows.[6]

(6) a. Heads project as they "discharge" their features (selectional features, agreement features, etc.).
    b. Iteration is possible, particularly at the single-bar level.
    c. One and the same operation ("Adjunction") is responsible for both structure building and movement.
    d. There is no X-bar schema. (Thus, the notion of "maximal projection" cannot be defined in terms of bar-levels, and ought to be characterized contextually.)
    e. Agreement closes projections.

Claim (6a) is based on the intuition that phrases are constructed around their heads, and that heads are driven to project in terms of their inherent features; (6b) is assumed to account for the infinitude of phrase structure composition (but see note 4). The simplification of transformations makes it possible to search for a fundamental operation (or a small number of fundamental operations), and (6c) is one possible answer to this important question. Given the idea expressed in (6a), the X-bar schema in the traditional X-bar theory seems eliminable. This is, in fact, a desirable result, not only because of Occam's razor but also because of the highly specific, rather stipulative nature of the postulated X-bar schema. If the effects of X-bar schema can be shown to derive from more natural, simpler principles, that would be a highly desirable result. The last claim, (6e), is based on the observation that in some type of languages (e.g., Japanese), phrases seem to be never "closed," in the sense that given a phrase, it is always possible (in syntax) to expand that phrase by combining it with some other element, as long as the combination is licensed by being assigned an appropriate interpretation. This is of course not the case in, say, English. And a hypothesis is put forth that the "closure" property of phrases seems to be linked to the presence of agreement. Thus, in a language such as Japanese, where there is no conventional φ-feature agreement, phrases are never closed, while in English-type languages, agreement closes projections of phrases, from which a variety of other differences also follow. See Fukui (1986). See also Kuroda (1988) for a different approach to the "agreement parameter."

It is perhaps worth pointing out here some fundamental differences between Kuroda's and Fukui's approaches to phrase structure and comparative syntax (in particular, the "agreement parameter" just mentioned). Kuroda's theory, as it is stated in Kuroda (1988), is "geometric" in nature. This orientation seems to derive from the spirit of modern geometry as laid out in Felix Klein's well-known Erlangen Program (1872), whose basic idea is that each geometry (Euclidean, affine, projective, etc.), given a certain space, can be characterized by a "group of transformations," and that a geometry is really concerned with invariants under this group of transformations (rather than a space itself). Simply put, Kuroda attempts to establish the geometry of human language. For Kuroda, then, the space is (universally) given by the X-bar schema in this case. English and Japanese are exactly the same in this regard (apart from linear order, of course). A group of transformations, particularly an abstract relation "Agreement" is also universal. English and Japanese are minimally different with respect to the enforcement of this operation: Agreement is forced in English, but it is unforced in Japanese. While the very nature of this "parametric" statement remains unclear, it is clear that Kuroda's approach is (i) geometric (and thus, in part, tends to be "representational" in the familiar linguistic terminology) and (ii) universalist (in that both the space and the group of transformations—Agreement, in particular—are taken to be universal). Fukui's approach, on the other hand, is couched in a more conventional "economy/last resort" paradigm (as we just saw earlier). It attempts to eliminate the X-bar schema, claiming that structures are built from the bottom up, starting out with a head and continuing on as long as syntactic objects are licensed (by feature-checking, for example). There is no superfluous structural position, and there is no superfluous operation. Since Japanese lacks the relevant agreement-inducing heads (e.g., ϕ-features) in its lexicon, agreement simply doesn't occur in the language, although even in Fukui's system, the operations are universally available as they are provided by UG. Thus, despite the widely held view that Kuroda's and Fukui's approaches exhibit many similarities (and they actually do share many insights), their background philosophies are very different, yielding quite a few important empirical differences. As it turns out, Fukui's approach went along with subsequent developments of linguistic theory (leading to bare phrase structure theory, for instance), while Kuroda's representational approach remained rather isolated. But his geometric insight offers interesting future research topics and is not to be discounted, in my opinion.

Returning to our main discussion, the total and explicit elimination of X-bar theory is carried out by Chomsky's (1995a) "bare phase structure" theory (see also Kayne 1994 for a different approach). The bare theory is couched within the minimalist program, according to which all the principles and entities of UG must be motivated and justified either by the properties of (at least) two interfaces that language has with the other performance systems—sensorimotor and conceptual-intentional systems—or by "third factor" conditions (see Chomsky 2005) that are not specific to language and that govern the way language satisfies the conditions imposed by the interfaces. Most of the basic claims of the approach mentioned earlier are actually incorporated into the bare theory in a greatly refined form, and the fundamental operation is identified as Merge, with respect to which various interesting theoretical and empirical problems arise, as discussed in the following section.

3 Merge and Related Issues

3.1 Merge

Chomsky (1995a) argues that standard X-bar theory specifies much redundant information, while the only structural information needed is that a "head" and a "non-head" combine to create a new unit. He then proposes that a phrase structure is constructed in a bottom-up fashion by a uniform operation called "Merge" which combines two elements, say α and β, and projects one of them as the head. Since Merge combines (not "concatenates") two[7] elements and does not specify the linear order between the two, the resulting object can be more accurately represented as in (7).

(7) $K = \{\gamma, \{\alpha, \beta\}\}$, where $\gamma \in \{\alpha, \beta\}$

Equation (7) states that Merge forms a new syntactic object K by combining two objects α and β, and specifies one of them (γ) as the projecting element (hence the "head"/"label" of K). Merge applies iteratively to form indefinitely many structures. Note incidentally that in this formulation, the operation Merge—Merge $(\alpha, \beta) = \{\gamma, \{\alpha, \beta\}\}$, where $\gamma \in \{\alpha, \beta\}$—is an *asymmetric* operation, projecting either α or β, the head of the syntactic object that "projects" becoming the head/label of the complex object formed by Merge.

How are the basic properties of human language listed in (1) captured by the bare theory, particularly by the simple operation Merge? Property (1a), hierarchic structure, can be straightforwardly captured by assuming iterative Merge to be non-associative (i.e., [A # B] # C ≠ A # [B # C], where # denotes Merge).[8] It requires some discussion to see how (and whether) this simple elementary operation captures the other properties listed in (1), to which we now turn.

3.2 Labeling

Notice that in the formulation of Merge (7), headedness (labeling) is a part of the operation, thereby rendering Merge asymmetric, as we just saw. However, the status of labeling under minimalist assumptions does not seem obvious. It is not entirely clear whether labels are indeed required by either of the two—sensorimotor and conceptual-intentional—interfaces, nor is it likely that labels as such are derived from some third-factor considerations. To sharpen the fundamental operation of Merge, therefore, it is desirable to dissociate the labeling part from Merge itself and see if labels are predictable by general principles. Under this scenario, Merge is formulated simply as a *symmetric* set-formation operation: Merge $(\alpha, \beta) = \{\alpha, \beta\}$.

How are labels determined, then? Since Chomsky (1995a), there have been various attempts to determine the label optimally (i.e., without reference to idiosyncrasies, without stipulating a special rule, without look-ahead to check eventual convergence of a derivation, etc.). One line of such attempts converges on the elimination of labeling. Collins (2002) examines various areas of syntax (X-bar theory, selection, Minimal Link Condition, etc.) in which the notion of labels has been used, and proposes that the notion of labels can be totally eliminated from the theory of syntax if we assume the mechanism of "saturation/discharge"—and the derived notion "locus"—similar to the one employed in an approach discussed earlier (see (6a); see also the references cited in note 6). In a series of works (e.g., Chomsky 1995a, 1995b, 2000, 2001, 2007, 2008a), Chomsky explores various possibilities of predicting labels in major cases, and reaches the conclusion that the notion "labels" may be illusory with no theoretical status, and that it can be eliminated entirely (along with Collins's notion of locus), by virtue of the third-factors such as minimal search conditions. Thus, in a structure of the form H-XP (where H is a(n) L(exical) I(tem), order irrelevant), a representative case of merger, minimal search conditions trivially determine that H is the element that enters into further computations, since the other element, XP, has no information available with its head too deep down within it. Headedness is simply an epiphenomenon under this approach.

Another line of research takes labeling/headedness to be a fundamental property of human language and proposes that this property be explicitly expressed by the theory of grammar (see Boeckx 2008, Hornstein 2009, among many others, and the references cited). For example, Fukui (2005) proposes that in addition to Merge, which is, as Chomsky formulates it, a simple set-formation operation, we need another operation called *Embed* which is responsible for expressing the "local self-embedding" character of the linguistic structure. Operating on the workspace—called the Base Set (BS)—created by an application of Merge (i.e., BS = $\{\alpha_1, \ldots, \alpha_n\}$, which is yielded by Merge $(\alpha_1, \ldots, \alpha_n) = \{\alpha_1, \ldots, \alpha_n\}$), Embed picks out one member of the BS, say α_i, and forms a union of α_i and the BS.

(8) Embed $(\alpha_i, \mathrm{BS}) = \alpha_i \cup \mathrm{BS} = \{\alpha_i, \{\alpha_1, \ldots, \alpha_n\}\}$[9]

The α_i, the target of the operation Embed, is the "head" of the resulting structure. As discussed earlier, the number *n* is usually 2 in human language. So, BS is of the form $\{\alpha, \beta\}$, and applying Embed to, say, α, we get the self-embedding structure $K = \{\alpha, \{\alpha, \beta\}\}$, where α is the label/head. By adding Embed to the structure-building component of grammar (the Merge/Embed system), properties (1a) (hierarchical structure) and (1c) (endocentricity/headedness) are naturally accounted for.

Fukui (2005, 2008) argues that more refined analyses become available in many areas of grammatical investigation within the Merge/Embed system than within the standard Merge-alone system. In fact, these works factor out three relevant factors to look at in examining the properties of phrase structure, (i) Merge, (ii) Embed, and (iii) iterativity. By combining these, we have (at least) the following possibilities.[10]

(9) a. non-iterative Merge without Embed
     b. iterative Merge without Embed
     c. non-iterative Embed
     d. iterative Embed

The last possibility (with all three factors in action) represents unbounded endocentric structures found in the core of human language, as traditional X-bar theory indicates. The other three possibilities have rarely been considered, but there may be cases in which they are attested. Thus, the data on Japanese Broca's aphasics indicate the following basic properties (see Fukui 2004 and references cited there).

(10) a. Word order is retained in general.
      b. Case and sentence-final particles such as *-ga* "NOM," *-o* "ACC," *-ka* "Q" are generally dropped.
      c. Postpositions (e.g., *-kara* "from," *-made* "until") are generally retained.

    d. The maximal number of constituents in a noun phrase is two.[11] That is, only one *-no* "GEN" is allowed within a single noun phrase, e.g., *ore-no kyoodai* "my brother," *Sapporo-no sigai* "the town of Sapporo," but **Taro-no imooto-no yoofuku* "Taro's sister's clothes," **a-no uti-no mon-no mae* "in front of the gate of that house."

Property (10a) could indicate the importance of the "head-parameter" (linear order) in the core part of language, but let's set this aside for the moment. Properties (10b), (10c), and (10d) all point to the conclusion that only sister elements can be related in Japanese Broca's aphasics. While the exact mechanism of case-marking in Japanese is still largely unknown, it is relatively clear that particles such as *-ga* and *-o* (as well as the question particle *-ka*) require "non-sister information" for their licensing, i.e., it is necessary to look at portions of a phrase marker that are not in a sister relation to these elements. Postpositions, on the other hand, require only "sister information" for their licensing, as they generally theta-mark their sisters. (10d) indicates that X and Y are linked within a noun phrase and *-no* can be attached to X (i.e., [X-*no* Y]), but one more application of Merge/Embed is impossible (i.e., *[Z-*no* [X-*no* Y]]). All of these properties can receive a natural account if we assume that iterativity is lost in Japanese aphasics.[12] Note incidentally that the traditional "working memory" account cannot explain why the crucial line is actually drawn where it is (rather than between, say, three and four, etc.).

Note also that the complement vs. non-complement distinction, which plays a major role in various modules of grammar, including the theory of movement, is grounded in a kind of third-factor considerations. Merge can be taken to provide a recursive definition of syntactic objects. Thus, its first application (first-Merge), which—apart from the case of singleton-formation (see note 18)—yields a head-complement configuration, directly corresponds to the base of a recursive definition, while subsequent applications of Merge, which introduce non-complements (specifiers), correspond to the recursion part of a recursive definition. The complement vs. non-complement distinction, therefore, is based on the independently motivated base vs. recursion distinction in the characterization of recursive definitions. The concept of recursive definition is certainly not specific to language (UG); thus, to the extent that the complement vs. non-complement distinction is reduced to the nature of recursive definition, the former distinction is justified on a kind of third-factor grounds. This reasoning holds under either interpretation of Merge we're discussing, but the distinction between first-Merge and subsequent applications of Merge is highlighted under the approach taking iterativity as a separate property (see Chapter 7 of this volume for some related discussion).

As this brief discussion indicates, it is generally the case that by considering the three factors separately, it becomes possible to address the questions of their respective roles in evolution, acquisition (development), and, as we just saw, (partial) loss of the human language capacity (see also Fujita 2007 for relevant discussion). Thus, it seems that the Merge/Embed system—with the treatment of iterativity as a separate property—offers a certain descriptive promise, although the addition of a new operation like Embed, thereby enriching UG, may run counter to general minimalist guidelines. The plausibility of this type of approach seems to depend in part on the "naturalness" of the additional operation (Embed or whatever), as well as the empirical significance of labels/headedness in the syntax and at the interfaces. The matter is still contested in the literature.

A recent proposal by Narita (2009, 2010) presents a rather radical view on the notion of labels and related concepts such as projection and feature percolation. He is in agreement with the first type of approach discussed here, i.e., an approach under which the role of label/headedness is being diminished to almost zero. He goes on to take a stronger view that when α and β are merged, forming a new object K, no feature of α/β is transmitted to K. That is, there is no projection, let alone feature percolation. Narita then assumes the following claim made by Chomsky (2008: 139).

> For an LI to be able to enter into a computation, merging with some SO [Syntactic Object], it must have some property permitting this operation. A property of an LI is called a *feature*, so an LI has a feature that permits it to be merged. Call this feature the *edge feature* (EF) of the LI. If an LI lacks EF, it can only be a full expression in itself: an interjection. When merged with a syntactic object SO, LI forms {LI, SO}; SO is its *complement*. The fact that Merge iterates without limit is a property at least of LIs—and optimally, only of LIs, as I will assume. EF articulates the fact that Merge is unbounded, that language is a recursive infinite system of a particular kind. (emphasis original)

Adopting the concept of EF discussed in this quote, Narita assumes that EF triggers Merge, and that only an LI can utilize its EF to do so. Notice that EF is a feature of an LI, and if there is no projection/feature-percolation, no features of an LI, including its EF, can be transmitted to a larger structure created by merging the LI and a syntactic object SO. Thus, an LI, once merged, can no longer trigger further application of Merge, which is clearly against "[t]he fact that Merge iterates without limit" (see the earlier quotation). To solve this problem, Narita assumes a multiple transfer model (e.g., Chomsky 2000, 2008), according to which syntax interfaces with the performance systems multiple times at well-defined steps of a derivation (called "phases"). Each application of Transfer strips off the complement of a designated LI, a phase head, thereby rendering the phase head a kind of "revived" LI. Thus, only phase heads allow more than one application of Merge, and only phase heads can "move" with the apparent effect of pied-piping in disguise. In this way, the system proposed by Narita (2009,

2010) permits a specific type of unbounded Merge. He goes on to explore an impressive array of consequences of this proposal, including a new analysis of freezing effects (Boeckx 2008), an account of an asymmetry in coordinate structures, and so on. The next subsection attempts to reinterpret Narita's proposal by recasting the notion of EF.

3.3 The Edge Feature

Whether an application of Merge is triggered or spontaneous has been a matter of debate. One line of inquiry sees Merge as a free-standing option made available by UG that can be utilized any time in a derivation, and the result is acceptable or unacceptable, depending on whether the merged element is properly licensed (at the interfaces). In this view (see Chomsky 1995a, 1995b), Merge is a cost-free operation, not "triggered" by anything, and is not subject to Last Resort. There is empirical evidence that this may in fact be true (cf. Saito and Fukui 1998), and thus this possibility is not to be discounted (see also section 4.3–4).

Another view on Merge is that its application is on a par with the other operations in a grammar in that it should be triggered by some kind of feature-checking (selection and other requirements). This view is motivated by the general (minimalist) guideline according to which there is no superfluous step in a derivation and every operation has the "reason" for it to apply. The notion of EF seems to have developed from these lines of inquiry as an abstract concept covering various cases that have been treated separately.

The EF of an LI is taken to be a "feature" (along with the other features) of the LI, and it indicates that the LI can be merged. As a feature, however, EF exhibits some peculiar properties. First, it is a feature associated with virtually every LI, apart from interjections or frozen expressions. Features in the lexicon are generally for the purposes of distinguishing different classes of lexical items. Thus, it is not entirely clear why such a feature should exist at all if it is universally associated with every lexical item. In fact, EF seems to be equivalent to being a lexical item, at least a part of its definition. Second, EF does not play any direct interpretive role at the interfaces. Thus, assuming some sort of full interpretation to hold at the interfaces (not a trivial assumption, though), EF is surely an "uninterpretable" feature that is not allowed to exist (survive) at the interfaces. So it must be deleted, but it cannot be deleted when Merge applies, because if EF is always deleted when satisfied (by an application of Merge), then there will never be second-Merge, third-Merge, etc. (i.e., specifiers/non-complements) per given LI. Empirical evidence indicates that specifiers/non-complements do exist. In particular, only this choice permits Internal Merge. When merging X to Y (the asymmetric phrasing here is only for expository purposes), X can be either external to Y or part of Y. In the former case, we have External Merge (responsible for predicate-argument structures), whereas the latter possibility represents Internal Merge, which comes free and which is assumed in the bare theory to be an equivalent to Move/transformations.[13] And Internal Merge is responsible for one of the fundamental properties of human language, i.e., property (1d), "the duality of semantics." Thus, if the expressive potential of human language is to be used in full, EF must be undeletable, and undeletability of EF provides the basis for the duality of semantics via Internal Merge. Moreover, unlike other uninterpretable features which get deleted when checked under certain structural conditions, deletion of EF is presumably carried out as part of the operations of Transfer (see Chomsky 2007: 11).[14] In all of these respects, EF is a unique "feature," quite distinct from all other features generally assumed to be associated with lexical items—which casts serious doubt about EF as a lexical feature. A natural conclusion, then, seems to be that EF is not a lexical feature *per se*, but rather a term describing the general properties of Merge (as it relates to lexical items).

If Merge applies freely without any drive (cf. the first view just discussed), then there is no need for EF anyway. But if an application of Merge indeed requires a driving force, we need to state the conditions, replacing EF, under which Merge applies. It is important to note in this connection that in the overwhelming number of cases of Merge applications, Merge always operates on a head (H or LI) and another syntactic object α, i.e., H-α (order irrelevant).[15] That is, merger almost always occurs between a head and some other syntactic object, and if we look at the actual cases, it is again almost always the case that α is a non-head (typically a phrase). Thus, the situation is such that when Merge applies to two syntactic objects, one of them must be a head, and the other non-head, i.e., there is a certain "(structural) asymmetry" (in some sense to be made precise) between the two objects. This suggests the following generalization concerning an application of Merge.[16]

(11) Merge is driven by asymmetry.

The intuition behind (11) is that syntax is unwilling to tolerate asymmetries, and tries to fix one by applying Merge. Merge in this scenario has the important function of maximizing symmetry. The asymmetry that exists between H (a head) and α (a non-head) is covered and eliminated by an application of Merge yielding a set {H, α}, a symmetric object. Human language has an intrinsic source of asymmetries, namely, the lexicon—lexical items with their selectional properties. As these LIs enter into the computation, they will necessarily create asymmetries, triggering Merge.

If a condition like (11) is sustainable, and if Merge applies only when it is driven (this is not obvious; see the earlier discussion), then there is no merger between two "symmetric" objects, such as head-head and XP-YP. In fact, this is what the preceding discussion predicts. But there are well-known "exceptions." One notable exception is an external merger of an external argument, which has all sorts of exceptional properties, as Chomsky (2007, 2008) discusses. As briefly discussed earlier, Narita (2009, 2010) tries to deal with this case by means of a phase-by-phase multiple Transfer mechanism. The phase head v in the complex $\{v, \{\text{V, Obj}\}\}$ can eliminate its complement by Transfer ($\{v, \{\text{V, Obj}\}\}$), so that the revived phase head v, an LI, can utilize its EF again, triggering an application of Merge, which merges an external argument. We are assuming EF is not a feature of a lexical item, so the same problem does not arise. But the insight of Narita's analysis, i.e., that merger of XP and YP is possible only when one of them constitutes a phase (whose head LI can Transfer its complement and thus become a revived head), can be stated as follows.[17]

(12) Transfer creates asymmetry.

Transfer strips off the complement portion of a phase, and by doing so, it makes the whole structure asymmetric and unstable, which triggers an application of Merge (External or Internal). Thus, the external merger of an external argument is properly motivated by the independently established fact that vP is a phase (and v is a phase head). This approach also accounts for the fact that movement (Internal Merge) only occurs at the phase level (basically at vP and CP, in informal terms), since only a phase head can trigger Transfer, which in turn creates asymmetry, thereby driving an application of (Internal) Merge.

As for the head-head merger case, particularly the first step of a derivation, when two LIs are to be merged, condition (11) does not force Merge to apply. Here we might adopt Kayne's (2011) idea that one option for Merge is the direct formation of the singleton set $\{x\}$, and that the singleton formation applies only to nouns (see Kayne 2011). Thus, when N and V are to be merged, Merge (singleton formation) first applies to N,[18] forming $\{N\}$, and this creates an asymmetry (V vs. $\{N\}$) that prompts an application of Merge, in accordance with the condition (11), yielding a set $\{V, \{N\}\}$ as desired.

In this way, we might be able to account for the conditions under which Merge should apply, without recourse to EF as an actual feature associated with a lexical item.

Our discussion is rather sketchy and inconclusive, and to make the proposal more substantive, it is certainly necessary to sharpen the notion of "asymmetry" invoked in condition (11). This is hard to do, however. The reason is that there is no general agreement as to what information Merge can obtain when it is to apply to syntactic objects X and Y. It is widely claimed that LIs are "atoms" for computations. If they are indeed atoms, Merge cannot obtain any information stored inside LIs' bundles of features, including, I suppose, EF, if it is really a feature of an LI. Then how does Merge know X or Y is an LI (with EF)? Bar-levels and other diacritics are excluded in the bare theory as violations of inclusiveness. So they are not available. The only entity that seems to be available to Merge is the "braces," (i.e., the information regarding the layers of sets formed by (prior) applications of Merge (i.e., the concept of nth order). Thus, x and $\{x\}$

should be distinguishable, if braces are indeed ontological entities (not an innocuous assumption) and Merge is able to "see" them (ditto). In this way, Merge should be able to detect the existence of asymmetry (or lack thereof), to see whether it should apply. Beyond this, it is hard to determine how much information (of syntactic objects) is accessible to Merge. This casts some doubt on any system in which Merge is "triggered" by some feature—including EF, if it is indeed a feature of a lexical item. The proposal suggested earlier is to barely get around this fundamental problem of feature-triggered Merge approaches. Note also that throughout the discussion, it remains open whether Merge can apply when not driven by asymmetry. It may be that Merge is always available and is free to apply without a trigger, but it is forced to apply when driven by a condition like (11). As briefly mentioned at the outset of this subsection, this possibility is not to be discounted.

As an alternative view, one might propose that Merge freely and blindly applies to X and Y without caring about what they are, what features they have, etc., and that some other mechanism (e.g., the labeling algorithm of Chomsky 2008: 145) deals with various properties of the structures constructed by Merge. Although the same "atom" problems arise for the mechanism at hand (how it distinguishes LI and non-LI, etc.), Merge itself could maintain the simplest possible form under this approach.

In the absence of crucial evidence at the moment, I leave all these possibilities open for future research, and turn to a brief discussion of Japanese syntax in the following subsection, as it appears to show some basic properties of Merge (and licensing mechanisms) in a straightforward way.

3.4 Merge and Japanese Syntax

It is by now widely known that expressions in Japanese—clauses in particular, but noun phrases show a very similar pattern—exhibit a certain iterativity property at the edge that is not generally observed in languages such as English.[19] Thus, given the sentence (13), which looks like a complete sentence, it is possible to keep expanding the sentence indefinitely by adding an expression (a noun phrase with a nominative marker) at the edge, as illustrated in (14).

(13) Dare-mo   (sono gakkai-ni)   ko-nakat-ta.
      anybody-MO(even)   that conference-to   come-NOT-PAST

    Lit. "Anybody did not come (to that conference)."
    "Nobody came (to that conference)."

(14) a. Daigakuinsei-ga [dare-mo (sono gakkai-ni) konakatta].
       graduate.students-NOM

       Lit. "Graduate students, anybody did not come (to that conference)."
       "As for the graduate students, none of them came (to that conference)."

b. Seisuuron-ga   [daigakuinsei-ga   [dare-mo   (sono   gakkai-ni)
    number.theory-NOM
    konakatta]].

    Lit. "Number theory, graduate students, anybody did not come (to
        that conference)."
    "As for number theory, none of the graduate students (in that field)
        came (to that conference)."

c. Suugakuka-ga   [seisuuron-ga   [daigakuinsei-ga   [dare-mo   (sono
    Mathematics.department-NOM
    gakkai-ni) konakatta]]].

    Lit. "Mathematics department, number theory, graduate students,
        anybody did not come (to that conference)."
    "As for the mathematics department, in the area of number the-
        ory, none of the graduate students (in that field) came (to that
        conference)."

d. Harvard-ga [suugakuka-ga [seisuuron-ga [daigakuinsei-ga [dare-
    mo (sono gakkai-ni) konakatta.

    Lit. "Harvard, mathematics department, number theory, graduate
        students, anybody did not come (to that conference)."
    "As for Harvard, none of the graduate students in the mathematics
        department in the area of number theory came (to that conference)."

And so on.

While the actual acceptability of a sentence depends on how easily one can
think of an appropriate relation holding between the added nominative
phrase and the rest of the sentence, it is safe to claim that the syntax of
Japanese allows indefinite expansions of a sentence at the edge, and submits
the resultant structure to interpretation.[20] More generally, given a sentence
(S) and a phrasal category (XP), typically a noun phrase or a postpositional
phrase—these are of course informal terms only for expository purposes—
it is always possible in Japanese to combine them, yielding the structure
{XP, S}. It is then necessary to submit the structure to interpretation, to
see if an appropriate interpretive relation holds between XP and S. This
"appropriate interpretive relation" includes all sorts of semantic/discourse
(or even pragmatic) relations such as topic-comment, focus-presupposition,
part-whole, predication, "aboutness," which seems to indicate that the situation is such that, as suggested by Wolfram Hinzen, Juan Uriagereka, and
others (see Hinzen 2006, Chomsky 2007, and references therein), that syntax carves the path interpretation must blindly follow (cf. Uriagereka 2002:
64), i.e., the output of syntax (the Japanese syntax, in this case) prompts the
semantic/pragmatic interface to try its best to come up with an appropriate
interpretation. If such a relation holds, then the structure is appropriately
interpreted. If not, the resulting expression is judged to be unacceptable or

unnatural. Abstracting away from all the important issues concerning the case, cartography (which I think provides us with valuable data, calling for minimalist explanations), and others, I maintain that this is basically all that happens at the edge of a sentence (and a noun phrase) in Japanese. In other words, "unbounded Merge" is in full force in the syntax of Japanese.

This basic property can be taken to be responsible for a variety of phenomena, apart from the obvious "topic prominence" of Japanese, listed in random order as follows.

(15) a. multiple *ga/no* (see the aforementioned)
    b. scrambling
    c. gapless topic constructions
    d. gapless relative clauses
    e. indirect passives
    f. multiple-headed constructions (multiple-headed relative clauses and clefts)

These phenomena have been noted widely in the literature, and have been listed as peculiar properties characterizing the Japanese language—as opposed to, say, English, where these constructions are generally impossible. But they all conform to the pattern just discussed, i.e., they all fall under the schematic structure {XP, S}, where the appropriate interpretation is required to obtain between XP and S. The syntax of Japanese permits the structure quite freely and sends it off to interpretation. Speakers' acceptability judgments may naturally vary depending on the availability of an appropriate interpretive relation between XP and S, but crucially, the structure does not violate the laws of form (syntax) and thus is not ungrammatical (even though it may be unnatural or nonsensical).[21]

Interestingly, the iterative mechanism sometimes comes into play, circumventing allegedly deviant island violations. Thus, it has been long noted that subjacency effects with scrambling or relativization in Japanese are rather "weak," in that some of the examples supposedly violating the condition are actually quite acceptable. For example, (16a) and (16b) are acceptable, even though they apparently involve subjacency violations. (The underscored portion indicates a position where the noun phrase supposedly receives a theta-role.)

(16) a. Sono-haiyuu-ni [s boku-wa ima [NP [s sensyuu
         that-actor-DAT   I-TOP   now   last.week
         Tokyo-de __ atta] hito]-o   sagasite-iru tokoro da].
            -in   met   person-ACC   be-looking.for

       Lit. "That actor, I'm now in the process of looking for the person who met in Tokyo last week."
    b. [s [NP [s __ kawaigatte ita] inu]-ga kyonen sindesimatta] otokonoko
                 took.loving.care.of dog-NOM last.year died boy

       Lit. "the boy who the dog he was taking good care of died last year"

Example (16a), involving scrambling from within a relative clause, is not perfect,[22] but as compared to the English counterpart (which is hopeless), it can be arguably regarded as grammatical. And it is quite easy to construct similar examples for the other types of island violations—the subject condition, the adjunct condition, the non-relative complex NP cases, etc. (16b) (adapted from Kuno 1973: 239) is a case of one relative clause embedded in another relative clause, and is plainly grammatical in Japanese. In both cases, the structure in which an XP is merged with an S is created by Merge at the top of the structure, and as long as an appropriate interpretive relation can be established between the XP and the S, the XP is locally licensed where it is merged, effectively nullifying the movement (if any) which violates the subjacency condition.

Thus, unbounded Merge not only provides the basis for the constructions in (15) but also offers a kind of repair strategy for certain island violations, as illustrated by the examples in (16). Note that there is no need to stipulate anything to account for these "peculiar" facts in Japanese. They are direct consequences of unbounded Merge along with necessary interface (interpretive) licensing. Japanese syntax, on this view, exhibits the nature of UG in its purest form. What needs to be accounted for are the cases where such unbounded Merge appears to be prohibited, e.g., the lack of those constructions (15) in, say, English.[23]

In brief, the discussion in this subsection indicates that the syntax of Japanese seems to exhibit how the bare minimum of UG—Merge and interface requirements—works in its barest form. A class of properties of Japanese, which has been treated as peculiar properties of the language, can be reduced simply to unbounded Merge and interpretive licensing conditions at the interface. Properties of Japanese seem to support the view that Merge applies rather freely without any drive, unless a reasonable concept of "(a)symmetry" may come up so that structures in this language can be appropriately characterized as inherently asymmetric (i.e., "open").

3.5 Summary

Let us summarize our discussion on Merge and related issues. Merge is a simple set-formation operation. Applying to two SOs, α and β, it forms a set $\{\alpha, \beta\}$. This symmetric view on Merge leaves unaccounted for the notion of labels/headedness, the core insight of traditional X-bar theory as we saw in section 2. We discussed this problem in section 3.2. One approach to this problem simply states that labeling is not part of the structure-building operation; rather, it is an epiphenomenon and to the extent that it holds, it's predictable by general principles of minimal search. Another approach takes labeling to be an essential part of the structure-building processes of human language, and claims that there is an additional operation of self-embedding (Embed) that directly accounts for headedness/labeling. Furthermore, it is argued that by factoring out combination (Merge), self-embedding (Embed), and their iterativity (recursiveness), more refined analyses become available, which has implications for the issues of the evolution, development, and (partial) loss of the human language faculty. A radical variant of the first approach claims that there is no notion of "projection" in syntax. Merge is assumed to be triggered by EF, but since EF (a feature of an LI) cannot project on this view, Merge cannot apply more than once per LI. This problem is resolved by assuming that Transfer, which applies only at the phase level, has a side effect of reviving the head as an LI. Thus, only phase heads permit specifiers/non-complements, only phase heads can "move," etc.

The notion of EF is critically examined in section 3.3. It is pointed out that EF is a unique feature, distinct from all the other "conventional" lexical features. It plays no direct interpretive role at the interfaces, so it is definitely an "uninterpretable" feature. However, unlike other uninterpretable features, it doesn't seem to be deleted when satisfied. All of these properties cast some doubt on the treatment of EF on a par with other lexical features. It is thus suggested that EF is a term describing the general conditions under which Merge applies as it relates to an LI. There are two views on the applicability of Merge. One is that Merge applies freely and blindly, without any need for a trigger. Under this view, there is basically no need for EF.

The other view is that Merge is driven by some factor such as EF. Based on the observation that Merge almost always operates on a head and another non-head syntactic object, it is suggested that a certain kind of "structural asymmetry" that holds between the two syntactic objects is actually the driving force for Merge. Basically, Merge applies to reduce asymmetries, maximizing symmetry in syntax. The special role of Transfer, mentioned earlier, with respect to applications of Merge is attributed to the fact that Transfer creates asymmetry, thereby making it possible for Merge to apply more than once per LI.

In section 3.4, certain well-known characteristics of Japanese syntax (cf. (15) and (16)) are discussed in light of general properties of Merge. These characteristics have been noted as peculiar properties of Japanese in the literature. In the present context, however, they can be analyzed as direct consequences of unbounded Merge, backed up with interface mechanisms that attempt to assign appropriate interpretations to the structures generated by syntax. Thus, they are no longer peculiar properties of Japanese, but rather, the situation in which free applications of Merge appear to be prohibited calls for an explanation.

4 Concluding Remarks

After going over the historical background briefly (section 2), I focused on the core of the bare phrase structure theory, the operation Merge, in section 3, to see how the fundamental properties of human language listed at the outset of this chapter can be naturally accounted for by this simple operation. As our discussion in the preceding section indicates, the current

situation seems to be as follows. Property (1a), the existence of a hierarchical structure, is straightforwardly handled by Merge, if we assume the
operation to be iterative and non-associative. The unboundedness/discrete
infinity (property (1b)) is expressed by EF, although there is an issue as to
whether EF (or structural asymmetry of some sort) triggers Merge or Merge
freely applies without any trigger. Either way, unbounded Merge directly
accounts for the unboundedness/discrete infinity exhibited by human language (but see note 4). The status of property (1c), endocentricity/head-
edness (labeling), which is the core insight of traditional X-bar theory, is
actually rather controversial. It is either a non-property of human language
per se, determined by a third-factor principle such as minimal search, or it is
indeed an essential property of the human language faculty that needs to be
captured by UG, by means of an additional operation such as Embed (or its
equivalent). Finally, property (1d), the duality of semantics, which is one of
the basic motivations for transformations in earlier models of grammar, is
also captured by Merge, Internal Merge in this case, as we saw earlier (but
see note 13 for a potential problem).

In this way, the bare phrase structure theory, with the elementary operation Merge, successfully accounts for all the fundamental properties listed
in (1) at the outset of our discussion. This is a remarkable and certainly
welcome result, given minimalist goals. On the other hand, this situation
may give rise to a fear that there is little left for future research, as far as the
core phrase structure theory is concerned. Notice that iterative Merge is the
simplest possible mode of recursive generation, and thus, apart from a few
interesting issues (e.g., multiple dominance, the role of linear order, labeling), the story is pretty much finished once we have reached this operation.
Does this mean there are no "deep" results to be obtained from the study of
phrase structure theory in the future? I don't think so.

I maintain that one promising area of study in this connection is the mathematical study of strong generative capacities of grammars, as they relate
to questions of empirical significance (with respect to explanatory adequacy
and beyond). Despite its importance for theoretical linguistics, the study of
strong generative capacity has been, after the classical study by Chomsky
and Schützenberger (1963), set aside for a long time. Kuroda's (1976) topological study of a strong generation of phrase structure languages, although
it has not been widely recognized, takes a significant step forward, unveil-
ing important mathematical problems embedded in this domain of inquiry.
Kuroda introduces a class of topological spaces associated with finite sets
of phrases of a phrase-structure (tree) language, and then defines the notion
of "continuous function" from one tree language to another as a continuous function with respect to these topological spaces. Then, grammars that
generate tree languages can be classified nicely into structurally homeomor-
phic types. He argues that the topological method introduced in this fashion
provides a better and more appropriate means, both mathematically and

linguistically, than the notion of strong equivalence in the traditional sense for investigating the structural similarity of languages and grammars.

Recent discoveries by Kuroda (2008) further confirm, in a rather unexpected way, the conviction that the mathematical studies of strong generation offer a rich area of inquiry with significant empirical import. Kuroda notes some similarities between phrase-structure languages and ζ functions. ζ functions, first explicitly noticed by Euler in the eighteenth century and later developed by a number of mathematicians (Riemann, Dirichlet, Hecke, to name just a few), are a "major" mathematical object in the sense that they show up at virtually every corner of mathematical structures—particularly in number theory,[24] but sometimes even in elementary particle theory in physics—with profound mathematical substance. Kuroda invents a formal procedure for transforming the Euler product representations of certain ζ functions into phrase structure representations (in the extended form); by arithmetizing such phrase structure languages, the values of ζ functions can be calculated, leading to the situation where one can say that a ζ function has a representation as an accumulative sum of a phrase structure language. It is demonstrated in Kuroda (2008) that this procedure holds for Ramanujan's second-degree ζ functions (it trivially holds for first-degree ζ functions such as Riemann's and Dirichlet's), and it can be conjectured (though not explicitly considered in Kuroda 2008) that the procedure can be naturally extended to the cases of higher-degree ζ functions, possibly even including congruence ζ functions.[25] Kuroda's procedure is stated in terms of concatenative systems such as context-free phrase structure grammars, but his results ought to be readily translatable into the Merge-based generative system.

Mathematical studies of phrase structure as represented by these works have not yet attracted much attention in theoretical linguistics. But if the Galilean dictum that "Nature's great book is written in mathematical language" indeed holds, and if the human language capacity is part of the natural world, as has been assumed throughout the development of biolinguistic inquiries, then the linkage between language and mathematics might actually turn out to be much more substantial than it first appears to be, giving real substance to the claim (see Chomsky 1980) that the language faculty and the "number faculty" may be rooted in the same origin.

Notes

* I have given talks and lectures at various places discussing part of the material presented here, and I thank the audiences on these occasions for their comments and questions. I also would like to thank Cedric Boeckx, Teresa Griffith, Terje Lohndal, Hiroki Narita, and Mihoko Zushi for their valuable input.
1 The discussion in this section is overly simplified, as it serves just to set the stage for the discussion in the following section. See Fukui (2001), for a more comprehensive historical survey.

2 The original reasons for the need for grammatical transformations are not strictly restricted to the duality of semantics. See Chomsky (1956, 1957) for details. Also, the concept of transformations has important precursors in pre-generative structural linguistics, particularly in Zellig Harris's work (Harris 1957). See Introduction to Chomsky (1955/1975) for relevant discussion.

3 The observation goes back to the pre-generative era. See Harris (1951). The endocentric-exocentric distinction is even older (see, for example, Bloomfield 1933), though the intended meaning of the distinction is somewhat different.

4 By allowing iteration at one or more levels of projection. It is not entirely clear how the "global" recursion of the type expressed by the use of recursive symbols in phrase structure grammar (see the earlier discussion) is to be captured by X-bar theory, or in any subsequent theory for that matter.

5 Care must be taken to interpret the adjunction/substitution dichotomy, as it has carried different contents over the years, depending on the theory of transformations at the time. See Fukui (2001, notes 11 and 12) for relevant discussion.

6 Fukui (1986), Fukui and Speas (1986), Speas (1986, 1990), among others. The exposition here is based largely on Fukui (1986) and naturally benefits from hindsight.

7 In general, n number of objects. In human language, however, the number seems to be restricted to 2, yielding only binary structures. See Chomsky (2004a: 115) for the relevant discussion regarding why n should be 2 under the probe-goal system. The possibility of allowing n-ary structures ("non-configurational" structures) may still be open, if/when the probe-goal mechanism is not in operation. See Chomsky (2004b: 167–168) for discussion.

8 As argued in Fukui and Zushi (2003, 2004: 12).

9 Note the similarity between Embed and the von Neumann version of the successor function $n^+ = n \cup \{n\}$. Merge, on the other hand, is very similar to Zermelo's formulation of the successor function $n^+ = \{n\}$. Although these two versions are generally assumed to be equivalent in regard to the construction of natural numbers, it is not clear whether two (mathematically) "equivalent" operations always represent perform the "identical" operations, in human cognition, in this case.

10 Note that Embed presupposes Merge.

11 There is, of course, no such restriction in non-aphasic Japanese, so the cited examples are all grammatical. See also the discussion that follows.

12 Fukui (2004) puts forth the hypothesis that Embed is also lost in Japanese Broca's aphasics. But the crucial evidence is hard to come by, and the available evidence does not seem compelling.

13 It is not entirely clear, however, exactly how two (or more) non-sister copies in the case of Internal Merge can be appropriately linked to each other in a way that can be carried out within the bounds of Merge, which is a very local operation.

14 Problems may arise for Narita's analysis if Transfer (of a complement) always deletes the EF of a phase head.

15 See Chomsky (2008: 145). Narita (2009, 2010) calls this the "H-α schema."

16 Condition (11) shares a spirit similar to (but not quite the same as) the one in the antisymmetric approach initiated by Kayne (1994), or to the proposal by Moro (2000), both mainly for motivating movement.

17 See also Boeckx (2009).

18 What motivates this application of Merge remains a problem. The apparent lack of "complements" in Japanese noun phrases—as opposed to verb phrases in the same language—discussed in Fukui (1986) may constitute empirical evidence for the singleton-formation applying to nouns (but not to, say, verbs).

19 The relevant literature is too numerous to mention. The reader is particularly referred to the references mentioned in note 6. See also papers in such collections/handbooks as Fukui (1995) and Miyagawa and Saito (2008), and sources cited therein.
20 As mentioned, this conclusion largely carries over to noun phrases.
21 See Hoji (2009) for an extensive study of methodology to sort out various factors involved in linguistic judgments.
22 This is actually the hardest kind of scrambling out of an island for salvaging, because of the associated particle -*ni*, taken by the verb *atta* "met." If the scrambled phrase is marked by -*o*, interpretive licensing will be much easier, thanks to the hidden possibility of taking the fronted phrase as a reduced form of -*no koto-o* Lit. "-*no*-formal noun-ACC," i.e., as a kind of "major object" akin to a topic.
23 Given the vital role of agreement in English-type languages vis-à-vis the apparent lack of such processes in Japanese, there have been attempts to deal with the problem by stipulating that agreement somehow "closes" the projection (cf. (6e)). While such a stipulative account cannot count as a true explanation in the current minimalist setting, its main insights, i.e., that additional requirements of English (including agreement) render the constructions impossible, should somehow be incorporated into the ultimate explanation.
24 Thus, according to Goro Shimura, a prominent number theorist, "Seisuuron, itarutokoro ζ kansuu ari" (Lit. "Number theory, ζ functions are everywhere"), i.e., "In number theory, ζ functions show up everywhere" (quoted by Kato 2009: 69).
25 See Fukui (1998: 209) for a brief remark about how (portions of) the "Weil Conjectures" (Weil 1949) might be related to human language structure.

References

Bloomfield, Leonard. 1933. *Language.* New York: Holt, Rinehart & Winston.

Boeckx, Cedric. 2008. *Bare syntax.* Oxford: Oxford University Press.

Boeckx, Cedric. 2009. On the locus of asymmetry in UG. *Catalan Journal of Linguistics* 8: 41–53.

Chomsky, Noam. 1955/1975. The logical structure of linguistic theory. Ms., Harvard University, 1955. Published in part in 1975, New York: Plenum.

Chomsky, Noam. 1956. Three models for the description of language. *IRE Transactions on Information Theory* IT-2: 113–124. [Reprinted, with corrections, in *Readings in mathematical psychology*, volume 2, ed. R. Duncan Luce, Robert R. Bush, and Eugene Galanter. New York: Wiley. (1965).]

Chomsky, Noam. 1957. *Syntactic structures.* The Hague: Mouton. 2nd edition, Mouton de Gruyter, 2002.

Chomsky, Noam. 1965. *Aspects of the theory of syntax.* Cambridge, MA: MIT Press.

Chomsky, Noam. 1970. Remarks on nominalization. In *Readings in English transformational grammar*, ed. Roderick A. Jacobs and Peter S. Rosenbaum, 184–221. Waltham, MA: Ginn.

Chomsky, Noam. 1980. *Rules and representations.* New York: Columbia University Press.

Chomsky, Noam. 1986. *Barriers.* Cambridge, MA: MIT Press.

Chomsky, Noam. 1995a. Bare phrase structure. In *Evolution and revolution in linguistic theory: Essays in honor of Carlos Otero*, ed. Héctor Ramiro Campos and

Paula Marie Kempchinsky, 51–109. Washington, DC: Georgetown University Press.

Chomsky, Noam. 1995b. *The minimalist program*. Cambridge, MA: MIT Press.

Chomsky, Noam. 2000. Minimalist inquiries: The framework. In *Step by step: Minimalist essays in honor of Howard Lasnik*, ed. Roger Martin, David Michaels, and Juan Uriagereka, 89–155. Cambridge, MA: MIT Press.

Chomsky, Noam. 2001. Derivation by phase. In *Ken Hale: A life in language*, ed. Michael Kenstowicz, 1–52. Cambridge, MA: MIT Press.

Chomsky, Noam. 2004a. Beyond explanatory adequacy. In *Structures and beyond: The cartography of syntactic structures*, volume 3, ed. Adriana Belletti, 104–131. Oxford: Oxford University Press.

Chomsky, Noam. 2004b. *The generative enterprise revisited: A conversation with Riny Huybregts, Henk van Riemsdijk, Naoki Fukui, and Mihoko Zushi*. Berlin: Mouton de Gruyter.

Chomsky, Noam. 2005. Three factors in language design. *Linguistic Inquiry* 36: 1–22.

Chomsky, Noam. 2007. Approaching UG from below. In *Interfaces + recursion = language? Chomsky's minimalism and the view from syntax-semantics*, ed. Uli Sauerland and Hans-Martin Gärtner, 1–29. Berlin: Mouton de Gruyter.

Chomsky, Noam. 2008. On phases. In *Foundational issues in linguistic theory: Essays in honor of Jean-Roger Vergnaud*, ed. Robert Freidin, Carlos P. Otero, and Maria Luisa Zubizarreta, 133–166. Cambridge, MA: MIT Press.

Chomsky, Noam, and Marcel Paul Schützenberger. 1963. The algebraic theory of context-free languages. In *Computer programming and formal systems*, ed. Paul Braffort and David Hirschberg, 118–161. Amsterdam: North-Holland.

Collins, Chris. 2002. Eliminating labels. In *Derivation and explanation in the minimalist program*, ed. Samuel David Epstein and T. Daniel Seely, 42–64. Oxford: Blackwell.

Fujita, Koji. 2007. Kaiki-sei kara mieru bunpou-no hattatu to sinka [The development and evolution of grammar in light of recursion]. *Gengo* 36 (11): 16–24.

Fukui, Naoki. 1986/1995. A theory of category projection and its applications. Doctoral dissertation, MIT. Published in 1995 with revisions as *Theory of projection in syntax*, Tokyo: Kurosio Publishers and Stanford: CSLI publications.

Fukui, Naoki. 1995. The principles-and-parameters approach: A comparative syntax of English and Japanese. In *Approaches to language typology*, ed. Masayoshi Shibatani and Theodora Bynon, 327–372. Oxford: Oxford University Press. [Reprinted in *Theoretical comparative syntax: Studies in macroparameters*, 100–131. London: Routledge. (2006).]

Fukui, Naoki. 1998. Kyokusyoo-moderu-no tenkai: Gengo-no setumei-riron-o mezasite [The development of a minimalist program: Toward a truly explanatory theory of language]. In *Seisei bunpo [Generative grammar]*, ed. Yukinori Takubo, Toshiaki Inada, Shigeo Tonoike, Heizo Nakajima, and Naoki Fukui, 161–210. Tokyo: Iwanami Shoten.

Fukui, Naoki. 2001. Phrase structure. In *The handbook of contemporary syntactic theory*, ed. Mark Baltin and Chris Collins, 374–406. Oxford: Blackwell. [Reprinted in *Theoretical comparative syntax: Studies in macroparameters*, 258–288. London: Routledge. (2006).]

Fukui, Naoki, ed. 2003. Formal Japanese syntax and universal grammar: The past 20 years. *Lingua Special Issue* 113 (4–6): 315–320.

Fukui, Naoki. 2004. Broca's aphasics: A generative approach. Paper presented at the Sophia International Workshop on Speech Pathology, Sophia University, Tokyo.

Fukui, Naoki. 2005. Embed. Paper presented at the Third International Conference on Formal Linguistics, Hunan University, Changsha.

Fukui, Naoki. 2008. Gengo no kihon enzan o meguru oboegaki [Some notes on the basic operations of human language]. In *Gengo kenkyu no genzai: Keisiki to imi no intaafeisu [The state of the art in linguistic research: The interface of form and meaning]*, ed. Yoshiaki Kaneko, Akira Kikuchi, Daiko Takahashi, Yoshiki Ogawa, and Etsuro Shima, 1–21. Tokyo: Kaitakusha. [Reprinted in *Sin sizen kagaku to site no gengogaku: Seisei bunpoo towa nanika [A new and expanded edition of linguistics as a natural science: What is generative grammar?]*, 241–274. Tokyo: Chikumasyoboo. (2012).]

Fukui, Naoki, and Magaret Speas. 1986. Specifiers and projection. *MIT Working Papers in Linguistics* 8: 128–172. [Reprinted in *Theoretical comparative syntax: Studies in macroparameters*, Naoki Fukui, 9–37. London: Routledge. (2006).]

Fukui, Naoki, and Mihoko Zushi. 2003. Yakusya-niyoru zyosetu [Translator's introduction]. In *Seiseibunpou no kuwadate [The generative enterprise revisited]*, ed. Noam Chomsky and trans. Naoki Fukui and Mihoko Zushi, 1–34. Tokyo: Iwanami Shoten.

Fukui, Naoki, and Mihoko Zushi. 2004. Introduction. [Abridged English translation of Fukui and Zushi 2003.] In *The generative enterprise revisited: A conversation with Riny Huybregts, Henk van Riemsdijk, Naoki Fukui, and Mihoko Zushi*, ed. Noam Chomsky, 1–25. Berlin: Mouton de Gruyter.

Harris, Zellig S. 1951. *Methods in structural linguistics*. Chicago: University of Chicago Press.

Harris, Zellig S. 1957. Co-occurrence and transformation in linguistic structure. *Language* 33: 283–340. [Reprinted in *The structure of language: Readings in the philosophy of language*, ed. Jerry A. Fodor and Jerrold J. Katz, 155–210. Englewood Cliffs, NJ: Prentice Hall. (1964).]

Hinzen, Wolfram. 2006. *Mind design and minimal syntax*. Oxford: Oxford University Press.

Hoji, Hajime. 2009. A foundation of generative grammar as an empirical science. Ms., University of Southern California.

Hornstein, Nobert. 2009. *A theory of syntax: Minimal operations and universal grammar*. Cambridge: Cambridge University Press.

Hornstein, Nobert, Jairo Nukes, and Kleanthes K. Grohmann. 2005. *Understanding minimalism*. Cambridge: Cambridge University Press.

Kato, Kazuya. 2009. *Fermat-no saisyuuteiri, Sato-Tate yosoo kaiketu-eno miti* [Fermat's last theorem and the paths towards the proof of the Sato-Tate conjecture]. Tokyo: Iwanami Shoten.

Kayne, Richard S. 1994. *The antisymmetry of syntax*. Cambridge, MA: MIT Press.

Kuno, Susumu. 1973. *The structure of the Japanese language*. Cambridge, MA: MIT Press.

Kuroda, S.-Y. 1976. A topological study of phrase-structure languages. *Information and Control* 30: 307–379.

Kuroda, S.-Y. 1988. Whether we agree or not: A comparative syntax of English and Japanese. *Linguisticae Investigationes* 12: 1–47. [Reprinted in *Japanese syntax and semantics*, 315–357. Dordrecht: Kluwer. (1992).]

Kuroda, S.-Y. 2008. Suugaku to seiseibunpoo: Setumeiteki datoosei-no kanatani sosite gengo-no suugakuteki zituzairon [Mathematics and generative grammar: Beyond explanatory adequacy and mathematical realism of language] (with an extended English summary). *Sophia Linguistica* 56: 1–36.

Lyons, John. 1968. *Introduction to theoretical linguistics.* Cambridge: Cambridge University Press.

Miyagawa, Shigeru, and Mamoru Saito, ed. 2008. *The handbook of Japanese linguistics.* Oxford: Oxford University Press.

Moro, Andrea. 2000. *Dynamic antisymmetry.* Cambridge, MA: MIT Press.

Narita, Hiroki. 2009. Multiple transfer in service of recursive Merge. Paper presented at the 32nd GLOW Colloquium. Abstract published in *GLOW Newsletter* 62: 89–91.

Narita, Hiroki. 2010. Phase cycles in service of projection-free syntax. Ms., Harvard University.

Post, Emil L. 1943. Formal deductions of the general combinatorial decision problem. *American Journal of Mathematics* 65 (2): 197–215.

Saito, Mamoru, and Naoki Fukui. 1998. Order in phrase structure and movement. *Linguistic Inquiry* 29: 439–474. [Reprinted in *Theoretical comparative syntax: Studies in macroparameters*, Naoki Fukui, 179–208. London: Routledge. (2006).]

Speas, Margaret J. 1986. Adjunctions and projections in syntax. Doctoral dissertation, MIT.

Speas, Margaret J. 1990. *Phrase structure in natural language.* Dordrecht: Kluwer.

Uriagereka, Juan. 2002. *Derivations.* London: Routledge.

Weil, André. 1949. Numbers of solutions of equations in finite fields. *Bulletin of the American Mathematical Society* 55: 497–508. [Reprinted in *Oeuvres scientifiques: Collected papers*, volume 1, 399–410. New York: Springer. (1979).]

Wells, Rulon S. 1947. Immediate constituents. *Language* 23: 81–117. [Reprinted in *Readings in linguistics: The development of descriptive linguistics since 1925*, ed. Martin Joos, 186–207. Washington, DC: American Council of Learned Societies. (1957).]

2 Merge and (A)symmetry*

With Hiroki Narita

1 Introduction

Under the most general formulation, the basic operation of human language—Merge—reduces to a generative procedure that takes n (typically two) syntactic objects (SOs) and forms an unordered pair (i.e., a set) of them thereby effectively combining the SOs, without specifying any other information such as labels or projection that has been stipulated in X-bar theory. The widely assumed "bare phrase structure" model thus holds that the mechanism of structure-generation minimally consists of the following two components: one is narrow syntax, whose core function is unbounded application of Merge, and the other is the Lexicon, which stores a finite set of lexical items (LIs) that constitute atoms for Merge. Primitive though it seems, this simple apparatus, when applied freely, yields a rather intricate array of hierarchically structured SOs, feeding various modes of interpretation at the interfaces with the conceptual-intentional (CI) system and the sensorimotor (SM) system (called SEM and PHON, respectively).

A cursory look at available linguistic data suggests that the arrangement of forms and interpretations, though fed by unconstrained Merge, is by no means random or arbitrary. For example, consider the long-standing observation that the distinction between External Merge and Internal Merge is systematically tied with the so-called "duality of semantics" (see Chomsky 2004, 2007, 2008 for recent formulation). For any instance of Merge(α, β), it is either that α and β are separate SOs or that one is part of the other. This yields the bifurcation of External Merge and Internal Merge as defined in (1):

(1) Merge(α, β) counts as *Internal Merge* if one of α, β is a term of the other. When α and β are separate SOs, Merge(α, β) counts as *External Merge*. (Chomsky 2004 *et seq.*)

For example, if Merge applies to two independent SOs, say *eat* and {*the, apple*}, it yields a case of External Merge, creating another SO {*eat*, {*the*, *apple*}}. (2) represents the input and the output of the external merger in terms of informal but familiar diagram-based notations, order irrelevant.

(2) a.   b.

     eat   eat

          the   apple   the   apple

In contrast, Internal Merge combines one SO and one of its terms, say {C, {*we*, {Infl, {*see*, *what*}}}} (3a) and its term *what*, and it creates another occurrence of *what* at the edge of (3a), yielding the "copy theory of movement" (Chomsky 1993, 1995b), as depicted in (3b).

(3) a.   b.

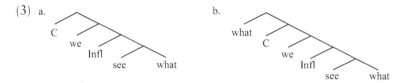

Chomsky (2007, 2008) observes that these two modes of Merge are systematically tied with quite different syntactic and semantic consequences. Broadly speaking, the bifurcation of External and Internal Merge closely correlates with two classes of semantic properties, the so-called "d(eep)-structure" and "s(urface)-structure" interpretations. D-structure interpretation typically involves θ-related properties such as selection and predicate-argument structure, and s-structure interpretation involves various discourse-related properties such as new/old information, topic-focus, operator-scope, specificity, and so on. Chomsky's observation is that this duality of semantics finds a close correspondence to the bifurcation of External and Internal Merge: thus, External Merge typically feeds d-structure interpretation, and Internal Merge s-structure interpretation. This observation, call it Approximation 1, uncovers a corner of hidden regularity that the system of unconstrained Merge incorporates.

(4) Approximation 1: External vs. Internal Merge ≈ Duality of Semantics: The bifurcation of External and Internal Merge correlates with the duality of "d(eep)-structure" and "s(urface)-structure" interpretations (Chomsky 2007, 2008).

In addition to Chomsky's observation (4), we point out a couple of more rather intriguing correlations of structures and their interpretations. The second approximation is concerned with the endocentricity of d-structure semantics. Recall that d-structure interpretation involves selection and θ-marking. Under the traditional assumption, these d-structure relations are typically established in the so-called head-complement relation: for example, a transitive verb takes a noun phrase or a clause as its complement, and assigns an object θ-role to it; T selects *v*P/AspP and associates tense-related/ aspectual semantics to it; C selects TP, assigning finiteness, modality and other propositional properties to it, and so forth. More generally, properties of d-structure semantics are in most cases primarily configured by a designated lexical head.

(5) Approximation 2: D-structure semantics ≈ Endocentricity:
Properties of d-structure interpretation are primarily configured by a designated head LI.

In contrast, it is not clear whether s-structure semantics is endocentric in any meaningful sense. What would be the "head" of the operator-scope construction, for example? Operators and their scope domains are typically two locally related XPs of certain types of salience in discourse, and they have *prima facie* no relation to any designated head LIs in linguistic expressions. The same holds for specificity and new-old information, and also for topic-focus or theme-rheme structure. While the contemporary literature of linguistic cartography attempts to provide a rich set of stipulations on covert head LIs in the domain of left periphery (see Rizzi 1997, 2004 and Cinque 1999, 2002), it seems reasonable to say that there is by far less evidence to stipulate headedness or endocentricity for these s-structure interpretations.

Another important observation, obviously related, is that structures feeding d-structure interpretation are often encoded in binary SOs, each of which consists of an LI H and a phrase XP:

(6) Approximation 3: D-structure interpretation ≈ Asymmetric branching:
D-structure interpretation (selectional properties, predicate-argument structure) is typically encoded in an "asymmetric" branching of the form {H, XP}, where H is an LI and XP is a phrasal SO.

(7a-e) exemplify some of the canonical configurations feeding selectional or θ-related interpretation, each of which is asymmetric in the described sense.[1]

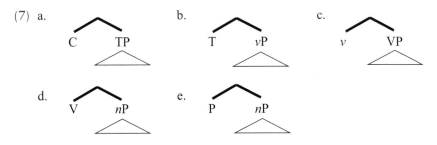

(7) a. C TP   b. T *v*P   c. *v* VP
     d. V *n*P   e. P *n*P

These are traditionally called "head-complement configurations," so (5) and (6) point to the close connection between d-structure semantics, the structural asymmetry of head-complement (H-XP) configurations, and the semantic endocentricity (though with an important exception of the merger of an external argument, a case which we will discuss shortly).

In contrast with configurations like those in (7), the opposite pattern is true for Internal Merge. As we mentioned, s-structure semantics that Internal Merge feeds is non-endocentric, and further, Internal Merge typically "moves" a phrase (XP) to the edge of another phrase (YP), yielding a "symmetric" branching of the form {XP, YP} ("symmetric" in the sense that both of the constituents are phrasal/non-LIs). For example, *wh*-movement dislocates a *wh*-phrase to the Spec-C position, and A-movement or Subject-raising moves an *n*P to the Spec-T position (t_{wh} and t_{nP} indicate copies of *which picture* and *the boy*, respectively).

(8) a.   *Wh*-movement:

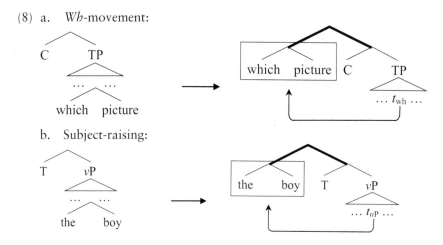

b.   Subject-raising:

Thus, it is a curious fact about Internal Merge that, unlike External Merge, it almost always generates symmetric XP-YP structures.

(9) Approximation 4: Internal Merge ≈ Symmetric branching:
     Internal Merge typically yields a "symmetric" branching, {XP, YP}.

These four observations point to an interesting generalization concerning Merge and its effect on the syntax-semantics interface. We reviewed that there are four conceptual dimensions pertaining to the Merge-based linguistic computation: External vs. Internal Merge, asymmetric vs. symmetric branching, d-structure vs. s-structure semantics, and endocentric vs. non-endocentric interpretations (i.e., interpretations primarily carved out by designated head LIs vs. interpretations in which headedness/endocentricity plays virtually no role). It seems that these four dichotomies closely correlate with one another. Thus, External Merge typically results in asymmetric H-XP branching and endocentric "d-structure" semantics, whereas Internal Merge results in symmetric XP-YP branching and non-endocentric "s-structure" semantics.

(10) *Generalization* (preliminary version):

a. External Merge	b. Internal Merge
≈ "d-structure" semantics (predicate-argument structure, selection)	≈ "s-structure" semantics (discourse-related properties)
≈ endocentric	≈ non-endocentric
≈ asymmetric branching ({H, XP})	≈ symmetric branching ({XP, YP})

This systematic pattern is a rather remarkable fact about human language. If we take the empirical hypothesis that Merge is unconstrained and applies freely, if only for the account of the discrete infinity of human language, then we would expect that it generates all sorts of SOs with mixed forms and properties. But this is not what we find at the syntax-semantics interface. Then, an investigation into the nature of (10) is expected to reveal an important aspect of Merge-based syntax, and humanly configured semantics it interfaces with.

The purpose of this chapter is to refine and sharpen the rough generalization in (10), and attempt to provide a possible explanation for this systematic dichotomy. The rest of the chapter is organized as follows. Section 2 will first examine two important cases of apparent exception to (10), namely head-movement and the merger of an external argument, and refine the concept of structural symmetry in order to incorporate these cases into the proposed generalization. Section 3 will then put forward the hypothesis that syntactic computation is essentially driven for symmetry as defined in section 2. Section 4 will discuss several consequences of our symmetry-driven syntax, and section 5 will conclude the chapter.

2 Sharpening the Generalization

Obviously, the preliminary generalization in (10) is quite rough as it stands now, and it faces a couple of difficulties in explaining the whole variety of linguistic structures. One of the most obvious problems is that it fails to explain cases where External Merge yields symmetric structures. Two obvious cases that fall under this category are head-movement and the merger of an external argument. We will discuss them one by one, and sharpen (10) in such a way that it can accommodate these apparent exceptions.

2.1 *Exceptional Case 1: Head-movement*

The first case we would like to discuss is *head-movement* (X^0-movement). Although whether head-movement is syntactic or not is currently contested (see, e.g., Boeckx and Stjepanović 2001, Chomsky 2001; see also Roberts 2010), the traditional assumption is that it is really a form of syntactic movement that adjoins an LI X^0 to another LI Y^0 that c-commands it. According to the traditional description, head-movement of X^0 effectively replaces Y^0 in an SO with the so-called "Y^{0max}" category that consists of X^0 and a segment of Y^0, as shown in (11), but still behaves as Y^0 as a whole.

(11) a.   b.

However, if Chomsky (2007, 2008) is right in claiming that every application of Merge satisfies the *No-tampering Condition* (NTC) (12), then X^0-Y^0-merger should not be able to modify the internal composition of Y^0.

(12) *No-tampering Condition*:
   Merge of X and Y leaves the two SOs unchanged (Chomsky 2008: 138).

Under the NTC, instances of X^0-Y^0-merger should not be able to replace Y^0 in (11a) with "Y^{0max}" = $\{X^0, Y^0\}$. Rather, it is predicted that such an application of Merge just generates another set $\{X^0, Y^0\}$, without tampering the SO in (13a)/(13a'). If this operation really exists as an instance of Merge (not an innocuous assumption), and if we keep to the definition of Merge as a simple set-formation operation, then, what it yields is two SOs, $\{X, Y\}$ and $\{Y, \{X, ZP\}\}$ as shown in (13b').

(13) a.   b.

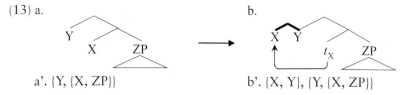

   a'. $\{Y, \{X, ZP\}\}$ b'. $\{X, Y\}, \{Y, \{X, ZP\}\}$

The informal tree notation in (13b) looks as though the operation counts as a kind of "sideways movement," yielding partially overlapping SOs that share Y as their immediate terms. No matter how we grasp the intuition behind (13), the point is that the replacement of Y^0 in an SO with an "Y^{0max}"-category is beyond the generative power of Merge. Traditional examples of head-movement, such as T-to-C and V-to-v, should be reanalyzed along these lines of reasoning.

(14) a. T-to-C-raising, forming $\{T, C\}$:

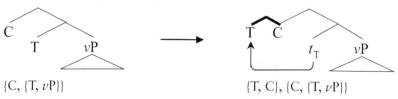

   $\{C, \{T, vP\}\}$ $\{T, C\}, \{C, \{T, vP\}\}$

b. V-to-*v*-raising, forming {V, *v*} (or root-incorporation more generally):

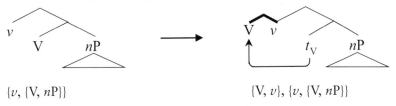

$\{v, \{V, nP\}\}$ $\{V, v\}, \{v, \{V, nP\}\}$

Notice that the occurrence of Y^0 is obviously not a term of X^0 (and *vice versa*). Then, such instances of Merge should count as External Merge under Chomsky's definition (1), reproduced here.

(1) Merge(α, β) counts as Internal Merge if one of α, β is a term of the other. When α and β are separate SOs, Merge(α, β) counts as External Merge. (Chomsky 2004 *et seq.*)

However, External Merge in head-movement is quite different in a number of respects from the canonical instances of External Merge. On the other hand, its similarity to Internal Merge is obvious: first of all, head-movement is obviously a movement operation just like Internal Merge, and it yields copies of X^0. Further, head-movement also patterns with Internal Merge in terms of our preliminary generalization in (10): just like core cases of Internal Merge, head-movement results in a kind of "symmetric" branching, in this case of the form $\{X^0, Y^0\}$. In addition, if head-movement has any semantic effect at all, it is always discourse-related (For example, Neg^0-raising alters the scope of negation, T^0-to-C^0-raising results in the interrogative force, etc.; see Lechner 2006). Therefore, if there is some truth to the generalization in (10), and if head-movement really exists as a syntactic phenomenon (again, not an obvious matter), it seems natural to pursue a theory of Merge that assimilates head-movement to the category of Internal Merge.

To achieve this goal, we propose to replace the Chomskyan definition of Internal vs. External Merge by (15):

(15) Merge (α, β) counts as *Internal Merge* if α and β are terms of a single SO. Otherwise, Merge (α, β) counts as *External Merge*.

This definition naturally accommodates the case of head-movement: the head-movement in (13a)/(13a'), understood as Merge(X^0, Y^0), is an instance of Internal Merge according to (15), since both X^0 and Y^0 are terms of a single SO (13a)/(13a'). Moreover, since 'term-of' is a reflexive relation, any SO is a term of itself (see Chomsky 1995b: 247). Therefore, canonical instances of XP-movement correctly fall under the category of Internal Merge as defined in (15): when α is a term of β, Merge(α, β) counts as Internal Merge, since both α and β are terms of a single SO β.[2]

In what follows, then, we will adopt the alternative definition in (15) and assume that head-movement falls within the category of Internal Merge for the sake of our account.

2.2 Exceptional Case 2: External Argument

A more serious problem arises with regard to another case of External Merge. It has to do with the merger of an external argument as in (16).

(16)

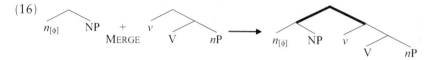

Clearly, this is a case of External Merge, and also this structure feeds d-structure interpretation that is allegedly endocentric (the standard description says that v is the alleged head of (16)). However, it is also a case of symmetric branching consisting of two phrasal constituents. Thus it is a clear deviation from the proposed generalization in (10). The situation is summarized as follows.

(17) (16) involves:
    a. External Merge
    b. d-structure interpretation (θ-role assignment to the external argument)
    c. endocentricity (v is the alleged head of (16))
    d. symmetric branching {XP, YP}

As is obvious from (17), in this case, we would rather like to assimilate this exceptional case to the category of asymmetric External Merge, with which endocentricity and d-structure semantics are closely associated.

To maintain the generalization in (10) in its essence *vis-à-vis* the merger of an external argument (16), we need to construct an alternative characterization of structural (a)symmetry that classifies SOs like (16) into the class of *asymmetric* structures. To achieve this goal, consider (16) again. Although this SO is a "symmetric" structure of the form {XP, YP}, if we also take *heads* of the relevant XP/YP into consideration, there is a certain sense in which the structure is "asymmetric." Specifically, the n-head of the external argument contains various nominal features such as person, number, and gender (so-called ϕ-features), while the v-head of the other SO is characterized by its verbal features, including interpretable features determining aspect and other eventuality properties. By the standard assumption, nominal features and verbal features are as distinct as they can be, so it is tempting to make use of the distinction in the wanted formulation of structural asymmetry.[3]

Compare (16) with (8) reproduced here as (18), cases of XP-YP structures that we still want to characterize as "symmetric."

(18) a. *Wh*-movement:

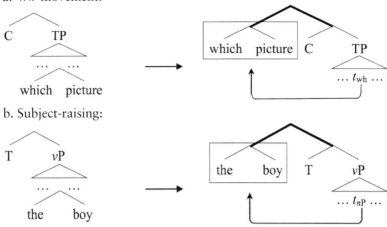

b. Subject-raising:

Indeed, the SOs in (18) differ from (16) in featural contents of the relevant heads. Consider first the XP-YP structure of subject-raising in (18b). Morphological evidence suggests that the heads of XP and YP, *n*/D (realized as *the*)[4] and T, undergoes φ-feature-agreement, presumably as a result of the probe-goal relation established by Agree (Chomsky 2000 *et seq.*), and thus these two heads share a matching set of φ-features.[5] The agreement relation can naturally be extended to cover the cases of *wh*-movement like the one in (18a), involving agreement of Q(uestion)-features or perhaps Foc(us)-features (see Cable 2007, 2010, Narita 2011, 2014, and Chomsky 2012 for arguments that moved *wh*-phrases are uniformly headed by a designated category Q). In contrast, this sort of feature-matching is clearly absent in (16).

It is tempting to hypothesize that the relevant type of feature-matching is a necessary condition for making such XP-YP structures as (18) symmetric. Pursuing these lines of reasoning, we would like to propose the following concept of *feature-equilibrium* in (19), and present a new characterization of symmetry (20) in terms of this new concept.

(19) *Feature-equilibrium:*
For a formal feature F, an SO $\{\alpha, \beta\}$ is in an *F-equilibrium.* $\equiv_{def.}$ α and β share a matching formal feature F that is equally prominent in α and β.

(20) *Featural symmetry:*
Given a formal feature F in an SO $\{\alpha, \beta\}$, the SO is *symmetric* with respect to F (or *F-symmetric*) if it is in an F-equilibrium. Otherwise, the SO $\{\alpha, \beta\}$ is (F-)asymmetric with respect to F.

According to the proposed definition, {XP, YP} counts as symmetric when it forms an F-equilibrium with respect to some formal feature F. Familiar XP-YP structures created by Internal Merge are classified as symmetric in this very sense: (18a) and (18b) are symmetric in that they form a

Q-equilibrium and a φ-equilibrium, respectively. In contrast, the case of the external argument (16) cannot count as symmetric under the definition in (20), given the lack of matching features shared by n and v. In particular, the existence of *bona fide* formal feature [φ] on n ensures that (16) is correctly classified as asymmetric according to (20b). In this approach, then, the case of the external argument ceases to be exceptional in the face of the otherwise valid correlation of structural asymmetry and asymmetric (endo-centric) d-structure semantics.

Note that the notion of featural symmetry is defined in (20) relative to some feature F present in {α, β}. If a relevant feature does not exist in the SO, F-(a)symmetry is not even defined and the notion becomes simply irrelevant. Therefore, the XP-YP structure in (18b) does count as φ-symmetric, but it is neither symmetric nor asymmetric with respect to, say, [Q], given the lack of [Q] in the SO (see also note 14 for an important clarification).

Recall that we still want to classify cases of H-XP structures like (7) (re-produced here) as asymmetric SOs, typical of External Merge. How does our new concept of featural symmetry achieve this goal?

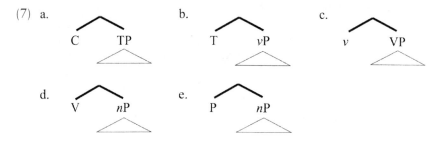

(7) a.   b.   c.

C   TP   T vP v VP

d.   e.

V nP   P nP

It is not clear whether H and XP share any matching feature in these cases. Observationally, there are various sorts of dependencies between H and the head of XP in those structures: C assigns finiteness to T in (7a); T determines tense and aspectual properties of v in (7b); $v/n/a/p$ assigns their categorial-features to V/N/A/P in SOs like (7c) (which may originally be an uncategorized root LI; see Halle and Marantz 1993 *et seq.*); V and P selects/subcategorizes n in (7d-e); and so on, and a variety of linguistic theories hypothesize abstract features and mechanisms of feature-checking thereof to capture these dependencies. Be that as it may, it is clear that these struc-tures invoke endocentric d-structure semantics, so the desirable result is that {H, XP} generally counts as asymmetric and cannot form any feature-equilibrium, irrespective of whether a matching feature F exists in H and XP. Intuitively speaking, SOs of the form {H, XP} are "unbalanced" with respect to the size of the two constituents, or the "depth" of features embedded in H and XP: H is an LI, and therefore a smallest syntactic element that imme-diately presents its features by assumption, but XP is a phrasal composite whose featural content can only be determined by further inspection of its

LI-terms. Building on this observation, we defined the notion of feature-equilibrium in (19) in such a way as to require that the matching feature F must be "equally prominent" in α and β in order for $\{\alpha, \beta\}$ to become symmetric. Here we characterize *feature prominence* inductively as in (21), which yields the result that $\{$H, XP$\}$ can never be symmetric with respect to any feature.

(21) *Feature prominence*:
       Suppose that Prom(F) = n ($n \geq 0$) is the order of prominence associated with a feature F, with, let us say, lower prominence indicated by a higher number, 0 being the highest order of prominence. Then, we can say:
       a. Prom(F of an LI H) = 0
       b. If Prom(F in an SO α) = n, then Prom(F in $\{\alpha, \beta\}$) = $n + 1$.

(21a) says that any feature F of an LI H is of the highest order of prominence (0) and immediately accessible in that LI, and (21b) maintains that the order of prominence of F decreases as H gets further embedded into a larger SO. Then, it follows that no feature F of H and XP can be equally prominent in $\{$H, XP$\}$: while Prom(F of H) = 0, it is necessarily the case that Prom(F in XP) > 0. Therefore, $\{$H, XP$\}$ can never count as symmetric according to the definition in (21).

Exploring these lines of reasoning, we put forward a revised version of our proposed generalization in (22), where the notion of symmetry/asymmetry is redefined in terms of feature-equilibrium.

(22) *Generalization* (revised):
       a. External Merge   b. Internal Merge
           $\approx$ asymmetric branching $\approx$ symmetric branching
               (forming a feature-equilibrium)
           $\approx$ endocentric $\approx$ non-endocentric
           $\approx$ "d-structure" semantics $\approx$ "s-structure" semantics
               (predicate-argument structure,   (discourse-related
               selection)   properties)

In particular, the alternative characterization of symmetry established in this section naturally incorporates otherwise exceptional cases of the external argument and, as we will see shortly, head-movement as well.

3 The Theory of Symmetry-Driven Syntax

Building on the generalization established in the preceding discussion, this section will advance a theory of syntax in which linguistic derivation is fundamentally driven for stable representations characterized by featural symmetry.

Without stipulation, Merge can freely combine SOs (generating both asymmetric and symmetric structures), but we observed that Internal Merge typically results in symmetric structures: Subject-raising and ϕ-feature-agreement result in a ϕ-equilibrium, while *wh*-movement and Q-feature-agreement result in a Q-equilibrium (in what follows, we will adopt the familiar notation where [uF] stands for a formal feature F whose value is unspecified, and [vF] stands for a valued F—hence inherently interpretable).

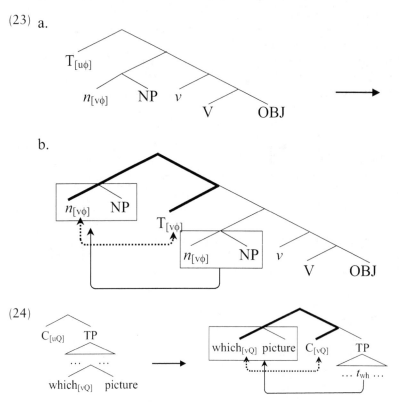

(23) a.

b.

(24)

In contrast, External Merge, the first application of Merge for each SO, typically yields asymmetric structures as we saw earlier. This pattern seems to be systematic, and we would like to know why this is almost always the case. To capture this state of affairs, we propose that syntactic derivation is driven by the need for featural symmetry. This idea can be stated as (25):

(25) *Dynamic Symmetrization Condition (DSC):*
Each formal feature F must form an F-equilibrium in the course of the derivation.

LIs are associated with their own feature contents. External Merge freely introduces LIs and their features (including formal features) into a syntactic derivation, but DSC (25) essentially states that once a formal feature F is introduced, the subsequent derivation must guarantee that F moves to a position where it can form an F-equilibrium. This is achieved by Internal Merge. For instance, Subject-raising is driven by the need for φ-equilibrium, and *wh*-movement is driven by the need for Q-equilibrium.

Further, the earlier discussion naturally points to the conclusion that head-movement is also driven for symmetry (see Chomsky 1995b, van Riemsdijk 1998b, Matushansky 2006, Citko 2008, 2011, and Roberts 2010 for earlier explorations of head-movement in the theory of projection). Recall that the prototypical case of head-movement is Root-incorporation (such as V-to-*v* and N-to-*n*), which is supposed to be driven by the need for categorizing the root. We may describe this situation by assuming that root categories are associated with an unvalued Cat(egorial)-feature that is in need of valuation by a neighboring categorizer. Then, root-incorporation can also be seen as driven by the need for categorial-feature symmetry. (26) illustrates the situation with V-to-*v* Internal Merge, where V/root's [uCat] enters into a Cat-equilibrium with *v*'s [V-Cat] (a categorial feature valued as [V(erb)]).[6]

(26)

$\{v, \{V, nP\}\}$ $\{V, v\}, \{v, \{V, nP\}\}$

Notice further that, if we follow Chomsky (2007, 2008) and Richards (2007) in assuming that T's tense-feature is dependent on C, then we might also say that T-to-C incorporation is just another instance of Internal Merge driven by feature-equilibrium. Adapting the analysis from the Chomsky-Richards theory of feature-inheritance, we assume that T has an unvalued T(ense)-feature [uT] that undergoes matching with an interpretable counterpart in C. Thanks to this T-feature-matching, T-to-C movement results in a symmetric structure {T, C}, just like root-incorporation. [7]

(27)

$\{C, \{T, vP\}\}$ $\{T, C\}, \{C, \{T, vP\}\}$

Thus, the formation of {T, C} can also be seen as driven by T(ense)-feature symmetry.

Under this approach, head-movement is assumed to fulfill an important function of fixing the asymmetry of {X⁰, YP} and forming a feature-equilibrium. Therefore, (25) provides an important rationale for head-movement, reducing it to a special case of symmetry-forming Internal Merge.

More generally, DSC (25) is articulating the view that asymmetric structures are unstable and must get stabilized by Internal Merge. Then, linguistic computation is irreversibly directed toward symmetrization, and this idea provides a natural ordering of operations in (28).

(28) External Merge → Internal Merge:
For any formal feature F, an application of External Merge that creates an F-asymmetric SO (i.e., an SO that is asymmetric with respect to F) entails a later application of Internal Merge that yields an F-equilibrium.

This completes our rationalization of the proposed generalization in (29):

(29) *Generalization* (final version):

a. External Merge
⇒ creates an F-asymmetric SO (forming a feature-equilibrium)
⇒ endocentric
⇒ "d-structure" semantics (predicate-argument structure, selection)
⇒ applies before (b)

b. Internal Merge
⇒ yields an F-symmetric SO
⇒ non-endocentric
⇒ "s-structure" semantics (discourse-related properties)
⇒ applies after (a)

Unconstrained Merge naturally yields the bifurcation of External Merge and Internal Merge, but since External Merge of some LI may introduce a new formal feature F into a derivation, it effectively drives a later application of Internal Merge for fixing the F-asymmetry. F-equilibrium is achieved either by XP-movement or head-movement, yielding symmetric {XP, YP} and {X, Y}, respectively. Empirical evidence suggests that, once generated by unconstrained Merge, the bifurcation of asymmetric and symmetric structures is utilized differently by CI: the former yields various endocentric, d-structure semantics such as predicate-argument structure and selection, whereas the latter yields non-endocentric, s-structure semantics such as topic-focus, operator-scope, theme-rheme structures, and so on. This way, the pattern in (29) can be systematically accounted for by the overarching hypothesis that syntactic derivation is geared and driven for symmetry (see also Fukui 2011 [Chapter 1, this volume]).

4 Further Consequences

In this section, we will discuss a number of further consequences of symmetry-driven syntax developed in the previous section. We will specifically argue that the notion of abstract Case can be entirely eliminated from the theory of grammar (section 4.1), and that we may provide an alternative explanation for why human language employs formal features (section 4.2). We will further argue that the reductionist approach to abstract Case provides room for a certain parametric variation as to the distribution of argumental *n*Ps across languages, focusing on English and Japanese as representative examples (section 4.3). Further remarks on the notion of endocentricity/asymmetry will also be provided in section 4.4.

4.1 Eliminating the Notion of Abstract Case

Since Vergnaud (1977/2008) and Chomsky (1981), it has become the orthodox presumption in the generative linguistic literature that the distribution of argument *n*Ps in linguistic structure is predominantly characterized by the notion of *abstract Case*. It is a concept distinguished from morphological case, and various theories have been proposed to derive its target function of determining *n*P-distribution. For example, Chomsky (1986b) proposes that Case is not an interpretable feature, but its assignment/checking is a necessary condition for an *n*P to become visible for θ-marking (his Visibility Condition on chains). In Chomsky's (1995b: 278–279) terms, Case is the "formal feature *par excellence*" that is always [–Interpretable]. Another way to characterize Case is to build on the idea that Case-assignment and φ-feature agreement go hand in hand (George and Kornfilt 1981). Chomsky (1995b, 2000) specifically proposes that an *n*P's Case-feature is checked and deleted as a reflex of the φ-feature agreement. Those theories of Case further propose that A-movement is essentially a "last-resort" operation that applies only when necessary to dislocate *n*Ps into Case-positions (Chomsky 1986b, 1995b). This way, a number of properties have been attributed to the concept of abstract Case, as summarized in (30).

(30) *Abstract Case* (under the traditional conception):
    a. distinguished from morphological case
    b. "formal feature *par excellence*" that is always uninterpretable (Chomsky 1995b: 278–279)
    c. a necessary condition for argumenthood (cf. Chomsky's 1986b Visibility Condition on chains)
    d. the trigger for A-movement (cf. Last resort)
    e. to be checked as a reflex of φ-feature agreement (George and Kornfilt 1981, Chomsky 1995b, 2000)

These assumptions are made to collectively derive the basic function of abstract Case, namely the function of determining the distribution of *n*Ps. Apart from this theory-internal motivation, however, the concept of abstract Case remains purely stipulative, lacking its justified *raison d'être* as a constituent of efficient mapping to SEM and PHON. (Apart from the visibility at the PHON interface, the situation is in fact similar in the case of φ-features. See section 4.2 for relevant discussion.) It is an abstract, narrowly syntactic entity distinguished from the morphological case (30a), hence it does not receive any phonetic interpretation by definition. Therefore, its existence cannot be justified in terms of conditions imposed on the PHON interface. Considerations from CI are not relevant, either, given that there is no evidence that it receives any semantic interpretation by itself (hence regarded as always [–Interpretable]; see (30b)). We are thus left with syntax-internal stipulations in (30c-e), clearly falling short of a principled explanation for why syntax has to come to obey these conditions. It seems then that abstract Case (and possibly φ-features as well) constitutes a genuine imperfection of linguistic system if present.

Contrary to the traditional approach outlined earlier, however, we argue that the basic function of abstract Case can be derived from our DSC (25), thus nullifying the need for this worrisome technical concept. Specifically, we would like to propose that canonical "Case-positions" such as Spec-T or Spec-V should be recast as positions where *n*Ps enter into φ-equilibrium.[8]

For concreteness, let us provide a list of LIs stored in the lexicon of English, which will serve as the basis for the following discussion.

(31) Lexicon (e.g., of English):
    a.   √root (including V, N, . . .) : [uCat(egory)], [uφ]
    b.   *n*: [N-Cat], [vφ]
    c.   *v*: [V-Cat]
    d.   *p*: [P-Cat]
    e.   T: [uT(ense)], [uφ]
    f.   C: [vT] (plus [uQ] for interrogative clauses)

The basic idea is that √root categories (to be realized as V, N, . . . etc.) and T (probably just another variety of √root; see note 7) are the most underspecified in terms of feature-values, here specifically associated with unvalued Cat(egorial)-features and φ-features. As to the source of [uφ], we may alternatively adopt the Chomsky-Richards hypothesis that unvalued φ-features (and tense) are not inherent to √root/T, but rather get inherited from phasehead categories like C and *v* (Chomsky 2007, 2008, Richards 2007). In what follows, little hinges on the choice between the two assumptions.

Bearing (31) in mind, let us turn to specific cases of Case-checking configurations. Representative examples are shown in (32–34).

(32) "Nominative" Case position:

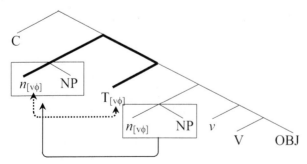

(33) "Accusative" Case position:

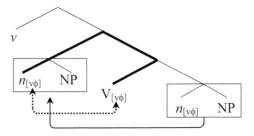

(34) "Oblique" Case position:

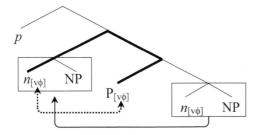

Consider first the Nominative Case position in (32), i.e., the so-called "Spec-T" position.[9] Subject *n*P A-moves into this position, and φ-feature agreement holds between *n* and T. Thanks to the A-movement and feature-matching, {*n*P, T'} forms a φ-equilibrium in (32), satisfying DSC. In this case, then, A-movement and agreement collectively yield the result that *n* and T's φ-features appropriately enter into a symmetric structure.

Moreover, if we follow Chomsky's (2008) hypothesis that the Accusative Case position is Spec-V, the same sort of analysis can be applied to (33) as well. Under this approach, it is V that is associated with [uφ], just like T (see note 7).[10] It undergoes feature-matching with the object *n*P, and the A-movement for Accusative Case targets its specifier position. In this case, too, the relevant A-movement and φ-feature-matching result in a φ-equilibrium at {*n*P, V'}. Recall that V also undergoes head-movement to *v* and forms {V, *v*}, which effectively puts V's [uCat] and *v*'s [V-Cat] in a Cat-equilibrium, satisfying DSC (see (26)).

We might further extend this line of approach to the Oblique Case position in (34) by, e.g., adapting Svenonius's *p*P-shell analysis of adpositional phrases (see Svenonius 2003, 2010). Let's assume that P is also a variety of √root in (31d), hence associated with [uCat] and [uφ], and that P's [uCat] enters into a Cat-equilibrium with *p*'s [P-Cat] via head-movement, just as in V-to-*v* incorporation. We further assume that the remaining [uφ] of P gets symmetrized by *n*P's complement-to-specifier movement as shown in (34). This way, we may analogize Oblique Case-configuration to the case of

Accusative in (33). Again, we see that A-movement and ϕ-feature-agreement work in tandem to reach a ϕ-equilibrium.[11]

In this context, it may be worth recalling that Chomsky (1986a, 1995b, 2000, 2001, 2004, 2008) among others provided various conceptions of the relevant Case-related movement/agreement correlation. For example, it was hypothesized in Chomsky (1986a, 1995b) that locating nPs in Case-positions via A-movement (overt or covert) is a necessary condition for ϕ-feature-agreement ("Spec-head agreement," Spec as the checking do-main, etc.). Chomsky (2000 *et seq.*) reversed the picture and claimed that Agree can operate on ϕ-features without movement but it might occasion-ally trigger subsequent nP-movement, depending on the presence of extra "EPP-feature" on the probe. However, here we are articulating the third view, namely that A-movement and ϕ-feature-agreement are both uniformly driven by the same force, i.e., of dynamic symmetrization.

It is important to note here that no notion of abstract Case needs to be invoked in the characterization of these Case-related operations. nPs move and agree as required, not because some abstract entity (Case) orders it, but rather because formal features, including [ϕ], are generally in need of feature-equilibrium (though the very existence of such features in human language—ϕ-features in particular—may pose a deeper problem). The ef-fects of Case as a trigger for A-movement (30d) and as a correlative of ϕ-feature-agreement (30e) are thus independently derived from DSC, reduc-ing the burden of this technical concept.

In order to further incorporate the "last-resort" nature of Case-driven A-movement, we may further propose that symmetric structures stabilize, and become invisible for further computations. This idea can be formulated as (35).

(35) *Equilibrium Intactness Condition (EIC)*:
    Fs in an F-equilibrium are stable and invisible for further F-related computation.

This condition explains why nPs embedded into Case-positions, i.e., ϕ-equilibrium, are not visible for further ϕ-feature-related operations. This derives, for example, the absence of superraising as shown in (36b).[12] The subject nP *John* already reaches the embedded Spec-T position and gets sta-bilized there (and hence frozen, due to the EIC), thus it becomes invisible for the [uϕ]-probe in the matrix clause.

(36) a.   *It* seems that *John$_i$* is believed t_i to be a great linguist.
    b. * *John$_i$* seems that t'_i is believed t_i to be a great linguist.

We advance (35) as a principle applicable to formal features in general, not limited to ϕ-features. Thus, we expect that the effect of (35) can be observed for features other than [ϕ]. Indeed, the contrast in examples like (37a)/(37b) seems susceptible of an analogous account, involving Q-features.[13,14] Thus, the "halting problem" of *wh*-movement can be solved on principled grounds.

(37) a. ??(Guess) *which book*$_i$ he wonders [*who*$_j$ t_j read t_i]?
      b. * (Guess) *who*$_i$ he wonders [t'_i t_i read *which book*]?

Finally, we argue that the role of Case as a marker of argumenthood (30c), or specifically the effect of the traditional Visibility Condition (Chomsky 1986b), largely follows as a straightforward consequence of our symmetry-driven syntax. Chomsky's (1986b) version of the Visibility Condition is formulated as (38):

(38) *Traditional Visibility Condition:*
      An element is visible for θ-marking only if it is assigned Case (Chomsky 1986b: 94).

Recall that our theory of structural (a)symmetry defines θ-positions as φ-asymmetric positions, and Case-positions as φ-symmetric positions. Then, what (38) states is essentially (39):

(39) *Revised Visibility Condition:*
      An element that enters into φ-feature asymmetry must also enter into φ-feature symmetry.

(39) follows just as a straightforward consequence of DSC. It is simply that φ-feature asymmetry, which serves for θ-marking, cannot count as φ-feature symmetry at the same time. Thus, A-movement for Case-positions becomes an automatic consequence of our mechanism of symmetry-driven syntax. Again, we don't need any *ad hoc* stipulation on Case to account for the effect of the Visibility Condition (38)/(39).

This completes our reduction of abstract Case. We have shown that the roles and functions traditionally attributed to abstract Case (30c-e) can find independent explanations under symmetry-driven syntax. Thus, we can entirely eliminate recourse to the worrisome "formal feature *par excellence*," a genuine imperfection of linguistic system if present. Of course, the theory of UG must be supplemented with particular theories of the morphological (lower-case) case for each I-language, but they are required independent of abstract Case, so the need for theories of the morphological case (probably purely morpho-phonological) does not entail stipulations on a narrowly syntactic mechanism of Case-checking. Thus, elimination of abstract Case from the theory of UG is a significant step toward the goal of principled explanation of human language, which we can achieve just as a straightforward consequence of our overarching hypothesis of dynamic symmetrization.

4.2 Why Formal Features?

The proposed elimination of the notion of abstract Case may have a significant implication for the notion of *formal features* in human language. The contemporary theory of syntax typically posits various formal features with the properties in (40).

(40) *Formal features:*
    a.   are distinguished from the class of features that are interpretable (either at SEM or at PHON).
    b.   must be "checked-off" before the derivation reaches the interfaces.

If we hypothesize that human syntax is the barest solution to interface legibility conditions (Chomsky 2000 *et seq.*), then the class of interpretable features appears to be sufficient for syntax to satisfy interface needs of expressiveness. Then, *prima facie*, human language would be "better off" if there is no such thing as formal features distinct from interpretable features, an apparent "imperfection." However, empirical facts suggest that there are a variety of "agreement" phenomena in natural language, where two (or more) distinct elements come to share values of morphological features under certain syntactically determined locality conditions. The class of φ-features (person, number, and gender) relevant to "subject-verb" agreement is a representative example. Agreement features apparently receive no interpretation at SEM (e.g., "2nd-person" feature on T), and thus constitute a prototypical instance of formal features.

Notice that another traditional example of formal features is (abstract) Case-feature. However, now that the notion of abstract Case is suggested to be entirely eliminable from the theory of syntax (see the discussion in the preceding section), we might entertain the stronger hypothesis that the class of formal features can be exhaustively characterized by agreement features. And as to agreement features, the idea of symmetry-driven syntax might provide a possible rationale for its existence in human language.

We have seen that agreement features such as [φ] and [Q] are crucially at stake in providing the basis for the definition of structural symmetry and asymmetry: External Merge brings them into a derivation, forming featurally asymmetric structures, and they necessitate later applications of Internal Merge to form feature-equilibrium. The bifurcation of asymmetric and symmetric structures in turn closely correlates with the duality of endocentric d-structure interpretation and non-endocentric s-structure interpretation, as we argued in the previous discussion. Then, we may posit a possible rationale for the presence of formal features (that is, agreement features) as in (41):

(41) Human language is designed to employ formal features/agreement features as the device to encode the duality of semantics in terms of featural (a)symmetry.

The duality of d-structure and s-structure interpretation has been recognized as a fundamental fact about the Conceptual-Intentional (CI) system, since the outset of generative linguistics. While we have little understanding of why CI comes to exhibit that property, (41) is articulating the view that the system of formal agreement features constitutes part of the solution to this design specification. Although we need more evidence to establish (41), it provides what appears to be an interesting insight into the role and functioning of formal features.

Note that (41) does not specify *which feature* is to be employed for the duality of semantics. We will propose that features other than φ-features may also be utilized for encoding predicate-argument structure. We will see in the next section that Japanese exhibits exactly this kind of situation.

4.3 Syntax without φ-features: The Case of Japanese

It is a traditional observation that Japanese is a language that exhibits no active φ-features for nominal declensions and subject-verb agreement. Thus, regardless of the semantic person, number, and gender of the subject nP, the verb form always stays the same, as exemplified in (42).

(42) Watasi-ga/anata-ga/gakusei-ga maitosi   ronbun-o   kak-u.
     I-NOM/you-NOM/student-NOM   every.year   paper-ACC   write-PRES
     "I/you/a student (students) write(s) a paper (papers) every year."

This traditional observation has been carried over to the generative literature at least since Kuroda (1965). Adopting the Principles-and-Parameters approach, Fukui (1986, 1988, 2006)—and Kuroda (1988, 1992), with some important and substantive qualifications (see Fukui 2011 for much relevant discussion)—puts forward the hypothesis that the lack of obligatory φ-feature-agreement in Japanese yields a highly intricate array of facts about this language that are unobservable in languages like English. In this section, we would like to maintain that our theory of symmetry-driven syntax may provide an interesting set of links between certain peculiar facts about Japanese, incorporating some of the major insights behind Fukui's (and Kuroda's, with qualifications) macro-parametric accounts.

Let us adopt (43) as a starting point, a particular formulation of the aforementioned observation put forward by Fukui (1986, 1988, 2006):

(43) Hypothesis (Fukui 1986, 1988, 2006):
     Japanese is a language that lacks active formal φ-features in its lexicon.

An immediate consequence of this hypothesis is that there is no notion of φ-feature symmetry/asymmetry in Japanese. We saw that φ-features plays a major role in creating featural asymmetry in languages like English: {√root, XP} is asymmetric because of √root's [uϕ], and {nP, v'} is asymmetric because of n's [vϕ], and so on. Such φ-feature asymmetry strongly correlates with endocentric d-structure semantics, in particular predicate-argument structure, and its presence drives later applications of symmetry-forming movement and agreement operations. Then, if a language lacks φ-features altogether in its lexicon, we predict the following two consequences:

(44) Consequence 1:
      Predicate-argument structure cannot be encoded by φ-feature asymmetry in Japanese-type languages.

(45) Consequence 2:
      There is no syntactic operation driven for φ-feature symmetry in Japanese-type languages.

   Let us discuss (44) first. We need to see what would happen in the two representative cases of predicate-argument structure: the internal argument in (46a) and the external argument in (46b).

(46) a.   b.

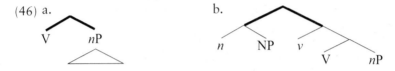

As we mentioned briefly, asymmetries of these structures can receive a uniform characterization in terms of φ-features in languages like English, but this option is unavailable in Japanese. However, at least as far as the internal argument (46a) is concerned, it is relatively easy to find a way to characterize {V, *n*P} as asymmetric. As discussed in section 2.2, {H, XP} generally fails to be symmetric, because the unbalanced H-XP branching can never form any feature-equilibrium. Thus, such an SO counts as asymmetric with respect to any formal feature of H. For example, we may say that (46a) is asymmetric even in Japanese with respect to another formal feature of V/√root, namely [uCat]. On the other hand, the asymmetry of XP-YP structure such as (46b) can only be characterized by making recourse to feature contents of the relevant SOs. How can we achieve this result, then, without reference to φ-features? Notice that by the time (46b) is formed, *n*'s [N-Cat] and *v*'s [V-Cat] enter into Cat-equilibrium via N-to-*n* and V-to-*v* head-movement, respectively. We maintain that the Cat-equilibrium effectively makes those Cat-features invisible due to EIC (35), and that, therefore, they are ineffective for further determination of featural (a)symmetry (see also note 14 for relevant discussion). Therefore, unlike the case in (46a), these Cat-features are insufficient to encode the asymmetry of (46b) in Japanese.

   It is quite interesting to observe in this connection that Japanese exhibits a peculiar set of morphological complexity that seems to make up for the lack of φ-features. It is a long noticed traditional observation, though less known in the generative literature, that Japanese has a rather complex system of verbal conjugations. We refer to the set of grammatical conjugational features as *χ-features*, and claim that they instantiate a variety of formal features in Japanese. There are two subcategories of χ-features in this language: one is the so-called *group feature* ([Group]) that differentiates five classes of verbs, and the other is the so-called *stem-form feature* ([Stem-form]) whose morphological realization mainly depends on the type of verbal suffixes.

(47) Values for χ-feature in Japanese:
    a. Group: I. (5-row Group (Godan))
                      II. (Upper 1-row/*i*-row Group (Kami-itidan))
                    III. (Lower 1-row/*e*-row Group (Simo-itidan))
                    IV. (Sa-Group (Sa-hen))
                    V. (Ka-Group (Ka-hen))
    b. Stem-form: Irrealis (Mizen)
                        Continuative/Adverbial (Ren'yoo)
                        Conclusive (Syuusi)
                        Adnominal/Attributive (Rentai)
                        Conditional/Hypothetical (Katei)
                        Imperative (Meirei)

For instance, (48) and (49) illustrate the Group I and Group III paradigms of verbal conjugation, respectively. Clearly, the two classes of verbal forms change according to the C/T suffix attached to it.

(48) a. Taro-ga   ronbun-o   kak-a-nakat-ta.
         Taro-NOM   paper-ACC   write.I-IRR-not-PAST
         "Taro did not write a paper."
    b. Taro-ga   ronbun-o   kak-i-nagara, . . .
         Taro-NOM   paper-ACC   write.I-CONT-while
         "While Taro was writing a paper, . . ."
    c. Taro-ga   ronbun-o   kak-u.
         Taro-NOM   paper-ACC   write.I-CONCL.PRES
         "Taro writes a paper."
    d. Taro-ga   ronbun-o   kak-u   toki, . . .
         Taro-NOM   paper-ACC   write.I-ADN   time
         "The time when Taro writes a paper, . . ."
    e. Taro-ga   ronbun-o   kak-e-ba, . . .
         Taro-NOM   paper-ACC   write.I-COND-if
         "If Taro writes a paper, . . ."
    f. Ronbun-o   kak-e.
         paper-ACC   write.I-IMP
         "Write a paper."

(49) a. Taro-ga   siken-o   uk-e-nakat-ta.
        Taro-NOM   exam-ACC   take.III-IRR-not-PAST
        "Taro did not take an exam."
     b. Taro-ga   siken-o   uk-e-nagara, . . .
        Taro-NOM   exam-ACC   take.III-CONT-while
        "While Taro is taking an exam, . . ."
     c. Taro-ga   siken-o   uk-**eru**.
        Taro-NOM   exam-ACC   take.III-CONCL.PRES
        "Taro takes an exam."
     d. Taro-ga   siken-o   uk-**eru**   toki, . . .
        Taro-NOM   exam-ACC   take.III-ADN   time
        "The time when Taro takes an exam, . . ."
     e. Taro-ga   siken-o   uk-ere-ba, . . .
        Taro-NOM   exam-ACC   take.III-COND-if
        "If Taro takes an exam, . . ."
     f. Siken-o   uk-**ero**.
        exam-ACC   take.III-IMP
        "Take an exam."

Based on this observation, we'd like to put forth the hypothesis that it is
χ-features that fulfill the function of encoding the asymmetric predicate-
argument structure for SOs like (46b)/(50b) in Japanese. (50b) counts as
asymmetric due to the presence of χ-features on v, which is different from
the English-type structure in (50a), whose featural asymmetry is characterized by the presence of φ-features on n.

(50) a. English-type: b. Japanese-type:

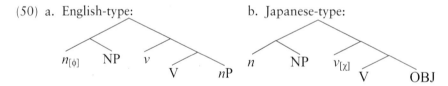

We propose the lexicon in (51) for Japanese, which is minimally different
from English in that it lacks φ-features but its v and C have χ-features.

(51) Lexicon (Japanese):
     a. root (including V, N, . . .) : [uCat(egory)]
     b. *n*: [N-Cat]
     c. *v*: [V-Cat], [χ: vGroup, uStem-form]
     d. *p*: [P-Cat]
     e. T: [uT]
     f. C: [vT], [χ: uGroup, vStem-form]

Japanese verbs are lexically specified with respect to group-features and exhibit
conjugation paradigms in regard to the force of C. We accommodate this

morphological fact about Japanese by stipulating that v has a valued group-feature and C has a valued Stem-form-feature, and that v and C undergo χ-feature agreement in this language. Recall our earlier proposal that formal features are generally required to enter into feature-equilibrium. Then, how does the χ-feature asymmetry of (50b) get symmetrized in the course of the derivation? Presumably, the χ-feature agreement between C and v is responsible. Exploring this idea, we present two possible analyses of the χ-feature symmetry formation. The first analysis is shown in (52), which involves a kind of head-movement that moves the V-v complex to the edge of the T-C complex:

(52) Analysis 1: Movement of V-v to the edge of T-C:

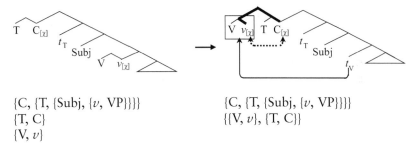

{C, {T, {Subj, {v, VP}}}}   {C, {T, {Subj, {v, VP}}}}
{T, C}   {{V, v}, {T, C}}
{V, v}

This movement yields a χ-feature-equilibrium, matching χ-features of C and v. Another possibility is the merger of v and C independently of T-to-C and V-to-v. This yields the structure in (53).

(53) Analysis 2: Movement of v to C, independent of T-to-C and V-to-v:

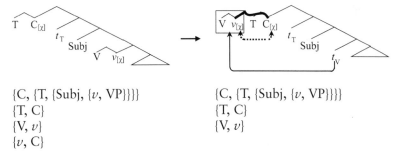

{C, {T, {Subj, {v, VP}}}}   {C, {T, {Subj, {v, VP}}}}
{T, C}   {T, C}
{V, v}   {V, v}
{v, C}

Either way, the χ-feature asymmetry gets fixed by relating v to C, satisfying the need for featural symmetry as desired.

In this manner, the proposed approach makes a novel connection between two peculiar facts about Japanese: the lack of φ-features and a rich system of χ-features. We are articulating the view that φ-features and χ-features are two sides of the same coin at a certain abstract level, uniformly characterizable as devices to encode predicate-argument structure, especially of the external argument as in (50).

Let us turn to the discussion of Consequence 2, namely that there can be no syntactic operation driven for φ-feature symmetry in φ-feature-free languages like Japanese. Recall first that various instances of ("Case-driven") A-movement have an important function of forming φ-feature symmetry. Due to the presence of φ-features on *n*, this symmetry-forming operation is obligatory in languages like English.

(54) English-type: A-movement obligatory for φ-feature symmetry:

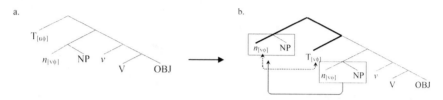

In contrast, if φ-features are totally absent, it is expected that the language also lacks A-movement driven for φ-feature symmetry. This is exactly what happens in Japanese, which is independently known as a language that shows no evidence for obligatory A-movement: see Fukui (1986), Kuroda (1988), Ishii (1997), Kato (2006), and Narita (2011, 2012b, 2014) among others for the view that Japanese subjects can (at least optionally) stay in-situ.

(55) Consequence 2–1:
     Japanese lacks obligatory A-movement into Case-positions.

(56) Japanese-type: Lack of obligatory A-movement:

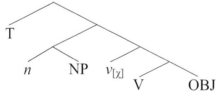

A related consequence is that the "Spec-T" position remains as a vacant site in Japanese-type languages. We maintain that this position can be optionally (and iteratively; see the following) filled by a "major subject," an *n*P that does not participate in a predicate-argument structure of the main verb and receives a topic-like interpretation.

(57) Consequence 2–2:
     Japanese Spec-T can be optionally filled by a major subject, yielding multiple subject constructions.

(58)

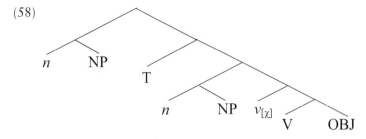

Examples of the major subject construction in Japanese is provided in (59):

(59) Japanese:
    a. Taro-ga   musuko-ga   nyuugakusiken-ni   sippaisita.
       Taro-NOM   son-NOM   entrance.exam-DAT   failed
       "As for Taro, his son failed the entrance examination."
    b. Aki-ga   sanma-ga   umai.
       autumn-NOM   saury-NOM   tasty
       "As for autumn, saury is tasty."

The merger of such an extra *n*P into Spec-T is unproblematic in Japanese, not only because this position is not designated for φ-equilibrium but also because the merger of *n*P alone does not entail formation of feature asymmetry (recall again that *n*'s [N-Cat] forms a Cat-equilibrium with N's [uCat] and becomes unable to determine feature asymmetry). Thus, it is predicted that *any number* of *n*Ps can be merged into this domain. Indeed, more than one major subject can be freely merged to a sentential structure in Japanese as shown in (60) (see Kuno 1973, Fukui 1986, 1988, 2006).

(60) Japanese: Sentence with more than one major subject (Kuno 1973)
    Bunmeikoku-ga   dansei-ga   heikinzyumyoo-ga   mizikai.
    civilized.countries-NOM male-NOM   average.lifespan-NOM   is.short
    "It is civilized countries that men, their average lifespan is short in."

Compare the situation with English, where each merger of an *n*P with [vφ] always result in a φ-asymmetric SO, necessitating later applications of symmetry-forming movement and agreement. Positions entering into φ-equilibrium are limited in English. Thus no free merger of a major subject *n*P is possible in this language:

(61) English:
    a. * Taro, his son failed the entrance examination.
    b. * Autumn, saury is tasty.
    c. * Civilized countries, male, the average lifespan is short (with the
         intended meaning "it is civilized countries that men, their average
         lifespan is short in.")

Still another consequence of φ-free syntax is that *n*Ps do not form any F-equilibrium with their Merge-mates in Japanese-type languages. Thus, they *never* stabilize or become invisible via EIC, reproduced here.

(35) *Equilibrium Intactness Condition (EIC)*:
Fs in an F-equilibrium are stable and invisible for further F-related operations.

Therefore, not having any "magnetic" power around, *n*Ps can freely undergo scrambling (optional dislocation).

(62) Consequence 2–3:
Japanese *n*Ps can freely undergo scrambling.

Japanese has been a textbook example of scrambling languages, where *n*Ps can freely move around as exemplified in (63). This peculiarity now follows as a consequence of the lack of φ-features in the language.

(63) Japanese:

a. John-ga   Mary-ni   sono hon-o   watasita
   John-NOM   Mary-DAT   that book-ACC   handed
   "John handed that book to Mary."

b. *Mary-ni$_i$*   John-ga t_i sono hon-o   watasita
   Mary-DAT   John-NOM   that book-ACC   handed
   "*To Mary$_i$*, John handed that book t_i."

c. *Sono hon-o$_i$*   John-ga   Mary-ni t_i watasita
   that book-ACC   John-NOM   Mary-DAT   handed
   "*That book$_i$*, John handed t_i to Mary."

d. *Sono hon-o$_i$*   *Mary-ni$_j$*   John-ga t_i t_j watasita
   that book-ACC   Mary-DAT   John-NOM   handed
   "*That book$_i$, to Mary$_j$*, John handed t_i t_j."

e. *Mary-ni$_j$*   *sono hon-o$_i$*   John-ga t_i t_j watasita
   Mary-DAT   that book-ACC   John-NOM   handed
   "*To Mary$_j$, that book$_i$*, John handed t_i t_j."

Contrasting with Japanese, English among many other languages does not exhibit optional scrambling. Thus, multiple fronting of *n*Ps is impossible in English-type languages.

(64) *English*:
a. John handed that book to Mary.
b. *To Mary$_i$*, John handed that book t_i.
c. *That book$_i$*, John handed t_i to Mary.
d. **That book$_i$, to Mary$_j$*, John handed t_i t_j.
e. **To Mary$_j$, that book$_i$*, John handed t_j t_i.

The impossibility of *n*P-scrambling in English follows from the fact that such *n*Ps have φ-features and they are "frozen" in positions forming a φ-equilibrium as in (65).

(65) English-type: *n*Ps are "frozen" in positions forming a φ-equilibrium:

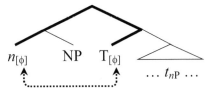

In contrast, there is no φ-equilibrium in Japanese-type languages. Thus *n*Ps can freely move around without getting frozen via EIC.[15]

(66) Japanese-type: *n*Ps can freely raise to "Spec-T."

a.

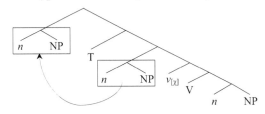

b.

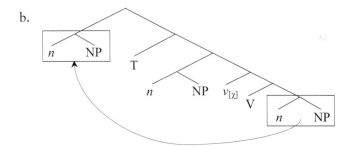

We have seen in this section that the single parametric statement, namely that Japanese lacks active φ-features, yields a number of intricate consequences in Japanese syntax. Note that the "macro"-parametric variation discussed here simply results from the underspecified nature of UG. Recall our hypothesis that the existence of formal features is grounded in the need for (a)symmetry-coding (see section 3.2), but UG does not specify which feature is to be utilized for that purpose. Thus, UG allows the possibility that English utilizes φ-features on *n*, while Japanese utilizes χ-features on *v* for the same purpose of encoding asymmetric d-structure semantics. Therefore, no brute-force stipulation on the constituents of UG is necessary to account for the "macro-parametric" variation, simplifying linguistic theory to a considerable extent.

4.4 Remarks on the Departure from Universal Endocentricity/Asymmetry

In this chapter, we proposed a theory of syntax in which linguistic derivation is fundamentally driven and geared for symmetry defined in terms of feature-equilibrium. Before concluding this chapter, we would like to note that the proposed theory of symmetry-driven syntax constitutes a rather radical departure from the traditional approach to the endocentricity/headedness of phrase structure.

Merge, understood as an elementary set-formation operation, recursively generates SOs without providing any additional information such as labels and projection. The theory of bare phrase structure thus renders the traditional concept of "label/projection" entirely superfluous, and "reference to labels [becomes] a departure from [the Strong Minimalist Thesis]." (Chomsky 2007: 23) We take this conclusion seriously, and put forward a certain analysis of Merge-based computation that makes no recourse to labels/projection.

It may be worth noting that the present approach appears to run afoul of the commonly held assumption that linguistic structures are always labeled by projections of designated head LIs and hence universally endocentric. We may refer to this conventional stipulation as the "universal endocentricity" hypothesis.

(67)   *"Universal Endocentricity" Hypothesis*:
       All SOs are endocentric, i.e., headed by a designated LI.

This idea of universal endocentricity essentially originates from Chomsky's (1970 *et seq.*) introduction of X-bar theory. The so-called X-bar schemata provide strict formats on the class of possible phrase structure rules (PSRs), and it excludes non-endocentric structures such as "S→NP VP" as a matter of principle.[16] Universal endocentricity is thus deduced as an automatic consequence of X-bar theory, which was regarded as a highly desirable achievement in the Government-and-Binding framework. Even after the X-bar-theoretic notion of projection was eliminated from the theory of syntax (Chomsky 1995a, 1995b), the universal endocentricity hypothesis (67) still remains as the standard assumption.

Contrary to (67), however, what we are pursuing in this chapter is a possibility, rarely explored in the literature, that endocentricity is not the norm for phrase structure but rather fundamentally unstable. In our system of symmetry-driven syntax, endocentric structures are regarded as prototypical instances of featurally asymmetric structures, triggering a variety of symmetry-forming operations (Internal Merge and Agree) to remedy them. In this manner, syntactic derivation is directed toward non-endocentric/

symmetric structures. Our argument thus points to the rational (but by and large unnoticed) conclusion that the universal endocentricity hypothesis (67) is an illegitimate residue of X-bar theory, hence to be discarded along with the concept of labels/projection (see also Fukui 2011 and Narita 2012a, 2014).

Note that our theory of symmetry-driven syntax is also distinct from a comparable hypothesis of universal asymmetry, related in various ways to universal endocentricity and thereby put forward by the majority of researchers:[17]

(68) *"Universal Asymmetry" Hypothesis*:
        All binary SOs are (featurally) asymmetric.

Both (67) and (68) were inescapable consequences of universal projection under X-bar theory, but successful elimination of the latter opens up the possibility of questioning the empirical basis for these traditional stipulations.[18]

It is exactly due to our rejection of (67) and (68) that we can entertain the full-fledged strength of symmetry-driven syntax. Insofar as various arguments put forward in this chapter are on the right track, then, the validity of (67) and (68) is correspondingly undermined.[19]

We hasten to add that Chomsky's (2013) theory of labeling algorithm points to a picture that somewhat parallels with our system of symmetry-driven syntax. The notion of projection is eliminated entirely in his theory of bare phrase structure, while Chomsky hypothesizes that the mechanism of head-detection (called the "labeling algorithm") is still necessary to assign appropriate interpretation to each SO. Thus, he argues, "For a syntactic object SO to be interpreted, some information is necessary about it: what kind of object is it? Labeling is the process of providing that information. . . . We assume, then, that there is a fixed labeling algorithm LA that licenses SOs so that they can be interpreted at the interfaces." (Chomsky 2013: 43) He further argues that, in the best case scenario, the labeling algorithm reduces to minimal search of head LIs for each SO. SOs of the form {H, XP} are defined by this algorithm as labeled H and hence interpretable at the interfaces. On the other hand, SOs of the form {XP, YP} are seemingly unlabelable and hence cannot receive interpretation. Part of Chomsky's solution to this problem was to hypothesize (69):

(69) Chomsky (2013):
        Labeling via minimal search can be bifurcated for SOs of the form {XP, YP}. If the bifurcated search into XP and YP hits an identical formal feature F, then {XP, YP} gets labeled F.

For example, if the labeling algorithm is applied to the case of TP-structure in (70), which constitutes a ϕ-equilibrium in our terms, the bifurcated search into nP and T' ends up finding a pair of matched [ϕ], and thus the SO gets labeled by [ϕ].

(70)

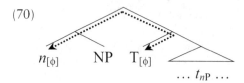

$n_{[\phi]}$　　NP　$T_{[\phi]}$

$\ldots t_{n}\mathrm{P} \ldots$

Generally speaking, SOs in an F-equilibrium for some formal feature F are properly labeled F, according to Chomsky's hypothesis in (69). Note that the class of SOs that get labeled F via (69) corresponds to the class of F-symmetric SOs in our theory of featural symmetry. If we understand the process of Chomskyan labeling as licensing for interpretation, then, by hypothesizing (69), Chomsky is effectively providing room for non-endocentric/symmetric structures like (70) as interface-legitimate objects. In this manner, we find an interesting parallel between our system of symmetry-driven syntax and Chomsky's theory of efficient labeling.

It constitutes an interesting research topic to investigate whether there really exists an operation of labeling that is independent of symmetry-formation or one can be reduced to the other, and whether the guiding principle of dynamic symmetrization described in this chapter is ultimately related in some manner to considerations of labeling. We leave the inquiry for future research.

5　Conclusion

In this chapter, we tried to establish the generalization in (71) (=(29)), and discussed its implications:

(71) *Generalization* (final version):
  a.　External Merge
  $\Rightarrow$　creates an asymmetric SO
  　　　(forming a feature-equilibrium)
  $\Rightarrow$　endocentric
  $\Rightarrow$　"d-structure" semantics
  　　　(predicate-argument structure,
  　　　selection)
  $\Rightarrow$　applies before (b)

  b.　Internal Merge
  $\Rightarrow$　yields a symmetric SO

  $\Rightarrow$　non-endocentric
  $\Rightarrow$　"s-structure" semantics
  　　　(discourse-related
  　　　properties)

  $\Rightarrow$　applies after (a)

The foundational hypothesis of bare phrase structure theory (Chomsky 1995b *et seq.*) is that Merge is unconstrained and applies freely, yielding the discrete infinity of human language. Merge thus can generate all sorts of SOs with mixed forms and properties, but what we find at the syntax-semantics interface is a rather remarkable systematicity described in (71): External Merge serves for creating featural asymmetry and yields endocentric d-structure interpretation, while Internal Merge fixes and stabilizes the asymmetry by forming feature-equilibrium as defined in (72) (=(19)), and yields non-endocentric s-structure interpretation.

(72) *Feature-equilibrium:*
    For a formal feature F, an SO {α, β} is in an *F-equilibrium.* $\equiv_{def.}$ α and β
    share a matching formal feature F that is equally prominent in α and β.

We argued that the systematic pattern in (71) follows as a consequence of
the fundamental hypothesis that linguistic computation is essentially driven
and geared for symmetry. The condition is formulated as DSC (73) (=(25)),
in which the notion of featural symmetry (74) (=(20)) plays a major role.

(73) *Dynamic Symmetrization Condition (DSC):*
    Each formal feature F must form an F-equilibrium in the course of the
    derivation.

(74) *Featural symmetry:*
    Given a formal feature F in an SO {α, β}, the SO is *symmetric* with
    respect to F (or *F-symmetric*) if it is in an F-equilibrium. Otherwise, the
    SO {α, β} is (F-)asymmetric with respect to F.

We argued that DSC is an overarching principle that provides a unifying account
of various properties in linguistic computation, summarized as follows:

(75) a. Head-movement, XP-movement, and feature-matching (Agree) are
        uniformly characterized as serving for symmetry-formation.
    b. The generalization in (71) is derived as a consequence of DSC.
    c. DSC further deduces various effects of abstract Case while elimi-
        nating stipulations of Case-features from the theory of lexicon.
    d. DSC provides a possible rationale for the existence of formal fea-
        tures as a device to encode the duality of semantics via featural
        (a)symmetry.
    e. DSC alone provides room for φ-feature-less languages like Japa-
        nese with their intricate properties (χ-features, lack of obligatory
        A-movement, availability of major subjects and optional scram-
        bling, etc.) while not invoking any syntactic "macro-parameter."

Although a number of important implications of the proposal remain to be
explored and examined carefully, we hope that the analysis presented in this
chapter provides a promising insight into the nature of linguistic computation and the syntax-semantic interface of human language.

Notes

*   Part of this research was supported by a grant from Japan Science and Technol-
    ogy Agency (CREST) and a grant from Japan Society for the Promotion of Sci-
    ence (Grant-in-Aid for Scientific Research(A), 23242025). This chapter, a rough
    draft of which was essentially completed in 2012, is a written-up and revised
    version of an oral presentation under the same title at the Kyoto Conference on
    Biolinguistics held at Kyoto University (March 12, 2012).

1 Here and in what follows, we will freely use notations like XP, YP to refer to any phrasal constituents, but it should be noticed that we are not granting any ontological status to such nonterminal label-symbols as XP, YP. That is to say, no notion of labeling or projection is implied in our informal usage of the terms. Thus, notations like TP, *v*P, and so on, just refer to nothing more than phrasal constituents containing T, *v*, etc. See Collins (2002), Seely (2006), Chomsky (2007, 2012, 2013), and Narita (2011, 2012a, 2012b, 2014) for relevant discussion on the prospects for label-free syntax.

2 Alternatively, we may attempt to abandon the External vs. Internal Merge dichotomy and replace it with a new, not-so-unnatural bifurcation of Base-Merge and Non-Base-Merge as defined in (i):

   (i) Merge(α, β) counts as *Base-Merge* if either α or β (or both) is drawn from the Lexicon. Otherwise, Merge(α, β) counts as *Non-Base-Merge*.

   The notion of Non-Base-Merge correctly encapsulates the Chomskyan notion of Internal Merge and instances of head-movement under a single category, as desired. However, this alternative dichotomy makes an apparently problematic prediction that instances of Chomskyan External Merge applying to two XPs also fall under the same category of Non-Base-Merge as Internal Merge and head-movement. However, there appear to be clear instances of Non-Base-Merge that externally merges two XPs and feed *bona fide* d-structure interpretation, such as the merger of an external argument as we will discuss shortly. Thus it seems that the Base-Merge vs. Non-Base-Merge dichotomy does not fit well with our purpose of accounting for the proposed generalization in (10).

3 There are theories in which the little *v* in the transitive verb construction is associated with a set of uninterpretable ϕ-features (see Richards 2007, Chomsky 2008 among others). However, even in these theories the ϕ-features are eventually inherited to V at the end of the derivation, thus the relevant ϕ-feature-based asymmetry arises consequentially.

4 We may say that relevant nominals are headed by D(eterminer) (Fukui 1986, 1988, Fukui and Speas 1986, and Abney 1987) or by the categorizer head *n* into which D incorporates (Chomsky 2007). We refrain from making specific assumptions regarding the exact nature of the nominal head, for want of better understanding of nominal-internal syntax.

5 We may regard agreement as achieved by probe-goal search operations (as hypothesized in Chomsky 2000 *et seq.*) or as a reflexive compensation for symmetry-formation, perhaps for the purpose of labeling.

6 See section 4.1 and in particular note 13 for other cases of root-incorporation.

7 We might further entertain the null hypothesis that T really *is* a root category with [uCat] that matches with C's categorial-feature valued as C/T (or something like "Finite" or "Inflectional," to adopt terms naturally applicable to both C and T). This approach eliminates T as an independent category, reducing it to a special case of underspecified root elements. We leave the exploration of this idea for future research.

8 See also Haeberli's (2001) earlier attempt to reduce part of abstract Case effects to D- and T-categorial features. See also Pesetsky and Torrego (2001, 2004).

9 The use of the term *Spec(ifier)* is only for expository ease, and no theoretical import is intended for this X-bar-theoretic notion throughout the chapter. See Starke (2004), Jayaseelan (2008), Chomsky (2012, 2013), Narita (2011, 2014) and Lohndal (2012) for various approaches to specifier-free syntax. Note incidentally that Fukui's (1986, 1988 *et seq.*) earlier attempt at eliminating the notion of *Spec(ifier)* as a structural notion (such as "a phrase that is immediately dominated by a maximal projection"), and instead characterizing *Spec* solely as a site for feature checking, indeed shares the basic insight with the approach being pursued here.

10 [uφ] on √root/T may be sometimes *defective* (lacking, e.g., [uPerson]), and such categories cannot form a φ-equilibrium with *n*Ps with full-fledged φ-features, as in cases with unaccusative/passive V and T in raising/ECM infinitivals. See, among others, Chomsky (2001) for the notion of defective [uφ].

11 The discussion leaves an account of Genitive Case for possessor *n*P. For want of better understanding of nominal-internal syntax, we have to leave the topic largely for future research, but a variety of analyses can be made to accommodate Genitive in our symmetry-driven syntax. We may, for example, adopt the idea that possessor *n*P is in the specifier of a covert D with independent Case-assigning property, which in our theory means a full-fledged set of [uφ] (see Szabolcsi 1984, Fukui 1986, 1988, Abney 1987). Alternatively, we may assume that possessor *n*P is underlyingly [$_{pp}$ P *n*P] located in the complement of N, whose adpositional head (something like a covert *of*) incorporates into D and *n*P moves into Spec-D (see, e.g., de Vries 2006).

12 But see note 15.

13 A word of caution is in order regarding N-to-*n* head-movement. Everything else being equal, we would like to provide an analysis of N-to-*n* √root-incorporation analogous to V-to-*v* and P-to-*p* discussed earlier. However, if √root/N is with full-fledged [uφ] like V/P and head-moves to *n*, the resultant structure {N, *n*} would constitute not only a Cat-equilibrium but also a φ-equilibrium, provided that N has [uCat] and [uφ] while *n* has [N-Cat] and [vφ] (31a-b). EIC then predicts that the φ-features of N and *n* become invisible for further computation, but we have reasons to suppose that [vφ] on *n* remains active/visible even after N-to-*n* head-movement, especially because *n*'s φ-features enter into feature-equilibrium with "Case-assigning" heads like T and V. One way to resolve this difficulty is to stipulate (i) (see note 10 for the notion of defectiveness):
(i) N's [uφ] is always defective (lacking, e.g., [uPerson]).
We argue that it is due to (i) that N's [uφ] cannot form a φ-equilibrium with *n*'s full-fledged [vφ], leaving the latter active for further symmetry-forming operations (Internal Merge, Agree).

   Although we have to leave open the question of why (i) should hold, it is not an entirely unreasonable assumption, given that the class of √root/T categories with defective [uφ] is independently observed for unaccusative/passive V and raising/ECM infinitival T. It may be that √root/T can freely appear either as φ-complete or as φ-defective, but that only certain choices may result in a successful derivation. For example, the choice of a φ-complete N terminates the derivation as soon as symmetric {N, *n*} is formed: such nominal structures may be represented by vocatives or interjections like *Gosh*, etc., which stand alone as complete expressions and do not participate in any interesting syntax with other elements.

14 We maintain that EIC also plays an important role in the determination of featural (a)symmetry (20). Recall that this notion is defined relative to the presence of some formal feature F in {α, β}, thus {*n*P, T'} in (18b) does count as φ-symmetric thanks to the presence of [φ] in *n*, but not as, say, Q-symmetric or Q-asymmetric given the lack of [Q] in the SO. However, one may still wonder whether the same holds if the subject *n*P or the T' does contain Q-features that are more deeply embedded: for example, [*the question of what John bought yesterday*] or [*the boy who John met last week*]. Obviously, the desirable result is that these occurrences of [Q] within those embedded clauses are irrelevant to the featural (a)symmetry defined for *n*Ps containing them. We argue that this desideratum can be achieved once we allow [Q] and other features in these lower domains (probably demarcated by notions like "phase"; see Chomsky 2000 *et seq.*) to become invisible due to EIC, after forming an equilibrium on their own.

More generally, we maintain that the calculation of F-(a)symmetry also counts as "F-related computation" in the definition of EIC (35).

15 Still another prediction is that, unlike English as shown in (36b), superraising (and possibly "long-distance" passive as well) in φ-feature-free languages like Japanese is not ruled out by EIC alone, because there is no notion of φ-equilibrium in which *n*Ps get stabilized and become invisible. It is interesting to note that Japanese is sometimes claimed to exhibit suggestive cases of superraising (see, e.g., Ura 1994a, 1994b, 1996), a fact that constitutes, if true, an interesting piece of evidence for the lack of φ-features and feature-equilibrium thereof in this language. Note that this conclusion is different from the one drawn by Ura (1994a, 1994b, 1996), which invokes a variety of (strong) φ-features and Case-features in this language (that may further be associated with another feature [+multiple], serving to provide room for multiple specifiers in the sense of Chomsky 1995b).

16 It is worth noting that Chomsky (1970) first puts forward the X-bar schemata in such a way that they could be interpreted not as strict laws governing PSRs but as a kind of evaluation measure that merely sets preference for (unmarked) X-bar-theoretic projections, leaving the possibility of (marked) non-endocentric structures.

17 Specifically, (68) is one of the leading ideas behind the so-called "antisymmetry" research program initiated by Kayne (1994), which argues for (68) as a necessary condition for proper linearization. See Kayne (1994, 2009, 2011), Chomsky (1995a, 1995b), Uriagereka (1999), Moro (2000), to name just a few (but see Narita 2010, 2011/2014: Ch.4 for criticism of the Kaynean antisymmetry approach).

18 See van Riemsdijk (1998a) and Citko (2008, 2011) for elaborated theories of universal projection that allow more than one LI to project in limited contexts. See also Grimshaw (2005). For much relevant discussion, see Fukui (1999).

19 However, see Narita (2011, 2012b, 2014) for various arguments for his projection-free but still universally endocentric/asymmetric syntax, which cannot be easily accommodated to the theory developed in this chapter.

References

Abney, Steven Paul. 1987. The noun phrase in its sentential aspect. Doctoral dissertation, MIT.

Boeckx, Cedric, and Sandra Stjepanović. 2001. Head-ing toward PF. *Linguistic Inquiry* 32: 345–355.

Cable, Seth. 2007. The grammar of Q. Doctoral dissertation, MIT.

Cable, Seth. 2010. *The grammar of Q: Q-particles, wh-movement, and pied-piping.* Oxford: Oxford University Press.

Chomsky, Noam. 1970. Remarks on nominalization. In *Readings in English transformational grammar*, ed. Roderick A. Jacobs and Peter S. Rosenbaum, 184–221. Waltham, MA: Ginn.

Chomsky, Noam. 1981. *Lectures on government and binding.* Dordrecht: Foris.

Chomsky, Noam. 1986a. *Barriers.* Cambridge, MA: MIT Press.

Chomsky, Noam. 1986b. *Knowledge of language: Its nature, origin, and use.* New York: Praeger.

Chomsky, Noam. 1993. A minimalist program for linguistic theory. In *The view from Building 20: Essays in linguistics in honor of Sylvain Bromberger*, ed. Ken Hale and Samuel J. Keyser, 1–52. Cambridge, MA: MIT Press.

Chomsky, Noam. 1995a. Bare phrase structure. In *Evolution and revolution in linguistic theory: Essays in honor of Carlos Otero*, ed. Héctor Ramiro Campos and Paula Marie Kempchinsky, 51–109. Washington, DC: Georgetown University Press.

Chomsky, Noam. 1995b. *The minimalist program*. Cambridge, MA: MIT Press.

Chomsky, Noam. 2000. Minimalist inquiries: The framework. In *Step by step: Essays on minimalist syntax in honor of Howard Lasnik*, ed. Roger Martin, David Michaels, and Juan Uriagereka, 89–155. Cambridge, MA: MIT Press.

Chomsky, Noam. 2001. Derivation by phase. In *Ken Hale: A life in language*, ed. Michael Kenstowicz, 1–52. Cambridge, MA: MIT Press.

Chomsky, Noam. 2004. Beyond explanatory adequacy. In *Structures and beyond: The cartography of syntactic structures*, volume 3, ed. Adriana Belletti, 104–131. New York: Oxford University Press.

Chomsky, Noam. 2007. Approaching UG from below. In *Interfaces + recursion = language? Chomsky's minimalism and the view from semantics*, ed. Uli Sauerland and Hans-Martin Gärtner, 1–29. Berlin and New York: Mouton de Gruyter.

Chomsky, Noam. 2008. On phases. In *Foundational issues in linguistic theory*, ed. Robert Freidin, Carlos Otero, and Maria Luisa Zubizarreta, 133–166. Cambridge, MA: MIT Press.

Chomsky, Noam. 2012. Introduction. In *Gengokisoronsyu* [*Foundations of biolinguistics: Selected writings*], ed. and trans. Naoki Fukui, 17–26. Tokyo: Iwanami Shoten.

Chomsky, Noam. 2013. Problems of projection. *Lingua* 130: 33–49.

Cinque, Guglielmo. 1999. *Adverbs and functional heads: A cross-linguistic perspective*. Oxford: Oxford University Press.

Cinque, Guglielmo. 2002. *Functional structure in DP and IP: The cartography of syntactic structures*, volume 1. Oxford: Oxford University Press.

Citko, Barbara. 2008. Missing labels. *Lingua* 118: 907–944.

Citko, Barbara. 2011. *Symmetry in syntax: Merge, Move, and labels*. Cambridge: Cambridge University Press.

Collins, Chris. 2002. Eliminating labels. In *Derivation and explanation in the minimalist program*, ed. Samuel David Epstein and T. Daniel Seely, 42–64. Oxford: Blackwell.

de Vries, Mark. 2006. Possessive relatives and (heavy) pied-piping. *Journal of Comparative Germanic Linguistics* 9: 1–52.

Fukui, Naoki. 1986/1995. A theory of category projection and its applications. Doctoral dissertation, MIT. Published in 1995 with revisions as *Theory of projection in syntax*, Tokyo: Kurosio Publishers and Stanford: CSLI publications.

Fukui, Naoki. 1988. Deriving the differences between English and Japanese: A case study in parametric syntax. *English Linguistics* 5: 249–270.

Fukui, Naoki. 1999. UG and parametric theory: A plenary lecture at the 118th annual meeting of the Linguistic Society of Japan, Tokyo Metropolitan University. An abridged version was published in 1999 as "Gengo no fuhensei to tayoosei" [Universals and diversity of human language]. *Gengo* 28 (12): 36–43. [Reprinted in Fukui (2012).]

Fukui, Naoki. 2006. *Theoretical comparative syntax: Studies in macroparameters*. London and New York: Routledge.

Fukui, Naoki. 2011. Merge and bare phrase structure. In *The Oxford handbook of linguistic minimalism*, ed. Cedric Boeckx, 73–95. Oxford: Oxford University Press. [Chapter 1, this volume.]

Fukui, Naoki, and Margaret Speas. 1986. Specifiers and projection. *MIT Working Papers in Linguistics* 8: 128–172. [Reprinted in Fukui (2006).]

George, Leland M., and Jaklin Kornfilt. 1981. Finiteness and boundedness in Turkish. In *Binding and filtering*, ed. Frank Heny, 105–127. London: Croom Helm; Cambridge, MA: MIT Press.

Grimshaw, Jane. 2005. Extended projection. In *Words and structure*, ed. Jane Grimshaw, 1–73. Stanford: CSLI.

Haeberli, Eric. 2001. Deriving syntactic effects of morphological case by eliminating abstract case. *Lingua* 111: 279–313.

Halle, Morris, and Alec Marantz. 1993. Distributed morphology and the pieces of inflection. In *The view from Building 20*, ed. Kenneth Hale and Samuel Jay Keyser, 111–176. Cambridge, MA: MIT Press.

Ishii, Toru. 1997. An asymmetry in the composition of phrase structure and its consequences. Doctoral dissertation, University of California, Irvine.

Jayaseelan, Karattuparambil. 2008. Bare phrase structure and specifier-less syntax. *Biolinguistics* 2: 87–106.

Kato, Takaomi. 2006. Symmetries in coordination. Doctoral dissertation, Harvard University.

Kayne, Richard S. 1994. *The antisymmetry of syntax*. Cambridge, MA: MIT Press.

Kayne, Richard S. 2009. Antisymmetry and the lexicon. *Linguistic Variation Yearbook* 8: 1–31. [Reprinted in *The biolinguistic enterprise: New perspectives on the evolution and nature of the human language faculty*, ed. Anna Maria Di Sciullo and Cedric Boeckx, 329–353. Oxford: Oxford University Press. (2011).]

Kayne, Richard S. 2011. Why are there no directionality parameters? In *Proceedings of the 28th West Coast Conference on Formal Linguistics*, ed. Mary Byram Washburn, Katherine McKinney-Bock, Erika Varis, Ann Sawyer, and Barbara Tomaszewicz, 1–23. Somerville, MA: Cascadilla Proceedings Project.

Kuno, Susumu. 1973. *The structure of the Japanese language*. Cambridge, MA: MIT Press.

Kuroda, S.-Y. 1965. Generative grammatical studies in the Japanese language. Doctoral dissertation, MIT.

Kuroda, S.-Y. 1988. Whether we agree or not: A comparative syntax of English and Japanese. *Linguisticae Investigationes* 12: 1–47. [Reprinted in Kuroda (1992).]

Kuroda, S.-Y. 1992. *Japanese syntax and semantics: Collected papers*. Dordrecht: Kluwer.

Lechner, Winfried. 2006. An interpretive effect of head movement. In *Phases of interpretation*, ed. Mara Frascarelli, 45–70. Berlin: Mouton de Gruyter.

Lohndal, Terje. 2012. Without specifiers: Phrase structure and events. Doctoral dissertation, University of Maryland, College Park.

Matushansky, Ora. 2006. Head movement in linguistic theory. *Linguistic Inquiry* 37: 69–109.

Moro, Andrea. 2000. *Dynamic antisymmetry*. Cambridge, MA: MIT Press.

Narita, Hiroki. 2010. The tension between explanatory and biological adequacy: Review of Fukui (2006). *Lingua* 120: 1313–1323.

Narita, Hiroki. 2011. Phasing in full interpretation. Doctoral dissertation, Harvard University (Downloadable at http://ling.auf.net/lingBuzz/001304).

Narita, Hiroki. 2012a. Remarks on the nature of headedness and compositionality in bare phrase structure. *Proceedings of Sophia University Linguistic Society* 26: 81–126.

Narita, Hiroki. 2012b. Phase cycles in service of projection-free syntax. In *Phases: Developing the framework*, ed. Ángel J. Gallego, 125–172. Berlin: Mouton de Gruyter.

Narita, Hiroki. 2014. *Endocentric structuring of projection-free syntax*. Amsterdam: John Benjamins.

Pesetsky, David, and Esther Torrego. 2001. T-to-C movement: Causes and consequences. In *Ken Hale: A life in language*, ed. Michael Kenstowicz, 355–426. Cambridge, MA: MIT Press.

Pesetsky, David, and Esther Torrego. 2004. Tense, case, and the nature of syntactic categories. In *The syntax of time*, ed. Jacqueline Gueron and Jacqueline Lecarme, 495–538. Cambridge, MA: MIT Press.

Richards, Marc D. 2007. On feature inheritance: An argument from the phase impenetrability condition. *Linguistic Inquiry* 38: 563–572.

Rizzi, Luigi. 1997. The fine structure of the left periphery. In *Elements of grammar: Handbook of generative syntax*, ed. Liliane Haegeman, 281–337. Dordrecht: Kluwer.

Rizzi, Luigi, ed. 2004. *The structure of CP and IP: The cartography of syntactic structures*, volume 2. Oxford: Oxford University Press.

Roberts, Ian. 2010. *Agreement and head movement: Clitics, incorporation, and defective goals*. Cambridge, MA: MIT Press.

Seely, T. Daniel. 2006. Merge, derivational c-command, and subcategorization in a label-free syntax. In *Minimalist essays*, ed. Cedric Boeckx, 182–217. Amsterdam: John Benjamins.

Starke, Michal. 2004. On the inexistence of specifiers and the nature of heads. In *Structures and beyond: The cartography of syntactic structures*, volume 3, ed. Adriana Belletti, 252–268. Oxford: Oxford University Press.

Svenonius, Peter. 2003. Limits on P: Filling in holes vs. falling in holes. *Nordlyd* 31 (2): 431–445.

Svenonius, Peter. 2010. Spatial P in English. In *Mapping spatial PPs: The cartography of syntactic structures*, volume 6, ed. Guglielmo Cinque and Luigi Rizzi, 127–161. Oxford: Oxford University Press.

Szabolcsi, Anna. 1984. The possessor that ran away from home. *The Linguistic Review* 3: 89–102.

Ura, Hiroyuki. 1994a. Hyper-raising and the theory of *pro*. *MIT Working Papers in Linguistics* 23: 297–316.

Ura, Hiroyuki. 1994b. Superraising in Japanese. *MIT Working papers in Linguistics* 24: 355–374.

Ura, Hiroyuki. 1996. Multiple feature checking: A theory of grammatical function splitting. Doctoral dissertation, MIT.

Uriagereka, Juan. 1999. Multiple spell-out. In *Working minimalism*, ed. Samuel David Epstein and Norbert Hornstein, 251–282. Cambridge, MA: MIT Press.

van Riemsdijk, Henk. 1998a. Categorial feature magnetism: The endocentricity and distribution of projections. *Journal of Comparative Germanic Linguistics* 2: 1–48.

van Riemsdijk, Henk. 1998b. Head movement and adjacency. *Natural Language and Linguistic Theory* 16: 633–678.

Vergnaud, Jean-Roger. 1977/2008. Letter to Noam Chomsky and Howard Lasnik on "Filters and Control," April 17, 1977. Reprinted in *Foundational issues in linguistic theory*, ed. Robert Freidin, Carlos Otero, and Maria Luisa Zubizarreta, 3–15. Cambridge, MA: MIT Press.

3 Generalized Search and Cyclic Derivation by Phase*

A Preliminary Study

With Takaomi Kato, Masakazu Kuno, Hiroki Narita, and Mihoko Zushi

Summary

Merge builds syntactic objects, but Merge alone cannot capture the syntactic relations established between syntactic objects. These relations include Agree(ment), chain-formation, and binding. In order to capture them in a unified manner, this chapter proposes that syntax is equipped with a general search mechanism, which we call *Search*. We characterize Search as an operation that establishes a relation between identical (complexes of) features. We also pose the question: what might the basic operations of syntax be? In the course of investigating this question, we scrutinize some of the putative operations in syntax, such as feature-valuation, feature-inheritance, and Transfer, and draw the conclusion that they are unnecessary and therefore should be eliminated. Our answer to the above question will thus be that Merge and Search are the only basic operations of syntax. The possibility that Search might be formally reduced to Merge is further suggested, in which case there would be only one fundamental operation of syntax, i.e., Merge, with an additional operation Search derived from it.

1 Introduction

Merge has been taken to be an indispensable basic operation of the syntax of human language, since it has the fundamental function of constructing an infinite set of hierarchically structured syntactic objects (SOs) without which human language simply cannot have the properties it actually has, e.g., discrete infinity. It is further suggested in the literature (cf. Berwick 2011) that Merge is the only operation that exists in human language. If true, this is a highly desirable result for obvious minimalist reasons. But the actual situation is such that despite the "Merge-only" thesis, various other miscellaneous operations have been postulated to describe a variety of linguistic phenomena. The fundamental reason for this situation is that Merge alone does not seem to be sufficient to capture the "relations" that are established among (portions of) SOs and that receive interpretations at the Conceptual-Intentional (CI) and Sensorimotor (SM) interfaces (SEM and PHON, respectively). Such relations include Agree(ment), chains formed by Internal Merge (IM) and binding. The main purpose of this chapter is to unify these seemingly disparate operations, and to explore the nature of the unifying operation (vis-à-vis Merge). Given the basic characteristics of the relations in question, it seems that the unifying operation can be characterized as an "identity-searching" operation. Thus, Agree involves matching identical features (values aside), chain-formation relates copies of an SO, which are identical to one another, and binding yields a referential identity.

We therefore propose that the operation in question can be characterized as a general search mechanism, and that the search operation should count as another basic operation of syntax. The idea of a general search mechanism goes back to Fukui and Sakai's (2003: 368) suggestion:

> [W]hat UG provides is a general (downward) "search mechanism" which meets specific locality conditions, and [. . .] the particular operation Agree as it is formulated for feature checking purposes in narrow syntax is a realization of this general search mechanism when it applies to a specialized relation (feature checking) in a specific component of grammar (narrow syntax).

Building on their suggestion, we roughly characterize the operation of *Search* as in (1).

(1) Let α be an element which initiates Search and β be the c-command domain of α. Then, Search is an operation which searches through β for a feature or a complex of features identical to the one contained in α and establishes a relation between those (complexes of) features.

This characterization of Search covers the cases of Agree, chain-formation, and binding. In other words, Search functions as a kind of generalized probe-goal mechanism (see also Samuels 2011 for the notion of Search in phonology).

Then the next question is what initiates Search, i.e., what counts as a generalized probe. Given that the direction of Search is downward, there has to be a natural dividing line that distinguishes between the elements that belong to a higher domain, from which Search is initiated, and those that belong to a lower domain, which is targeted by Search. A good candidate is a phase (Chomsky 2000 *et seq.*), in which there is a distinction between the edge and the interior. Thus, we put forth the following hypothesis.

(2) *Edge = Probe Hypothesis (EPH):*
    Search is initiated by an element X (a *probe*) iff X appears at the edge of a phase.

In what follows, we provide supporting arguments for the EPH. This chapter is organized as follows. In Section 2, we explore the EPH and argue that it is indeed a sustainable and promising hypothesis. In Section 3, we scrutinize three putative operations in syntax, feature-valuation, feature-inheritance and Transfer, from the viewpoint of the No-Tampering Condition (NTC), and claim that they are superfluous and must be eliminated. We thereby establish that Merge and Search are the only basic operations of syntax. Section 4 concludes the chapter.

2 Exploring the EPH

In order to argue for the EPH, it is necessary to show that the class of "edge" elements can be identified with the class of probes. Specifically, we must show that the following two generalizations hold:

(3) All elements that appear in phase-edge positions act as probes (there is no element that appears in a phase-edge and does not initiate Search).

(4) All probes are located in phase-edge positions (there is no element that acts as a probe and is located in a non-edge position).

We will evaluate these propositions in what follows.

2.1 *Edge* ⇒ *Probe*

(3) holds that being located at the edge of a phase is a sufficient condition for acting as a probe for some Search operation. Then, we should examine each of the typical edge categories and try to see if they all initiate some Search operation.

We adopt the widely-assumed theory of phases advocated by Chomsky (2000 *et seq.*), according to which C and v form a distinct class of "phase heads" that determine the *edge* and the *interior* of each phase. (5) provides the relevant definitions.

(5) Let Σ be a phase determined by a phase head H, which we take to be completed when Transfer associated with H occurs:[1]
   a. The *interior* of Σ is the SO that is externally merged with H (i.e., H's sister).
   b. The *edge* of Σ is every element within Σ that does not belong to the interior.

Thus, H and the specifier(s) of H stand as the edge of the relevant phase.[2] To evaluate (3), then, our task is to check whether C, v, Spec-C, and Spec-v can all be characterized as probes.

First, let us examine C-T and v-V relations. Following Chomsky (2001, 2008), we assume that T and V are "defective" categories in the sense that T lacks an inherent tense interpretation, and that V is a root category √V lacking categorical specification, which we propose to characterize as T bearing an unvalued tense-feature [uT(ense)] and V an unvalued categorial feature ([uCat(egorial)]).[3] The defectiveness of T and V is complemented by C and *v*, respectively, with C assigning an appropriate tense interpretation to T and *v* categorizing V.[4] We thus take the C-T and *v*-V relations to be instantiations of Search in support of (3).[5]

Next consider Spec-C and Spec-*v*, which are introduced either by Internal Merge (IM) or by External Merge (EM). In the case of IM, the Spec is filled by a *copy* of some phase-internal SO. It is a property of IM that the set of occurrences/copies of the SO forms a *chain* that as a whole receives appropriate interpretations (θ-roles, scope, etc.). Therefore, CI/SM necessitate some chain-formation operation, and assign interpretations to each IMed Spec-C/*v* in relation to their phase-internal copies. It is natural to suppose that this function is carried out by Search, initiated by the copies at the phase-edge, conforming to our EPH.[6]

This leaves us with EMed Spec-*v*/C, instantiated by, e.g., the external argument (EA) in Spec-*v*, and *why*-type base-generated *wh*-phrases in Spec-C (see, e.g., Rizzi 1990, Ko 2005, Shlonsky and Soare 2011). Unlike the case of IM, they require no chain-formation, but we nevertheless argue that they still initiate some sort of Search operation, conforming to our EPH.

To illustrate this point, let us consider the derivation of a simple sentence *who does John love?* The *v*-phase is first constructed by recursive EM as in (6a), and then mapped to (6b-c) by phase-level applications of Search and IM (here, we adopt Chomsky's 2007, 2008 hypothesis that EM applies before all the other phase-level operations; see also Narita 2014). We will concentrate on the edge elements *v* and *who* here, while the discussion of object-verb agreement is deferred until Section 2.2.

(6) *v*-phase of *who does John love?*

    a.   EM constructs the *v*-phase:

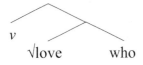

    b.   *v* initiates Search (resulting in categorization):

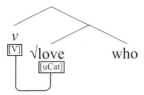

c. IM of *who* and Search (resulting in chain-formation):

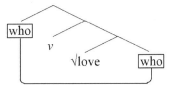

In (6b-c), *v* and *who* at the edge each probe the matching elements in conformity with the EPH. These Search operations establish the relevant identity relations, resulting in Agree(ment) and chain-formation relevant to CI- and SM-interpretation (operator-variable interpretation, phonological copy-deletion). Note that the *v*-phase in (6) does not involve the EA *John*. The EA has nothing to probe within the *v*-phase interior, and thus if it appears at the *v*-phase edge, its Search would end in vain, failing to establish any interpretive relation. For the purpose of the discussion here, let us suppose that such superfluous application of Search is disfavored from the viewpoint of computational efficiency. As is clearly exemplified by unaccusative/passive constructions, the *v*-phase generally need not include the EA, and we assume that this applies to transitive *v* (*v**) as well. We assume that Transfer applies freely and determines their phase domains, and that the *v*-phase need not involve the EA, keeping to the EPH. See note 1 for related discussion.

We argue that there are also cases in which the EA is introduced in the *v*-phase and initiates non-vacuous Search. This situation is exemplified by the case of anaphor-binding by the EA. Let us assume that there is some sort of feature-matching relation between the binder and the anaphor (say in φ-features or some independent referential feature [Ref]). Under this assumption, the EA may appear in the *v*-phase edge and initiate Search in conformity with the EPH.

(7) *v*-phase of *John loves himself*
  a. EM constructs the *v*-phase:

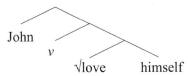

  b. *John* and *v* independently initiate Search:

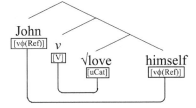

Thus, our hypothesis is that the EA is merged into the *v*-phase only if the EA can initiate non-vacuous Search within the *v*-phase.[7]

Incidentally, the notion of a "phrasal probe" is a distinct feature of our EPH-based approach. The conventional theory of Agree (Chomsky 2000 *et seq.*) maintains that only heads/LIs with unvalued features can probe, but this stipulation has no principled grounds, and there is no reason to exclude phrasal SOs initiating Search, whether they are externally merged or internally merged, and whether they are associated with unvalued or valued features (as mentioned in note 4, we also agree with Pesetsky and Torrego 2001, 2004 in assuming that valued features can act as probes, too).

The C-phase subsequent to (6) is first constructed by recursive EM (including EM of the EA), as in (8a), and phase-level applications of IM and Search map it to (8b) and then to (8c) (the discussion of A-movement will be postponed until Section 2.2).

(8)   C-phase of *who does John love?*
    a.   EM of *John*, T, and C:

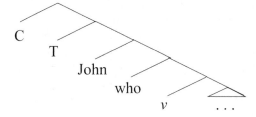

    b.   C initiates Search (resulting in Agree(ment)):

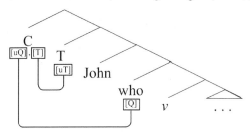

    c.   IM and Search (resulting in chain-formation):

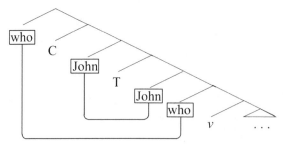

Here too, the relevant edge categories, C and IMed Spec-C, successfully conform to the EPH, independently initiating relevant Search operations.

Just like the case of EMed Spec-*v*, the C-phase may introduce EMed Spec-C in its edge, too, so long as it yields non-vacuous Search. This case is exemplified by the *why*-type *wh*-phrase, which is directly base-generated in Spec-C and matches with C in Q-features, according to Rizzi (1990) and others (see Ko 2005, Shlonsky and Soare 2011, and references cited therein). Thus, if the *v*-phase in, say, (7) is merged with T, C, and *why*, as in (9a), then the latter two edge elements can independently initiate Search, and *why* specifically finds C's Q-feature as its goal, as in (9b).

(9) C-phase of *why does John love himself?*

    a.   EM of T, C, and *why*:

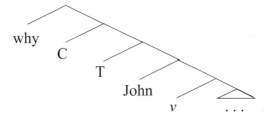

    b.   C and *why* independently initiate Search:

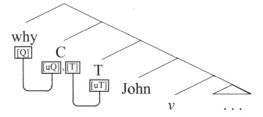

    c.   IM and Search (resulting in chain-formation):

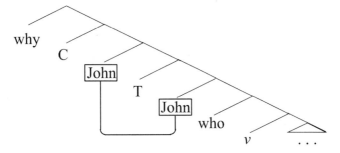

In (9b), the edge element *why* stands as a phrasal probe, and the phase head C rather acts as a goal for this higher probe within the same phase. This possibility is allowed in our EPH-based approach.

We will discuss A-movement of the EA *John* shortly. Here, let us just confirm that it is possible to characterize all the relevant edge elements (Spec-C, C, Spec-*v* and *v*) as probes that independently initiate generalized Search, conforming to (3).

2.2 Probe ⇒ Edge

The preceding discussion establishes that (3) can be maintained, namely that an SO Σ being in a phase-edge can be characterized as a sufficient condition for Σ acting as a probe for a Search operation. The next question is whether the converse (4) can be maintained, i.e., whether being located in some phase-edge is also a necessary condition for being a probe for generalized Search.

(4) holds that no non-edge elements should be able to act as probes. In the traditional theory of phases (Chomsky 2000 *et seq.*), it is assumed that T and Spec-T count as *bona fide* non-edge categories and are included within the interior of the C-phase. However, these categories should be able to establish relations involving agreement and IM: T is often assumed to be the locus of [uϕ] for subject-T agreement, and Spec-T is the landing site for A-movement of the subject. Then, exploring the theory of generalized Search, we must either dispense with (4), or show that no non-edge elements are involved as a probe in the above T-related phenomena. We argue that the latter approach is favorable on both conceptual and empirical grounds.

Recall that we adopt the definition of "edge" and "interior" in (5), according to which everything within the sister of a phase-head H counts as a non-edge of the H-phase. Putting aside T for a while, it remains to be determined whether the Spec-T belongs to the class of non-edges. It was stipulated in Chomsky's (2008) theory that IM of the subject NP to Spec-T results in the mapping from (10a) to (10b), and that, therefore, the Spec-T position in (10b) is properly subsumed within the complement/interior of C.

(10) a.

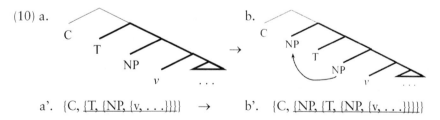

a'. {C, {T, {NP, {v, . . .}}}}   →   b'. {C, {NP, {T, {NP, {v, . . .}}}}}

Notice that the mapping from (10a) to (10b) involves a nontrivial form of tampering, which can be made clear by representing the relevant SOs in set-theoretic terms (10a'/b') (see N. Richards 2001 for the notion of "tucking-in"). Movement of the form in (10) transforms the internal structure of (10a), specifically replacing the underscored sub-constituent in (10a') with the one in (10b'). This mapping goes beyond the generative capacity of

Merge, understood as elementary set-formation, and it violates the general ban on tampering operations, which is referred to as the *No-tampering Condition (NTC)* (adapted from Chomsky 2008: 138, explored by Narita 2014).

(11) *No-tampering Condition (NTC):*[8]
No elements are deleted or modified in the course of the narrow syntactic derivation.

The NTC is a natural principle of computational efficiency, and it emerges as a direct consequence of the simplest formulation of Merge. Thus, from the viewpoint of the minimalist program (Chomsky 1995), an alternative characterization of A-movement is in order.

Epstein et al. (2012) and Narita (2014) provide a theory of A-movement that is free from NTC-violations. They propose that the original SO in (10a)/(12a) is fully preserved as demanded by the NTC, as in (12b'-i), and IM of the subject NP rather yields a "two-peaked" structure shown in (12b).

(12)

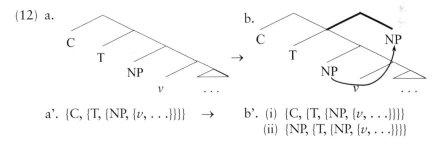

a'. {C, {T, {NP, {v, . . .}}}}   →   b'. (i) {C, {T, {NP, {v, . . .}}}}
(ii) {NP, {T, {NP, {v, . . .}}}}

Indeed, (12b) is exactly what the literal application of IM should generate: the subject NP is a term of {T, {NP, {v, . . .}}} (what is traditionally called T'), and the merger of these two SOs counts as IM, yielding the undominated root SO (12b'-ii) = {NP, {T, {NP, {v, . . .}}}}, which is distinct from but partially overlaps with the original C-phase structure (12a') = (12b'-i). Unlike Chomsky's (2008) formulation of A-movement, the mapping from (12a) to (12b) does not tamper with (12a/a'), and therefore, it satisfies the NTC, a desirable result.

Note that the intersection of (12b'-i) and (12b'-ii) is exactly what we call the interior of the C-phase, according to the definition in (5a), and that "Spec-T" does not belong to this domain. Since Spec-T may be created before the Transfer associated with C, which is assumed to complete the C-phase, it seems reasonable to assume that it can be regarded as being within the C-phase. If so, under the definition of the edge given in (5b), Spec-T should be able to count as an edge position and as such initiate a Search for chain-formation, as correctly predicted by our EPH. Building on these considerations, we propose that A-movement to Spec-T is also an instance of IM to the edge, thus conforming to our generalized theory of Search-based chain-formation.[9] The informal representations of A-movement in (8c) and (9c) should be revised accordingly.[10,11]

Incidentally, if we are right in claiming that both Spec-C and Spec-T may count as the edge of the C-phase (and that the same holds for Spec-v and Spec-V; see note 9), then it becomes mysterious why A'-movement always targets Spec-C and A-movement Spec-T, and not the other way round: they are both edge-positions and should therefore be able to initiate Search without any problem, so we have to provide some explanation for the fact that we do not normally find any instance of A-movement into Spec-C, or A'-movement into Spec-T.[12]

There are several ways to overcome this problem. First, it is possible (and indeed customary) to stipulate some sort of semantico-syntactic criteria according to which certain types of interpretation are required to be encoded in designated syntactic structures: for example, it is commonly assumed that Spec-C is the designated operator position and movement of a non-operator category into this position results in illegitimate interpretation, while Spec-T has the criterion of "subjecthood," and so on (see, e.g., Rizzi 1997, 2006). Though rather stipulative at this point, such a criterion-based approach is commonly adopted in the literature, and it readily provides a detailed description of what moves where.[13]

Another approach to explain the distribution of A- and A'-movement is proposed by Fukui and Narita (2012) [Chapter 2, this volume], according to which syntactic derivation is fundamentally driven by structural symmetry, or specifically what they call "feature-equilibrium." They attend to the fact that EM typically generates structures that are traditionally called "endocentric," i.e., asymmetric in terms of the prominence of a head LI (or its features) ({V, NP}, {T, vP}, {C, TP}, and so on), whereas IM in tandem with Agree generates structures that are symmetric with respect to agreement features: A-movement into Spec-T creates {NP, TP} and the immediate heads of NP and TP (N and T) share ϕ-features matched via Agree;[14] *wh*-movement into Spec-C generates {QP, CP}, and again the immediate heads of QP and CP share the agreeing Q-features, and so on (see Cable 2010 and Narita 2014 for the view that *wh*-phrases are uniformly headed by a distinct functional category Q). Building on the overall directionality from asymmetric structures towards symmetric structures, Fukui and Narita (2012) propose that IM uniformly targets positions that can yield the symmetric configuration defined in (13)–(14):

(13) *Feature-equilibrium:*
   For a formal feature F, an SO {α, β} is in an *F-equilibrium.* $\equiv_{def.}$ α and β share a matching formal feature F that is equally prominent in α and β.

(14) *Featural symmetry:*
   Given a formal feature F in an SO {α, β}, the SO is symmetric with respect to F (or F-symmetric) if it is in an F-equilibrium. Otherwise, the SO {α, β} is (F-)asymmetric with respect to F.

In this theory, the Spec-T structure {{N$_{[\phi]}$, . . .}, {T$_{[\phi]}$, . . .}} is in a ϕ-equilibrium, and the Spec-C structure {{Q$_{[Q]}$, . . .}, {C$_{[Q]}$, . . .}} is in a Q-equilibrium; in contrast, movement of $\{N_{[\phi]}, \ldots\}$ into Spec-$C_{[Q]}$ or movement of $\{Q_{[Q]}, \ldots\}$ into Spec-$T_{[\phi]}$ form no feature-equilibrium, and hence they never yield any stable structures and do not surface at SEM/PHON. In this manner, Fukui and Narita's theory of feature-equilibrium provides an alternative explanation of what category moves to which position, without necessarily making recourse to criterion-based stipulations (see Fukui and Narita 2012 for further discussion).[15,16]

In summary, we have shown that Epstein et al. (2012) and Narita's (2014) "two-peaked" characterizations of A-movement may yield a theory of phase-edges that can subsume Spec-T (and Spec-V; see note 9) for the purpose of the EPH, and that either criterion-based approaches or the notion of feature-equilibrium (or possibly yet other means) can provide a proper description of what category undergoes IM to which position.

Let us finally remark on T. Provided that it is a typical non-edge category, (4) predicts that it can never initiate Search/probing. However, it is commonly assumed that T bears (or inherits from C) a set of unvalued ϕ-features [uϕ] that act as a *bona fide* probe for subject-verb agreement. Then, does T's [uϕ] provide a piece of counterevidence to our EPH? Our answer is no. Recall our conclusion that Spec-T is an edge position and initiates its own Search operation. The application of Search initiated by an element in Spec-T is independently required for chain-formation, but now, provided that the single operation Search is by assumption responsible for both Agree(ment) and chain-formation, it is reasonable to suppose that the IMed SO $N_{[\phi]}P$ at Spec-T also triggers Search for ϕ-feature-agreement: in the configuration $\{\{N_{[\phi]}, \ldots\}, \{T_{[\phi]}, \ldots\}\}$, Search by the moved $N_{[\phi]}P = \{N_{[\phi]}, \ldots\}$ first necessarily hits T as its closest goal and inspects every feature within it, including [uϕ]. Then, nothing prevents this Search from establishing ϕ-feature-agreement between T and $N_{[\phi]}P$, in addition to the chain of the IMed $N_{[\phi]}P$ (see Bošković 2007 for the view that moved elements can probe). Therefore, this alternative approach accounts for subject-verb agreement as an instance of Search driven by the edge category Spec-T. Again, the same analysis may be extended to V: the A-moved NP at Spec-V initiates Search for A-chain formation and object ϕ-feature agreement (see note 9).

2.3 Interim Summary

In this section, we showed that the EPH is a promising way to offer a generalized theory of Search, and that being located at some edge position is both a necessary and a sufficient condition for initiating some Search-operation.

3 Further Reduction

We have shown that Agree, chain-formation, and binding can be subsumed under the general operation Search and that Search can be seen as a basic operation of syntax besides Merge. Then, the next task is to establish that only Search and Merge count as basic operations of syntax. To do so, we scrutinize three alleged "operations" in syntax, feature-valuation, feature-inheritance, and Transfer, and show that they are unnecessary and can (and must) be dispensed with.

First, let us take up feature-valuation. In the discussion thus far, we have assumed that Agree involves feature-valuation (Chomsky 2000, 2001). However, feature-valuation is a violation of the NTC as defined in (11), in that it alters a feature value of an LI. Therefore, if we are to pursue a theory of no-tampering syntax, feature-valuation must be eliminated. Here is where Search comes into play. Recall the characterization of Search repeated below.

(15) Let α be an element which initiates Search and β be the c-command domain of α. Then, Search is an operation which searches through β for a feature or a complex of features identical to the one contained in α and establishes a relation between those (complexes of) features.

The point is that Search is not only an identity-searching operation but also the one that establishes a relation between identical (complexes of) features. Thus, when Search applies in the form of Agree, it establishes an Agree(ment) relation between a searching element (probe) and a searched element (goal). In light of this characterization of Search, we can rework the process of Agree(ment) as follows.

(16) When an Agree(ment) relation is established between an unvalued feature and a valued feature, the interface systems access it, so that the unvalued feature will be processed at SEM/PHON in relation to the valued feature.

Notice that this reworked process of Agree(ment) does not involve "literal" feature-valuation, and, therefore, it can be eliminated, a welcome result from the viewpoint of the NTC.

Similarly, an effort to pursue a theory of no-tampering syntax leads us to abandon "feature-inheritance" proposed by Chomsky (2008), according to which unvalued ϕ-features are first introduced at C and then get inherited by T. For the sake of discussion, let us first briefly review how feature-inheritance is supported by M. Richards (2007). He points out that if it is assumed following Chomsky (2000, 2001, 2004) that T bears unvalued ϕ-features while the subject NP bears valued ϕ-features and that the former Agrees with (and gets valued by) the latter, a problem arises as to the timing of Transfer. If T's unvalued ϕ-features Agree with the subject NP's valued ϕ-features after Transfer, T's unvalued (and uninterpretable) ϕ-features will be sent to the interfaces, causing the derivation to crash. If, on the other hand, T's unvalued ϕ-features Agree with the subject NP's valued ϕ-features before Transfer, T's ϕ-features become indistinguishable from the lexically valued ϕ-features, in which case T's uninterpretable φ-features fail to be deleted by Transfer, causing the derivation to crash at SEM. Therefore, M. Richards (2007) concludes that in order to satisfy Full Interpretation, Transfer and Agree (valuation) must happen together. Given that Transfer is a C level operation, it follows that C bears φ-features and T gets them via inheritance.

By contrast, feature-inheritance is not necessary under our Search-based valuation-free approach, in which T's unvalued φ-features are simply related to the subject NP's valued φ-features via Search and are interpreted by the interface systems as having the same value as the valued counterpart. In this approach, even if T inherently bears unvalued φ-features, there is no point in the derivation where they get valued and become indistinguishable from their originally valued counterparts. Therefore, our approach does not need to resort to feature-inheritance, and as long as it can be maintained, feature-inheritance can and must be eliminated in favor of a theory of syntax in which the No-tampering Condition is fully respected.

Elimination of feature-valuation further leads us to rethink the status of Transfer. According to Chomsky (2004, 2008), it is an operation that cyclically strips off the interior of a phase and sends that portion to the CI and SM interfaces for interpretation upon the completion of the phase. Specifically, this operation is assumed to execute the following three functions:

(17) *Transfer* (under Chomsky's 2004, 2008 system):
   a. deletes uninterpretable/unvalued features [uF] within the phase that get valued by Agree,
   b. subjects the phase to SEM and PHON for CI- and SM-interpretations, and
   c. renders the interior of the phase inaccessible for further operations (the "Phase-Impenetrability Condition (PIC)").

Of these three, we take (17b) to be the essential and indispensable function of Transfer. So long as we characterize human language as the (hopefully optimal) computational system that generates an infinite array of "sound"-"meaning" linkages (i.e., pairs of SEM and PHON), there must be some "interfacing" operation that subjects Merge-based SOs to CI and SM, and this is exactly what (17b) amounts to. In contrast, we argue that the assumptions in (17a) and (17c) are eliminable in our valuation-free approach. First, (17a) essentially originates from the conventional hypothesis in (18).

(18) Valued [uF] cannot receive interpretation at SEM, and hence it needs to be deleted immediately upon valuation by Agree.

However, once we eliminate feature-valuation in favor of Search-based interpretive relations (16), we no longer have any reason to stick to (18). We can alternatively assume (19).

(19) In the absence of a lexically specified value, [uF] receives no interpretation at SEM, but it nevertheless satisfies Full Interpretation indirectly through Agree(ment) relations established with [vF] via Search.

According to our Search-based valuation-free approach, there is no representation of valued [uF], and we can keep to the simplest typology of feature values and their interpretation: [vF] receives interpretation, while [uF] does not. (19) naturally dispenses with the two stipulations in (17a) and (18), again a welcome result in light of the NTC (see Epstein et al. 2010 for related discussion).

Let us finally turn to (17c), whose effect is commonly referred to as the "Phase-Impenetrability Condition (PIC)" (Chomsky 2004 *et seq.*). Although space limitations prevent us from presenting a full-fledged analysis of the PIC effect (see, e.g., Narita 2014), there is good reason to cast doubt on the current formulation of the PIC. These doubts pertain to the clear existence of long-distance (i.e., cross-phasal) dependencies: for example, see Bošković (2007) and references cited therein for ample crosslinguistic examples of long-distance Agree(ment) that clearly violate the PIC. Moreover, binding (say, of pronouns or subject-oriented anaphors) can no doubt apply in a long-distance fashion as well, and thus binding is not constrained by the PIC, either. The theory of generalized Search, so long as we pursue it, has to subsume such cases by assumption, and these considerations support the view that the PIC (17c) must be reconsidered.[17,18]

If we dispense with (17a) and (17c), it becomes possible to replace the complex definition of Transfer in (17) with a bare conceptual minimum in (20) (corresponding to (17b)).

(20) Upon completion of each phase, the interface systems access elements and relations internal to it.

In this line of reasoning, we can even draw the conclusion that Transfer may ultimately lose its status as an independent syntactic operation, reducing to just a cover term for the simple fact that CI and SM have periodic access to SOs generated by narrow syntax. Although we have to leave fuller exploration of this reduction for future research, we argue that this is what the generalized theory of Search leads us to pursue.

Summarizing, we have shown a fruitful line of research that eliminates feature-valuation, feature-inheritance, and Transfer. Success in this endeavor supports our hypothesis that Merge and Search exhaustively characterize the basic operations of syntax.

4 Conclusion

In this chapter, we have argued that Search is a basic operation of syntax that establishes relations between SOs constructed by Merge. The relevant relations to be subsumed under Search include Agree(ment), chain-formation, and binding. We have also demonstrated that Search is always initiated by an element that appears at the edge of a phase, the EPH. A novel feature of this hypothesis is that it allows a probe to be phrasal as well as valued, contrary to the standard theory of Agree developed by Chomsky (2000 *et seq.*), according to which only LIs with [uF] can act as a probe. One of the empirical advantages is that we can account for the fact that there are cases in which an EMed Spec-H Agrees with H, as exemplified by the *why*-type *wh*-phrase. Another noteworthy feature of the EPH is its compatibility with the two-peaked structure analysis proposed by Epstein et al. (2012) and Narita (2014). This analysis makes it possible for Spec-T not to belong to the C-phase interior, hence it can initiate Search, Agreeing with T and forming a chain with its own copy. Fukui and Narita's (2012) approach to movement provides an important piece of the argument for the whole picture sketched in this chapter. In particular, their idea that movement takes place in search of featural symmetry enables us to explain why A-movement targets Spec-T whereas A'-movement targets Spec-C, not the other way around. Finally, we have argued for the elimination of feature-valuation, feature-inheritance, and Transfer in favor of a theory of syntax that is truly without tampering. Consequently, we draw the conclusion that Merge and Search are the only basic operations of syntax.

A final remark for future research is now in order. Let us compare Merge and Search formally. A standard formulation of Merge is Merge $(X, Y) = \{X, Y\}$, i.e., Merge applies to two SOs and forms a set of them. A corresponding formulation of Search (based on our informal characterization (1)) will necessarily involve the process of picking a probe and its goal and putting them in an ordered pair (not a set, because a probe and a goal will have to be distinguished): Search $(X, Y) = <X, Y>$, where X = probe, Y = goal. Since the ordered pair $<X, Y>$ is mathematically equivalent to the set $\{X, \{X, Y\}\}$ (a variant of the standard Kuratowski definition $<X, Y> = \{\{X\}, \{X, Y\}\}$), Search is in fact very similar formally to an asymmetric version of Merge. This suggests a possibility that Search is actually a derived operation, a special case of the very fundamental operation Merge. Thus, our Merge/Search hypothesis about the basic operations of human syntax, with all of its descriptive and theoretical advantages, may eventually turn out to be compatible with the "Merge-only" thesis mentioned at the outset of this chapter.

Notes

* We are indebted to Bridget Samuels for her helpful comments and suggestions. An earlier version of this work was presented at the 30th Annual Meeting of the English Linguistic Society of Japan held at Keio University, and we thank the audience for their comments and questions. Part of this research is supported by the Japan Science and Technology Agency (CREST) and by the Japan Society for the Promotion of Science (Grant-in-Aid for Scientific Research, Scientific

Research (A) (General) #23242025, and Challenging Exploratory Research #25580095).

1 It follows that if X is merged into the derivation after the Transfer associated with a phase head H, X counts as being outside the phase determined by H. We will see shortly as a concrete example that the external argument (EA) may or may not be included in the v-phase, depending on the rule ordering between Transfer and External Merge (EM) of the EA.

2 X-bar-theoretic projections (X′, XP, etc.), as well as notions like "complement" and "specifier," play no role in bare phrase structure, but we will sometimes use these terms solely for expository convenience.

3 Henceforth, we will sometimes use the notations [vF]/[uF] to refer to valued/ unvalued feature F.

4 See, e.g., Pesetsky and Torrego (2001, 2004) for the view that valued features can also act as probes in certain cases.

5 Moreover, C and v (or specifically its transitive variety, v^*) are known to be the loci of subject and object agreement. M. Richards (2007) and Chomsky (2007, 2008) propose that the relevant unvalued ϕ-features ([uϕ]) are first introduced at C and v^*, and then inherited by T and V via phase-level probing. We will return to the discussion of the Richards-Chomsky hypothesis in Section 3, where it will be proposed that the whole notion of "feature-inheritance" can be eliminated.

6 See Bošković (2007) for the view that IMed elements can probe from the chain-head position.

7 Bošković and Takahashi (1998), Hornstein (1998), Lasnik (1999) and others argue that θ-marking from v/V to NPs is mediated by checking/agreement of "θ-features" between these categories. If we adopt this approach, then we may alternatively hypothesize that the EA always appears at the v-phase edge and initiates Search for θ-feature matching. We leave investigation of this possibility for future research. See, e.g., Brody (1999, 2002) for some arguments against the notion of θ-feature-checking.

8 The original NTC in Chomsky (2008: 138), given in (i), was formulated specifically in terms of Merge:
(i) Merge of α and β leaves the two SOs unchanged.
Indeed, if we restrict our attention to the simplest formulation of Merge, namely an elementary binary set-formation, it is just an operation that does nothing more than combining SOs, and therefore it cannot modify the elements that constitute the input to this operation. The NTC as formulated in (11) is thus trivially satisfied. Here we reformulate the NTC as a more general ban on tampering of elements previously introduced by syntax.

9 The same analysis can be readily extended to A-movement to Spec-V, which is assumed to be the position that the object NP should overtly move to for Accusative Case-checking (Chomsky 2007, 2008). Here, too, the landing site should be able to count as the edge of v^*, according to (5).

10 Unlike our definition in (5), Epstein et al. (2012) and Narita (2014) build on the assumption that the interior of a phase is rather identified with the domain that is subjected to Transfer (the mapping to the SEM and PHON interfaces). They both propose that the whole second-peak SO (12b'-ii) is subjected to Transfer immediately after (or simultaneously with) the phase-level application of IM, and that the Spec-T position belongs to the interior in their sense.

11 It is worth noting that the two-peaked structure like (12) may provide a neat explanation of why A-movement typically cannot range over multiple phases, while A'-movement can apply successive-cyclically and can yield a long-distance chain. The two-peak approach essentially holds that the landing site of A-movement (such as the Spec-T position within (12b'-ii)) is "on a different plane," isolated from the main phase domain (such as the one in (12b'-i)). It is

then simply impossible for such an A-moved category to get *re*-integrated by IM into the main phase domain, because IM is by definition an instance of Merge applying to two elements one of which is properly contained within the other. Thus, for example, the higher NP copy within (12b'-ii) can never be internally merged into the edge of (12b'-i), since the former can never be a term of the latter.

12 However, see George (1980) and Chomsky (1986, 2012, 2013) for the so-called Vacuous Movement Hypothesis.
13 However, this approach critically hinges on the notion of "Specifier" and "Spec-head licensing," which may turn out to be illegitimate residues of earlier X-bar-theoretic stipulations. See, e.g., Chomsky (2013), Fukui and Narita (2012) and Narita (2014) for theories that dispense with the concept of specifier altogether.
14 Depending on the analysis of nominal syntax, the highest head of a nominal phrase may be D, or *n*, or K(ase) as proposed by Bittner and Hale (1996), Narita (2014), and the references cited therein.
15 Fukui and Narita (2012) argue that the notion of feature-equilibrium enables us to provide a simple characterization of A-movement: it is IM of $N_{[\phi]}P$ driven for ϕ-equilibrium. They further argue that their theory of symmetry-driven syntax can dispense with the notion of abstract Case, a stipulative and now totally redundant device meant to capture the driving force of A-movement.
16 In both Fukui and Narita's (2012) system and the system being proposed here, it is predicted that subject raising is not obligatory in languages that lack ϕ-feature-agreement. However, those systems differ in the predictions they make concerning languages where T lacks ϕ-features and N/D/*n*/K bears them: In Fukui and Narita's (2012) system, such languages are predicted not to exist; in the present system, it is predicted that such languages can exist, and that subject raising is not obligatory in them.
17 We may, for example, follow Bošković (2007) and assume that IM is constrained by the PIC while Agree/Search is immune to the PIC. This approach also eliminates recourse to the stipulation in (17c), leaving the PIC as an independent constraint specific to IM. Further investigation is required to explain why there are two kinds of independent conditions. Note that the situation is reminiscent of the traditional division between subjacency/ECP and binding theory in the 1970s/1980s.
18 Note that one of the functions of the PIC (17c) has been to characterize the computational cyclicity of linguistic derivation. However, recall that we now establish an alternative motivation for the cyclic derivation by phase: under the EPH (2), Search is designed to operate from a well-defined subdomain of a phase (i.e., the edge), and thus all relation-formation operations, including IM, are initiated by some edge position, showing up cyclically per phase.

References

Berwick, Robert. 2011. All you need is Merge: Biology, computation, and language from the bottom up. In *The biolinguistic enterprise: New perspectives on the evolution and nature of the human language faculty*, ed. Anna Maria Di Sciullo and Cedric Boeckx, 461–491. Oxford: Oxford University Press.
Bittner, Maria, and Ken Hale. 1996. The structural determination of Case and agreement. *Linguistic Inquiry* 27: 1–68.
Bošković, Željko. 2007. On the locality and motivation of Move and Agree: An even more minimal theory. *Linguistic Inquiry* 38: 589–644.
Bošković, Željko, and Daiko Takahashi. 1998. Scrambling and last resort. *Linguistic Inquiry* 29: 347–366.

Brody, Michael. 1999. Relating syntactic elements: Remarks on Norbert Hornstein's "Movement and chains." *Syntax* 2: 210–226.

Brody, Michael. 2002. One more time. *Syntax* 4: 126–138.

Cable, Seth. 2010. *The Grammar of Q: Q-particles, wh-movement, and pied-piping.* Oxford: Oxford University Press.

Chomsky, Noam. 1986. *Barriers.* Cambridge, MA: MIT Press.

Chomsky, Noam. 1995. *The minimalist program.* Cambridge, MA: MIT Press.

Chomsky, Noam. 2000. Minimalist inquiries: The framework. In *Step by step: Essays on minimalist syntax in honor of Howard Lasnik*, ed. Roger Martin, David Michaels, and Juan Uriagereka, 89–155. Cambridge, MA: MIT Press.

Chomsky, Noam. 2001. Derivation by phase. In *Ken Hale: A life in language*, ed. Michael Kenstowicz, 1–52. Cambridge, MA: MIT Press.

Chomsky, Noam. 2004. Beyond explanatory adequacy. In *Structures and beyond: The cartography of syntactic structures*, volume 3, ed. Adriana Belletti, 104–131. Oxford: Oxford University Press.

Chomsky, Noam. 2007. Approaching UG from below. In *Interfaces + recursion = language? Chomsky's minimalism and the view from semantics*, ed. Uli Sauerland and Hans-Martin Gärtner, 1–29. Berlin and New York: Mouton de Gruyter.

Chomsky, Noam. 2008. On phases. In *Foundational issues in linguistic theory*, ed. Robert Freidin, Carlos Otero, and Maria Luisa Zubizarreta, 133–166. Cambridge, MA: MIT Press.

Chomsky, Noam. 2012. Introduction. In *Gengokisoronsyu [Foundations of biolinguistics: selected writings]*, ed. and trans. Naoki Fukui, 17–26. Tokyo: Iwanami Shoten.

Chomsky, Noam. 2013. Problems of projection. *Lingua* 130: 33–49.

Epstein, Samuel David, Hisatsugu Kitahara, and T. Daniel Seely. 2010. Uninterpretable features: What are they and what do they do? In *Exploring crash-proof grammars*, ed. Michael Putnam, 124–142. Amsterdam: John Benjamins.

Epstein, Samuel David, Hisatsugu Kitahara, and T. Daniel Seely. 2012. Structure building that can't be! In *Ways of structure building*, ed. Myriam Uribe-Etxebarria and Vidal Valmala, 253–270. Oxford: Oxford University Press.

Fukui, Naoki, and Hiroki Narita. 2012. Merge and (a)symmetry. Paper presented at the Kyoto Conference on Biolinguistics, Kyoto University, March 12, 2012. [Revised version published as Chapter 2 of this volume.]

Fukui, Naoki, and Hiromu Sakai. 2003. The visibility guideline for functional categories: Verb raising in Japanese and related issues. *Lingua* 113 (4–6): 321–375. [Reprinted in *Theoretical comparative syntax: Studies in macroparameters*, Naoki Fukui, 289–336. London: Routledge. (2006).]

George, Leland M. 1980. Analogical generalization in natural language syntax. Doctoral dissertation, MIT.

Hornstein, Norbert. 1998. Movement and chains. *Syntax* 1: 99–127.

Ko, Heejeong. 2005. Syntax of *why-in-situ*: Merge into [Spec, CP] in the overt syntax. *Natural Language and Linguistic Theory* 23: 867–916.

Lasnik, Howard. 1999. Chains of arguments. In *Working minimalism*, ed. Samuel D. Epstein and Norbert Hornstein, 189–215. Cambridge, MA: MIT Press.

Narita, Hiroki. 2014. *Endocentric structuring of projection-free syntax.* Amsterdam: John Benjamins.

Pesetsky, David, and Esther Torrego. 2001. T-to-C movement: Causes and consequences. In *Ken Hale: A life in language*, ed. Michael Kenstowicz, 355–426. Cambridge, MA: MIT Press.

Pesetsky, David, and Esther Torrego. 2004. Tense, case, and the nature of syntactic categories. In *The syntax of time*, ed. Jacqueline Gueron and Jacqueline Lecarme, 495–538. Cambridge, MA: MIT Press.

Richards, Marc D. 2007. On feature inheritance: An argument from the phase impenetrability condition. *Linguistic Inquiry* 38: 563–572.

Richards, Norvin. 2001. *Movement in language: Interactions and architectures*. Oxford: Oxford University Press.

Rizzi, Luigi. 1990. *Relativized minimality*. Cambridge, MA: MIT Press.

Rizzi, Luigi. 1997. The fine structure of the left periphery. In *Elements of grammar: Handbook of generative syntax*, ed. Liliane Haegeman, 281–337. Dordrecht: Kluwer.

Rizzi, Luigi. 2006. On the form of chains: Criterial positions and ECP effects. In *Wh-movement: Moving on*, ed. Lisa Lai-Shen Cheng and Norbert Corver, 97–133. Cambridge, MA: MIT Press.

Samuels, Bridget. 2011. *Phonological architecture: A biolinguistic approach*. Oxford: Oxford University Press.

Shlonsky, Ur, and Gabriela Soare. 2011. Where's 'why'? *Linguistic Inquiry* 42: 651–669.

4 Merge, Labeling, and Projection[*]

With Hiroki Narita

1 Introduction

Thousands of years of language study share the belief, commonly ascribed to Aristotle, that the grammar of human language is, in essence, a system of the pairing of "sound" (or "signs") and "meaning." The enterprise of generative grammar initiated by Chomsky (1955/1975, 1957) is just a recent addition to this long tradition, but it brought a couple of important insights into the nature of human language, which have massively revolutionized our perspective from which to study language. At the core of this "Chomskyan revolution" lies an old observation, essentially due to Descartes and other rationalists, that the capacity to pair sounds and meanings in human language exhibits unbounded creativity: humans can produce and understand an infinitude of expressions, many of which are previously unheard of or too long and/or senseless to be produced. This Cartesian observation specifically led Chomsky to suppose that the grammar of human language must be essentially "generative" and "transformational" in the following sense, setting the basis for sixty years of contemporary linguistic research:

(1) The grammar of human language is "generative" in the sense that it is a system that uses a finite number of basic operations to yield "discrete infinity" (i.e., the infinity created by combinations of discrete units) of linguistic expressions.

(2) Further, it is "transformational" in the sense that it has the property of mapping an abstract representation to another representation.

For example, any linguistic expression—say, *the boy read the book*—can be infinitely expanded by adding optional adjuncts of various types (3), coordinating its constituents (4), or embedding it into another expression (5), yielding various sorts of discrete infinity.

(3) Adjunction:
  a. the boy (often) (eagerly) read the book (carefully) (quickly) (at the station) (at 2 p.m.) (last week) . . .

    b. the (smart) (young) (handsome) . . . boy (who was twelve years old) (who Mary liked) (whose mother was sick) . . . read the book.

(4) Coordination:
    a. the boy read the book (and/or/but) the girl drank coffee (and/or/but) . . .
    b. [the boy (and/or/but not) the girl (and/or) . . .] read the book.

(5) Embedding:
    a. I know that [the girl believes that [it is certain that . . . [the boy read the book]. . .]]
    b. The boy [(that/who) the girl [(that/who) the cat [. . .] bit] liked] read the book.

Moreover, the same sentence can be "transformationally related" to many other sentences of different types, yielding the massive expressive potential of human language:

(6) Passive:
The book was read (by the boy).

(7) Interrogatives:
    a. Did the boy read the book?
    b. {Which book/what} did the boy read?
    c. {Which boy/who} read the book?

(8) Topicalization/Fronting:
    a. The book, the boy read (last week).
    b. Read the book, the boy did (last week).

The recognition of the generative and transformational aspects of human language led Chomsky to conclude that structural linguistics was fundamentally inadequate in that it restricted its research focus to the techniques of sorting finite linguistic corpora (see, e.g., Harris 1951). Linguists were instead urged to shift their focus of study from an arbitrarily chosen set of observable utterances to the mind-internal mechanism that generates that set and infinitely many other expressions (i.e., "I-language" in the sense of Chomsky 1986b). This shift of focus effectively exorcised the empiricist/behaviorist doctrine that attributes the knowledge of language in its entirety to the reinforcement of finite experience, resurrecting the rationalist/mentalist approach to the human mind and its innate mechanism (the topic of *Universal Grammar* (UG)). It further came to be recognized in subsequent years that (1)-(2) (or specifically the recursive property attributable to the operations underlying (1)-(2)) are unique properties of human language and apparently shared by no other species (Hauser et al. 2002, Fitch et al. 2005). The recognition of (1)-(2) as a species-specific trait (an "autapomorphy" in cladistical terms) stirred the interest of evolutionary biologists and comparative ethologists, leading to a lively discussion on the uniqueness of human language and its evolutionary origins (although the other themes of domain-specificity and theory-internal complexity largely prevented generative linguists from addressing the question of evolution for several decades).

The history of generative linguistics can be understood in significant part by the development of theories of the generative and transformational aspects of human language (1)-(2). The purpose of this chapter is to provide a brief overview of this development, which will be organized as follows. We will first see in section 2 how sixty years of generative research has emerged as a system of phrase structure rules and transformations and converged on the framework of "bare phrase structure" (BPS) (Chomsky 1995a, 1995b *et seq.*). We will see how this framework incorporates major insights of earlier approaches, and how a single operation hypothesized therein, called *Merge*, provides an arguably minimal but sufficient account of (1)-(2). Some possible refinement of Chomsky's (1995a, 1995b) theory of Merge will be suggested in section 3, and further research questions will be addressed in section 4.

2 A Historical Overview

2.1 *Phrase Structure Rules and Transformations: Grammar as a Rule-System*

In the earliest tradition of transformational generative grammar initiated by Chomsky (1955/1975, 1957), it was assumed that the syntax of natural language at its core is a bifurcated system of *phrase structure rules* (PSRs) and *transformational rules (grammatical transformations)*. According to this conception, the skeletal structure of a sentence is initially generated by a finite set of PSRs, each of which maps a nonterminal symbol to its ordered constituents. PSRs are illustrated in (9), which generates the basic structure of English sentences.

(9) a. S' → COMP S
    b. S → NP Infl VP
    c. Infl → Present, Past, will, . . .
    d. VP → V NP
    e. VP → V S'
    f. NP → (D) N
    g. D → the, a, . . .
    h. N → boy, mother, student, book, apple, . . .
    i. V → read, see, eat, make, open, touch, . . .

Starting with a designated initial symbol (S' in (9a)), each PSR converts a nonterminal symbol to a sequence of its internal constituents. Applied one by one, the PSRs in (9) generate phrase-markers such as the one in (10).

(10)

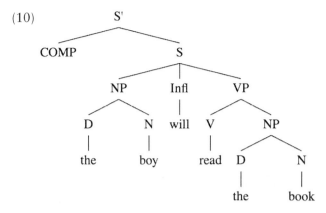

The phrase-marker (10) indicates, for example, that the largest constituent is an S' comprising COMP (Complementizer) and S (Sentence), lined up in this order; that S is made up of a constituent NP (Noun Phrase), Infl(ection), and VP (Verb Phrase) in this order; and so forth. In this manner, each PSR encapsulates three kinds of information about phrase-markers, namely the constituent structure, "label" symbol of a phrase, and left-to-right ordering of internal constituents:

(11) a.   Constituent structure: the hierarchical and combinatorial organization of linguistic elements ("constituents")
     b.   Labeling: the nonterminal symbol ("label") associated with each constituent
     c.   Linear order: the left-to-right order of the constituents

The part of transformational grammar that generates phrase-markers such as (10) by means of PSRs is referred to as the *phrase structure component*.

Structures generated by the phrase structure component are then mapped to the corresponding derived structures by the *transformational component*, which is characterized by a finite sequence of transformations or conversion rules by which a phrase-marker is mapped to (transformed into) another phrase-marker. For example, (12) is a transformation (called *wh*-movement) by which a *wh*-phrase is deleted at its original position and inserted at COMP, with t representing a trace assigned an index i identical to the *wh*-phrase. Applied to S' in (13a), (12) maps this phrase-marker to another phrase-marker in (13b), representing the underlying structure of (*Guess*) [*what the boy will read*].

(12) *wh*-movement:
     structural analysis (SA): $X—COMP—Y—NP_{[+wh]} —Z$
     structural change (SC): $X—NP_{[+wh]i}—Y—t_i \qquad —Z$

(13) a.

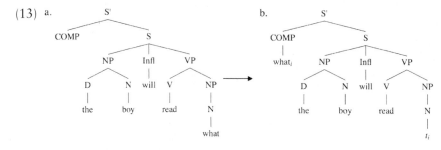

Another example of transformations is Coordination (14), which conflates two sentences into one by conjoining two constituents of the same category with *and* and reducing overlapping parts of the sentences. (15) represents some illustrations of its application.

(14) Coordination:
       SA of S'$_1$:   X—W$_1$—Y
         of S'$_2$:   X—W$_2$—Y (where W$_1$ and W$_2$ are of the same category)
       SC: X—W$_1$ and W$_2$—Y

(15) a. S'$_1$: the boy will read [$_{NP1}$ the book]
          S'$_2$: the boy will read [$_{NP2}$ the magazine]
          →   the boy will read [$_{NP1}$ the book] and [$_{NP2}$ the magazine]
      b. S'$_1$: the boy will [$_{V1}$ buy] the book
          S'$_2$: the boy will [$_{V2}$ read] the book
          →   the boy will [$_{V1}$ buy] and [$_{V2}$ read] the book
      c. S'$_1$: the boy will [$_{VP1}$ read the book]
          S'$_2$: the boy will [$_{VP2}$ drink coffee]
          →   the boy will [$_{VP1}$ read the book] and [$_{VP2}$ drink coffee]

The first type of transformation, exemplified by *wh*-movement (12), is referred to as the category of *singulary transformations*, in that they take a single phrase-marker as their input: Passivization, Topicalization, Auxiliary Inversion, Heavy NP-Shift, and a number of other rules have been proposed as instances of singulary transformations (see Chomsky 1955/1975, 1957 and many others). On the other hand, Coordination (14) represents another type of transformation, referred to as *generalized transformations*, which take more than one phrase-marker (say two S's) as their input and conflate them into a single unified phrase-marker: Relative Clause Formation and Nominalization are other instances of generalized transformations. See Chomsky (1955/1975) and others for details.

   In this sort of traditional generative grammar, the generative and transformational aspects of language (1)-(2) are characterized by the interplay of PSRs and transformations: first of all, the transformational capacity of language (2) is straightforwardly ascribed to the set of transformations such as (12) and (14). Moreover, discrete infinity naturally results, for example, from an indefinite application of generalized transformations. For instance, Coordination may expand a sentence to an unlimited length, say *the boy will read [the book and the magazine and the report and . . .]*. Chomsky (1965) further notices that PSRs can also be devised to yield discrete infinity once we allow the initial symbol S' to appear on the right-hand side of PSRs, as in rule (9e) = VP → V S', whose application results in embedding of an S' within another S', as in (16):

(16)

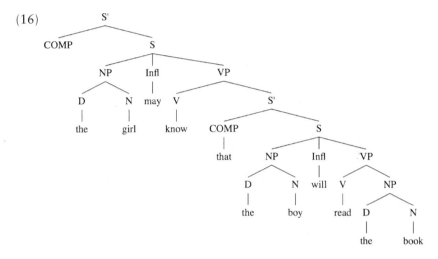

(16) or any other S' of an arbitrary size may be further embedded into another sentence by means of rule (9e) over and over again, thus yielding discrete infinity.

2.2 X-bar Theory and Move-α: The Emergence of Principles and Parameters

As described in the previous subsection, the theory of transformational generative grammar (Chomsky 1955/1975, 1957) held that human language is essentially a complex system of conversion rules. The rules posited in this framework were, as we have seen, quite abstract as well as language- and construction-specific, and, therefore, linguists were led to face the problem of language acquisition (also called "Plato's problem"): how can the child learn the correct set of highly complex rules from limited experience? In order to address this question, it was necessary for linguists of the day to set the following two tasks for their inquiry (see Chomsky 1965: Ch. 1):

(17) a. To reduce, as much as possible, the complexity and language-specificity (i.e., properties specific to particular languages) of rules that the child is supposed to learn without sacrificing descriptive adequacy of the proposed rule system.

b.   To enrich the power of the innately endowed language acquisition device (*Universal Grammar*, *UG*) so that it can reduce the burden of the child's language learning.

Though challenging, the research agenda in (17) turned out to be valuable as a heuristic, yielding a number of novel insights into the architecture of UG. By the early 1980s, research oriented by these goals converged on what we now call the *Principles-and-Parameters* (P&P) framework. According to this model of UG, the body of adults' linguistic knowledge is characterized in significant part by a finite set of innately endowed *principles*, which are invariant and universal across languages, and *parameters*, whose values are open to being set by a child learner with the help of linguistic experience, allowing certain forms of linguistic variation. In this conception of linguistic knowledge, what the child has to learn from experience reduces to the values for the parameters and the set of lexical entries in the lexicon, a radical simplification of the problem of language acquisition.

Specifically, serious efforts to achieve the goals in (17) in the domain of phrase structure resulted in the crystallization of *X-bar theory* (Chomsky 1970 *et seq.*). Historically, this UG principle was put forward as a way to remedy one of the fundamental inadequacies of earlier PSRs, pointed out by Lyons (1968). Lyons correctly argued that the system of PSRs is inadequate or insufficient in that it fails to capture the fact that each XP always dominates a unique X (NP dominates N, VP dominates V, etc.). That is to say, nothing in the formalism of PSRs excludes rules of the following sort, which are unattested and presumed to be impossible in human language but formally comparable to the rules in, say, (9), in that one symbol is rewritten (converted) into a sequence of symbols in each rule.

(18)   a.   NP → VP PP
  b.   PP → D S Infl V
  c.   AP → COMP NP

X-bar theory was put forward by Chomsky (1970) essentially to overcome this inadequacy of PSRs, and has been explored in much subsequent work. X-bar theory holds that the class of possible PSRs can be radically reduced by postulating the following two general schemata, where an atomic category X (X^0) is necessarily dominated by an intermediate category X', which in turn is necessarily dominated by the maximal category X" (XP) (see also Jackendoff's 1977 tripartite X-bar structure).

(19)   *X-bar schemata*:
  a.   X' = X (Y") or (Y") X   (where Y" is called the *Complement* of X)
  b.   X" = (Z") X'   (where Z" is called the *Spec(ifier)* of X)

For example, the X-bar schemata yield the following phrase-marker from the same set of terminal elements as those in (10), assuming the DP-analysis of nominals (Brame 1981, 1982, Fukui 1986, Fukui and Speas 1986, Abney 1987) and the head-initial linear order in (19a) (X (Y")) for English:

(20)

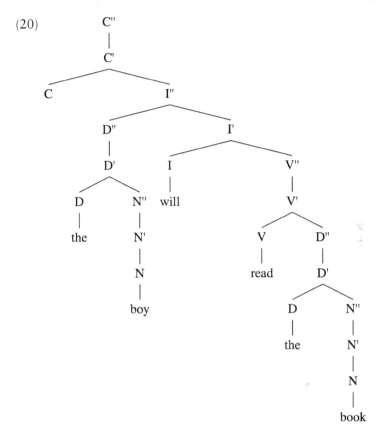

Note that, in (20), S' and S from earlier theories were replaced by C" and I", respectively (Chomsky 1986a). This move is motivated by X-bar theory's fundamental hypothesis that phrasal nodes are obtained essentially by projecting the lexical features of X and attaching bar-level indices (' or ") to them. In this theory, there is a strong sense in which all phrasal nodes, X' and X", are "projections" of X: N' and N" are projections of N, V' and V" are projections of V, and so on. We may refer to this consequence of X-bar theory as "labeling by projection."

(21) *Labeling by Projection*:
Each phrasal constituent is a projection of a lexical item (LI, X^0) it contains.

The class of possible constituent structures is hence restricted to those "endocentric" projections, while "exocentric" (non-headed) structures like (18), together with traditional S' and S, are ruled out as a matter of principle.

Lyons's criticism is thus naturally overcome as a result of (21). However, it is worth noting that Chomsky (1970) first put forward the X-bar schemata in such a way that they could be interpreted not as strict formats for PSRs but as a kind of evaluation measure that merely sets a preference for (unmarked) X-bar-theoretic projections, leaving open the possibility of (marked) exocentric structures such as S' and S. The C" analysis of S' and the I" analysis of S were introduced only later by Chomsky (1986a).

X-bar theory is so strong a generalization over the possible forms of PSRs that idiosyncratic PSRs of the sort exemplified in (9) can be entirely eliminated (with the help of other "modules" of grammar), a highly desirable result acknowledged by Stowell (1981) and Chomsky (1986a), among others. This is not only a considerable simplification of the child's acquisition task but also constitutes an indispensable building block of the emergent P&P framework: according to the P&P model of UG, the grammar of human language is essentially "ruleless" and conversion rules such as PSRs and transformations play no role in the account of the human linguistic capacity. Elimination of PSRs in favor of the X-bar schemata was a real step toward embodying this radical conceptual shift.

Furthermore, X-bar theory also takes part in reducing the class of transformations, essentially by providing the structural notion of *Spec(ifier)* (19b). Thanks to the X-bar schemata, Spec positions are distributed throughout the clausal architecture, with each of these Specs being further assumed to hold some special relation to the head (so-called "Spec-head agreement"; Chomsky 1986a), so they can serve as the target of various movement transformations: *wh*-movement targets Spec-C in order for the *wh*-phrase to be licensed under Spec-head agreement with C, a subject DP moves to Spec-I in order to receive Nominative Case under Spec-head agreement with I, and so on. More generally, the notion of Spec allows us to characterize various movement transformations as serving Spec-head relations in which categories have to participate. Pushing this line of approach to its limit, then, we may generalize various movement transformations into a single, highly underspecified transformation schema (called *Move-α*), which can be utilized for establishing various Spec-head relations:

(22) *Move-α* (Chomsky 1981):
    Move anything anywhere.

If we can indeed reformulate all language- and construction-specific transformations in the form of Move-α, serving different Spec-head relations at different times, then we may envisage the complete picture of "ruleless grammar," eliminating all PSRs and specific transformations in favor of X-bar theory and Move-α interacting with various other modules of UG. This is indeed the shift generative linguistics has taken to solve the problem of language acquisition (17), setting the stage for the full-blown P&P

research program, which has turned out to be remarkably successful in a number of research domains (comparative grammar, language acquisition, and so on).

2.3 Merge: Unifying the Phrase Structure and Transformational Components

In the original conception of transformational generative grammar (summarized in section 2.1), the phrase structure component generates the class of underlying structures by means of PSRs, and the transformational component maps those structures to various transformed structures (S-structures, LF, etc. in standard and extended standard theories) by means of transformations. The separation of these two components was then assumed to be a necessary device to capture the generative and transformational aspects of human language (1)-(2). However, we saw in section 2.2 that the P&P framework paves the way for eliminating PSRs and specific transformational rules as a matter of principle. Thus, it is interesting to ask if the distinction between the phrase structure and transformational components has any ground within the P&P framework.

This problem is addressed by Chomsky (1993, 1995a, 1995b), who eventually proposes the replacement of the relevant distinction with the notion of *Merge*. According to Chomsky, UG is endowed with an elementary operation, Merge, whose function is to recursively combine two syntactic objects (SOs) α, β and form another SO, which is just a set of α and β with one of them projected as the label γ (23a). (23b) visualizes the relevant set-theoretic object using a familiar tree-diagram, but it should be understood that, unlike traditional PSRs and X-bar theory, the linear order between α and β is not specified by Merge, since $\{\alpha, \beta\}$ is defined as an unordered set.

(23) Merge(α, β) =   a. $\{\gamma, \{\alpha, \beta\}\}$, where the label γ = the label of α or β.

b.

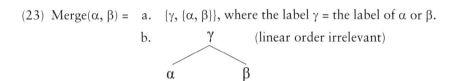

(linear order irrelevant)

Chomsky argues that, once recursive Merge constitutes an inborn property of UG, its unconstrained application immediately derives the basic effects of X-bar theory and Move-α in a unified fashion, as we will see below.

Consider first the case where Merge applies to two lexical items (LIs) drawn from the lexicon: say, *the* and *book*, as in (24). It yields an SO comprising a determiner *the* and a noun *book*, with the former projected (for the DP-analysis of nominals, see Brame 1981, 1982, Fukui 1986, Fukui and Speas 1986, Abney 1987).

(25) Merge(the, book)   =   a.   {the, {the, book}}
b.

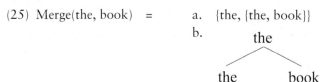

This SO can constitute another input to Merge, as in (25), for example, where it is combined with a verb *read*, projecting the latter.

(25) Merge(read, {the, {the, book}})   =   a.   {read, {read, {the, {the, book}}}}
b.

read

read   the

the   book

SOs such as (24)-(25) can provide minimal but sufficient information about constituent structure and labeling: (25) is a phrasal SO that is labeled "verbal" by *read*; it contains (or "dominates" in earlier terms) a subconstituent SO (24) labeled "nominal" by *the*; and so on. Recursive applications of Merge can generate SOs of an arbitrary size in a bottom-up fashion, including sentential SOs such as (26) that can be further subjected to Merge, yielding discrete infinity.

(26)

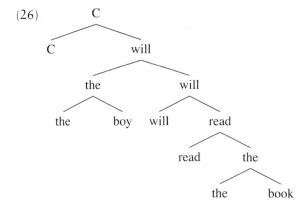

In articulating a Merge-based theory of phrase-markers, Chomsky (1995a, 1995b) capitalizes on Muysken's (1982) proposal that the notions of minimal and maximal projections are relational properties of categories and not inherently marked by additional devices such as bar-level indices (see also Fukui 1986, 1988, Fukui and Speas 1986, and Speas 1990 for their relational approaches to X-bar theory). Chomsky's relational definition of maximal and minimal projections is stated in (27):

(27) *Relational definition of projection* (Chomsky 1995a: 61):
Given a phrase-marker, a category that does not project any further is a maximal projection X^{max} (XP), and one that is not a projection at all is a minimal projection X^{min} (X^0); any other is an X', invisible for computation.

For example, the SO in (24) embedded within (25) or (26) counts as a maximal projection X^{max} of *the*, given that it does not project any further in those phrase-markers, and its immediate constituent *the* is a minimal projection X^{min}, since it is an LI and not a projection at all. In this manner, Merge supplemented by the relational definition of projection (27) can derive the effects of X-bar theory. In particular, Merge as defined in (23) incorporates the basic insight of X-bar theory, namely that each phrase is a projection of an LI (labeling by projection (21)).

In the earlier cases, the two operands of Merge, α and β, are distinct from, or external to, each other. This type of Merge represents what Chomsky calls *External Merge* (EM). Chomsky further notes that, if Merge applies freely, it should also be able to apply to α and β, one of which is *internal* to the other. This case represents the second type of Merge, called *Internal Merge* (IM). For example, if there is an SO_i = {*the*, {*the*, *book*}} (23) and some other SO that contains SO_i—for example, (26)—Merge applying to the two SOs yields an SO_j = {SO_i, {. . . SO_i . . .}} with two copies of SO_i:

(28)

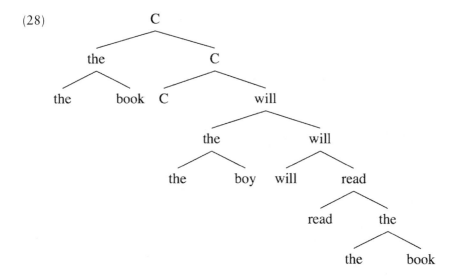

Chomsky (1993) proposes that the excessively powerful operation of Move-α may be eliminated in favor of IM, with traces in earlier theories replaced by copies created by IM (compare (28) with, for example, the trace-based conception of *wh*-movement in (13)). This consequence is called the "copy theory of movement" and has proven to be highly advantageous for the account of various properties of movement transformations, such as reconstruction (see Chomsky 1993). If we follow this line of approach, then we may regard (28) as the representation of a sentence with Topicalization, *the book, the boy will read*, with the lower copy of SO$_i$ deleted at its phonetic form. If this reductionist approach to movement proves to be successful, then the whole spectrum of movement transformations, which was once reduced to Move-α, can be further reformulated as an aspect of the basic operation Merge.

Without any stipulation, then, the ubiquity of discrete infinity and movement with copy-formation (Chomsky 1993, 1995a, 1995b) becomes an automatic consequence of the unbounded character of Merge. This simple device immediately yields the bifurcation of EM and IM, and these two types of Merge incorporate a significant part of X-bar theory and Move-α. It thus naturally unifies the theories of the phrase structure component and the transformational component.

These considerations suggest that the theory of Merge-based syntax, called the framework of *bare phrase structure* (BPS) (Chomsky 1995a, 1995b), arguably provides a minimal explanation of the generative and transformational aspects of human language (1)-(2). This completes our historical review of how the theory of transformational generative grammar converged on the current BPS framework.

3 Towards the "Barest" Phrase Structure

In the previous section, we saw that the theory of phrase structure evolved into the simple theory of Merge by critically examining the technical devices proposed earlier and reducing them to a conceptual minimum that can still satisfy their target functions. Such an endeavor of reductionist simplification is sometimes termed the "Minimalist Program" (MP) (Chomsky 1993, 1995a, 1995b *et seq.*), but it just exemplifies an ordinary practice of science, persistent throughout the history of generative linguistics, which seeks the best account of empirical data with a minimal set of assumptions.

In this section, we will turn to the discussion of how we may advance further simplification of Merge-based syntax, even more radically departing from earlier theories of conversion rules and X-bar theory.

3.1 The Labeling Algorithm and Projection-Free Syntax

Consider again the formulation of Merge (23) advocated by Chomsky (1995a, 1995b). We saw that this operation is a simple device to incorporate the major insight of X-bar theory, namely labeling by projection (21). However, the open choice of the label γ in (23) is admittedly too unrestricted. It is typically specified either as the label of α or β, but then nothing in (23) precludes, for example, D of the object from projecting over VP, instead of V, as in (29).

(29) Merge(read, {the, {the, book}}) = a. {the, {read, {the, {the, book}}}}
                                            b.

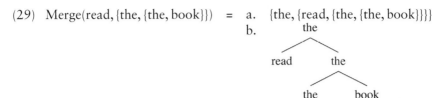

This sort of "wrong choice" would make a number of ill-advised predictions: for example, that this SO can act as a DP and can be merged with another V (*the boy will touch [read the book]*). Therefore, there must be some mechanism that determines the "correct" label/head for each Merge-output. Following the standard convention, we may refer to this mechanism as the *labeling algorithm* (LA).

The exact nature of the LA is one of the major research topics in the current literature, and, indeed, a great variety of proposals have been advanced, with more in press. For example, Chomsky (1995b, 2000) hypothesizes that determining the label of a set-theoretic object {α, β} correlates with a selectional or agreement dependency between α and β, an idea followed by a number of researchers:

(30) LA (Chomsky 1995b, 2000):
      The output of Merge(α, β) is labeled by α if
      a. α selects β as its semantic argument, or
      b. α agrees with β: that is, β is attracted by α for the purpose of Spec-head agreement (feature-checking).

This LA excludes the wrong choice in (29) by (30a), since it is the V *read* that selects/theta-marks DP, not the converse. Moreover, the merger of the subject DP to the edge of I(nfl) (or, as it is more recently called, T(ense)) results in projection of I, given that I agrees with the DP in person, number, and gender (these agreement features are also called "φ-features"). As intended, (30) closely keeps to the basic result of X-bar theory. However, recourse to such external relations as (semantic) selection and agreement may be regarded as a potentially worrisome complication of the LA. As a possible reformulation of the LA, Chomsky (2008: 145, (2)-(3)) puts forward another algorithm in (31).

(31) LA (Chomsky 2008: 145):
      The output of Merge(α, β) is labeled by α if
      a. α is an LI, or
      b. β is internally merged to α.

According to this version of the LA, the output of Merge(V, DP) is labeled V by virtue of V being an LI, and movement of subject DP to Spec-I/T lets I/T be the label, by virtue of the merger being an instance of IM. Chomsky (2013) further suggests eliminating (31b) from the LA, reducing it to minimal search for an LI for each phrase (31a), a proposal to which we will return (see also Fukui and Narita 2012 [Chapter 2, this volume], Lohndal 2012, Narita 2012, 2014, Ott 2012, for various explorations).

(32) LA (Chomsky 2013):
      The label/head of an SO Σ is the most prominent LI within Σ.

See also Boeckx (2008, 2009, 2014), Hornstein (2009), Narita (2009, 2014), Fukui (2011) [Chapter 1, this volume], and many others for different approaches to labeling.

Incidentally, it should be noted that, once we decide to let UG incorporate an LA in addition to Merge, it becomes questionable whether Merge itself has any role to play in labeling/projection at all. In particular, the specification of the label γ in (23) becomes superfluous, because the choice of the label is independently determined by the LA. As redundancies are disfavored in scientific theories, Chomsky (2000) proposes further simplification of the definition of Merge, as in (33):

(33) Merge(α, β) =   a. $\{\alpha, \beta\}$.

                     b.   ⎯⎯⎯⎯⎯⎯   (linear order irrelevant)

                 α β

In this simpler theory, Merge reduces to an elementary set-formation operation, and SOs generated thereby are all "bare" sets. That is, such SOs are associated with no nonterminal symbols such as projections, while the reduced notion of "label," which now amounts to nothing more than the syntactically or interpretively relevant "head" of a phrase, is determined independently by the LA. Indeed, any version of the LA in (30)-(32) can be understood as a mere search mechanism for head-detection, free from additional steps of projection. In this manner, theories of labeling can render BPS really "bare": that is, completely projection-free (see Collins 2002, Chomsky 2007, 2013, Narita 2012, 2014).

It is instructive to recall that nonterminal symbols such as S, VP, NP, etc., used to constitute the necessary input to and/or output of conversion rules in the earlier system of PSRs: cf., for example, S → NP Infl VP (9b). However, the BPS framework now invites us to ask if there is any strong empirical evidence that requires an extraneous mechanism of nonterminal symbol-assignment or projection, in addition to the simplest means of constituent structuring (i.e., Merge). See Collins (2002), Chomsky (2007, 2008, 2013), Fukui (2011), Fukui and Narita (2012), Narita (2012, 2014) for a variety of explorations along these lines.

3.2 Linearization as Part of Post-Syntactic Externalization

Recall that PSRs embody the following three kinds of information regarding phrase-markers (11): constituent structure, labeling, and linear order. For example, PSR (9d), VP → V NP, represents that a phrase is labeled VP, that VP immediately dominates V and NP, and that V precedes NP. We saw that Merge takes over the role of constituent structuring while eliminating labeling. Moreover, as Merge creates unordered sets, it is also ineffective in determining the linear order of constituents. Therefore, BPS bears the burden of providing an independent account of linear order. Conventionally, this hypothesized mechanism of linear order-assignment is referred to as *linearization*, for which a variety of proposals have been made in the growing literature.

It is obvious that linear order appears at the "sound"-side of linguistic expressions. In contrast, observations in the literature suggest that linear order plays little role in the "meaning"-side of linguistic computation: for example, there is no evidence that linear order is relevant to core syntactic-semantic properties such as predicate-argument structure or theta-role assignment. Reinhart (1976, 1983), among others, further points out that purely hierarchically determined relations such as c-command are sufficient to encode the conditions on binding, scope, and other discourse-related properties. This strongly suggests that linear order may not be a core property of phrase-markers that persists throughout the derivation, as the system of PSRs predicts, but rather may be assigned relatively "late" in linguistic computation, probably post-syntactically. Obviously, the less relevant linear order is shown to be to syntactic computation, the less necessary, desirable, or even plausible it becomes to encapsulate linear order into the core of structure-generation. These considerations strongly suggest that linear order should not belong to syntax or the mapping to the syntax-semantics interface (called SEM). Given that linear order must be assigned before SOs get "pronounced" at the syntax-phonetics interface (called PHON), we conjecture that linearization may most plausibly be part of the syntax-PHON mapping, or what is sometimes called *externalization* (Chomsky 2013).

(34) Linear order is only a peripheral part of human language, related solely to externalization (the syntax-PHON mapping).

Various attempts are currently being made to approach the theory of linearization under the working hypothesis in (34). However, see, for example, Fukui (1993), Kayne (1994, 2011), and Saito and Fukui (1998) for indications that linear order may play some role in syntax.

We would like to deepen our understanding of linearization, whether it is located in the core of syntax or only at externalization. It seems that various competing theories of linearization proposed in the literature more or less share the goal of reformulating the basic results of X-bar theory (19), namely:

(35) a. the variability of head-complement word order (cf. "directionality parameter" in (19a))
     b. the apparent universal "specifier-left" generalization (cf. (19b))

See Epstein et al. (1998), Saito and Fukui (1998), Richards (2004, 2007), and Narita (2014) for various attempts to reformulate the directionality parameter in BPS. In this context, it is worth noting that some researchers attempt to provide a parameter-free account of word order by advocating a single universal word order template. By far the most influential approach of this sort is Kayne's (1994) "antisymmetry," which proposes a universal Spec-Head-Complement word order and typically analyzes apparent head-final, Spec-Complement-Head order as being derived from the movement of the Complement to some intermediate Spec-position (for various implementations, see Kayne 1994, 2009, 2011, Chomsky 1995a, 1995b; Epstein et al. 1998, Uriagereka 1999, and Moro 2000, to name just a few). The Kaynean approach can be contrasted with Takano (1996) and Fukui and Takano's (1998) hypothesis that the universal template is rather Spec-Complement-Head (see also Gell-Mann and Ruhlen 2011), while apparent Spec-Head-Complement order is derived by moving the Head to some intermediate position. Attractive though it seems, imposing a particular word order template appears to be generally costly, in that it invites a number of technical stipulations to explain cases of disharmonic word order, as pointed out by Richards (2004) and Narita (2010, 2014).

It is interesting to note that most of the previous theories of linearization make crucial recourse to projection, as is expected since they aim to recapture the basic results of X-bar theory (35). Exceptions are Kayne (2011) and Narita (2014), who approach linearization from a truly projection-free perspective, but they still rest on the notion of "head" (LA) and involve complications in some other domains (Kayne reformulates Merge as ordered-pair formation; Narita relies on a specific formulation of cyclic Spell-Out). Thus, it is a curious open question whether linearization necessitates projection or how linearization relates to the LA.

3.3 Summary: A Modular Approach to Constituent Structure, Labeling, and Linearization

We saw that the treatment of three kinds of information (constituent structure, labeling, and linear order) was once encapsulated into PSR-schemata. However, the theory of Merge holds that they should rather be fully modularized into different components of UG (or even a third factor which governs the functioning of UG): constituent structuring is fully taken care of by unbounded Merge; the identification of the head/label of each SO is carried out by some version of the LA (30)-(32) or others;

and the mechanism of linearization may be properly relegated to post-syntactic externalization (34).

4 Questions for Future Research

The BPS theory is at a very initial stage of inquiry, leaving a number of important problems for future research. The following were already mentioned earlier.

[1] *Is BPS free from nonterminal symbols/projection? Cf.* section 3.1.

[2] *What is the exact nature of the LA? In particular, does it involve projection? Cf.* section 3.1.

[3] *Does linear order play any role in syntax or SEM, or is it only a property of externalization? Cf.* section 3.2.

[4] *What is the exact nature of linearization? In particular, does it make recourse to projection or the notion "head?" Cf.* section 3.2.

And we will review some others in the rest of this section. First, let us consider an open question about Merge:

[5] *How is unbounded Merge constrained?*

As we saw earlier, we would like to keep the application of Merge unbounded, if only to provide a principled account of discrete infinity and movement with copy-formation (Chomsky 1993, 1995a, 1995b). However, it is of course not true that any random application of Merge yields a legible output. Therefore, there must be some constraints on Merge-application that limit the space of interface-legible outputs of Merge.

It is quite likely that the relevant constraints on Merge include proper theories of labeling and linearization. Moreover, many proposals have been made regarding "economy" conditions on IM/Move, such as the principle of "Last Resort" (Chomsky 1986b) ("Move only when necessary"), a variant of which is the idea that an application of IM is contingent on the presence of "Agree(ment)" (feature-checking, or more recently "probe-goal" relations; see Chomsky 2000 *et seq.*). Further, current research provides interesting pieces of evidence for the view that the Merge-based computation is demarcated into several well-defined cycles of derivation, called *phases*: see Uriagereka (1999), Chomsky (2000, 2001, 2004, 2007, 2008, 2013), Boeckx (2009, 2014), Gallego (2010, 2012), and Narita (2014), among others, for various explorations of phase theory. See also Fukui (2011) and Fukui and Narita (2012), who argue, on different grounds, that Merge-based computation is fundamentally driven by the need for symmetric {XP, YP} structures (or what Fukui and Narita call "feature-equilibrium").

[6] *Is the notion of label/head relevant to narrowly syntactic computation,
or does it appear only at SEM (and linearization)?*

We saw that the notion of "label" is now reduced to nothing more than the computationally or interpretively relevant "head" of each SO, detected by the LA, and that it may well be free from the now-superfluous notion of projection. Clearly, at least some aspect of the syntax-semantics interface (SEM) is dependent on the notion of label/head: the semantics of VP is prototypically configured by the head V, and the same obviously applies to NP-N, AP-A, CP-C, etc., as well. Therefore, it seems reasonable to assume that the LA feeds information to SEM. Questions remain regarding where, or at which point of linguistic computation, the LA applies. Does it apply at each and every point of Merge-application, just as in Chomsky's (1995a, 1995b) earlier theory of Merge, or only at particular points in a syntactic derivation, say at the level of each phase, as hypothesized in Chomsky (2008, 2013) and Ott (2012), or only post-syntactically at SEM, as suggested by Narita (2014)? These possibilities relate to question [2], and depending on the answer, they may also invite particular answers to [4] as well.

It is worth recalling in this connection that virtually all the past theories of linearization make crucial recourse to the concept of label/head (see references cited in section 3.2). Thus, the LA appears to feed information not only to SEM but also to linearization. Under the conception of syntax as *the* mechanism of "sound"-"meaning" pairing, a natural conclusion from this observation seems to be that the LA should be regarded as an operation internal to narrow syntax, applying before the computation branches off into the semantic and phonological components (this argument was put forward by Narita 2009).

What remains curious in this approach is the fact that there is actually less and less evidence for the relevance of labeling/headedness to narrowly syntactic computation under minimalist assumptions. C(ategorial)-selection/subcategorization used to constitute a *bona fide* instance of a label-dependent operation, but it is often assumed in the modern framework that c-selection is reducible to s(emantic)-selection applying at SEM (Pesetsky 1982), and that selection (categorial or semantic) plays virtually no role in narrow syntax (Chomsky 2004: 112–113).

However, consider also Chomsky's (2013) hypothesis that the LA reduces to minimal search for the most prominent LI for each SO (32). He further suggests that the minimality property of the LA can be regarded as a reflection of the laws of nature, specifically the principle of computational efficiency in this case, i.e., that minimal search is attributable to the so-called "third factor" of language design (see Chomsky 2007, 2008). Third-factor principles are by definition domain-general and, thus, they may be simultaneously applicable to any aspect of linguistic computation, be it narrowly syntactic computation or post-syntactic mapping to SEM and PHON. It may turn out that further inquiry into the LA provides some empirical support for this "LA-as-third-factor" hypothesis, a possibility left for future research.

[7] *Is every SO endocentric: that is, headed by an LI?*

The earlier PSR-based conception of phrase-markers holds that each phrase is associated with nonterminal symbols, and X-bar theory further maintains that phrases are all projections of head LIs (labeling by projection, (21)). Under the assumption that projection imposes headedness, the X-bar-theoretic approach in effect subscribes to the "Universal Endocentricity" hypothesis:

(36) *Universal Endocentricity*:
    Every phrase is headed by an LI.

(36) has become a standard assumption since the advent of X-bar theory, followed by the majority of subsequent theories in the generative framework. However, it should be noted that, once X-bar theory is replaced with the theory of Merge, universal labeling by projection can be correspondingly eliminated from the BPS framework. (36) thus loses its theorem-like status, and it becomes open to scrutiny. Does (36) receive real support from empirical data, or should it be regarded as an unwarranted residue of X-bar theory that is to be discarded as well?

In fact, (36) becomes less obvious when we seek to reduce the LA to a bare minimum. For example, while Chomsky's (2013) LA in (32) is able to determine the head LI H in {H, XP}, it is not clear whether it is effective at all in determining the label/head of SOs with two phrasal constituents, {XP, YP}, where no LI immediately stands as the most prominent. In the earlier X-bar-theoretic approach, such SOs are generally characterized as involving one of the two phrases: say XP, being the "specifier" of the other, YP, thereby letting the latter project. But this projection-based characterization of Spec and universal endocentricity becomes unavailable in the approach based on (32). Chomsky (2013) argues that this result is indeed desirable, and that there should be room for certain non-endocentric structures appearing at SEM (see also Narita 2014).

X-bar theory was originally proposed to replace earlier idiosyncratic PSRs. This was a real step toward the simplification of UG, setting the basis for the later P&P framework, but, in hindsight, it also effectively brought the stipulation of universal endocentricity (36) into the theory of phrase structure. However, now that X-bar theory has been eliminated in favor of projection-free Merge (33), any {XP, YP} structures, regardless of whether they are created by EM or IM, are open to non-endocentric characterizations. Inquiry into the nature of non-endocentric structures appears to be a potentially fruitful research topic. See, in this connection, Fukui and Narita (2012), who put forward the hypothesis that endocentric (asymmetric) structures {H, XP}, typically created by EM, are generally in need of being mapped to "symmetric," non-endocentric {XP, YP} structures via IM, exploring the significance of symmetry/non-endocentricity in BPS (see also Fukui 2011).

The earlier discussion also raises the following question:

[8] *Is the notion of Spec(ifier) relevant to linguistic computation?*

The radical thesis put forward by Chomsky (2012a, 2013) is that the notion of specifier is an illegitimate residue of X-bar theory and has no place in BPS—that is, projection-free syntax. See Narita (2009, 2012, 2014), Chomsky (2012a, 2013), Fukui and Narita (2012), and Lohndal (2012) for various explorations of Spec-free syntax.

[9] *Is Merge always restricted to binary set-formation?*

So far, we have restricted our attention to cases where Merge is limited to a binary set-formation: (33). This was partly because linguistic structures are generally assumed to involve binary branching in almost every case (see Kayne's (1981) influential work on "unambiguous paths"). Indeed, considerations on binding, quantifier scope, coordination, and various other phenomena seem to lend support to the universal binary branching hypothesis. However, we do not know why human language is structured that way. Binarity is a nontrivial constraint on Merge and, if possible, we would like to remove this constraint, generalizing the Merge operation to the simplest conception of *n-ary* set-formation:

(37) $\text{Merge}(SO_1, \ldots, SO_n) = \{SO_1, \ldots, SO_n\}$.

What is the factor that almost always restricts n to two? Again, it is likely that theories of labeling and linearization play major roles in this binarity restriction. Moreover, the relevance of third-factor principles of efficient computation has been suggested at times, though arguments are inconclusive (Collins 1997, Chomsky 2008, Narita 2014).

[10] *What is the nature of adjunction?*

Finally, we would briefly like to mention another case that has been put aside so far, namely *adjunction*. In any natural language, there are classes of adjectives, adverbials, and other modifiers that can be optionally adjoined, indefinitely many times, to relevant constituents (Harris 1965). Multiple adjunction, as in (3), may expand a sentence to an unlimited length, yielding another type of discrete infinity. Curiously, the presence of those optional adjuncts does not affect the core architecture of the sentence, a distinct property of adjunction that has to be captured in some way or another in the BPS framework.

It is desirable if the theory of adjunction can be devised to make no recourse to projection. One such proposal is actually made by Chomsky (2004), who proposes that Merge has two varieties, one being the usual set-formation Merge (called *set-Merge*, producing {α, β}) and the other being an operation that creates an ordered pair of constituents (called *pair-Merge*, producing <α, β>). Chomsky proposes that adjunction, in general, can be reformulated as instances of pair-Merge, where the head-nonhead asymmetry is built in the asymmetry of order. Another approach originates from Lebeaux (1991), among others, who holds that, while usual instances of Merge apply cyclically from the bottom up, adjuncts are introduced to the structure only after the main clausal structure is constructed in the derivation (this operation is called "late-Merge"). Still another approach is to eliminate the notion of adjunction as a distinct mechanism and assimilate adjuncts to the class of Specs. This approach is most notably carried out by Kayne (1994 *et seq.*) and other proponents of antisymmetry (see section 3.2). All these possibilities are open to future inquiry.

Further Reading

Readers may find it useful to consult Fukui (2001, 2011) as supplementary reading to this chapter. After reading this chapter, which provides a general background in the theory of phrase structure, readers are referred to more technical and advanced works on this topic, such as the papers collected in Chomsky (1995b, 2012b), among many others. See also Narita (2014), which explores various empirical consequences of a truly projection-free approach to labeling, linearization, and universal endocentricity.

Acknowledgments

Part of this research is supported by a grant from Japan Science and Technology Agency (JST, CREST) and a grant from Japan Society for the Promotion of Science (Grant-in-Aid for Scientific Research, Scientific Research (A) #23242025, and Challenging Exploratory Research #25580095). We would like to thank Noam Chomsky, Bridget Samuels, and Yosuke Sato for their detailed written comments and suggestions on earlier versions of this paper.

References

Abney, Steven Paul. 1987. The English noun phrase in its sentential aspect. Doctoral dissertation, MIT.
Boeckx, Cedric. 2008. *Bare syntax*. Oxford: Oxford University Press.

Boeckx, Cedric. 2009. On the locus of asymmetry in UG. *Catalan Journal of Linguistics* 8: 41–53.

Boeckx, Cedric. 2014. *Elementary syntactic structures*. Cambridge: Cambridge University Press.

Brame, Michael. 1981. The general theory of binding and fusion. *Linguistic Analysis* 7 (3): 277–325.

Brame, Michael. 1982. The head-selector theory of lexical specifications and the nonexistence of coarse categories. *Linguistic Analysis* 10 (4): 321–325.

Cable, Seth. 2010. *The grammar of Q: Q-particles, wh-movement, and pied-piping*. Oxford: Oxford University Press.

Chomsky, Noam. 1955/1975. *The logical structure of linguistic theory*. Ms., Harvard University, 1955. Published in part in 1975, New York: Plenum.

Chomsky, Noam. 1957. *Syntactic structures*. The Hague: Mouton. 2nd edition, Mouton de Gruyter, 2002.

Chomsky, Noam. 1965. *Aspects of the theory of syntax*. Cambridge, MA: MIT Press.

Chomsky, Noam. 1970. Remarks on nominalization. In *Readings in English transformational grammar*, ed. Roderick A. Jacobs and Peter S. Rosenbaum, 184–221. Waltham, MA: Ginn.

Chomsky, Noam. 1981. *Lectures on government and binding: The Pisa lectures*. Dordrecht: Foris.

Chomsky, Noam. 1986a. *Barriers*. Cambridge, MA: MIT Press.

Chomsky, Noam. 1986b. *Knowledge of language*. New York: Praeger.

Chomsky, Noam. 1993. A minimalist program for linguistic theory. In *The view from Building 20: Essays in linguistics in honor of Sylvain Bromberger*, ed. Ken Hale and Samuel J. Keyser, 1–52. Cambridge, MA: MIT Press.

Chomsky, Noam. 1995a. Bare phrase structure. In *Evolution and revolution in linguistic theory: Essays in honor of Carlos Otero*, ed. Héctor Ramiro Campos and Paula Marie Kempchinsky, 51–109. Washington, DC: Georgetown University Press.

Chomsky, Noam. 1995b. *The minimalist program*. Cambridge, MA: MIT Press.

Chomsky, Noam. 2000. Minimalist inquiries. In *Step by step: Essays on minimalist syntax in honor of Howard Lasnik*, ed. Roger Martin, David Michaels, and Juan Uriagereka, 89–155. Cambridge, MA: MIT Press.

Chomsky, Noam. 2001. Derivation by phase. In *Ken Hale: A life in language*, ed. Michael Kenstowicz, 1–52. Cambridge, MA: MIT Press.

Chomsky, Noam. 2004. Beyond explanatory adequacy. In *Structures and beyond: The cartography of syntactic structures*, volume 3, ed. Adriana Belletti, 104–131. Oxford: Oxford University Press.

Chomsky, Noam. 2007. Approaching UG from below. In *Interfaces + recursion = language? Chomsky's minimalism and the view from semantics*, ed. Uli Sauerland and Hans-Martin Gärtner, 1–29. Berlin: Mouton de Gruyter.

Chomsky, Noam. 2008. On phases. In *Foundational issues in linguistic theory: Essays in honor of Jean-Roger Vergnaud*, ed. Robert Freidin, Carlos Otero, and Maria Luisa Zubizarreta. 133–166. Cambridge, MA: MIT Press.

Chomsky, Noam. 2012a. Introduction. In *Gengokisoronsyu* [*Foundations of biolinguistics: Selected writings*], ed. and trans. by Naoki Fukui, 17–26. Tokyo: Iwanami Shoten.

Chomsky, Noam. 2012b. *Chomsky's linguistics*, ed. Peter Graff and Coppe van Urk. Cambridge, MA: MIT Working Papers in Linguistics.

Chomsky, Noam. 2013. Problems of projection. *Lingua* 130: 33–49.

Collins, Chris. 1997. *Local economy*. Cambridge, MA: MIT Press.

Collins, Chris. 2002. Eliminating labels. In *Derivation and explanation in the minimalist program*, ed. Samuel David Epstein and T. Daniel Seely, 42–64. Oxford: Blackwell.

Epstein, Samuel David, Erich M. Groat, Ruriko Kawashima, and Hisatsugu Kitahara. 1998. *A derivational approach to syntactic relations*. Oxford: Oxford University Press.

Fitch, W. Tecumseh, Marc D. Hauser, and Noam Chomsky. 2005. The evolution of the language faculty: Clarifications and implications. *Cognition* 97: 179–210.

Fukui, Naoki. 1986/1995. A theory of category projection and its applications. Doctoral dissertation, MIT. Published in 1995 with revisions as *Theory of projection in syntax*, Tokyo: Kurosio Publishers and Stanford: CSLI publications.

Fukui, Naoki. 1988. Deriving the differences between English and Japanese: A case study in parametric syntax. *English Linguistics* 5: 249–270.

Fukui, Naoki. 1993. Parameters and optionality. *Linguistic Inquiry* 24: 399–420. [Reprinted in Fukui (2006).]

Fukui, Naoki. 2001. Phrase structure. In *The handbook of contemporary syntactic theory*, ed. Mark Baltin and Chris Collins, 374–406. Oxford: Blackwell. [Reprinted in Fukui (2006).]

Fukui, Naoki. 2006. *Theoretical comparative syntax: Studies in macroparameters*. London and New York: Routledge.

Fukui, Naoki. 2011. Merge and bare phrase structure. In *The Oxford handbook of linguistic minimalism*, ed. Cedric Boeckx, 73–95. Oxford: Oxford University Press. [Chapter 1, this volume.]

Fukui, Naoki, and Hiroki Narita. 2012. Merge and (a)symmetry. Paper presented at the Kyoto Conference on Biolinguistics, Kyoto University, March 12, 2012. [Revised version published as Chapter 2 of this volume.]

Fukui, Naoki, and Margaret Speas. 1986. Specifiers and projection. *MIT Working Papers in Linguistics* 8: 128–172. [Reprinted in Fukui (2006).]

Fukui, Naoki, and Yuji Takano. 1998. Symmetry in syntax: Merge and Demerge. *Journal of East Asian Linguistics* 7: 27–86. [Reprinted in Fukui (2006).]

Gallego, Ángel J. 2010. *Phase theory*. Amsterdam: John Benjamins.

Gallego, Ángel J., ed. 2012. *Phases: Developing the framework*. Berlin: Mouton de Gruyter.

Gell-Mann, Murray, and Merritt Ruhlen. 2011. The origin and evolution of word order. *Proceedings of the National Academy of Sciences* 108 (42): 17290–17295.

Harris, Zellig S. 1951. *Methods in structural linguistics*. Chicago: University of Chicago Press.

Harris, Zellig S. 1965. Transformational theory. *Language* 41 (3): 363–401.

Hauser, Marc D., Noam Chomsky, and W. Tecumseh Fitch. 2002. The faculty of language: What is it, who has it, and how did it evolve? *Science* 298 (5598): 1569–1579.

Hornstein, Norbert. 2009. *A theory of syntax: Minimal operations and universal grammar*. Cambridge: Cambridge University Press.

Jackendoff, Ray. 1977. *X'-syntax: A study of phrase structure*. Cambridge, MA: MIT Press.

Kayne, Richard S. 1981. Unambiguous paths. In *Levels of syntactic representation*, ed. Robert May and Jan Koster, 143–183. Dordrecht: Foris.

Kayne, Richard S. 1994. *The antisymmetry of syntax*. Cambridge, MA: MIT Press.

Kayne, Richard S. 2009. Antisymmetry and the lexicon. *Linguistic Variation Yearbook* 8: 1–31. [Reprinted in *The biolinguistic enterprise: New perspectives on the evolution and nature of the human language faculty*, ed. Anna Maria Di Sciullo and Cedric Boeckx, 329–353. Oxford: Oxford University Press. (2011).]

Kayne, Richard S. 2011. Why are there no directionality parameters? In *Proceedings of the 28th West Coast Conference on Formal Linguistics*, ed. Mary Byram Washburn, Katherine McKinney-Bock, Erika Varis, Ann Sawyer, and Barbara Tomaszewicz, 1–23. Somerville, MA: Cascadilla Proceedings Project.

Lebeaux, David. 1991. Relative clauses, licensing, and the nature of the derivation. In *Perspectives on phrase structure: Heads and licensing*, ed. Susan Rothstein, 209–239. New York: Academic Press.

Lohndal, Terje. 2012. Without specifiers: Phrase structure and events. Doctoral dissertation, University of Maryland, College Park.

Lyons, John. 1968. *Introduction to theoretical linguistics*. Cambridge: Cambridge University Press.

Moro, Andrea. 2000. *Dynamic antisymmetry*. Cambridge, MA: MIT Press.

Muysken, Pieter. 1982. Parametrizing the notion 'head'. *Journal of Linguistic Research* 2: 57–75.

Narita, Hiroki. 2009. Full interpretation of optimal labeling. *Biolinguistics* 3: 213–254.

Narita, Hiroki. 2010. The tension between explanatory and biological adequacy: Review of Fukui (2006). *Lingua* 120: 1313–1323.

Narita, Hiroki. 2012. Phase cycles in service of projection-free syntax. In *Phases: Developing the framework*, ed. Ángel J. Gallego, 125–172. Berlin: Mouton de Gruyter.

Narita, Hiroki. 2014. *Endocentric structuring of projection-free syntax*. Amsterdam: John Benjamins.

Ott, Dennis. 2012. *Local instability*. Berlin and New York: Walter de Gruyter.

Pesetsky, David. 1982. Paths and categories. Doctoral dissertation, MIT.

Reinhart, Tanya. 1976. Syntactic domain of anaphora. Doctoral dissertation, MIT.

Reinhart, Tanya. 1983. *Anaphora and semantic interpretation*. London: Croom Helm.

Richards, Marc D. 2004. Object shift, scrambling, and symmetrical syntax. Doctoral dissertation, University of Cambridge.

Richards, Marc D. 2007. Dynamic linearization and the shape of phases. *Linguistic Analysis* 33: 209–237.

Saito, Mamoru, and Naoki Fukui. 1998. Order in phrase structure and movement. *Linguistic Inquiry* 29: 439–474. [Reprinted in Fukui (2006).]

Speas, Margaret J. 1990. *Phrase structure in natural language*. Dordrecht: Kluwer Academic.

Stowell, Tim. 1981. Origins of phrase structure. Doctoral dissertation, MIT.

Takano, Yuji. 1996. Movement and parametric variation in syntax. Doctoral dissertation, University of California, Irvine.

Uriagereka, Juan. 1999. Multiple spell-out. In *Working minimalism*, ed. Samuel David Epstein and Norbert Hornstein, 251–282. Cambridge, MA: MIT Press.

5   A Note on Weak vs. Strong Generation in Human Language*

The last section of Chapter 1 of *Aspects* states that "[p]resumably, discussion of weak generative capacity marks only a very early and primitive stage of the study of generative grammar. Questions of real linguistic interest arise only when strong generative capacity (descriptive adequacy) and, more important, explanatory adequacy become the focus of discussion" (p. 61). This is a clear and explicit statement of Chomsky's perception of the linguistic relevance of formal and mathematical investigations of grammars and languages, which he had initiated and explored in the 1950s and early 1960s. Clearly the concept of weak generation (the size of the set of output strings) plays only a marginal role, if any, in the formal investigation of human language. Rather, the nature of human language lies in its strong generative capacity, i.e., what kind of structural descriptions it generates, and more deeply, what kind of generative procedures it involves in generating those structural descriptions.[1]

However, this understanding has been largely ignored and forgotten in the literature of formal investigations of grammars and languages, particularly in fields such as computational linguistics, biology, or more recently, neurosciences.[2] Thus, many recent studies in the brain science of language (or in the study of animal communications as compared to human language) deal with the alleged formal properties of languages, e.g., local dependencies, nested dependencies, cross-serial dependencies, etc. However, as indicated in many places in the literature (see note 2), these studies suffer from two major drawbacks.

One, the object "languages" are all finite, showing no discrete infinity. Since finite languages are outside of (or "below") the popular hierarchy (the so-called Chomsky hierarchy) assumed in the relevant literature, the finitary status of the object languages is crucial, rendering the comparison between, say, finite-state properties and context-free properties simply irrelevant. This drawback can be partially overcome by some clever experimental tricks, such as letting the subjects "suppose" that the object language exhibits discrete infinity—even though it is, in fact, necessarily finite in actual experiments. The possibility of such a treatment indicates something significant about human cognition. That is, when objects proceed from one, two, and three, humans are most likely led to suppose that the sequence of that object will go on indefinitely, rather than stopping at some arbitrary number. This is certainly true for natural numbers, and should also hold when the object is a linguistic element. While this is an important point, I will not delve into this issue any further here.

Second, the focus of discussion so far in the literature has been on formal dependencies defined on the strings, and little attention has been paid to the abstract (hierarchical) structures assigned to the strings. This is a serious problem—because, as indicated ever since the earliest phase of contemporary generative grammar (see the aforementioned), the nature of human language lies in the way it assigns abstract structures to strings (of words, phonemes, etc.) and not the set of such strings *per se*. That is, one should look for the nature of human language in its "strong generation" (the set of structures)—or ultimately, its *procedures* strongly generating the structures—rather than its "weak generation," which is related to the set of strings it generates.

From this viewpoint, it is not at all surprising that human language does not quite fit nicely into the hierarchy in terms of weak generation (the Chomsky hierarchy). Human language is clearly beyond the bounds of finite-state grammar, and is "mildly" beyond the scope of context-free phrase structure grammar, but perhaps stays within the weak generative capacity of a certain subclass of context-sensitive phrase structure grammar (Joshi 1985). However, these results may not imply any substantive point, because even if a given grammar is adequate in its weak generation, the potential inadequacy in its strong generation will be sufficient for its exclusion as an appropriate model of human language. This is indeed true in the case of phrase structure grammars, regardless of whether it is context-free, where it seems inadequate even in its weak generation, or context-sensitive, where the way it strongly generates the structures for human language clearly exhibits its inadequacy. In short, the hierarchy in terms of weak generation, despite its naturalness and usefulness for other purposes, simply cannot provide a relevant scale along which human language is properly placed.

Let us consider some of the well-known types of dependencies in this light. For concreteness, let us take up the artificial languages discussed in Chomsky (1956, 1957): $L_1 = \{a^n b^n\}$ ($n \geq 0$) (counter language), $L_2 = xx^R$ ($x \in \{a, b\}^*$, x^R stands for the reversal of x) (mirror-image language), and $L_3 = xx$ ($x \in \{a, b\}^*$) (copying language). All these languages are shown to be beyond the bounds of finite-state grammar, and L_1 and L_2 are shown to be within the bounds of context-free phrase structure grammar. L_3, on the other hand, is proven to be beyond the scope of context-free phrase structure grammar, since it shows cross-serial dependencies; however, its sentences can be generated by context-sensitive phrase structure grammar.

How does human language fit in this picture? It is well known that human language exhibits nested dependencies (cf. L_2) all over the place. It is also observed that human language sometimes shows cross-serial dependencies (cf. L$_3$). If we look at the actual cases, however, the distribution of these dependencies (among terminal elements) remains rather mysterious. For example, consider the following schematic Japanese example.

(1) NP$_1$-*ga* NP$_2$-*ga* NP$_3$-*ga* . . . NP$_n$-*ga* . . . V$_n$-*to* . . . V$_3$-*to* V$_2$-*to* V$_1$
(-*ga* = Nom, *to* = that)

If we have n number of NP-*ga*s and n number of Vs in this configuration, we can only have NP-V matching as indicated earlier, i.e., the nested dependency. Thus, "John-*ga* Bill-*ga* Mary-*ga* *waratta* (laughed) *to omotta* (thought) *to itta* (said)" can only mean "John said that Bill thought that Mary laughed." It can never mean, for example, that Mary said that Bill thought that John laughed (a case of cross-serial dependency). In a configuration such as (1), a typical sentence-embedding configuration, the linking pattern forming a nested dependency is the only possible option.

On the other hand, if we have the following coordinate configuration:

(2) NP$_1$-*to* NP$_2$-*to* NP$_3$-*to* . . . NP$_n$-(*to*-)*ga*, (*sorezore* (respectively)) *warai* (laughed) (V$_1$), *omoi* (thought) (V$_2$), *hanasi* (spoke) (V$_3$), . . ., *itta* (said) (V$_n$)

[*to* = and; it can be replaced by other elements with the same meaning, e.g., *ya* (and)]

it can mean that NP$_1$ laughed (V$_1$), NP$_2$ thought (V$_2$), NP$_3$ spoke (V$_3$), . . ., and NP$_n$ said (V$_n$). That is, a cross-serial dependency is certainly allowed here. In addition, other dependencies are also possible. Specifically, the so-called "group reading" is possible, where the interpretation is such that a group of people comprising NP$_1$, NP$_2$, . . ., NP$_n$ collectively laughed, thought, spoke, . . ., and said. The nested dependency and other (mixed order) dependencies are probably impossible to obtain. The question is *why* this should be the case. Why is it that in a configuration like (1), only nested dependencies are allowed, whereas in (2), group readings and cross-serial dependencies (but perhaps no other dependencies) are allowed?

The answer to this question is difficult to obtain if we only look at terminal strings. However, if we look at the structures of these configurations, the answer seems obvious. In (1), neither of the sequences NP$_1$, . . ., NP$_n$ (subjects of different clauses) and V$_1$, . . ., V$_n$ (predicates belonging to different clauses) forms a *constituent*, whereas in (2), each of the sequences NP$_1$, . . ., NP$_n$ (NP$_1$ and NP$_2$ and . . . and NP$_n$, conjoined NPs) and V$_1$, . . ., V$_n$ (V$_1$-V$_2$- . . . -V$_n$, conjoined predicates) forms a constituent. Thus, the generalization here can be stated as follows: cross-serial dependencies in human language are possible only when the relevant terminal elements form a constituent. This constituency requirement strongly suggests that a transformation—a structure-dependent operation—plays an important role here. The actual way of deriving the cross-serial dependencies may be due to Copying Transformation, as suggested in Chomsky (1957) (p. 47, note 11, Chapter 5)—although in the cases considered here, "Copying" cannot be literal copying and should be characterized in a more abstract way, abstracting away from terminal elements and their immediate categorial status and focusing only on structural isomorphisms.[3] Note that such a copying operation is more readily formulable in the current Merge-based system than in the classical theory of grammatical transformations. While grammatical transformations in the earlier theory operate on terminal strings with designated structures (structure indices), Merge directly operates on syntactic objects (structures), rather than strings, and with no direct reference to terminal strings which are not even "strings" at the point where Merge applies, since terminal elements are yet to be linearized. In this sense, Merge is even more structure-oriented than classical transformations, and leaves room for an operation that cannot be performed by classical transformations.[4]

The observed linking patterns can be accounted for along the following lines. In (1), as we mentioned earlier, the nested dependency is naturally and directly obtained by applying Merge in a phase-by-phase fashion, a conventional way of embedding sentences. Since neither the sequence of NPs nor that of predicates forms a constituent, the group reading is impossible. Cross-serial dependency is also impossible, because there is no structural basis (constituency) for such a dependency.

By contrast, the NPs and the Vs in (2) each form a constituent, and since there is a "copying" relation between the two constituents (the NP_1, . . ., NP_n sequence and the V_1, . . ., V_n sequence), group reading, which only requires the matching constituents (with no requirement on the order of terminal elements), is readily possible. Cross-serial dependency is also possible under the assumption that the structures generated by Merge ought to be maximally preserved through the linearization process, i.e., the structural properties should be directly mapped onto sequences, yielding a kind of maximal "copying" relation between the two constituents created by copying Merge. Nested dependency would force a departure from maximal copying, and hence is virtually impossible. Other mixed-order dependencies are even more difficult to obtain, yielding unintelligible interpretations.

If this line of reasoning is on the right track, the aforementioned generalization can be stated as follows:

(3) Cross-serial dependencies are possible only to the extent that they are "transformationally" derivable.

That is, item-by-item matching on terminal strings—which is necessary when the relevant item sequences do not form a constituent, as in case (1)—is not possible in human language. Consequently, context-sensitive phrase structure grammar is also disqualified in this regard as an adequate model for human language (cf. Chomsky 1963 for relevant discussion).

Given the basic properties of the current Merge-based system briefly discussed earlier, the same insight can be stated even in a more general (and stronger) form, which constitutes the main hypothesis of this chapter.

(4) *Hypothesis*:
Dependencies are possible in human language only when they are Merge-generable.

This is a generalization that cannot be made when the rule system of human language is divided into phrase structure rules and grammatical transformations, and when only a weak generation of human language is intensively investigated.

Merge is a crucial operation (perhaps the only core operation) of the human language faculty, a biological endowment. Thus, when humans deal with a given dependency, the language faculty comes into play if the dependency is Merge-generable (directly or indirectly), but if the dependency is not Merge-generable, humans have to utilize other cognitive resources to handle it. More specifically, Merge does not specify linear order, does not count, and applies to structured objects (constituents) under certain structural conditions (characterizable by No-tampering, etc.). It follows, then, that L_1 (counter language) cannot be dealt with by humans in terms of "finite-state grammar with counters," since Merge does not provide counters. In this case, however, there is an alternative approach to characterize this language by Merge alone, without recourse to counters. Thus, this may well be the "right" account of L_1 if we are concerned with what is actually happening in the human brain. Note that in terms of weak generation, there is no right-or-wrong issue concerning the choice between the two ways to characterize L_1. L_2 (mirror-image language) is also Merge-generable. Thus, dependencies observed in (1)—nested dependencies—are easily generated by applying Merge cyclically (phase-by-phase). This is why nested dependencies abound in human language. However, cross-serial dependencies are Merge-generable only if the relevant items form constituents (note that Merge does not provide counters, nor does it give us linear order). Therefore, the distribution of cross-serial dependencies is extremely limited in human language. Such a dependency is possible in (2), where the constituency requirement is fulfilled, but is disallowed in (1), where it is not.

Dependencies observed/defined on terminal strings are, in fact, epiphenomena, obtained as a consequence of Merge. Merge-generable dependencies are handled by the faculty of language, while non-Merge-generable dependencies are processed, perhaps as a kind of a puzzle or an intellectual exercise, by other cognitive capacities. It is thus predicted that the brain regions responsible for syntax, such as the left inferior frontal gyrus (L. IFG) and the left supramarginal gyrus (L. SMG) (Ohta et al. 2013a, 2013b), will be significantly activated when Merge-generable dependencies are being processed, whereas brain activation patterns will be quite different when non-Merge-generable dependencies such as non-constituent cases of cross-serial dependencies are being processed. Reasonable and well-designed neuroscience experiments are likely to demonstrate these points. In fact, an experimental research is being conducted in an attempt to shed light on how Merge-generable and non-Merge-generable dependencies are differentiated in the brain (cf. Ohta et al. 2014).

In closing the discussion on generative capacity of grammars in *Aspects*, Chomsky argues for the utmost importance of explanatory adequacy/feasibility requirement as follows.

> It is important to keep the requirements of explanatory adequacy and feasibility in mind when weak and strong generative capacities of theories are studied as mathematical questions. Thus one can construct hierarchies of grammatical theories in terms of weak and strong generative capacity, but it is important to bear in mind that these hierarchies do *not* necessarily correspond to what is probably the empirically most significant dimension of increasing power of linguistic theory. This dimension is presumably to be defined in terms of the scattering in value of grammars compatible with fixed data. Along this empirically significant dimension, we should like to accept the least "powerful" theory that is empirically adequate. It might conceivably turn out that this theory is extremely powerful (perhaps even universal, that is, equivalent in generative capacity to the theory of Turing machines) along the dimension of weak generative capacity, and even along the dimension of strong generative capacity. It will not necessarily follow that it is very powerful (and hence to be discounted) in the dimension which is ultimately of real empirical significance.
>
> (p. 62; emphasis original)

These remarks, which appear to have been mostly forgotten or otherwise disregarded in the past fifty years or so, seem to hold true almost verbatim even now, or since the current theory is supposedly trying to go "beyond explanatory adequacy," perhaps the empirically most significant dimension is to be defined by factors that lie beyond the feasibility requirement. The status of evaluation procedure that is behind the notion of "the scattering in value of grammars compatible with fixed data" in *Aspects* has been blurred particularly after the principles-and-parameters approach emerged around 1980.[5] Thus, it is presently not even clear how to address what seems to be the most important theoretical question for the mathematical study of grammars. Perhaps it is premature to tackle such a question until we come up with a reasonable mathematical theory of the Merge-based generative system, which in turn should be based on a fuller understanding of the properties of human language. What has been suggested in this chapter is a much more modest proposal, i.e., that we should shift our focus from weak generative capacity to, at least, strong generative capacity, i.e., the matter concerning descriptive adequacy, hoping for future development of the formal study of generative procedures themselves (category theory comes to mind as a promising framework).

Notes

* I thank Noam Chomsky for his comments on an earlier version of this chapter. The research reported in this chapter was supported in part by a Core Research for Evolutionary Science and Technology (CREST) grant from the Japan Science and Technology Agency (JST).

1 See Chomsky (1986), Chapters 1 and 2 for much relevant discussion.

2 References are too numerous to mention. See Everaert and Huybregts (2013) for an illuminating review. See also Ohta et al. (2013a, 2013b) and the references cited therein for a detailed discussion on the importance of hierarchical structures and the Merge operation in the neuroscience of human language.

3 See Stabler (2004) for some related discussion on copying operations.

4 In various other respects, Merge is much more restricted and thus much less powerful than classical transformations (and phrase structure rules). Although there has been much interesting work in the literature (see, among others, Stabler (2010), Collins and Stabler (2011), and references cited therein), the issue of the overall generative power of the Merge-based system, particularly with respect to its strong generative capacity, seems to remain largely open. In the current Merge-based bare phrase structure theory, where no specification of linear order and labeling is made by Merge itself, the status of such classical concepts (and all the "theorems" and generalizations based on the concepts) as right- vs. left-branching structures, nesting vs. self-embedding structures, cross-serial dependencies, etc., does not seem obvious. Thus, Merge alone cannot, of course, distinguish right- vs. left-branching structures. The distinction should be made in the process of linearization (as part of the externalization processes). Merge, applying phase-by-phase, does generate nesting, as discussed in the text, but it underspecifies it, specifying no linear order. The distinction between nesting and self-embedding cannot be made by Merge, but it ought to be handled in the course of labeling. And so on. Also, even in narrow syntax, most of the dependencies are defined not (solely) by Merge, but via Agree, "predication," and other miscellaneous relations/operations whose status is not crystal clear at this point. All of these problems should be cleared to seriously address the issue of the generative power of the Merge-based syntax. See Chapter 6 of this volume for some relevant discussion.

5 It is important to note in this connection that the logical possibility of eliminating the evaluation procedure is already hinted at (and disregarded) in *Aspects* (pp. 36–37).

References

Chomsky, Noam. 1956. Three models for the description of language. *I.R.E. Transactions on Information Theory*, vol. IT-2, Proceedings of the symposium on information theory, September, 113–124. [Reprinted, with corrections, in *Readings in mathematical psychology*, volume II, ed. R. Duncan Luce, Robert R. Bush and Eugene Galanter, 105–124. New York: John Wiley & Sons. (1965).]

Chomsky, Noam. 1957. *Syntactic structures*. The Hague: Mouton. 2nd edition, Mouton de Gruyter, 2002.

Chomsky, Noam. 1963. Formal properties of grammars. In *Handbook of mathematical psychology*, volume II, ed. R. Duncan Luce, Robert R. Bush, and Eugene Galanter, 323–418. New York: John Wiley & Sons.

Chomsky, Noam. 1965. *Aspects of the theory of syntax*. Cambridge, MA: MIT Press.

Chomsky, Noam. 1986. *Knowledge of language: Its nature, origins, and use*. New York: Praeger.

Collins, Chris, and Edward Stabler. 2011. A formalization of minimalist syntax. Ms., New York University and University of California, Los Angeles.

Everaert, Martin, and Riny Huybregts. 2013. The design principles of natural language. In *Birdsong, speech, and language: Exploring the evolution of mind and brain*, ed. Johan J. Bolhuis and Martin Everaert, 3–26. Cambridge, MA: MIT Press.

Joshi, Aravind. 1985. How much context-sensitivity is necessary for characterizing structural descriptions. In *Natural language processing: Theoretical, computational and psychological perspectives*, ed. David Dowty, Lauri Karttunen, and Arnold Zwicky, 206–250. New York: Cambridge University Press.

Ohta, Shinri, Naoki Fukui, and Kuniyoshi L. Sakai. 2013a. Syntactic computation in the human brain: The degree of merger as a key factor. *PLoS One* 8 (2): 1–16. [Chapter 8, this volume.]

Ohta, Shinri, Naoki Fukui, and Kuniyoshi L. Sakai. 2013b. Computational principles of syntax in the regions specialized for language: Integrating theoretical linguistics and functional neuroimaging. *Frontiers in Behavioral Neuroscience* 7 (204): 1–13. [Chapter 9, this volume.]

Ohta, Shinri, Masatomi Iizawa, Kazuki Iijima, Tomoya Nakai, Naoki Fukui, Mihoko Zushi, Hiroki Narita, and Kuniyoshi L. Sakai. 2014. An on-going research: The experimental design. Paper presented at the CREST Workshop with Noam Chomsky, The University of Tokyo.

Stabler, Edward. 2004. Varieties of crossing dependencies: Structure dependence and mild context sensitivity. *Cognitive Science* 28: 699–720.

Stabler, Edward. 2010. Computational perspectives on minimalism. In *The Oxford handbook of linguistic minimalism*, ed. Cedric Boeckx, 617–641. Oxford: Oxford University Press.

6   0-Search and 0-Merge

With Hiroki Narita, Hironobu Kasai,
Takaomi Kato, and Mihoko Zushi

Summary

In this chapter, we put forward the hypothesis that all syntactic operations can be uniformly characterized as a composite of two most primitive operations, which we refer to as 0-Search (S_0) and 0-Merge (M_0). 0-Search is an operation such that it picks out n elements contained in a given domain as an input to linguistic computation. 0-Merge is an operation such that given n objects, it forms a set of these objects. We argue that not only "Merge" (be it external or internal) but also various other "relation-forming" operations, such as labeling, Agree(ment), chain-formation, and binding, can be unified under a composite operation $M_0 {\circ} S_0$, incorporating and further extending the notion of generalized Search proposed by Kato et al. (2014) [Chapter 3, this volume]. We also propose a generalized minimality condition on $M_0 {\circ} S_0$, and demonstrate that it can capture various locality constraints on Merge, labeling, Agree(ment), chain-formation, and binding.

1 Introduction

The syntax of human language has the function of constructing an infinite array of hierarchically structured syntactic objects (SOs), which are transferred to the "Conceptual-Intentional" (CI) and "Sensorimotor" (SM) Interfaces (SEM and PHON, respectively). It has been conjectured that a single recursively applicable operation *Merge* is sufficient to characterize the discrete infinity exhibited by human language (cf. Boeckx 2009, Berwick 2011, Fujita 2013). However, Merge as commonly construed only serves to construct hierarchically organized SOs, while it falls short of capturing various "linguistic relations" among SOs. A number of other operations have been proposed in the literature for the purpose of capturing the linguistic/syntactic relations that Merge as commonly construed cannot handle. Such linguistic relations include Agree(ment), chain-formation, binding, etc. Kato et al. (2014) [Chapter 3, this volume] attempt to unify these seemingly disparate relation-formation operations under a general search operation, which is referred to as *Search*, and conclude that Merge and Search are the only basic operations of syntax.

The purpose of this chapter is to explore further unification.[1] We will put forward the hypothesis that Merge as commonly formulated in the literature actually consists of more elementary operations, and consequently, it is not really the most elementary syntactic operation, contrary to the widely-held belief. We will argue that it should rather be analyzed as a *composite* of two most primitive operations, i.e., (i) the selection of n elements, $\alpha_1, \ldots, \alpha_n$, from a designated domain of computation, and (ii) the formation of an unordered set of these n elements, $\{\alpha_1, \ldots, \alpha_n\}$. We will propose that Search, like Merge, should also be decomposed into the two primitive operations (i) and (ii). Decomposing Merge and Search in this way leads to unification of these two syntactic operations into a single composite operation.

This chapter is organized as follows. In Section 2, we will propose the decomposition of Merge into two most primitive operations: the first operation, which we will call *0-Search*, is the selection of n (typically two) elements, corresponding to what are generally called the "probe" and the "goal"; then, the second operation *0-Merge* is the formation of an unordered set of these n elements. In Section 3, we will propose that Search is also decomposed into 0-Search and 0-Merge. Therefore, Merge and Search are unified as a composite of the two most primitive operations in syntax (i.e., 0-Merge and 0-Search). In Section 4, we will refine the notion of occurrence, adopting Chomsky's (2001) idea that each occurrence of an SO is defined in terms of its "mother" node SO. This mother-based definition of occurrence will be extended to the agreement relation established between features of lexical items (LIs). We will also address the issue as to whether there are any cases where 0-Search/0-Merge applies independently of the other primitive operation, rather than as part of the composite operation. In Section 5, we will make some speculative remarks on this issue. In Section 6, we will show how various locality constraints on Merge, labeling, Agree(ment), chain-formation, and binding are captured in a unified way. In Section 7, we will suggest a new way of looking at the nature of agreement, where agreement is obtained as a by-product of labeling. Section 8 will conclude the chapter.

2 Decomposing Merge

Merge as commonly conceived in the literature (cf. Chomsky 2005, 2007, 2008, among others) is an operation that performs the following computations: (i) it takes n (typically two) objects from a designated domain of computation, and (ii) it forms a set of the n objects. In view of these two sub-functions, it is natural and rather accurate to analyze Merge as a composite operation. Thus, we propose in this chapter that Merge is a composition of two most primitive operations, which we call 0-Search and 0-Merge, formulated as in (1) and (2), respectively (the formulation of 0-Search will be slightly modified in Section 5).

(1) 0-Search (S_0):
0-Search is an operation such that it picks out n elements contained in a given domain as an input to 0-Merge.

(2) 0-Merge (M_0):
0-Merge is an operation such that given n objects, it forms a set of these objects (i.e., $M_0(\alpha_1, \ldots, \alpha_n) = \{\alpha_1, \ldots, \alpha_n\}$).

0-Search (S_0) takes a designated workspace WS as its input, and picks out n objects from WS: $S_0(WS) = \alpha_1, \ldots, \alpha_n$ and 0-Merge (M_0) takes the *output* of 0-Search, $\alpha_1, \ldots, \alpha_n$, as its input, and forms an unordered set of them: $M_0(\alpha_1, \ldots, \alpha_n) = \{\alpha_1, \ldots, \alpha_n\}$. In this manner, we analyze Merge as a composite operation of 0-Search and 0-Merge, namely $M_0(S_0(WS))$, or equivalently, $M_0 \circ S_0(WS)$. It is assumed that WS is a set consisting of SOs already constructed $\Sigma_1, \ldots, \Sigma_n$ and LIs in the Lexicon, that is, WS = $\{\Sigma_1, \ldots, \Sigma_n\} \cup$ Lexicon = $\{\Sigma_1, \ldots, \Sigma_n, LI_1, \ldots, LI_m\}$ (note that the Lexicon is a set of LIs, which we tentatively take to be finite).

Let us begin our discussion with External Merge (EM).[2] Consider first the cases where both of the targets of EM are LIs.[3] Suppose that *the* and *book* undergo EM. 0-Search takes WS as an input and picks out *the* and *book*, which are contained in the Lexicon: $S_0(WS)$ = *the*, *book*. Then 0-Merge forms a set of them: $M_0(the, book) = \{the, book\}$. The proposed analysis also accommodates the cases where at least one of the targets of EM is not an LI. For example, let us consider the derivational step where *read* undergoes EM with *the book*, as shown in (3).

(3) *read* ← EM → {*the, book*}

In order to yield the effect of this EM, 0-Search in $M_0 \circ S_0$ must be able to pick out an object contained in the Lexicon (*read*) and an object not contained in the Lexicon ({*the, book*}). Given the definition of WS noted earlier, we successfully accommodate this effect because LIs and non-LI SOs are both contained in WS.

0-Search can also pick out two non-LI SOs Σ_i, Σ_j contained in WS. In that case, $M_0 \circ S_0(WS) = \{\Sigma_i, \Sigma_j\}$. This takes place, for example, in the EM of {*the, woman*} and {*v*, {*criticize, John*}} to form *v*P:

(4) {*the, woman*} ← EM → {*v*, {*criticize, John*}}

Now, let us turn to Internal Merge (IM). Under our proposal, IM involves an application of $M_0 \circ S_0$ as shown below:

(5) Internal Merge (IM):
$M_0 \circ S_0(WS) = \{\alpha, \Sigma\}$ (where a copy of α is contained in Σ)

Given WS, 0-Search picks out Σ contained in WS and an element α contained in Σ. Then, 0-Merge applies to these objects and forms a set $\{\alpha, \Sigma\}$. Let us consider the following example:

(6) a.   What did John buy?

    b.   [$_{vP}$ John [v [$_{VP}$ buy what]]]

Suppose that the derivation of (6a) has reached the stage shown in (6b), where *John* has been merged with {v, {*buy*, *what*}} to form {*John*, {v, {*buy*, *what*}}}. 0-Search applies to WS and picks out {*John*, {v, {*buy*, *what*}}} and *what*. 0-Merge applies to these objects and forms a set of them. In short, $M_0 \circ S_0$ works as in (7).

(7) $M_0 \circ S_0$(WS) = {*what*, {*John*, {v, {*buy*, *what*}}}}

The output of this application of $M_0 \circ S_0$ becomes an input to another application of $M_0 \circ S_0$ for chain-formation (see Section 3 for details).[4]

3 Decomposing Search

As mentioned at the outset of this chapter, various miscellaneous operations have been postulated to describe a variety of linguistic phenomena. Merge as usually construed cannot handle them. Such phenomena include Agree(ment), chain-formation, and binding. Kato et al. (2014) characterize those operations as "identity-searching" operations and attempt to unify them under a general search operation. The relevant operation is referred to as *Search*, and characterized as in (8).

(8) Let α be an element which initiates Search and β be the c-command domain of α. Then, Search is an operation which searches through β for a feature or a complex of features identical to the one contained in α and establishes a relation between those (complexes of) features. (Kato et al. 2014: 204)

Search functions, as it were, as a generalized probe-goal mechanism, and covers the cases of Agree, chain-formation, and binding.

Let us briefly see how Search applies in the course of a derivation, taking a case of *wh*-movement as an example.[5] Consider the derivation of (9a), shown in (9b, c).

(9) a.   What did John buy?

    b.   [C [T [John [what v [buy what]]]]]

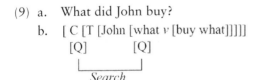

c.   [what C [T [John [what v [buy what]]]]]
     └──────────────┘
         Search

At the derivational stage illustrated in (9b), C initiates Search, so that an agreement relation is established between the Q-feature ([Q]) of C (which Kato et al. take to be unvalued) and the Q-feature of *what* (which they take to be valued) at the edge of vP.[6] After *what* is internally merged to the edge of CP from the edge of vP as in (9c), it also initiates Search from the higher position and a chain is created between the two copies of the *wh*-phrase. Agree and chain-formation are thus unified under the single operation Search.[7]

Kato et al. (2014) present Search as one of the basic operations of syntax (or a version of the basic operation of syntax, Merge). It is implicitly assumed there that Search (as well as Merge) is a primitive operation, which cannot be decomposed any further. As can be seen in (8), however, Search clearly consists of two parts: the one that picks out two elements—that is, a feature or feature complex which the Search initiator contains and a feature or feature complex identical to it contained in the c-command domain of the Search initiator—and the one that establishes a relation between them. Thus, it seems quite plausible to regard Search as being decomposable, or a composite operation. We propose that Search is also a composition of two more, in fact most, primitive operations, namely $M_0 \circ S_0$.

It is suggested in Kato et al. (2014: 218) that the output of Search should be represented as an ordered pair, not a(n unordered) set, because a probe and a goal have to be distinguished. Departing from Kato et al. (2014), we claim that the output of $M_0 \circ S_0$(WS) is represented as a set, not an ordered pair. This departure is reasonable to the extent that the traditional notion of probe/goal is to be abandoned under the current proposal.[8] Obviously, a set {X, Y} itself does not represent a relation R holding between X and Y. Our claim is that the interface systems somehow derive R from {X, Y} (and other information available to them). When the output of $M_0 \circ S_0$(WS) is a two-membered set {X, Y}, it is interpreted as "there is a relation between X and Y" at SEM and/or PHON. See Section 6 for details.

Let us see how agreement, chain-formation, and binding, which Kato et al. (2014) try to unify under Search, are recaptured under $M_0 \circ S_0$(WS).[9] First, consider ϕ-agreement between T and the subject nP. In this chapter, we use "nP" to refer to nominal phrases. Suppose that the derivation has reached the stage where T and vP have been merged to form {T, vP}. First, 0-Search applies to WS and picks out the (unvalued) ϕ-features ([ϕ]) of T and the (valued) ϕ-features of the subject nP, located at the edge of vP. Then, 0-Merge applies to these sets of features and forms a set containing them.

Thus, $M_0 \circ S_0$ takes WS as an input and yields $\{[\phi]$ (of T), $[\phi]$ (of the subject *n*P)$\}$ as the output, as shown in (10).[10,11]

(10) $M_0 \circ S_0$(WS) = $\{[\phi]$ (of T), $[\phi]$ (of the subject *n*P)$\}$

We propose that the output of this application of $M_0 \circ S_0$(WS) will be interpreted as "there is a ϕ-agreement relation between T and the subject *n*P" at PHON (see note 6 for relevant discussion).[12]

Next, let us see how $M_0 \circ S_0$ works for chain-formation, taking (11a) as an example. Consider the derivational stage where, as a result of IM, a copy of *what* has been created at the edge of *v*P, as shown in (11b).

(11) a. What did John buy?
      b. $[_{vP}$ what [John *v* $[_{VP}$ buy what]]]

First, 0-Search picks out the two copies of *what* contained in WS. Then, 0-Merge applies to these copies and forms a set of them. Thus, $M_0 \circ S_0$(WS) works as shown in (12) here.

(12) $M_0 \circ S_0$(WS) = $\{$*what* (at the edge of *v*P), *what* (within VP)$\}$

The set on the right-hand side of (12) will be interpreted as a chain of *what* at PHON and SEM.

Anaphor-binding as in (13a) also falls under $M_0 \circ S_0$(WS).

(13) a. John criticized himself.
      b. $[_{vP}$ John $[_{VP}$ criticize himself]]

Departing from Kato et al. (2014), we assume that binding is a relation established between two *n*Ps (see Section 6.4). At the derivational stage given in (13b), 0-Search first picks out *himself* and *John*. Then, 0-Merge applies to these *n*Ps and forms a set of these objects, as shown in (14).

(14) $M_0 \circ S_0$(WS) = $\{$*John, himself*$\}$

This output of $M_0 \circ S_0$(WS) will be interpreted as "there is a binding relation between *John* and *himself*" at SEM (in order for *John* to be interpreted as a "binder" and *himself* as a "bindee," SEM also needs to access information on the configurational relation between the two *n*Ps, namely that *John* is structurally higher than (or "c-commands") *himself*).

Unlike the Search operation proposed by Kato et al. (2014), which establishes a relation only between identical elements (i.e., identical features or feature complexes), $M_0 \circ S_0$(WS) can form a pair of non-identical elements as well. We argue that pairing of non-identical elements occurs in the case of labeling.[13] More specifically, assuming that what has to be done in labeling is to form a(n "is headed by") relation between an SO and its label, we claim that, in labeling, $M_0 \circ S_0$(WS) works in such a way that 0-Search first picks out the SO Σ and its label, and then 0-Merge forms a set of these objects, as shown in (15) (where λ = the label of Σ).[14,15,16] This set is read as "Σ is headed by λ" at the interfaces.

(15) $M_0 \circ S_0$(WS) = {Σ, λ}

For example, in the labeling of the SO {*criticize*, *himself*}, 0-Search picks out the SO itself and *criticize*, and 0-Merge applies to these objects and forms a set of them, as in (16). As a result of this application of $M_0 \circ S_0$(WS), *criticize* will be interpreted as the label of the relevant constituent.

(16) $M_0 \circ S_0$(WS) = {{*criticize*, *himself*}, *criticize*}

If the discussion so far is on the right track, labeling is successfully unified with the other operations such as Agree, binding, and chain-formation, and we now have a very general unifying mechanism. This is one of the most notable results obtained under our approach. Chomsky has suggested in his various writings that (minimal) search is involved in labeling (see, for example, Chomsky 2005, 2007, 2008). Although it is safe to bet that some search mechanism is also involved in operations like Agree (see, for example, Chomsky 2015b), it is not clear under the standard probe-goal system how to unify these operations with labeling. This is because, under the standard system, the two items to be related (that is, the probe and the goal) must be located in such a way that one c-commands the other, but in the case of labeling, an SO and its label are not—in fact, never—in such a structural relationship. A similar point applies to Search in Kato et al. (2014). In contrast, under the current approach, in which the traditional notion of probe/goal is abandoned, we can unify labeling and other operations such as Agree in a very natural way. They are all instances of the single operation $M_0 \circ S_0$(WS) (see note 8 for relevant discussion).

To sum up the discussion in this and the previous sections: we have proposed that Merge ought to be analyzed as a composition of the two most primitive operations—0-Search and 0-Merge—namely $M_0 \circ S_0$. 0-Search picks out n objects and 0-Merge forms a set of these picked-out objects. We have also shown that the Search operation, which is originally proposed by Kato et al. (2014), ought to be another instance of $M_0 \circ S_0$. Under the proposed mechanism, labeling is naturally unified with the other operations such as Agree, binding, and chain-formation. If the discussion so far is on the right track, all the syntactic operations are unified under $M_0 \circ S_0$(WS), a welcome result from a minimalist perspective.

4 Refining the Notion of Occurrence

In the preceding discussion, we established that Merge and Search, as well as labeling (Chomsky 2005, 2007, 2008), can be uniformly characterized as $M_0 \circ S_0$(WS). We specifically hypothesized that 0-Merge always yields an unordered set in every case, regardless of whether the result is chain-formation, Agree, labeling, or binding. As a concrete example, consider again the vP structure in (17), and specifically the instance of $M_0 \circ S_0$ that serves to generate a chain with two copies of *what* in (18).

(17) vP = {*what*, {*John*, {*v*, {*buy*, *what*}}}}

(18) $M_0 \circ S_0$(WS) = {*what* (at the edge of vP), *what* (within VP)}

In (18), the two copies of *what* are identical and indistinguishable from each other, assuming that there are no indices or other representational tricks that differentiate the two tokens (cf. the Inclusiveness Condition of Chomsky 1995 *et seq.*). Then, one might wonder if chain-notations like (18) cause a problem from the perspective of set theory. The reason is that the output of (18) should be equivalent to that of (19) in terms of extension.

(19) $M_0 \circ S_0$(WS) = {*what*}

(19) can be obtained when S_0(WS) picks out only one instance of *what* within vP. The two sets in (18) and (19) contain exactly the same (in fact unique) element, and hence should count as identical, if we assume the basic postulate of set theory according to which a set is determined uniquely by its members, excluding multisets (the Zermelo-Fraenkel axiom of extensionality). This situation is problematic, because the conception that (18) = (19) fails to capture the chain relation between the two occurrences of *what* in (17).

One way to avoid this problem is to adopt Chomsky's (2001) idea that each occurrence of an SO is in fact defined in terms of its "mother" node SO. According to this hypothesis, the chain corresponding to (18) is represented as in (20).

(20) $M_0 \circ S_0$(WS) = {{*what*, {*John*, {*v*, {*buy*, *what*}}}}, {*buy*, *what*}}

This approach nicely resolves the problem of extensional equivalence just mentioned, since the indistinguishable copies of *what* in (18) are successfully replaced by their "mother" SOs, which are clearly distinguishable from each other.

Moreover, the mother-based definition of chains can also offer a unified analysis of the notion of "feature-chain," that is, the agreement relation established between features of LIs.[17] Recall that we defined the output of $M_0 \circ S_0$ in service of ϕ-agreement informally as in (21):

(21) $M_0 \circ S_0$(WS) = {[ϕ] (of T), [ϕ] (of the subject nP)}

If a valued feature and its unvalued counterpart count as identical to each other (cf. Chomsky's (2000: 124) remark, "We therefore understand "feature-identity" [. . .] to be identity of choice of feature, not of value."), then the two sets of ϕ-features may yield another case of extensional equivalence as shown in (22).

(22) $M_0 \circ S_0(WS) = \{[\phi], [\phi]\} = \{[\phi]\}$

Here, our mother-based solution to chains can be applied to the cases of feature-chains as well. Suppose that feature-chains are defined in terms of the "mothers" of relevant feature-occurrences. Note that LIs have been traditionally understood as bundles (i.e., sets) of features. Thus, each LI counts as the "mother" of the features it contains, if we assume that a set in the set-theoretic notation of phrase structure is regarded as the "mother" of its members. Then, we might say that what $M_0 \circ S_0$ creates, when applying in the case of feature-chain formation, is in fact a set of two LIs, $\{T, n\}$ in the case of (21) (assuming that n is the LI that contains ϕ-features within a nominal). The two LIs each define an occurrence of the relevant agreement features.

(23) $M_0 \circ S_0(WS) = \{T, n\}$

Based on these considerations, we propose that chains are uniformly characterized as *sets of the mothers of* the relevant elements. This approach not only eliminates the potential problem of extensional equivalence but also has broader empirical applications, unifying chains of movement and feature-chains created by Agree(ment).[18]

5   Cases Where 0-Search/0-Merge Applies on Its Own: Some Speculations

So far, we have argued that primitive operations of syntax are 0-Search and 0-Merge, and that various operations assumed in the literature, including the major and fundamental operations such as Merge and Agree, can be solely reduced to the composite of the two primitive operations $M_0 \circ S_0$. Given this claim, a question that naturally arises is: Are there any cases where 0-Search/0-Merge applies independently of the other, rather than as part of the composite operation $M_0 \circ S_0$? Obviously, if there are such cases, the view that 0-Search and 0-Merge are independent primitive operations would be reinforced. Below, we will make some suggestions about where 0-Search/0-Merge applies on its own.

Let us begin with 0-Search, which was formulated earlier as in (24).

(24) 0-Search (S_0):
     0-Search is an operation such that it picks out n elements contained in a given domain as an input to 0-Merge.

Since Chomsky (2004), it has been widely assumed that objects constructed in narrow syntax are handed over to SEM and PHON by the operation Transfer. But what is the nature of this operation? Do we have to assume it as an independent syntactic operation? In Kato et al. (2014), it is claimed that Transfer must be eliminated from narrow syntax, and that once it loses its status as a syntactic operation, it would reduce to just a cover term for the fact that the interface systems periodically access objects generated by narrow syntax. Given this insight, a possibility that we think is worth pursuing is that the interface systems make use of 0-Search to draw objects from narrow syntax. More specifically, we would like to suggest entertaining the hypothesis in (25) along with a concomitant extension of 0-Search as in (26), where "linguistic computation" includes not only 0-Merge but also interpretations at the interfaces.

(25) Objects (i.e., sets) generated by $M_0 \circ S_0$ in narrow syntax are taken to SEM and PHON as a result of S_0(WS) triggered by the respective interfaces.

(26) 0-Search (S_0) (a generalized version):
0-Search is an operation such that it picks out n elements contained in a given domain as an input to linguistic computation.

We leave full investigation of issues raised by the above hypothesis for future research. But if it turns out to be correct, Transfer would no longer need to be assumed as an independent syntactic operation: it would be reduced to a more primitive operation (i.e., 0-Search), hence further reduction of syntactic operations. In addition, since the above hypothesis implies that 0-Search can apply on its own, the view that 0-Search is a primitive operation of syntax would be reinforced.

Let us now turn to 0-Merge, the formulation of which is repeated in the following:

(27) 0-Merge (M_0):
0-Merge is an operation such that given n objects, it forms a set of these objects (i.e., $M_0(\alpha_1, \ldots, \alpha_n) = \{\alpha_1, \ldots, \alpha_n\}$).

Note that if 0-Merge applies independently of 0-Search, receiving nothing as an input, it should yield a set with no member, namely, the empty set ($\varnothing$).

(28) 0-Merge $\rightarrow \{\ \} = \varnothing$

In axiomatic set theory, the existence of the empty set is often postulated as an axiom. But why should it exist? What assures its existence? Given (28), we are tempted to speculate that the conception of the empty set is a direct consequence of the availability of 0-Merge (in the human mind/brain).[19] If this speculation is basically on the right track, it follows that 0-Merge can apply on its own in principle, constituting a good case for the claim that 0-Merge is an independent primitive operation.[20]

6 Unifying Minimality Constraints on 0-Search

We saw that $M_0 \circ S_0$ not only derives unbounded structure-generation via Merge, which constantly extends and rearranges the elements within WS, but it also provides a unified account of various relation-forming computations, such as chain-formation, Agree(ment), binding, and labeling. In this section, we will provide arguments for the idea that an application of $M_0 \circ S_0$ obeys a generalized minimality condition (cf. Rizzi 1990).

6.1 Label

Let us first consider the case of labeling, which takes the following form.

(29) $M_0 \circ S_0(WS) = \{\Sigma, \lambda\}$ (where λ is an LI or a (bundle of) feature(s))

It has been proposed in various forms that labeling obeys a strong locality condition, or what Chomsky (2012, 2013) calls a "minimal search" requirement (see also Narita 2014). For example, consider the case of labeling in (30), which yields (31a).

(30) $v\mathrm{P} = \{v, \{read, \{n, books\}\}\} \in WS$

(31) $M_0 \circ S_0(WS) =$ a. $\{v\mathrm{P}, v\}$
                      b.   *$\{v\mathrm{P}, read\}$
                      c.   *$\{v\mathrm{P}, n\}$

Whenever labeling targets an SO Σ within WS, it must select the highest possible element λ within Σ as the label of Σ. Thus, only (31a) among (31a-c) counts as a legitimate instance of labeling.

What seems to be at work here is the requirement that the two outputs of 0-Search, Σ and λ, be minimally distant. In order to formulate this requirement, let us introduce the notion of "Depth relative to Σ" (henceforth Depth$_\Sigma$) as a measure for structural distance:

(32) Depth$_\Sigma$:[21]
     Suppose that Depth$_\Sigma(\alpha) = m$ ($m \geq 0$) is the order of depth—the inverse relation of structural height—associated with α relative to an SO Σ. Then, we can say:
     a.   Depth$_\Sigma(\Sigma) = 0$ for any SO Σ.
     b.   If Depth$_\Sigma(\alpha) = m$, then Depth$_\Sigma(\beta) = m + 1$ for any β such that β is a daughter of α (i.e., $\beta \in \alpha$).

(32a) states that for any SO Σ, Σ is of depth 0 to Σ itself. (32b) states that the value of Depth$_\Sigma(\alpha)$ increases as α gets more deeply embedded within Σ. In (30), for example, Depth$_{v\mathrm{P}}(v\mathrm{P}) = 0$, Depth$_{v\mathrm{P}}(v) = 1$, Depth$_{v\mathrm{P}}(read) = 2$, Depth$_{v\mathrm{P}}(n) = 3$, etc. As shown in (31), $\{v\mathrm{P}, v\}$ but not $\{v\mathrm{P}, read\}$ or $\{v\mathrm{P}, n\}$ is a legitimate output of $M_0 \circ S_0$ for labeling, given that v is the most prominent lexical element that can define a label.

Capitalizing on the notion of Depth$_\Sigma$, we can formulate a minimality condition on 0-Search as in (33). The relevant notion of "formal restrictions on Label(ing)" is defined as in (34).

(33) Minimality Condition on 0-Search (first version):
　　0-Search may pick out α, β for a linguistic relation R only if
　　a.　α, β meet the formal restrictions on R, and
　　b.　There is no γ ($\gamma \neq \beta$) such that α, γ also meet the formal restrictions
　　　　on R and $\text{Depth}_\alpha(\gamma) < \text{Depth}_\alpha(\beta)$.

(34) Formal Restrictions on Label:
　　a.　β is a (bundle of) feature(s) (typically an LI),[22] and
　　b.　β is contained in α.

(34) holds that α, β must be of a particular sort in order to define a legitimate instance of "Label." Specifically, β must be a (bundle of) feature(s) contained in α. (33) serves to minimize the distance between the two outputs of 0-Search, α, β, in such a way that β is the most prominent (least embedded) element within α that satisfies the relevant formal restrictions. (33b) specifically holds that a linguistic relation R between α and β cannot be established if there is any intervening element γ that could formally participate in R with α and is "closer" to α than β.

Given the formal restrictions in (34), the minimality condition in (33) can explain cases of labeling like (31): S_0(WS) can access any terms of vP, v, *read*, n, etc., in (30), but since $\text{Depth}_{v\text{P}}(v) < \text{Depth}_{v\text{P}}(read) < \text{Depth}_{v\text{P}}(n)$, v is the most prominent term of vP that could participate in Label, and hence it is the only LI that can enter into a labeling relation with vP via minimal 0-Search.

In the discussion above, we hypothesized that 0-Search in service of Label takes an SO α first, and then looks through α and finds its label β. This ordering of α, β seems to be a natural assumption, since it is the SO α that requires the label β for Full Interpretation. Here, we are assuming with Chomsky (2013: 43) that each SO must be assigned a label in order to be interpreted at SEM and PHON. Under this assumption, every SO is forced to trigger Label-formation via $M_0 \circ S_0$, due to the principle of Full Interpretation. Thus, whenever 0-Search first hits an SO α that is yet to be labeled, then the instance of 0-Search proceeds to find its label β in accordance with the formal restrictions in (34).

In what follows, we will make certain proposals regarding the order in which 0-Search picks out the output elements α, β. The overall hypothesis is that the order of α, β is determined by the need to satisfy Full Interpretation. We will specifically argue that the first output α is the one that is in need of establishing certain linguistic relations to another output β. For Label, α is the SO that is in need of labeling by β, as we saw above. Further, we will also claim that for chain-formation, 0-Search first picks out the newest occurrence α that is in need of being related to the older occurrence β. We will also argue that 0-Search for binding first takes a "bindee" element α that is in need of being bound by a referential, "binder" element β, etc. More generally, Full Interpretation determines which object α within a given WS is in need of being related to some other element β via 0-Search.

6.2 *Chain*

If we are right in claiming that every operation of syntax in fact involves $M_0 \circ S_0$, then it is expected that the proposed minimality condition generally applies to any instance of 0-Search, irrespective of which relation R it serves to establish. We will argue that this expectation can be met, though with slight elaboration.

First, we will show that cases of chain-formation also satisfy (33). Building on the discussion in Section 4, we define the formal restrictions on the Chain-relation as in (35).

(35) Formal Restrictions on Chain (cf. Chomsky 2001):
    a. $\text{Depth}_\Sigma(\alpha) < \text{Depth}_\Sigma(\beta)$ for some SO Σ, and
    b.   There exists an element γ such that $\gamma \in \alpha$ and $\gamma \in \beta$.

If γ is the moving element, the occurrences of γ are the mothers of the copies of γ. Within some SO Σ, α, the first output of 0-Search, is structurally higher than β, the second output of 0-Search. We formulate (35) under the assumption that for each internal merger of γ, 0-Search for Chain always picks out the "newest"/highest occurrence α first, and then finds an "older," more deeply embedded occurrence β. This is a natural assumption, for every time a new copy of γ is created, it is in need of participating in Chain, presumably due to the effect of Full Interpretation.

To see how 0-Search and 0-Merge serve to generate the Chain-objects, consider the derivation of *who will kiss Mary*, summarized in (36).

(36) (Guess) $[_{CP}$ *who* C $[_{TP}$ *t'* will $[_{vP}$ *t v* $[_{VP}$ kiss Mary]]]]
    a.   *v*P = {*who*, {*v*, {kiss, Mary}}}
    b.   T' = {will, {*who*, {*v*, {kiss, Mary}}}}   : EM
    c.   TP = {*who*, {will, {*who*, {*v*, {kiss, Mary}}}}}   : IM
    d. $M_0 \circ S_0$(WS) = {TP, *v*P}   : Chain 1
    e.   C' = {C, {*who*, {will, {*who*, {*v*, {kiss, Mary}}}}}}   : EM
    f.   CP = {*who*, {C, {*who*, {will, {*who*, {*v*, {kiss, Mary}}}}}}} : IM
    g. $M_0 \circ S_0$(WS) =   i.   {CP, TP}   : Chain 2
                          ii. *{CP, *v*P}

Recursive Merge (viz. $M_0 \circ S_0$(WS)) constructs *v*P in (36a), T' in (36b), and then TP in (36c). The final application of $M_0 \circ S_0$(WS) in (36c) is an instance of IM, yielding two copies of *who*. It thus feeds the formation of Chain in (36d): 0-Search picks out the highest occurrence of *who*, namely TP, and then the lower occurrence, vP, and 0-Merge forms a set of them, {TP, vP}. The derivation then continues, reaching CP in (36f). The internal merger of *who* in (36f) feeds another instance of Chain-formation in (36g-i): here, 0-Search first picks out CP as the first occurrence of *who*, and then seeks inside CP and finds the "closest" goal that meets the formal restrictions in (35), namely TP, feeding 0-Merge to form {CP, TP}.

Under the present approach, the minimality condition predicts that at each application of Chain-formation, only the highest and the next highest occurrences can be related via minimal 0-Search. Thus, the Chain-formation of {CP, vP} in (36g-ii) is blocked, because $Depth_{CP}(TP) < Depth_{CP}(vP)$, and TP stands as an "intervener" that is closer to CP than vP.

More generally, the proposed minimality condition can account for the general immobility of "trace" objects. To see this, consider the case in (37a), where the matrix subject position must be filled by some nP—the "Extended Projection Principle" (EPP) effect.

(37) a. ___ seems that [$_{TP}$ *John$_i$* will [$_{vP}$ t_i meet Mary]]
      b. * [$_\Sigma$ *John$_i$* seems that [$_{TP}$ t'_i will [$_{vP}$ t_i meet Mary]]]
      c. [$_\Sigma$ it seems that [$_{TP}$ *John$_i$* will [$_{vP}$ t_i meet Mary]]]

As shown in (37b), once *John* gets stabilized in the embedded subject position in (37a), it cannot move into another A-position, leaving *it*-insertion in (37c) as the only viable option for EPP-satisfaction. The traditional account says that since *John* already checks its Case in TP, it cannot move into another Case position, resulting in the immobility of *John* from the position of t' in (37b). See Fukui and Narita (2012) [Chapter 2, this volume] for an account of the relevant fact in terms of their "Equilibrium Intactness Condition." See also Rizzi (2006) for the notion of "Subject Criterion." However, these authors have nothing to say concerning why the lower occurrence of *John* within vP (indicated by t) can never move, skipping over the other occurrence in t' in (37b).[23] If this option is available in a derivation, then the un-Case-marked copy in a non-criterial position t may freely raise to satisfy another EPP/criterial requirement, and thus we will lose the account of why (37b) is deviant. For this matter, we argue that our minimality condition in (33) can explain the immobility of the copy in t. 0-Search cannot pick out Σ, vP for Chain due to the existence of TP, since Σ, TP meet the formal restrictions on Chain and $Depth_\Sigma(TP) < Depth_\Sigma(vP)$. Hence, TP is "closer" to Σ than vP, thereby preventing the formation of Chain(Σ, vP) under our minimality condition.

In this manner, our $Depth_\Sigma$-based minimality derives the "successive-cyclicity" of Chain-formation. Unbounded Merge generates structures from the bottom up, and whenever IM applies, $M_0 \circ S_0$ in service of Chain-formation must apply in a minimal fashion to relate the new/highest occurrence to the next highest one.

6.3 Agree and Feature-Chain

In the preceding discussion, our attention has been restricted to cases of IM and XP-chains thereof. However, recall that we also introduced the notion of "feature-chain" in Section 4 in order to account for Agree(ment). We assumed that each LI counts as the mother of the features it contains, and hence that occurrences of features can be defined by the LIs containing them. If, for example, *will* (T) and *who* in (36b) undergo ϕ-feature agreement via $M_0 \circ S_0(WS)$, then the feature-chain of $[\phi]$ should look like (38) (assuming that *will* and *who* are LIs with $[\phi]$).

(38) $M_0 \circ S_0(WS) =$ a.   {*will, who*}   : Feature-chain
                   b.   *{*will, Mary*}

It is easy to confirm that (38a) meets the formal restrictions on Chain in (35): $Depth_T(will) < Depth_T(who)$ (35a), and there exists a bundle of features, namely $[\phi]$, such that $[\phi] \in will$ and $[\phi] \in who$ (35b).

Incidentally, Agree has been said to obey a certain kind of minimality condition, too: under the traditional description (as in Chomsky 2000, 2001), Agree is an operation where the "probe" LI searches through its c-command domain and finds the closest possible "goal"; thus, in (36b), *will* undergoes ϕ-feature agreement only with the closest ϕ-bearer, *who*, and it can never ϕ-agree with a more distant element, say, *Mary*.

This minimality effect, however, cannot be captured by the present Minimality Condition in (33), since $Depth_{will}(who)$ and $Depth_{will}(Mary)$ are both undefined, and hence neither *who* nor *Mary* stands closer to *will* than the other under the definition in (33). In order to extend our account to the minimality of Agree (probe-goal relations) as well, we propose to revise the definition of minimality (33) to (39).

(39) Minimality Condition on 0-Search (revised version):
     0-Search may pick out α, β for a linguistic relation R only if
     a. α, β meet the formal restrictions on R, and
     b.   There is no γ ($\gamma \neq \beta$) such that α, γ also meet the formal restrictions
           on R and $Depth_\Sigma(\gamma) < Depth_\Sigma(\beta)$ for some SO Σ.

The difference between (33) and (39) lies in (39b), which states that what matters is not just $Depth_\alpha$, namely the structural height within α, but $Depth_\Sigma$ for any SO Σ that contains γ and β. Specifically for (38), *who* now stands closer to *will* than *Mary* under the definition in (39b), given $Depth_T(who) < Depth_T(Mary)$, thus the non-minimal formation of a feature-chain in (38b) is blocked by the revised minimality condition.

It can be easily confirmed that the revision does not affect the explanatory force of our minimality condition with regard to cases of labeling and

Chain-formation. We will further argue that the revised version receives further support from the analysis of Bind and Merge.[24]

6.4 Bind

Binding is known to be possible only when the binder c-commands the bindee (in fact, c-command is part of the definition of binding). Thus, *the boy* can bind *himself* in (40a) but not in (40b), since *the boy* c-commands *himself* in (40a) but not in (40b).

(40) a.   The boy$_i$ criticized himself$_i$.
     b. * The boy$_i$'s father criticized himself$_i$.

We argue that this "c-command requirement" can be seen as a natural consequence of minimality (39). To begin, let us introduce the notion of "referential feature" [Ref] as a cover term for features relevant to binding. We specifically hypothesize that referential expressions are associated with valued referential features [vRef], while non-referential expressions like pronouns, anaphors, etc., are associated with unvalued referential features ([uRef]) that need to be licensed via Bind-relations.[25] Now, we propose the formal condition on Bind as follows:[26]

(41) Formal Restrictions on Bind:
     a.   α has an unvalued referential feature ([uRef]), and
     b.   β has a referential feature not distinct from α's [uRef].

By formulating Bind as in (41), we intend to characterize 0-Search for Bind as a process that first picks out the "bindee" element α with [uRef], and then seeks to find a "binder" element β with non-distinct [Ref]. As for anaphor-binding in (40), for example, 0-Search first picks out *himself* with [uRef], and then seeks to find its binder nP. In (40a), the subject nP *the boy* occupies the "Spec-T" position as shown in (42a), while this position is occupied by nP$_1$ (= *the boy's father*) that contains nP$_2$ (= *the boy*) in (42b).

(42) a. $[_{TP} [_{nP}$ *the boy*$]$ $[_{T'}$ T $[_{vP}$ . . . *himself* . . .$]]]$
     b. $[_{TP} [_{nP1} [_{nP2}$ *the boy*$]$*'s father*$]$ $[_{T'}$ T $[_{vP}$ . . . *himself* . . .$]]]$

Now, observe that $Depth_{TP}(nP_1) < Depth_{TP}(nP_2)$ in (42b). Thus, nP_1, a possible binder, is closer to *himself* than nP_2, and hence the Bind-relation in (40b) is blocked by the minimality condition in (39), coupled with the formal restrictions in (41). In this manner, our theory of $M_0 \circ S_0$ effectively reduces the "c-command" requirement on binding to another consequence of minimality (39) (see Rooryck and Vanden Wyngaerd 2011 for a similar approach).

    Note that binding may apply in a long-distance fashion. Thus, it is possible that *every boy* binds *him* in (43), skipping *John*.

(43) [$_{CP}$ *every boy$_i$* thinks that John$_j$ criticized *him$_i$*]

Such cases of long-distance binding do not pose a problem to the idea that $M_0 \circ S_0$ is constrained by the Depth$_\Sigma$-based minimality condition in (39). Recall our hypothesis that 0-Search in service of Bind is a process that first picks out the "bindee," and then seeks to find a "binder." Thus, in (43), 0-Search first picks out *him*, and then tries to find the most prominent element within CP, which is *every boy* (cf. Depth$_{CP}$(*every boy*) < Depth$_{CP}$(*John*)). In this manner, long-distance binding follows as a consequence of unconstrained 0-Search, reaching the bindee *n*P with [uRef] and then finding the most prominent (least embedded) element within a given SO as a binder.[27]

6.5 Merge

Finally, let us turn to Merge, understood here as another instance of $M_0 \circ S_0$(WS). Merge can be regarded as the most basic function of $M_0 \circ S_0$, and its application is the most unconstrained among the various functions of $M_0 \circ S_0$. Indeed, it can freely take any two SOs of any form (lexical or constructed) within WS, α and β, and creates a new SO {α, β}. We take this to mean that the formal restriction on Merge is null.

(44) Formal Restriction on Merge:[28]
     No formal restriction is imposed on α, β.

Now, let us ask what consequence this null restriction may bring to the workings of our generalized minimality condition. Consider the case of IM in (45). Before the application of IM in (45a), an SO X is a proper term of another SO Z, and Z is further embedded in a "root" ("undominated") SO Y ∈ WS. Given this structure, it is possible to internally merge X with Y, as shown in (45b).

(45) a.   b.

This state of affairs can be seen as a natural consequence of unconstrained $M_0 \circ S_0$. Suppose that 0-Search looks through the root SO Y and picks out X first. It then seeks to find the most prominent element within WS in accordance with the minimality condition. Now, any element can satisfy the (null) formal restriction on Merge, and thus every term of Y (including Y itself, as well as Z, X, etc.) is a potential candidate for Merge. However, the minimality condition allows only the highest (least embedded) element among them to be picked out by the application of 0-Search. Y, being a root SO, is one such element, hence 0-Search may pick out X and then Y for 0-Merge, yielding {X, Y}. Note that $Depth_Y(Y) < Depth_Y(Z)$, and hence that Merge(X, Z) is excluded as a minimality violation.

(46) a.   b.

More generally, the proposed minimality condition restricts the possible target of IM to root SOs, since they are the highest (least embedded) SOs.[29] This consequence closely corresponds to the effect of the so-called "Extension Condition" proposed in Chomsky (1995).

(47) Extension Condition (Chomsky 1995: 248, 254):
      Merge and Move (EM and IM in current terms) always apply in the simplest possible form: at the root.

This is a natural consequence of our $Depth_\Sigma$-based minimality, because it holds that root SOs have a privileged status of being the least embedded (most prominent) within WS.

Now, let us see if our account can derive the Extension Condition effect on EM as well.[30] Consider a case of EM in (48), where an LI X drawn from the Lexicon is combined with a root SO Y (lexical or constructed).

(48) a.   b.

Such cases of EM pose no problem to our $Depth_\Sigma$-based minimality, since there is no γ (γ ≠ Y) such that $Depth_\Sigma(\gamma) < Depth_\Sigma(Y)$ for any SO Σ. This account can be naturally generalized to EM of non-lexical (phrasal) SOs. Thus, a root SO X with a proper term W may be externally merged with another root SO Y with a proper term Z, as shown in (49).

(49) a.   b.

Notice that the existence of a proper term W of X does not cause a problem for 0-Search picking out X, Y, because, again, there is no γ (γ ≠ Y) such that $Depth_\Sigma(\gamma) < Depth_\Sigma(Y)$ for any SO Σ. Notice, moreover, that 0-Search cannot pick out X, Z for Merge, since $\text{Depth}_\gamma(Y) < \text{Depth}_\gamma(Z)$ and hence Y stands as an "intervener." Therefore, our Depth_Σ-based minimality predicts that a root SO can only be externally merged with another root SO, which is exactly the effect of the Extension Condition.

In this manner, when coupled with the vacuous formal restriction on Merge, our Depth_Σ-based minimality straightforwardly derives the Extension Condition effect on EM and IM.

6.6 Interim Summary

In this section, we proposed a generalized minimality condition on $M_0 \circ S_0$ in terms of Depth_Σ, summarized in (50).

(50) Minimality Condition on 0-Search (summary):
0-Search may pick up α, β for a linguistic relation R only if
a. α, β meet the formal restrictions on R, and
b. There is no γ ($\gamma \neq \beta$) such that α, γ also meet the formal restrictions on R and $\text{Depth}_\Sigma(\gamma) < \text{Depth}_\Sigma(\beta)$ for some SO Σ.

We showed that this condition can account for various locality conditions imposed on $M_0 \circ S_0$, when coupled with the formal restrictions on the relevant linguistic relations (51)–(54).

(51) Formal Restriction on Merge:
No formal restriction is imposed.

(52) Formal Restrictions on Label:
a. β is a (bundle of) feature(s) (typically an LI), and
b. β is contained in α.

(53) Formal Restrictions on Chain:
a. $\text{Depth}_\Sigma(\alpha) < \text{Depth}_\Sigma(\beta)$ for some SO Σ, and
b. There exists an element γ such that $\gamma \in \alpha$ and $\gamma \in \beta$.

(54) Formal Restrictions on Bind:
a. α has an unvalued referential feature ([uRef]), and
b. β has a referential feature not distinct from α's [uRef].

We may say that our minimality condition in (50) essentially reformulates the intuition behind Rizzi's (1990) "relativized minimality," and incorporates it into the theory of generalized $M_0 \circ S_0$, although this new minimality condition yields a quite different set of empirical consequences. (55) summarizes the empirical generalizations achieved by our minimality condition.

(55) Our generalized minimality condition on 0-Search (50) can capture:
a. the minimal search requirement on labeling
b. the minimality of chain-formation

    c.   the minimal search requirement on Agree(ment)
    d.   the "c-command" requirement on binding
    e.   the effect of Chomsky's (1995) Extension Condition

Notice that these results can be established and unified only under the assumption that various relation-forming operations (labeling, Agree(ment), chain-formation, binding, Merge, etc.) are uniformly characterizable by the notion of generalized $M_0 \circ S_0$.

7 Agree as a Consequence of Labeling?

We have proposed that Agree is unified with other syntactic operations under $M_0 \circ S_0$, and we have introduced the notion of "feature-chain" to capture the agreement relation established between features of LIs. In this section, we will suggest a new and alternative view of agreement, where agreement is reduced to the process of labeling. If this speculation turns out to be correct, the notion of feature-chain could be entirely dispensed with, as suggested below. The discussion on labeling so far has been limited to the form {H, XP}, where H is an LI and XP is not an LI. In order to explore fuller details of the process of labeling, we will shift our focus to the labeling of the form {XP, YP}, where neither XP nor YP is an LI.

Let us now briefly review Chomsky's (2013) labeling algorithm (henceforth, LA). He proposes that under the hypothesis that Merge(α, β) yields a set {α, β} without any label, another independent process operates in order to find the label for the SO through "minimal search." Chomsky's LA works in the following way.

(56) a. Suppose SO = {H, XP}, H a head and XP not a head. Then LA will select H as the label, and the usual procedures of interpretation at the interfaces can proceed.
      b. Suppose SO = {XP, YP}, neither a head. Here minimal search is ambiguous, locating the heads X, Y of XP, YP, respectively. There are, then, two ways in which SO can be labeled: (A) modify SO so that there is only one visible head, or (B) X and Y are identical in a relevant respect, providing the same label, which can be taken as the label of the SO. (Chomsky 2013: 43)

According to Chomsky, there are two ways to label SOs of the form {XP, YP}. One is to move either XP or YP so that there is only one visible head. The other possibility is that X and Y are identical in the sense that they share the same feature via Agree and the shared feature is taken to be the label of {XP, YP}.

Our analysis also faces a similar "ambiguity" problem of labeling with the form {XP, YP}.[31] Let us take an example the case of the labeling of {nP, TP} given in (57), on the assumption that the locus of ϕ-features of a nominal phrase is *n*.

(57)

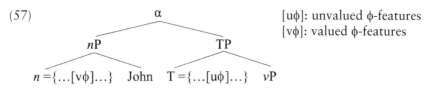

[uϕ]: unvalued ϕ-features
[vϕ]: valued ϕ-features

In (57), n and T are both candidates for the label of α in terms of the Minimality Condition, because $\text{Depth}_{\alpha}(n) = \text{Depth}_{\alpha}(T)$.

We adopt Chomsky's (2013) hypothesis that a (bundle of) feature(s) can be a label as well. Given the definition of the formal restrictions on Label, 0-Search is allowed to pick out features as well as LIs for a label. In (57), [vϕ] of n and [uϕ] of T are not excluded as a candidate for the label of α in terms of the Minimality Condition, because $\text{Depth}_{\alpha}([\text{v}\phi]$ of $n) = \text{Depth}_{\alpha}([\text{u}\phi]$ of T). Thus, the label of α is not determined uniquely.

One possible solution would be to simply adopt Chomsky's idea that the features which undergo Agree(ment) (feature-chain-formation, under our analysis presented in Section 4) are chosen as a label. Under this solution, some preceding, independent application of Agree(ment)/feature-chain-formation (58a) is a necessary condition for ϕ-features to be selected as the label of α, yielding (58b).

(58) a. $M_0 \circ S_0(\text{WS}) = \{T, n\}$: Feature-chain
      b. $M_0 \circ S_0(\text{WS}) = \{\alpha, \phi\}$: Label

This solution is worth pursuing; see Chomsky (2013, 2015a) for discussion. However, we would like to point out that this approach does not explain why Agree(ment)/feature-chain-formation in (58a) happens to play such an important role in labeling (58b). In an attempt to address this problem, we will also suggest an alternative hypothesis below.

Suppose that the interfaces are equipped with the strategy given in (59), whereby given multiple candidates for the label of an SO, the interfaces regard them as being identical in order to satisfy the condition on labeling given in (60), which might be regarded as one of the interface requirements.

(59) Suppose α, β meet the formal restrictions on Label, and there is γ such that α, γ meet the formal restrictions on Label and $\text{Depth}_{\Sigma}(\beta) = \text{Depth}_{\Sigma}(\gamma)$ for some SO Σ. Then β and γ must be regarded as being identical in order for the uniqueness condition on Label to be satisfied.

(60) Uniqueness Condition on Label (cf. Chomsky 2013):
      The label of any SO must be determined uniquely.

Let us see how the label of α in (57) is determined under this hypothesis. [uϕ] of T must be interpreted as having the same value as [vϕ] of n so that [vϕ] of n and [uϕ] of T can be regarded as being identical. The Uniqueness

Condition on Label (60) is thus satisfied by the interface strategy in (59), yielding Label {α, φ}.

(61) $M_0 \circ S_0(WS) = \{\alpha, \phi\}$ 　　　　　　　　　　　　　: Label
　　　　　　　　　　　　　　　　　　　　　　　　　　　　(=(58b))

At PHON, the Label-relation in (61) (or the identification of [uφ] of T and [vφ] of *n* due to (59)) leads to morphological agreement between T and *n*. Under the alternative hypothesis presented here, $M_0 \circ S_0$ does *not* apply to generate feature-chains between features of LIs, but morphological agreement is obtained as a consequence of Label in (61). This analysis not only dispenses with the apparent redundancy in (58a, b), but it may also give a possible explanation for why agreement typically appears in {XP, YP} structures.[32]

　　If the alternative proposal given in (59) is on the right track, agreement should be restricted to the so-called "Spec-head" configuration, which is independently argued by Fukui and Narita (2012) and Narita and Fukui (2016, forthcoming). This is because an unvalued feature and its valued counterpart are regarded as being identical only when they have the same value of Depth$_\Sigma$. However, the literature includes many cases in which agreement appears to take place in the non-Spec-head configuration where a probe asymmetrically c-commands a goal. Reanalyzing such "agreement in-situ" cases including *there*-constructions is what remains to be seen (see, e.g., Section 5 of Hornstein 2009 for relevant discussion).[33,34]

8 Conclusion

In this chapter, we put forward the hypothesis that External/Internal Merge is a composite of the two most primitive operations (i.e., 0-Search and 0-Merge). 0-Search is an operation such that it picks out *n* elements contained in a given domain as an input to linguistic computation. 0-Merge is an operation such that given *n* objects, it forms a set of these objects. Their formulations are repeated as in (62) and (63).

(62) 0-Search (S_0) (a generalized version):
　　　0-Search is an operation such that it picks out *n* elements contained in a given domain as an input to linguistic computation.

(63) 0-Merge (M_0):
　　　0-Merge is an operation such that given *n* objects, it forms a set of these objects (i.e., $M_0(\alpha_1, \ldots, \alpha_n) = \{\alpha_1, \ldots, \alpha_n\}$).

We proposed that Search, which is originally proposed by Kato et al. (2014), is also decomposed into 0-Search and 0-Merge. Labeling is also unified with other syntactic operations in a very natural way. Therefore, all the syntactic operations are unified under $M_0 \circ S_0(WS)$. We also suggested that there seem to be cases where 0-Search/0-Merge applies independently of the other operation, which might give further support for the decomposition approach proposed in this chapter. It was also shown how various locality constraints on Merge, labeling, Agree(ment), chain-formation, and binding are captured in a unified way. Finally, we suggested that Agree(ment) can be alternatively characterized as a consequence of labeling, eliminating an instance of $M_0 \circ S_0 (WS)$ for agreement as a syntactic operation (cf. Hornstein 2009).

If the core proposal in this chapter is essentially correct, we have arrived at the most primitive operations of human language syntax—the composite of which is responsible for a vast array of linguistic computations as well as linguistic relations. Exploring further the nature of these most primitive operations, and how they interact with computational efficiency coupled with the system of interface conditions, we will likely offer significant contributions to our understanding of the basic operations of syntax.

Notes

An earlier version of this chapter was presented at the 88th Annual Meeting of the English Literary Society of Japan held at Kyoto University. We are grateful to the audience for their comments and questions. Part of this research is supported by AMED-CREST and by the Japan Society for the Promotion of Science (Grant-in-Aid for Scientific Research, Scientific Research (A) (General) #23242025, Challenging Exploratory Research #25580095, and Scientific Research (C) #16K02779).

1 It is suggested in Kato et al. (2014: Section 4) that Search could ultimately be reduced to Merge. Next we will suggest a different way of unifying the two operations.
2 Since EM is an instance of $M_0 \circ S_0$ under our proposal, it is assumed here that $M_0 \circ S_0$ in principle can apply at any point of the derivation (see note 9).
3 See also Chomsky (2012: 23), where it is suggested that EM, as well as Internal Merge (IM), involves some kind of search.
4 We assume here that IM can occur not only at phase levels but also at other derivational points (contra Chomsky 2007, 2008, among others). Thus, subject-raising to "Spec-T" is assumed to occur before the phase head C is introduced into the derivation, satisfying the No-Tampering Condition (NTC). See Chomsky (2007, 2008, 2013, 2015a), Epstein et al. (2012), Kato et al. (2014), and Narita (2014) for various proposals to the effect that IM occurs at phase levels while satisfying the NTC.
5 Space limitations prevent us from providing a full review of how Search works. We refer the reader to Kato et al. (2014) for details.
6 Kato et al. (2014) argue that the mechanism of feature valuation must be eliminated if a theory of no-tampering syntax is seriously pursued (see Kato et al. 2014 for details). They instead put forward the following hypothesis:
   (i) When an Agree(ment) relation is established between an unvalued feature and a valued feature, the interface systems access it, so that the unvalued feature will be processed at SEM/PHON in relation to the valued feature. (Kato et al. 2014: 214)
   In this chapter, we also assume that feature valuation does not exist and adopt the hypothesis in (i).
7 It is assumed in Kato et al. (2014) that binding is a sort of agreement (in φ-features or some independent referential feature [Ref]). See also Section 6.4.

8 In this connection, it may be worth noting that Chomsky has recently suggested the possibility that there is no probe in the application of Agree, which should be reduced to some search procedure along with labeling (see Chomsky 2015b).

9 Kato et al. (2014) hypothesize that what initiates Search is all and only elements at phase-edges, but we do not adopt a similar hypothesis for $M_0 \circ S_0$(WS) here. We assume that $M_0 \circ S_0$(WS) can apply at any point of the derivation in principle and its application is not forced by phase-edge elements (see note 2).

10 We will discuss in Section 4 how the outputs of $M_0 \circ S_0$(WS) should be represented. Until then, we will represent them in an informal way as in (10).

11 Here we tentatively assume that subject-T agreement occurs as soon as T is introduced into the derivation (see Kato et al. 2014 for the argument that the mechanism of feature inheritance should be eliminated). An alternative hypothesis is that subject-T agreement occurs after C is introduced into the derivation (as suggested, for example, by Chomsky 2007, 2008, and Richards 2007). Whichever hypothesis may turn out to be correct, the discussion in this chapter will not be affected.

12 Note that $M_0 \circ S_0$(WS) can in principle establish agreement relations not only between a "higher" unvalued feature and a "lower" valued feature (as in traditional theories of Agree; see Chomsky 2000 *et seq.*) but also between a "higher" valued feature and a "lower" unvalued feature (see Baker 2008), and in fact between two valued features or between two unvalued features as well. See, e.g., Pesetsky and Torrego (2001, 2004) for the idea that some valued features are still uninterpretable and in need of probing via Agree(ment). See also note 24.

13 Kato et al. (2014) do not discuss labeling.

14 In Section 6, we will discuss how $M_0 \circ S_0$(WS) picks out a particular element within Σ as its label. We will provide further discussion on the labeling of {XP, YP} structures in Section 7.

15 The tentative assumption here is that labeling occurs every time a new SO is created. Alternatively, Chomsky (2013) suggests that labeling occurs at phase levels. The latter possibility is also compatible with the proposal here.

16 Note that IM and labeling are formally similar to each other, as indicated by (5) and (15). See also Fujita (2009, 2012) for the view that labeling is a special case of IM.

17 But see Section 7, where a view of agreement will be suggested under which the notion of feature-chain could be dropped.

18 Chomsky's (2000) earlier set-based approach to chain is to assume that each occurrence is defined in terms of its sister (not its mother). This approach has a much earlier origin in Chomsky (1955/1975), adapted from Quine's (1940) notion of "occurrence of a variable." Here we adopt Chomsky's (2001) mother-based definition of occurrence, since the sister-based definition is not readily applicable to occurrences of feature-chains. If it turns out, however, that agreement relations need not be captured in terms of feature-chains, as will be suggested in Section 7, the sister-based definition would work equally well for our present purposes.

19 Note that if 0-Search is allowed to pick out no element (or n in the definition of 0-Search can be 0), $M_0 \circ S_0$ can also generate the empty set. Here, we tentatively assume that 0-Search, whose raison d'etre is to pick out something for subsequent linguistic computations—including, crucially, Merge—must pick out at least one element.

20 Moreover, it might be the case that the "arithmetic" (the ability to "count," the concept of natural numbers) is obtained via 0-Merge and 0-Search in the following way: first 0-Merge applies and yields $\varnothing$, which we can call "zero"; then $M_0 \circ S_0$

applies to $\varnothing$ and yields $\{\varnothing\}$, which we can call "one"; and so on (see Fukui 2008 for relevant discussion).

(i) 0-Merge $\to \varnothing = 0$

$M_0{\circ}S_0(0) = \{\varnothing\} = 1$

$M_0{\circ}S_0(1) = \{\{\varnothing\}\} = 2$

$M_0{\circ}S_0(2) = \{\{\{\varnothing\}\}\} = 3$

$\vdots$

21 Similar/related notions are found in Ohta et al. (2013) [Chapter 8, this volume] ("Degree of Merger") and Oka (1993) ("shallowness"). See also Fukui and Narita (2012) and Narita and Fukui (2016, forthcoming).

22 Chomsky (2013) leaves room for cases where a (bundle of) feature(s) smaller than an LI (say a collection of ϕ-features) may participate in labeling. (34) can naturally incorporate such cases as well. See Section 7 for further investigations.

23 This effect may seem attributable to some other factor, such as the "Phase-Impenetrability Condition" (PIC) (Chomsky 2004 *et seq.*). As pointed out by Kato et al. (2014), however, there is good reason to cast doubts on the current formulation of the PIC. These doubts pertain to the clear existence of long-distance (i.e., cross-phasal) dependencies. See Bošković (2007) and references cited therein for ample crosslinguistic examples of long-distance Agree(ment) that clearly violate the PIC. Moreover, binding (say, of pronouns or subject-oriented anaphors) can no doubt apply in a long-distance fashion as well, and thus binding is not constrained by the PIC, either. Our theory of $M_0{\circ}S_0$ eventually has to subsume such cases by assumption, and these considerations support the view that the PIC must be reconsidered.

24 Recall our hypothesis that the application of 0-Search is guided by Full Interpretation, in such a way that the first output of 0-Search α is the element that is in need of establishing certain linguistic relations to another element β. Then, so long as there exists some interface requirement that the higher "probe" feature F of an LI X, valued or not, be related to some lower feature G of an LI Y, 0-Search is allowed to pick out X, Y (the occurrences of F and G, respectively) for (feature-)Chain. See note 12 for relevant discussion, particularly on Pesetsky and Torrego's (2001, 2004) hypothesis that certain valued features are uninterpretable and forced to act as probes for Agree(ment). Further, see Fukui and Narita (2012) and Narita and Fukui (2016, forthcoming) for the hypothesis that in fact *every* formal feature is in need of being mapped to a configuration dubbed "feature-equilibrium" via Agree(ment) plus movement.

25 It is possible for a pronoun with [uRef] to stay unbound in a sentence, as indicated by the grammaticality of *he criticized Mary*, etc. For such cases, we may assume that some contextual variable is located at C and it can optionally assign a contextually determined reference to pronouns with [uRef].

26 Obviously, (41) leaves many cases of binding failures unaccounted for. In order to achieve a full-fledged account of binding, much more than (41) should be supplied to constrain proper Bind-formation (conditions of binding theory, possibility of vehicle change, and so on), which falls beyond the scope of this chapter.

27 A quantifier phrase can bind a variable from a specifier position, as shown in (i) (Reinhart 1987, Kayne 1994).

(i) *Every girl*$_i$'s father thinks that *she*$_i$ is a genius.

One might wonder why such cases of "specifier binding" are not excluded in a way similar to (40b). For this matter, we hypothesize that QR or some equivalent may covertly raise *every girl* to a position where its [Ref] may stand higher than [Ref] of *every girl's father*. More generally, our analysis predicts that "specifier binding" is restricted to quantificational phrases, although we have to leave a fuller exploration of this prediction for future research.

28 We may call the relation established by Merge "Sister-of." See Kato et al. (2016).

29 Note that this also leaves root SOs other than Y to participate in Merge with X. Thus, if there is another root SO W $\in$ WS that is unrelated to Y, then Merge(X, W) is not excluded by our minimality condition in (39), since there is no γ (γ $\neq$X, W) such that $Depth_\Sigma(\gamma)$ < $Depth_\Sigma(W)$ for some SO Σ. This leads to a certain "sideward remerge" or "multidominance" structures as in (i).

(i) **a.**   **b.**

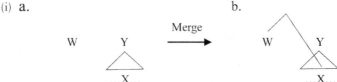

Here, we would like to argue that the two "occurrences" of X cannot be related by Chain, because they cannot satisfy the formal restrictions on Chain in (35): the two occurrences would be {W, X} and {V, X} for some term V of Y, but they cannot satisfy (35a), which requires that $Depth_\Sigma(\{W, X\})$ < $Depth_\Sigma(\{V, X\})$ for some SO Σ. More generally, we argue that sideward remerge or multidominance are severely restricted by the formal restrictions on Chain.

30 Some researchers argue that the Extension Condition can be violated. Thus, Citko (2011) argues that instances of EM violating the Extension Condition yield what she calls "parallel Merge." We will assume with Chomsky (2015b) that "parallel Merge" (which is also sometimes called "multidominance") leads to massive overgeneration, and hence they should be avoided in the theory of UG. See also note 29.

31 In this chapter, we will not discuss how to label the form {XP, YP} where either XP or YP undergoes movement.

32 We assume that the strategy in (59) is restricted to the features that belong to the same type, which correctly excludes undesirable results such as regarding a categorial feature and a tense feature as being identical, for example.

33 If defective intervention effects are characterized as a failure of agreement by the existence of an intervener (cf. Chomsky 2000, among others), they would not be captured under the idea suggested in this section. Bruening (2014) argues, however, that the relevant effects should not be analyzed as a failure of agreement.

34 We leave open how we can capture the minimality effect on Agree(ment) under the alternative approach suggested here, where the notion of feature-chain is dispensed with.

References

Baker, Mark. 2008. *The syntax of agreement and concord.* Cambridge: Cambridge University Press.

Berwick, Robert. 2011. All you need is Merge: Biology, computation, and language from the bottom up. In *The biolinguistic enterprise: New perspectives on the evolution and nature of the human language faculty,* ed. Anna Maria Di Sciullo and Cedric Boeckx, 461–491. Oxford: Oxford University Press.

Boeckx, Cedric. 2009. On the locus of asymmetry in UG. *Catalan Journal of Linguistics* 8: 41–53.

Bošković, Željko. 2007. On the locality and motivation of Move and Agree: An even more minimal theory. *Linguistic Inquiry* 38: 589–644.

Bruening, Benjamin. 2014. Defects of defective intervention. *Linguistic Inquiry* 45: 707–719.

Chomsky, Noam. 1955/1975. *The logical structure of linguistic theory.* Ms. Harvard University, 1955. Published in part in 1975, New York: Plenum.

Chomsky, Noam. 1995. *The minimalist program.* Cambridge, MA: MIT Press.

Chomsky, Noam. 2000. Minimalist inquiries: The framework. In *Step by step: Essays on minimalist syntax in honor of Howard Lasnik*, ed. Roger Martin, David Michaels, and Juan Uriagereka, 89–155. Cambridge, MA: MIT Press.

Chomsky, Noam. 2001. Derivation by phase. In *Ken Hale: A life in language*, ed. Michael Kenstowicz, 1–52. Cambridge, MA: MIT Press.

Chomsky, Noam. 2004. Beyond explanatory adequacy. In *Structures and beyond: The cartography of syntactic structures*, volume 3, ed. Adriana Belletti, 104–131. Oxford: Oxford University Press.

Chomsky, Noam. 2005. Three factors in language design. *Linguistic Inquiry* 36: 1–22.

Chomsky, Noam. 2007. Approaching UG from below. In *Interfaces + recursion = language? Chomsky's minimalism and the view from semantics*, ed. Uli Sauerland and Hans-Martin Gärtner, 1–29. Berlin: Mouton de Gruyter.

Chomsky, Noam. 2008. On phases. In *Foundational issues in linguistic theory: Essays in honor of Jean-Roger Vergnaud*, ed. Robert Freidin, Carlos Otero, and Maria Luisa Zubizarreta, 133–166. Cambridge, MA: MIT Press.

Chomsky, Noam. 2012. Introduction. In *Gengokisoronsyu [Foundations of biolinguistics: Selected writings]*, ed. and trans. Naoki Fukui, 17–26. Tokyo: Iwanami Shoten.

Chomsky, Noam. 2013. Problems of projection. *Lingua* 130: 33–49.

Chomsky, Noam. 2015a. Problems of projection: Extensions. In *Structures, strategies and beyond: Studies in honour of Adriana Belletti*, ed. Elisa Di Domenico, Cornelia Hamann, and Simona Matteini, 3–16. Amsterdam and Philadelphia: John Benjamins.

Chomsky, Noam. 2015b. A discussion with Naoki Fukui and Mihoko Zushi (March 4, 2014). In *The Sophia Lectures (Sophia Linguistica* 64), 69–97. Tokyo: Sophia Linguistic Institute for International Communication, Sophia University.

Citko, Barbara. 2011. *Symmetry in syntax: Merge, Move, and labels.* Cambridge: Cambridge University Press.

Epstein, Samuel David, Hisatsugu Kitahara, and T. Daniel Seely. 2012. Structure building that can't be! In *Ways of structure building*, ed. Myriam Uribe-Etxebarria and Vidal Valmala, 253–270. Oxford: Oxford University Press.

Fujita, Koji. 2009. A prospect for evolutionary adequacy: Merge and the evolution and development of human language. *Biolinguistics* 3: 128–153.

Fujita, Koji. 2012. Toogoenzan-nooryoku to gengo-nooryoku no sinka [The evolution of the capacity for syntactic operations and linguistic competence]. In *Sinkagengogaku no Kootiku: Atarasii Ningenkagaku o Mezasite [Constructing evolutionary linguistics: Toward a new human science]*, ed. Koji Fujita and Kazuo Okanoya, 55–75. Tokyo: Hituzi Syobo.

Fujita, Koji. 2013. Evolutionary problems of projection. Paper read at Tokyo Workshop on Biolinguistics, Sophia University, Tokyo.

Fukui, Naoki. 2008. Gengo no kihon enzan o meguru oboegaki [Some notes on the basic operations of human language]. In *Gengo kenkyu no genzai: Keisiki to imi no intaafeisu [The state of the art in linguistic research: The interface of form and meaning]*, ed. Yoshiaki Kaneko, Akira Kikuchi, Daiko Takahashi, Yoshiki Ogawa, and Etsuro Shima, 1–21. Tokyo: Kaitakusha. [Reprinted in Fukui 2012, *Sin sizen kagaku to site no gengogaku: Seisei bunpoo towa nanika [A new and expanded edition of linguistics as a natural science: What is generative grammar?]*, 241–274. Tokyo: Chikumasyoboo.]

Fukui, Naoki, and Hiroki Narita. 2012. Merge and (a)symmetry. Paper presented at the Kyoto Conference on Biolinguistics, Kyoto University, March 12, 2012. [Revised version published as Chapter 2 of this volume.]

Hornstein, Norbert. 2009. *A theory of syntax: Minimal operations and universal grammar*. Cambridge: Cambridge University Press.

Kato, Takaomi, Masakazu Kuno, Hiroki Narita, Mihoko Zushi, and Naoki Fukui. 2014. Generalized Search and cyclic derivation by phase: A preliminary study. *Sophia Linguistica* 61: 203–222. Tokyo: Sophia Linguistic Institute for International Communication, Sophia University. [Chapter 3, this volume.]

Kato, Takaomi, Hiroki Narita, Hironobu Kasai, Mihoko Zushi, and Naoki Fukui. 2016. On the primitive operations of syntax. In *Advances in biolinguistics: The human language faculty and its biological basis*, ed. Koji Fujita and Cedric Boeckx, 29–45. London and New York: Routledge.

Kayne, Richard S. 1994. *The antisymmetry of syntax*. Cambridge, MA: MIT Press.

Narita, Hiroki. 2014. *Endocentric structuring of projection-free syntax*. Amsterdam and Philadelphia: John Benjamins.

Narita, Hiroki, and Naoki Fukui. 2016. Feature-equilibria in syntax. In *Advances in biolinguistics: The human language faculty and its biological basis*, ed. Koji Fujita and Cedric Boeckx, 9–28. London and New York: Routledge.

Narita, Hiroki, and Naoki Fukui. forthcoming. *Symmetry-driven syntax*. London and New York: Routledge.

Ohta, Shinri, Naoki Fukui, and Kuniyoshi L. Sakai. 2013. Syntactic computation in the human brain: The degree of merger as a key factor. *PLoS One* 8 (2): 1–16. [Chapter 8, this volume.]

Oka, Toshifusa. 1993. Shallowness. *MIT Working Papers in Linguistics* 19: 255–320.

Pesetsky, David, and Esther Torrego. 2001. T-to-C movement: Causes and consequences. In *Ken Hale: A life in language*, ed. Michael Kenstowicz, 355–426. Cambridge, MA: MIT Press.

Pesetsky, David, and Esther Torrego. 2004. Tense, case, and the nature of syntactic categories. In *The syntax of time*, ed. Jacqueline Gueron and Jacqueline Lecarme, 495–538. Cambridge, MA: MIT Press.

Quine, Willard V. O. 1940. *Mathematical logic*. Cambridge, MA: Harvard University Press.

Reinhart, Tanya. 1987. Specifier and operator binding. In *The Representation of (in)definiteness*, ed. Eric J. Reuland and Alice G. B. ter Meulen, 130–167. Cambridge, MA: MIT Press.

Richards, Marc D. 2007. On feature inheritance: An argument from the phase impenetrability condition. *Linguistic Inquiry* 38: 563–572.

Rizzi, Luigi. 1990. *Relativized minimality*. Cambridge, MA: MIT Press.

Rizzi, Luigi. 2006. On the form of chains: Criterial positions and ECP effects. In *Wh-movement: Moving on*, ed. Lisa Lai-Shen Cheng and Norbert Corver, 97–133. Cambridge, MA: MIT Press.

Rooryck, Johan, and Guido Vanden Wyngaerd. 2011. *Dissolving binding theory*. Oxford and New York: Oxford University Press.

Part II
Merge in the Brain

7 The Cortical Dynamics in Building Syntactic Structures of Sentences

An MEG Study in a Minimal-Pair Paradigm

With Kazuki Iijima and Kuniyoshi L. Sakai

Abstract

The importance of abstract syntactic structures and their crucial role in analyzing sentences have long been emphasized in contemporary linguistics, whereas the linear order model, in which next-coming words in a sentence are claimed to be predictable based on lexico-semantic association or statistics alone, has also been proposed and widely assumed. We examined these possibilities with magnetoencephalography (MEG) and measured cortical responses to a verb with either object-verb (OV) or subject-verb (SV) sentence structures, which were tested in a minimal-pair paradigm to compare syntactic and semantic decision tasks. Significant responses to the normal OV sentences were found in the triangular part of the left inferior frontal gyrus (F3t) at 120–140 ms from the verb onset, which were selective for explicit syntactic processing. The earliest left F3t responses can thus be regarded as predictive effects for the syntactic information of the next-coming verb, which cannot be explained by associative memory or statistical factors. Moreover, subsequent responses in the left insula at 150–170 ms were selective for the processing of the OV sentence structure. On the other hand, responses in the left mediofrontal and inferior parietal regions at 240–280 ms were related to syntactic anomaly and verb transitivity, respectively. These results revealed the dynamics of the multiple cortical regions that work in concert to analyze hierarchical syntactic structures and task-related information, further elucidating the top-down processing of each next-coming word, which is crucial during on-line sentence processing.

Keywords: MEG; Sentence processing; Syntax; Semantics; Frontal cortex

Introduction

It has been proposed that syntactic computation, which recursively embeds phrases within phrases to produce hierarchical sentence structures, is a critical component of the uniquely human faculty of language (Chomsky 1995,

Hauser et al. 2002). The initial step toward clarifying such formal computation in systems neuroscience would be distinguishing between syntactic (form) and semantic (content) processes in the brain. Earlier functional imaging studies reported the distinction between syntax and semantics in the left frontal regions (Stromswold et al. 1996, Dapretto and Bookheimer 1999, Kang et al. 1999); however, different words were used for two contrasting conditions, and thus the distinction might be simply explained by lexical factors. To overcome this problem, we have developed a minimal-pair paradigm, in which the same set of words was used to make normal and anomalous sentences for each condition. Using this paradigm, our functional magnetic resonance imaging (fMRI) study has clarified that explicit syntactic processing, as compared with explicit semantic and phonological processing, selectively enhances the activation in the left inferior frontal gyrus (IFG) (Suzuki and Sakai 2003). Using transcranial magnetic stimulation (TMS) in the same minimal-pair paradigm, we have also reported selective priming effects on syntactic decisions when TMS was administered to the left IFG at 150 ms after the verb onset (Sakai et al. 2002). These results suggest the critical involvement of the left IFG in syntactic processing, but more detailed temporal aspects of syntactic processing must be further elucidated.

Recent fMRI and magnetoencephalography (MEG) studies have suggested that the left IFG activation is modulated by various linguistic factors, including grammaticality (Friederici et al. 2000a), the structure of the relative clause (Stromswold et al. 1996, Indefrey et al. 2001a), and canonicity (Röder et al. 2002, Ben-Shachar et al. 2004, Bornkessel et al. 2005, Grewe et al. 2006, Kinno et al. 2008). As a possible common operation among these linguistic computations that are subserved by the left IFG, we propose here that merging a pair of syntactic objects is most crucial, which is indeed a fundamental operation for building syntactic structures of a sentence (Chomsky 1995). In the present MEG study, we thus focus on the structure of a minimal sentence, which is formed by merging a single pair of noun and verb. Figures 7.1a and 7.1b show the basic structures of object-verb (OV) and subject-verb (SV) sentences we used, respectively. In the OV sentence, a noun phrase (NP) with an accusative case particle (Acc) -o is combined with a transitive verb (vt) to form a verb phrase (VP). Note that Japanese is a verb-final language, and that the phonetically null subject (pro-drop) is allowed in Japanese, as well as in Spanish and Italian (Jaeggli 1981). As shown in Figure 7.1a, the presence of an empty category (EC) has been proposed as a pronominal element (*pro*) (Chomsky 1981), which is combined with a VP to form a whole sentence (Saito and Fukui 1998). In the SV sentence, in contrast, an NP with a nominative case particle (Nom) -ga is combined with a VP, and indirectly with an intransitive verb (vi), to form a whole sentence (Figure 7.1b). The following examples clarify the distinction between these basic structures:

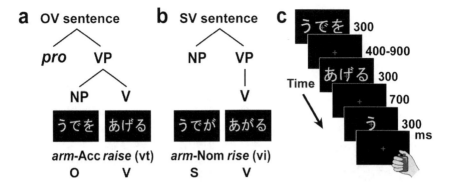

Figure. 7.1 A minimal-pair paradigm with a minimum sentence consisting of a noun phrase and a verb. A pair of sentences including an object-verb (OV) sentence ("*ude-o ag-e-ru*") (a) and a subject-verb (SV) sentence ("*ude-ga ag-ar-u*") (b) is shown. The same noun was used for both sentences; a transitive verb (vt) and an intransitive verb (vi) were morphologically related in a pair (Table 7.1). For both sentence structures, a sentence is divided into a subject (OV: pronominal element, *pro*; SV: noun phrase, NP) and a predicate (verb phrase, VP). The VP is further divided into an NP and V under the OV sentence condition, leading to a more complex structure than the structure under the SV sentence condition. (c) A sin-gle trial of a task. All tasks used the same set of visual stimuli, consisting of an NP, which was either O or S, and a V, which was either vt or vi. One kana letter (e.g., "*u*") was presented after a V to inform participants to initiate a response. For the explanation of a syntactic decision (Syn) task and a semantic decision (Sem) task, see Table 7.2.

(a) *Mary will raise her hand, and John will do so,*
(b) *Mary will rise, and John will do so,*

as "*do so*" substitutes for the entire VP in both sentences.

The distinction between vt and vi, i.e., verb transitivity, is one of the universal aspects of syntactic features, present in English, Japanese, and other natural languages. In Japanese, there are a number of morphologically related vt-vi pairs (e.g., "*ag-e-ru*" and "*ag-ar-u*"; Table 7.1) that are primarily determined by morphosyntax (Shibatani 1990), similar to the distinction of *raise/rise, fell/fall, lay/lie,* and *set/sit* in English. Each pair of OV and SV sentences was prepared with an identical noun in the present study, in which the verbs were also semantically related (Table 7.1). By simply exchanging the verbs within a vt-vi pair, a minimal pair of syntactically normal (N) and anomalous (A) sentences was produced under each of the OV and SV sentence conditions (Table 7.2). This experimental paradigm is one of the novel merits of the present study.

Table 7.1 A list of 48 normal sentences.

Group	Object-Verb (OV) sentence		Subject-Verb (SV) sentence		Translation of SV sentence
	Noun-Acc	vt	Noun-Nom	vi	
I	ude-o	ag-e-ru	ude-ga	ag-ar-u	the arm rises
	kagi-o	kak-e-ru	kagi-ga	kak-ar-u	the lock engages
	waza-o	kim-e-ru	waza-ga	kim-ar-u	techniques succeed
	neji-o	shim-e-ru	neji-ga	shim-ar-u	the screw gets tight
	nuno-o	som-e-ru	nuno-ga	som-ar-u	the cloth gets dyed
	oyu-o	tam-e-ru	oyu-ga	tam-ar-u	hot water collects
	ase-o	tom-e-ru	ase-ga	tom-ar-u	sweat ceases
	ana-o	um-e-ru	ana-ga	um-ar-u	the hole is filled
II	hada-o	ar-as-u	hada-ga	ar-e-ru	someone's skin gets rough
	uso-o	bar-as-u	uso-ga	bar-e-ru	the lie is exposed
	kabi-o	hay-as-u	kabi-ga	ha(y)-e-ru	mold grows
	hara-o	biy-as-u	hara-ga	hi(y)-e-ru	someone's stomach gets cold
	kizu-o	buy-as-u	kizu-ga	hu(y)-e-ru	the number of scratches increases
	ine-o	kar-as-u	ine-ga	kar-e-ru	the rice withers
	nabe-o	kog-as-u	nabe-ga	kog-e-ru	the pot gets burnt
	koe-o	mor-as-u	koe-ga	mor-e-ru	the voices are heard
	maki-o	moy-as-u	maki-ga	mo(y)-e-ru	firewood gets burnt
	kutsu-o	nur-as-u	kutsu-ga	nur-e-ru	the shoes get wet
	netsu-o	sam-as-u	netsu-ga	sam-e-ru	the fever wanes
	yuki-o	tok-as-u	yuki-ga	tok-e-ru	snow melts
	yuka-o	yur-as-u	yuka-ga	yur-e-ru	the floor shakes
III	tsume-o	nob-as-u	tsume-ga	nob-i-ru	someone's nails grow
	zure-o	nao-s-u	zure-ga	nao-r-u	the difference is corrected
	kaji-o	ok-os-u	kaji-ga	ok-i-ru	the fire starts

Morphologically related vt and vi are paired for each row. According to Shibatani (1990), the verbs are divided into three groups: groups I (-e-ru/-ar-u), II (-as-u/-e-ru), and III (others). There was no significant difference regarding the transition probability of adjacent NP and verb between the normal OV and SV sentences, according to either Google (http://www.google.co.jp/) [t(23) = −0.37, P = 0.7 (paired t-test)] or Yahoo (http://www.yahoo.co.jp/) [t(23) = 0.91, P = 0.4].

Based on this minimal-pair paradigm, we tested two main linguistic tasks (Table 7.2): a syntactic decision (Syn) task and a semantic decision (Sem) task. In the Syn task, participants judged whether sentences were syntactically correct or not (Figure 7.1c). To solve the Syn task, the identification of vt or vi, as well as the linguistic knowledge of a syntactic relationship between a case particle and a verb, was required. Moreover, the Syn task could not be solved on the basis of the lexico-semantic relationship between a noun and a verb, because it was always correct for both syntactically normal sentences and anomalous sentences. For the Sem task, we made semantically anomalous sentences by exchanging verbs among the whole set of sentences. Here we focused on the lexico-semantic relationship (selectional

Table 7.2 Examples of sentences used in a minimal-pair paradigm.

Task	Sentence structure	Anomaly	
		Normal (N)	Anomalous (A)
Syntactic decision task (Syn)	OV	"ude-o ag-e-ru" [1] arm-Acc raise (vt)	"ude-o ag-ar-u" [2] arm-Acc rise (vi)
	SV	"ude-ga ag-ar-u" [3] arm-Nom rise (vi)	"ude-ga ag-e-ru" [4] arm-Nom raise (vt)
Semantic decision task (Sem)	OV	"ude-o ag-e-ru" arm-Acc raise (vt)	"ude-o tam-e-ru" arm-Acc collect (vt)
	SV	"ude-ga ag-ar-u" arm-Nom rise (vi)	"ude-ga tam-ar-u" arm-Nom collect (vi)

We designed this minimal-pair paradigm so that anomalous sentences in the Syn task violated the syntactic relationship between a case particle and a verb, whereas anomalous sentences in the Sem task were unacceptable regarding the lexico-semantic relationship between a noun and a verb. The Syn task thus explicitly required syntactic processing but implicitly involved semantic processing, whereas the Sem task explicitly required semantic processing but implicitly involved syntactic processing. We did not use sentences with dual errors, such as "ude-o tam-ar-u" and "ude-ga tam-e-ru". In both tasks, the accusative (Acc) and nominative (Nom) case particles corresponded to OV and SV sentence structures, respectively.

[1] *someone raises one's own arm.*
[2] The sentence is syntactically incorrect since vi does not take an object, whereas the lexico-semantic relationship between the noun and verb is correct as in the case of the normal SV sentence.[3]
[3] *the arm rises* (e.g., while breathing deeply).
[4] The sentence is syntactically incorrect because there is a wrong case particle when compared with the normal OV sentence.[1] Note, however, that the sentence becomes grammatical in a rare case when an arm itself can be regarded as an *animate subject*, e.g., "[robotto-no] ude-ga [iwa-o] ag-e-ru" ([robot's] arm raises [a rock]). Other nouns are clearly *inanimate subjects* in SV sentences (Table 7.1).

restrictions) between a noun and a verb. For example, "*ude*" (gloss: *arm*) and "*ag-e-ru*" (vt, gloss: *raise*) are semantically associated, whereas "*ude*" and "*tam-e-ru*" (vt, gloss: *collect*) have little association. In the Sem task, participants judged whether sentences were semantically normal or anomalous, while the presented sentences were always syntactically correct with respect to the usage of vt and vi.

In our paradigm under the OV sentence condition, the preceding NP case-marked with an Acc predicts the syntactic information of vt *within* the VP, because vt is the only possible verb type within the VP (Figure 7.1a). Since the Syn task involved the judgment on a syntactic relationship between an NP and the next-coming verb, greater predictive effects for the syntactic information of the next-coming verb are expected in the Syn task than the Sem task. Under the SV sentence condition, in contrast, the preceding NP with a Nom specifies a VP, but not vi itself (Figure 7.1b). Thus, the Syn-selective predictive effects would be more distinct under the OV sentence condition than the SV sentence condition.

Besides the structural account of sentence processing, an alternative hypothesis is the linear order model for word sequences, which predicts next-coming words based on lexico-semantic association or statistics, i.e., transition probabilities between single words in a sentence (Cleeremans and McClelland 1991, Elman 1991). Greater predictive effects for the lexico-semantic information of the next-coming verb are expected in the Sem task than the Syn task, irrespective of sentence structures, because the Sem task required the linear order processing of associated words. However, a differential effect on the cortical responses between the normal OV and SV sentences, if any, cannot be explained by such associative memory or statistical factors alone, because there was no difference between the normal OV and SV sentences regarding the transition probability of adjacent NP and verb pairs (Table 7.1). To examine both the syntactic and semantic predictive effects on the cortical responses to *verbs*, we directly compared the Syn and Sem tasks under each of the normal OV and SV sentence conditions. For this purpose, we focused on the cortical responses to a verb from the verb onset. The interval between an NP and a verb was varied, so that the responses to verbs were not confounded with those to NPs (Figure 7.1c). A direct comparison of the Syn and Sem tasks on the normal sentences is also useful for clarifying the predictive effects independently from syntactic or semantic anomaly.

Materials and Methods

Participants

The participants in the present study were 12 native Japanese speakers. Two participants, whose data contained large amount of noise due to eye movement or blinking (noise-free data during – 100–300 ms: 70.3 and 76.2 % each for the excluded participants, 80.9–99.8 % for the others), were discarded from the analysis, leaving a total of 10 participants (2 females, 19–31 years). The 10 participants showed right-handedness (laterality quotients: 86–100) as determined by the Edinburgh inventory (Oldfield 1971). Informed consent was obtained from each participant after the nature and possible consequences of the studies were explained. Approval for these experiments was obtained from the institutional review board of the University of Tokyo, Komaba.

Stimuli

Visual stimuli were presented in yellow letters against a dark background, which were projected from outside of the shield room onto the translucent screen (within the visual angle of 5.7°). For fixation, a red cross was always shown at the center of the screen. Each visual stimulus was either an NP (a noun and a case particle) or verb (Figure 7.1c), which always consisted of three letters (three moras or syllables) spelled in kana letters (Japanese phonograms) to ensure a consistent reading time among words. Each stimulus was presented for 300 ms, and the interstimulus interval (ISI) between an NP and a verb was randomly varied for 400, 500, 600, 700, 800, and 900 ms. One kana letter was also presented 1,000 ms after the verb onset to inform participants to start pushing one of two buttons according to a task instruction. The identity of a kana letter is relevant only in a memory (Mem) task, but we presented a kana letter in the other tasks to keep stimuli identical. The inter-trial interval was randomly varied within the range of ± 10 % at 4 s to reduce any periodical noises. Stimulus presentation and behavioral data collection were controlled using the LabView software and interface (National Instruments, Austin, TX).

Tasks

Each of the Syn and Sem tasks was performed in a separate MEG run. In each run of the Syn task, there were 24 trials and 24 different sentences for each of normal OV, normal SV, syntactically anomalous OV, and syntactically anomalous SV sentences. In each run of the Sem task, there were 24 trials and 24 different sentences for each of normal OV, normal SV, semantically anomalous OV, and semantically anomalous SV sentences. As shown in Table 7.2, verb transitivity (vt, vi) was related to both sentence structure (OV, SV) and anomaly (N, A) in the Syn task, whereas verb transitivity corresponded to sentence structure alone in the Sem task. In this chapter, the normal OV sentence condition, for example, is denoted as (OV, N, vt). In both of the Syn and Sem tasks, a kana letter following a verb was chosen randomly from six letters of the stimuli in the same trial. The Syn task explicitly required syntactic processing but implicitly involved semantic processing, and vice versa in the Sem task.

Two additional tasks regarding the control of reading, evaluation, and memorization processes involved in the Syn and Sem tasks were tested in separate runs: an evaluation (Eva) task and a Mem task. In the Eva task, participants judged whether the impression of each sentence was positive or negative based on pragmatics, while the presented sentences were always normal in terms of syntax and lexico-semantics. For example, "*waza-ga kim-ar-u*" (*techniques succeed*) is positive, and "*hada-ga ar-e-ru*" (*someone's skin gets rough*) is negative. Correct answers in the Eva task were determined by a pilot study performed before the experiments. We used the Eva task for analyzing reaction times (RTs) and task selectivity of cortical responses alone. A kana letter was presented in the same manner as in the Syn and Sem tasks. In each run of the Eva task, there were 24 trials and 12 different sentences for each of positive OV (a half of the 24 normal OV sentences), negative OV (the other half of the 24 normal OV sentences), positive SV (a half of the 24 normal SV sentences), and negative SV (the other half of the 24 normal SV sentences) sentences. In the Mem task, participants judged whether or not a kana letter following a verb *matched* one of the six letters of the normal sentence in the same trial. In contrast to other tasks, the decision in the Mem task was delayed until the presentation of a kana letter. We used the Mem task for analyzing the accuracy and task selectivity of cortical responses alone. In each run of the Mem task, there were 24 trials and 24 different sentences for each of the matched OV, mismatched OV (with sentences identical to those for the matched OV), matched SV, and mismatched SV (with sentences identical to those for the matched SV) sentences. For all participants, four runs were tested for each of these four tasks, in which the orders of tasks, and sentence structures were fully randomized and counterbalanced. Only trials with participants' correct responses were used for analyzing RTs.

MEG Data Acquisition and Analyses

The raw MEG data were acquired with a 160-channel whole-head system (MEGvision, Yokogawa Electric Corporation, Kanazawa-city, Japan), and they were digitized with an on-line bandwidth of 0.3 Hz to 1000 Hz and a sampling rate of 2000 Hz. Using the BESA 5.1 software (MEGIS Software, Munich, Germany), the MEG signals evoked by a verb from – 100 to 300 ms were analyzed, where the signals from – 100 to 0 ms were used as a baseline (Figure 7.2). Only artifact-free trials (peak-to-peak amplitude < 2500 fT) with participants' correct responses were averaged for each condition, and the averaged MEG signals were band-pass filtered in the frequency domain from 2 to 30 Hz to eliminate large eye movement noises. For mapping with the individual brain, high resolution T1-weighted MR images (repetition time, 30 ms; echo time, 8.0 ms; flip angle, 60°; field of view, 256 × 256 mm²; resolution, 1 × 1 × 1 mm³) were acquired using a 1.5-T Scanner (Stratis II, Premium; Hitachi Medical Corporation, Tokyo, Japan). The sensor positions were coregistered to the MR images by aligning the five fiducial markers with their visible locations on the head surface, and final adjustments were completed by using a least-squares fit algorithm (MEG Laboratory, Yokogawa Electric Corporation, Kanazawa-city, Japan). Using the BrainVoyager QX software (Brain Innovation, Maastricht, Netherlands), each individual brain was normalized to the image of the Montreal Neurological Institute (MNI) standard brain, which was already transformed into the Talairach space (Talairach and Tournoux 1988). In order to perform a cortex-based data analysis, the gray and white matter of the transformed standard brain was segmented, and their boundary was then partitioned into 3256 cortical patches with a mean distance of 5.5 mm (Kriegeskorte and Goebel 2001).

For each participant, the MEG signals of each channel were averaged for a bin of 20 ms; the time bin was moved in 10 ms steps over the 100–300 ms period after the presentation of a verb. The distribution of cortical activation underlying the averaged MEG signals was modeled with the minimum norm estimates (MNEs) of currents using BESA 5.1. A current dipole was perpendicularly placed at the center of each cortical patch, approximating

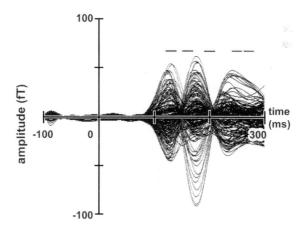

Figure 7.2 The averaged MEG signals for all trials from ten participants, shown for each sensor. The black bars above the waveforms indicate the time windows, where significant responses were observed in the contrasts shown in Table 7.3 and Figures 7.3–7.6.

any spatial distributions of currents on the cortex without assuming particular positions of the dipole sources (Dale and Sereno 1993, Hämäläinen et al. 1993). The current density at each cortical patch was calculated by dividing the current strength by the mean area of the cortical patches. The MNEs of currents without averaging for a bin of 20 ms were also obtained and shown in Figures 7.3–7.6 as the temporal changes of the current density.

Across all participants, a paired t-test on the current density was performed for two contrasting conditions (see the following). The statistical results for each time bin were further corrected for multiple comparisons across the whole cortical patches ($P_{corr} < 0.05$), using a permutation procedure for the current density of two conditions (Karniski et al. 1994, Pantazis et al. 2005). For example, in the comparison between the Syn and Sem tasks, the data of all cortical patches were exchanged between the two tasks in some of the participants. For such a permutation, a maximum t-value was determined among the cortical patches. There were $2^{10} = 1024$ permutations for 10 participants, which produced a reference distribution of t-values for determining the corrected P-values. Correction for multiple comparisons using t-values, each of which is a mean difference normalized by a variance, is superior in sensitivity than that using simple mean differences of the current density (Nichols and Holmes 2002). Note that this method requires no assumption of a normal distribution or of the correlation structure of the data requiring correction (Karniski et al. 1994). The dipoles with statistical significance were identified, each of which was further represented by a sphere with a diameter of 6 mm using ImageJ software (http://rsb.info.nih.gov/ij/). Using the MRIcro software (http://www.mricro.com/), a spatial Gaussian filter was applied to these spheres (full width of half maximum, 8 mm), which were then superimposed onto the transformed standard brain as a statistical parametric map of the cerebral cortex.

Procedures of Identifying Selective Responses

We first compared the tasks under the *normal* sentence conditions, in which *identical* sentences were presented (Table 7.2). To examine any Syn-selective responses, we adopted a two stage procedure with a statistical parametric map (a paired t-test), starting with contrasting the current density in the Syn task and the two control tasks, i.e., Syn − (Eva + Mem) / 2, with a liberal statistical threshold of uncorrected $P < 0.005$. To exclude false positive responses, we then focused on Syn-selective responses, i.e., Syn − Sem, at the level of $P_{corr} < 0.05$. Once Syn-selective responses were found at a particular time bin, a three-way repeated measures analysis of variance (rANOVA), further incorporating the factors of sentence structure and anomaly (Table 7.2), was performed for the cortical patch with a maximum t-value (Table 7.3). To examine any Sem-selective responses, we also started

Table 7.3 A list of statistical analyses.

Paired t-test	rANOVA	Figure
Syn – Sem, (OV, N, vt)	task × sentence structure × anomaly	7.3
Syn, (*OV*, N, *vt*) – (*SV*, N, *vi*)	sentence structure × verb transitivity	7.4
Syn, (*SV*, *A*, vt) – (*OV*, N, vt)	syntactic anomaly × sentence structure	7.5
Syn, (SV, A, *vt*) – (SV, N, *vi*)	verb transitivity × syntactic anomaly	7.6

The italicized factors in each condition for a paired *t*-test are main effects of interest. See the Materials and Methods for each analysis.

with Sem – (Eva + Mem) / 2 (uncorrected $P < 0.005$), and then performed Sem – Syn ($P_{corr} < 0.05$).

We next focused on three factors included in the Syn task: sentence structure (OV, SV), syntactic anomaly (N, A), and verb transitivity (vt, vi; see Table 7.2). To examine any selective responses to these factors, a statistical parametric map (a paired *t*-test) was obtained by contrasting the current density under two conditions ($P_{corr} < 0.05$). For example, with Syn, (*OV*, N, *vt*) – (*SV*, N, *vi*), we examined the effect of sentence structure (OV, SV) or verb transitivity (vt, vi), while syntactic anomaly (N) was held constant (Table 7.3). Once selective responses were found at a particular time bin, a two-way rANOVA was performed for the cortical patch with a maximum *t*-value. In the rANOVA of sentence structure × verb transitivity, the remaining factor of syntactic anomaly (held constant for a paired *t*-test) corresponds to an interaction of two main effects of interest (see the Syn task in Table 7.2). Similarly, Syn, (*SV*, *A*, vt) – (*OV*, N, vt) and Syn, (SV, A, *vt*) – (SV, N, *vi*) were also performed, in which two factors were selected in a cyclic manner (Table 7.3).

Results

Behavioral Data

For each task, behavioral data of accuracy and RTs are shown in Table 7.4. We focused on the normal sentence conditions, in which *identical* normal sentences were presented. Regarding the accuracy for normal sentences, a two-way rANOVA [task (Syn, Sem, Mem) × sentence structure (OV, SV)] showed marginal main effects of task [$F(2, 18) = 3.4, P = 0.055$] and sentence structure [$F(1, 9) = 4.7, P = 0.058$] with a significant interaction [$F(3, 27) = 5.8, P = 0.012$]. By analyzing the accuracy data separately for each sentence structure, paired *t*-tests showed no significant difference in accuracy among the tasks under the normal OV sentence condition ($P > 0.5$). Under the normal SV sentence condition, the accuracy of Syn was significantly higher than Sem [$t(9) = 2.4, P = 0.040$] and Mem [$t(9) = 4.7, P = 0.0011$], and that of Sem was also higher than Mem [$t(9)$ = 2.2, P = 0.054]. Regarding the RTs for normal sentences, a two-way rANOVA [task (Syn, Sem, Eva) × sentence structure (OV, SV)] showed a significant main effect of task [$F(2, 18)$ = 6.9, P = 0.0060] with neither main effect of sentence structure [$F(1, 9)$ = 2.3, P = 0.2] nor interaction [$F(2, 18)$ = 2.1, P = 0.1]. The RTs of Syn were significantly shorter than Eva [OV: $t(9)$ = 2.6, P = 0.028; SV: $t(9)$ = 2.6, P = 0.029]; the RTs of Sem were also significantly shorter than Eva [OV: $t(9)$ = 2.6, P = 0.031; SV: $t(9)$ = 3.1, P = 0.013]. In contrast, there was no significant difference in RTs between Syn and Sem (P > 0.2). These behavioral results indicate that the main linguistic tasks of Syn and Sem were comparable to or easier than the control tasks of Eva and Mem. Therefore, selective responses in Syn or Sem, if any, cannot be explained by task difficulty.

We next focused on the effects of sentence structure and syntactic anomaly within the Syn task (Table 7.4). Regarding the accuracy of Syn, a two-way rANOVA [sentence structure (OV, SV) × syntactic anomaly (N, A)] showed a significant main effect of sentence structure [$F(1, 9)$ = 6.1, P = 0.036; SV > OV] and a marginal main effect of syntactic anomaly

Table 7.4 Behavioral data for each task.

Task	Sentence structure	Anomaly	
		Normal (N)	Anomalous (A)
Syntactic decision task (Syn)	OV	92.9 ±1.4 575 ± 64	92.5 ± 1.9 611 ± 63
	SV	96.7 ± 1.1 572 ± 70	93.1 ± 1.9 609 ± 64
Semantic decision task (Sem)	OV	92.5 ± 2.1 589 ± 67	95.7 ± 1.3 601 ± 71
	SV	94.5 ± 1.6 565 ± 69	95.8 ± 1.2 598 ± 70
Evaluation task (Eva)	OV	89.6 ± 2.4 630 ± 63	
	SV	88.7 ± 2.0 625 ± 67	
Memory task (Mem)	OV	92.3 ± 1.3 789 ± 33	
	SV	91.5 ± 1.6 780 ± 32	

Data are shown as mean ± SEM. Upper row, accuracy (%); lower row, RTs (ms).

$[F(1, 9) = 4.8, P = 0.057; N > A]$ with no interaction $[F(1, 9) = 3.7, P = 0.09]$. Paired *t*-tests further revealed that the accuracy under the normal SV sentence condition (SV, N, vi) was significantly higher than the other conditions $[(OV, N, vt): t(9) = 3.0, P = 0.015; (OV, A, vi): t(9) = 2.9, P = 0.016; (SV, A, vt): t(9) = 2.5, P = 0.032]$, whereas there was no other significant difference in the accuracy $(P > 0.5)$. This result indicates that the normal SV sentence condition was the least demanding among the four conditions. Regarding the RTs of Syn, there was a significant main effect of syntactic anomaly $[F(1, 9) = 10, P = 0.011; A > N]$ with neither main effect of sentence structure $[F(1, 9) = 0.13, P = 0.7]$ nor interaction $[F(1, 9) < 0.1, P > 0.9]$. Paired *t*-tests showed that the RTs under the anomalous OV sentence condition (OV, A, vi) were significantly longer than the normal sentence conditions $[(OV, N, vt): t(9) = 3.3, P = 0.0087; (SV, N, vi): t(9) = 2.5, P = 0.032]$; the RTs under the anomalous SV sentence condition (SV, A, vt) were also significantly longer than the normal sentence conditions $[(OV, N, vt): t(9) = 3.0, P = 0.016; (SV, N, vi): t(9) = 2.5, P = 0.036]$. These results indicate that the anomalous OV and SV sentences were more demanding than the normal sentences. The longer RTs for the anomalous sentences, which are consistent with our previous studies using the same paradigm (Sakai et al. 2002, Suzuki and Sakai 2003), may be due to the reanalysis of anomalous sentences.

Cortical Responses to Task

First, we focused on the task effects by comparing the four tasks under the *normal* sentence conditions, in which *identical* sentences were presented (Table 7.2). In order to clarify selective cortical responses to the explicit syntactic processing, we examined a statistical parametric map with a paired *t*-test for directly contrasting the Syn and Sem tasks (Syn – Sem), first under the normal OV sentence condition (OV, N, vt). We found the earliest Syn-selective responses in the left pars triangularis of the IFG (F3t) [Talairach coordinates, $(x, y, z) = (-47, 35, 9)$; Brodmann's area (BA) 45; $P_{corr} = 0.025$] at 120–140 ms after the verb onset (Figure 7.3a). The temporal changes in this region also revealed enhanced Syn-selective responses, which started to rise as early as 110 ms (Figure 7.3b).

Paired *t*-tests on the current density of this region under the normal OV sentence condition showed that the responses to Syn were significantly larger than those to Sem $[t(9) = 7.5, P < 0.0001]$, Eva $[t(9) = 3.4, P = 0.0083]$, and Mem $[t(9) = 3.2, P = 0.010]$ (Figure 7.3c). On the other hand, there was no significant difference among all task pairs under the normal SV sentence condition $(P > 0.1)$. We further tested the task effect, additionally incorporating the factors of sentence structure and anomaly shown in Table 7.2. A three-way rANOVA [task (Syn, Sem) × sentence structure (OV, SV) × anomaly (N, A)] showed a significant main effect of task $[F(1, 9) = 7.2,$

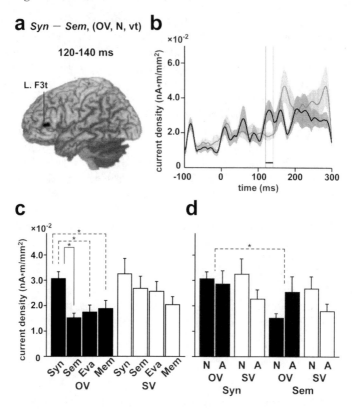

Figure 7.3 (**Plate 1**). Selective responses to the Syn task. (a) The cortical responses to Syn and Sem were compared with a paired *t*-test under the normal OV sentence condition, and mapped on the transformed standard brain ($P_{corr} < 0.05$). Note the significant responses in the left (L.) F3t. (b) The averaged temporal changes of the current density for the left F3t. The black and gray lines correspond to the current density for Syn, (OV, N, vt) and Sem, (OV, N, vt), respectively. Their SEMs are shown as shaded bands ($n = 10$). The interval which resulted in significant differences is shown with a bar. (c) Histograms for the current density (mean ± SEM) under each normal sentence condition for the left F3t. (d) Histograms for the current density, including the anomalous sentences for Syn and Sem. Filled and open bars denote the current density under the OV and SV sentence conditions, respectively. The solid and dashed lines with aster-isks above pairs of bars correspond to the significant contrasts used for the statistical parametric maps and other significant contrasts ($P < 0.05$, paired *t*-test), respectively.

$P = 0.025$; Syn > Sem] with neither other main effects [sentence structure: $F(1, 9) < 0.1$, $P > 0.9$; anomaly: $F(1, 9) = 2.5$, $P = 0.2$] nor interactions ($P > 0.1$) (Figure 7.3d). Even if the responses to the normal and anoma-lous sentences were averaged together under the OV sentence condition, the responses to Syn were significantly larger than those to Sem [$t(9) = 2.6$, $P = 0.029$]. Moreover, the responses to Sem under the normal OV sentence condition were significantly smaller than those to Syn under both normal and anomalous OV sentence conditions (i.e., with vt and vi) [Syn, (OV, N, vt): $t(9) = 7.5$, $P < 0.0001$; Syn, (OV, A, vi): $t(9) = 2.4$, $P = 0.042$]. Therefore, the responses of the left F3t were Syn-selective under the OV sentence condition, irrespective of syntactic anomaly or verb transitivity.

During the intervals of 100–120 and 140–300 ms, there was no significant Syn-selective response under the normal OV sentence condition. Regarding the normal SV sentence condition, there was no significant Syn-selective response during the entire searched interval of 100–300 ms. We also confirmed that there was no significant response in *Sem – Syn* under both the normal OV and SV sentence conditions during 100–300 ms. In Figure 7.3b, Sem might have enhanced the responses in the left F3t during 150–200 ms, but neither Sem – (Eva + Mem) / 2 (uncorrected $P > 0.08$) nor Sem – Syn ($P_{corr} > 0.17$) reached significance under the normal OV sentence condition.

Cortical Responses to Sentence Structure or Verb Transitivity

Following the elucidation of the Syn-selective responses, we examined the effect of sentence structure (OV, SV) or verb transitivity (vt, vi), while syntactic anomaly (N) was held constant (Table 7.3). In Syn, (OV, N, vt) – (SV, N, vi), we found significant responses in the left insula [(–33, 8, 19); $P_{corr} = 0.031$] at 150–170 ms (Figure 7.4a). The temporal changes in this region showed enhanced responses to the normal OV sentences, which started to rise around 130 ms (Figure 7.4b). Next we performed a two-way rANOVA [sentence structure × verb transitivity] on the current density of this region, in which the remaining factor of anomaly corresponded to an interaction (Table 7.3). This analysis revealed a significant main effect of sentence structure [$F(1, 9) = 13$, $P = 0.0054$; OV > SV] with neither main effect of verb transitivity [$F(1, 9) = 4.0$, $P = 0.08$] nor interaction [$F(1, 9) = 0.39$, $P = 0.6$] (Figure 7.4c). Paired t-tests showed that the responses to the SV sentences with vi were significantly smaller than those to the OV sentences [(OV, N, vt): $t(9) = 6.7$, $P < 0.0001$; (OV, A, vi): $t(9) = 2.6$, $P = 0.029$].

In the same contrast, significant responses were also present in the left supramarginal gyrus (SMG) [(–59, –23, 23); BA 40; $P_{corr} = 0.025$] at 190–210 (Figure 7.4d). The temporal changes in this region showed enhanced responses to the normal OV sentences, which started to rise around 150 ms (Figure 7.4e). A two-way rANOVA on the current density of this region showed neither main effects [sentence structure: $F(1, 9) = 2.5$, $P = 0.2$; verb transitivity: $F(1, 9) = 3.0$, $P = 0.1$] nor interaction [$F(1, 9) = 1.0$, $P = 0.3$] (Figure 7.4f). Paired t-tests showed that the responses to the SV sentences with vi were significantly smaller than those to the OV sentences [(OV,

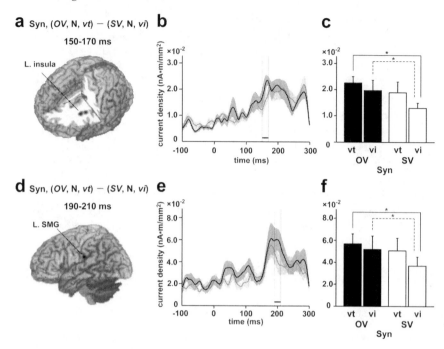

Figure 7.4 (**Plate 2**). Cortical responses to sentence structure or verb transitivity. (a, d) The OV and SV sentence conditions were compared within the Syn task (Table 7.3). Note the significant responses in the left insula and left supramarginal gyrus (SMG). (b, e) The averaged temporal changes of the current density for the left insula and left SMG, respectively. The black and gray lines correspond to the current density for Syn, (OV, N, vt) and (SV, N, vi), respectively. (c, f) Histograms for the current density under each condition are shown for the left insula and the left SMG. Filled and open bars denote the current density under the OV and SV sentence conditions, respectively.

N, vt): $t(9)$ = 7.7, P < 0.0001; (OV, A, vi): $t(9)$ = 2.4, P = 0.041]. During 100–300 ms, we confirmed that there was no significant response in the following contrasts, in which syntactic anomaly was held constant: Syn, (SV, N, vi) – (OV, N, vt); Syn, (OV, A, vi) – (SV, A, vt); and Syn, (SV, A, vt) – (OV, A, vi).

Cortical Responses to Syntactic Anomaly or Sentence Structure

We next examined the effect of syntactic anomaly (A, N) or sentence structure (SV, OV), while verb transitivity (vt) was held constant (Table 7.3). In Syn, (SV, A, vt) – (OV, N, vt), significant responses were observed in the left anterior cingulate cortex (ACC) [(–7, 41, 4); BA 32; P_{corr} = 0.016] and

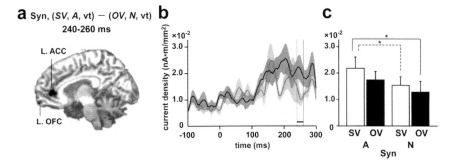

Figure 7.5 (**Plate 3**). Cortical responses to syntactic anomaly or sentence structure. (a) The anomalous and normal sentence conditions were compared within the Syn task (Table 7.3). A parasagittal section ($x = -7$) is shown for the left anterior cingulate cortex (ACC) and left orbitofrontal cortex (OFC). (b) The averaged temporal changes of the current density for the left ACC. The black and gray lines correspond to the current density for Syn, (SV, A, vt) and (OV, N, vt), respectively. (c) Histograms for the current density under each condition are shown for the left ACC; the left OFC showed a similar tendency.

orbitofrontal cortex (OFC) [(−4, 56, −9); BA 10; P_{corr} = 0.020] at 240–260 ms (Figure 7.5a). In Figure 7.5b, Syn, (SV, A, vt) might have also enhanced the responses in the left ACC during 170–220 ms, but the same contrast did not reach significance (P_{corr} > 0.19). A two-way rANOVA [syntactic anomaly × sentence structure] on the current density of the left ACC at 240–260 ms revealed significant main effects of syntactic anomaly [$F(1, 9) = 23$, $P = 0.0010$; A > N] and sentence structure [$F(1, 9) = 6.9$, $P = 0.028$; SV > OV] with no interaction [$F(1, 9) = 0.14$, $P = 0.7$] (Figure 7.5c). Paired t-tests showed that the responses to the anomalous SV sentences were significantly larger than those to the normal sentences [(OV, N, vt): $t(9) = 8.1$, $P < 0.0001$; (SV, N, vi): $t(9) = 4.1$, $P = 0.0028$]. During 100–300 ms, we confirmed that there was no significant response in the following contrasts, in which verb transitivity was held constant: Syn, (OV, N, vt) − (SV, A, vt); Syn, (OV, A, vi) − (SV, N, vi); and Syn, (SV, N, vi) − (OV, A, vi).

Cortical Responses to Verb Transitivity or Syntactic Anomaly

Finally, we examined the effect of verb transitivity (vt, vi) or syntactic anomaly (A, N), while sentence structure (SV) was held constant (Table 7.3). In Syn, (SV, A, vt) − (SV, N, vi), significant responses were observed in the left inferior parietal lobule (IPL) [(−20, −60, 45); BA 7; P_{corr} = 0.032] at 260–280 ms (Figure 7.6a). The temporal changes in this region showed distinct differences between two SV sentence conditions (Figure 7.6b). A two-way

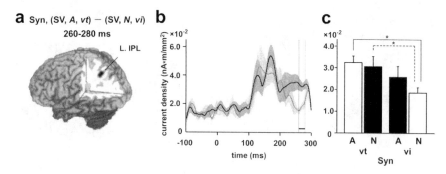

Figure 7.6 (**Plate 4**). Cortical responses to verb transitivity or syntactic anomaly. (a) The vt and vi sentence conditions were compared within the Syn task (Table 7.3). Note the significant responses in the left inferior parietal lobule (IPL). (b) The averaged temporal changes of the current density for the left IPL. The black and gray lines correspond to the current density for Syn, (SV, A, vt) and (SV, N, vi), respectively. (c) Histograms for the current density under each condition are shown for the left IPL.

rANOVA [verb transitivity × syntactic anomaly] on the current density of this region revealed a significant main effect of verb transitivity [$F(1, 9) = 8.7, P = 0.016$] with neither main effect of syntactic anomaly [$F(1, 9) = 3.1, P = 0.1$] nor interaction [$F(1, 9) = 1.3, P = 0.3$] (Figure 7.6c). Paired *t*-tests showed that the responses to the normal sentences with vi were significantly smaller than those to the sentences with vt [(SV, A, vt): $t(9) = 6.5$, $P = 0.0001$; (OV, N, vt): $t(9) = 3.0$, $P = 0.014$]. During 100–300 ms, we confirmed that there was no significant response in the following contrasts, in which sentence structure was held constant: Syn, (SV, N, vi) – (SV, A, vt); Syn, (OV, N, vt) – (OV, A, vi); and Syn, (OV, A, vi) – (OV, N, vt). These results further clarified the specific temporal dynamics of cortical responses selective for sentence structure, syntactic anomaly, and verb transitivity, all of which were included in the Syn task.

Discussion

The present study revealed the dynamics of the multiple cortical regions that are involved in the analysis of hierarchical syntactic structures and task-related information. The Syn-selective responses to the OV sentences suggest that the left F3t may be critically involved in building sentence structures of a sentence as early as 120 ms from the verb onset (Figure 7.3). Moreover, we found selective responses to the three factors included in the Syn task: sentence structure, syntactic anomaly, and verb transitivity. Subsequent responses in the left insula at 150–170 ms were selective for the processing of the OV sentence structure (Figure 7.4). On the other hand, responses in the left mediofrontal and inferior parietal regions at 240–280 ms were related to syntactic anomaly and verb transitivity, respectively (Figures 7.5 and 7.6). Taken together, these results support the account of sentence processing proposed in contemporary linguistics, rather than the linear order model for word sequences.

Cortical Responses to the Syn Task

The direct comparison between the Syn and Sem tasks revealed that the OV sentences evoked selective responses to explicit syntactic processing in the left F3t. The syntax-selective activation of the opercular and triangular parts of the left IFG (F3op/F3t), which is a putative grammar center (Sakai 2005), has been reported by our previous study with a minimal-pair paradigm (Suzuki and Sakai 2003), as well as by other studies (Stromswold et al. 1996, Dapretto and Bookheimer 1999, Kang et al. 1999, Embick et al. 2000, Hashimoto and Sakai 2002). The present study further demonstrated that the responses of the left F3t are selectively modulated by explicit syntactic processing as early as 120–140 ms. Cortical responses to visual words in this time window are often regarded as representing a pre-lexical process, as shown by lexical tasks (Helenius et al. 1998, Pylkkänen and Marantz 2003). However, in our paradigm under the OV sentence condition, the preceding NP with an Acc already specifies the syntactic information of vt within the VP (Figure 7.1a, see the Introduction). The Syn-selective responses of the left F3t can thus be regarded as predictive effects for the syntactic information of the next-coming verb. Under the OV sentence condition of our previous TMS study, we have reported the priming effects on syntactic decisions, when TMS was administered to the left F3op/F3t 150 ms after the verb onset (Sakai et al. 2002). The critical spatio-temporal window of the TMS study is thus consistent with that of the present study, namely, the left F3t and 120–140 ms.

Cortical Responses to Sentence Structure

The activation of the left insula, as well as the adjacent frontal operculum, has been reported in previous fMRI studies focusing on syntactic decision (Friederici et al. 2003, Newman et al. 2003, Suzuki and Sakai 2003, Tatsuno and Sakai 2005, Friederici et al. 2006), and in those focusing on sentence comprehension (Homae et al. 2002). In the present study, the selective responses to the OV sentence structures in the left insula may reflect the processing of more complex hierarchical structure of the OV sentences (Figure 7.1a), which is consistent with the behavioral results. On the other hand, the left SMG has been implicated in lexical processing (Corina et al. 2005), the activation of which was enhanced more by vt than vi in a lexical decision task (Thompson et al. 2007). In the present study, the responses in the left SMG, showing selectivity to the OV sentences with vt, may reflect the processing of more detailed lexical information for vt.

Cortical Responses to Syntactic Anomaly and Sentence Structure

As shown by the behavioral data, the syntactically anomalous sentences were more demanding than the normal sentences. Previous studies have suggested that the ACC and OFC are involved in the process of monitoring and choosing between decision options when the outcomes of those decisions are uncertain or conflicting (Bush et al. 2000, O'Doherty et al. 2001, Botvinick et al., 2004, Walton et al. 2004). The effects of syntactic anomaly in the ACC and OFC are consistent with these reports, in that this monitoring process involves an error detection, reanalysis, and correction as in our case of syntactically anomalous sentences, especially for anomalous SV sentences with inanimate subjects and vt (Table 7.2). On the other hand, it has been reported that the event-related potentials (ERPs) at 100–300 ms, known as early left anterior negativity (ELAN), showed selectivity to the syntactic anomaly, reflecting early phrase structure building processes (Friederici et al. 1993, Hahne and Friederici 1999). Using MEG, the generators of the ELAN were suggested to be localized in the inferior frontal and anterior temporal cortices (Friederici et al. 2000b), which were selected *a priori* as the seed points. It is possible that the left ACC and/or OFC, which showed greater responses under the syntactic anomalous conditions (Figure 7.5b), also contribute to the ELAN.

Cortical Responses to Verb Transitivity

It has been suggested that a lateral region of the IPL [MNI coordinates, (–44, –54, 46)] is critical for vocabulary knowledge (Lee et al. 2007), which may be related to the effect of verb transitivity observed here, i.e., increased responses to the sentences with vt. It is also possible that the decreased responses to the sentences with vi reflected simpler lexical processing with a single argument of a subject, consistent with the behavioral data, in which the condition (SV, N, vi) was the least demanding.

Conclusions

Using MEG with the minimal-pair paradigm to compare the Syn and Sem tasks, we found that the responses to the normal OV sentences in the left F3t at 120–140 ms were selective for explicit syntactic processing. The earliest left F3t responses can thus be regarded as predictive effects for the syntactic information of the next-coming verb, which cannot be explained by associative memory or statistical factors. Moreover, the selective responses to the OV sentence structures in the left insula at 150–170 ms may reflect the processing of more complex hierarchical structure of the OV sentences.

The responses in the left SMG at 190–210 ms, showing selectivity to the OV sentences with vt, may reflect the processing of more detailed lexical information for vt. On the other hand, the responses in the left ACC and left OFC at 240–260 ms were related to syntactic anomaly, reflecting an error detection, reanalysis, and correction. The responses in the left IPL at 260–280 ms were related to verb transitivity, probably reflecting lexical processing. These results revealed the dynamics of the multiple cortical regions that work in concert to analyze hierarchical syntactic structures and task-related information, further elucidating the top-down syntactic processing that is crucial during on-line sentence processing.

Acknowledgments

We thank M. Koizumi, T. Yasui, and F. Tani for their helpful discussion, N. Saeki and N. Komoro for their technical assistance, and S. Matsukura and H. Matsuda for their administrative assistance. This work was supported in part by a Core Research of Evolutional Science and Technology (CREST) grant from the Japan Science and Technology Agency (JST) and by a Grant-in-Aid for Scientific Research on Priority Areas ("Higher-Order Brain Functions," 17022013) from the Ministry of Education, Culture, Sports, Science, and Technology of Japan.

References

Ben-Shachar, Michal, Dafna Palti, and Yosef Grodzinsky. 2004. Neural correlates of syntactic movement: Converging evidence from two fMRI experiments. *NeuroImage* 21: 1320–1336.

Bornkessel, Ina, Stefan Zysset, Angela D. Friederici, D. Yves von Cramon, and Matthias Schlesewsky. 2005. Who did what to whom? The neural basis of argument hierarchies during language comprehension. *NeuroImage* 26: 221–233.

Botvinick, Mattew M., Jonathan D. Cohen, and Cameron S. Carter. 2004. Conflict monitoring and anterior cingulate cortex: An update. *Trends in Cognitive Science* 8: 539–546.

Bush, George, Phan Luu, and Michael I. Posner. 2000. Cognitive and emotional influences in anterior cingulate cortex. *Trends in Cognitive Science* 4: 215–222.

Chomsky, Noam. 1981. *Lectures on government and binding: The Pisa lectures.* Dordrecht: Foris.

Chomsky, Noam. 1995. *The minimalist program.* Cambridge, MA: MIT Press.

Cleeremans, Axel, and James L. McClelland. 1991. Learning the structure of event sequences. *Journal of Experimental Psychology* 120: 235–253.

Corina, David P., Erin K. Gibson, Richard Martin, Andrew Poliakov, James Brinkley, and George A. Ojemann. 2005. Dissociation of action and object naming: Evidence from cortical stimulation mapping. *Human Brain Mapping* 24: 1–10.

Dale, Anders M., and Martin I. Sereno. 1993. Improved localization of cortical activity by combining EEG and MEG with MRI cortical surface reconstruction: A linear approach. *Journal of Cognitive Neuroscience* 5: 162–176.

Dapretto, Mirella, and Susan Y. Bookheimer. 1999. Form and content: Dissociating syntax and semantics in sentence comprehension. *Neuron* 24: 427–432.

Elman, Jeffrey L. 1991. Distributed representations, simple recurrent networks, and grammatical structure. *Machine Learning* 7: 195–225.

Embick, David, Alec Marantz, Yasushi Miyashita, Wayne O'Neil, and Kuniyoshi L. Sakai. 2000. A syntactic specialization for Broca's area. *Proceedings of the National Academy of Sciences of the United States of America* 97: 6150–6154.

Friederici, Angela D., Christian J. Fiebach, Matthias Schlesewsky, Ina D. Bornkessel, and D. Yves von Cramon. 2006. Processing linguistic complexity and grammaticality in the left frontal cortex. *Cerebral Cortex* 16: 1709–1717.

Friederici, Angela D., Bertram Opitz, and D. Yves von Cramon. 2000a. Segregating semantic and syntactic aspects of processing in the human brain: An fMRI investigation of different word types. *Cerebral Cortex* 10: 698–705.

Friederici, Angela D., Erdmut Pfeifer, and Anja Hahne. 1993. Event-related brain potentials during natural speech processing: Effects of semantic, morphological and syntactic violations. *Cognitive Brain Research* 1: 183–192.

Friederici, Angela D., Shirley-Ann Rüschemeyer, Anja Hahne, and Christian J. Fiebach. 2003. The role of left inferior frontal and superior temporal cortex in sentence comprehension: Localizing syntactic and semantic processes. *Cerebral Cortex* 13: 170–177.

Friederici, Angela D., Yunhua Wang, Christoph S. Herrmann, Burkhard Maess, and Ulrich Oertel. 2000b. Localization of early syntactic processes in frontal and temporal cortical areas: A magnetoencephalographic study. *Human Brain Mapping* 11: 1–11.

Grewe, Tanja, Ina Bornkessel, Stefan Zysset, Richard Wiese, D. Yves von Cramon, Matthias Schlesewsky. 2006. Linguistic prominence and Broca's area: The influence of animacy as a linearization principle. *NeuroImage* 32: 1395–1402.

Hahne, Anja, and Angela D. Friederici. 1999. Electrophysiological evidence for two steps in syntactic analysis: Early automatic and late controlled processes. *Journal of Cognitive Neuroscience* 11: 194–205.

Hämäläinen, Matti, Riitta Hari, Risto J. Ilmoniemi, Jukka Knuutila, and Olli V. Lounasmaa. 1993. Magnetoencephalography: Theory, instrumentation, and applications to noninvasive studies of the working human brain. *Reviews of Modern Physics* 65: 413–497.

Hashimoto, Ryuichiro, and Kuniyoshi L. Sakai. 2002. Specialization in the left prefrontal cortex for sentence comprehension. *Neuron* 35: 589–597.

Hauser, Mark D., Noam Chomsky, and W. Tecumseh Fitch. 2002. The faculty of language: What is it, who has it, and how did it evolve? *Science* 298: 1569–1579.

Helenius, Päivi, Riitta Salmelin, Elisabet Service, and John F. Connolly. 1998. Distinct time courses of word and context comprehension in the left temporal cortex. *Brain* 121: 1133–1142.

Homae, Fumitaka, Ryuichiro Hashimoto, Kyoichi Nakajima, Yasushi Miyashita, and Kuniyoshi L. Sakai. 2002. From perception to sentence comprehension: The convergence of auditory and visual information of language in the left inferior frontal cortex. *NeuroImage* 16: 883–900.

Indefrey, Peter, Colin M. Brown, Frauke Hellwig, Katrin Amunts, Hans Herzog, Rüdiger J. Seitz, and Peter Hagoort. 2001a. A neural correlate of syntactic encoding during speech production. *Proceedings of the National Academy of Sciences of the United States of America* 98: 5933–5936.

Jaeggli, Osvaldo. 1981. *Topics in Romance syntax*. Dordrecht: Foris.

Kang, A. Min, R. Todd Constable, John C. Gore, and Sergey Avrutin. 1999. An event-related fMRI study of implicit phrase-level syntactic and semantic processing. *NeuroImage* 10: 555–561.

Karniski, Walt, R. Clifford Blair, and Arthur David Snider. 1994. An exact statistical method for comparing topographic maps, with any number of subjects and electrodes. *Brain Topography* 6: 203–210.

Kinno, Ryuta, Mitsuru Kawamura, Seiji Shioda, and Kuniyoshi L. Sakai. 2008. Neural correlates of noncanonical syntactic processing revealed by a picture-sentence matching task. *Human Brain Mapping* 29: 1015–1027.

Kriegeskorte, Nikolaus, and Rainer Goebel. 2001. An efficient algorithm for topologically correct segmentation of the cortical sheet in anatomical MR volumes. *NeuroImage* 14: 329–346.

Lee, Hwee Ling, Joseph T. Devlin, Clare Shakeshaft, Lauren H. Stewart, Amanda Brennan, Jen Glensman, Katherine Pitcher, Jenny Crinion, Andrea Mechelli, Richard S. J. Frackowiak, David W. Green, and Cathy J. Price. 2007. Anatomical traces of vocabulary acquisition in the adolescent brain. *The Journal of Neuroscience* 27: 1184–1189.

Newman, Sharlene D., Marcel Adam Just, Timothy A. Keller, Jennifer Roth, and Patricia A. Carpenter. 2003. Differential effects of syntactic and semantic processing on the subregions of Broca's area. *Cognitive Brain Research* 16: 297–307.

Nichols, Thomas E., and Andrew P. Holmes. 2002. Nonparametric permutation tests for functional neuroimaging: A primer with examples. *Human Brain Mapping* 15: 1–25.

O'Doherty, John, Morten L. Kringelbach, Edmund T. Rolls, Julia Hornak, and Caroline Andrews. 2001. Abstract reward and punishment representations in the human orbitofrontal cortex. *Nature Neuroscience* 4: 95–102.

Oldfield, Richard Charles. 1971. The assessment and analysis of handedness: The Edinburgh inventory. *Neuropsychologia* 9: 97–113.

Pantazis, Dimitrios, Thomas E. Nichols, Sylvain Baillet, and Richard M. Leahy. 2005. A comparison of random field theory and permutation methods for the statistical analysis of MEG data. *NeuroImage* 25: 383–394.

Pylkkänen, Liina, and Alec Marantz. 2003. Tracking the time course of word recognition with MEG. *Trends in Cognitive Science* 7: 187–189.

Röder, Brigitte, Oliver Stock, Helen Neville, Siegfried Bien, and Frank Rösler. 2002. Brain activation modulated by the comprehension of normal and pseudo-word sentences of different processing demands: A functional magnetic resonance imaging study. *NeuroImage* 15: 1003–1014.

Saito, Mamoru, and Naoki Fukui. 1998. Order in phrase structure and movement. *Linguistic Inquiry* 29: 439–474. [Reprinted in *Theoretical comparative syntax: Studies in macroparameters*, Naoki Fukui, 179–208. London: Routledge. (2006).]

Sakai, Kuniyoshi L. 2005. Language acquisition and brain development. *Science* 310: 815–819.

Sakai, Kuniyoshi L., Yasuki Noguchi, Tatsuya Takeuchi, and Eiju Watanabe. 2002. Selective priming of syntactic processing by event-related transcranial magnetic stimulation of Broca's area. *Neuron* 35: 1177–1182.

Shibatani, Masayoshi. 1990. *The languages of Japan*. Cambridge: Cambridge University Press.

Stromswold, Karin, David Caplan, Nathaniel Alpert, and Scott Rauch. 1996. Localization of syntactic comprehension by positron emission tomography. *Brain and Language* 52: 452–473.

Suzuki, Kei, and Kuniyoshi L. Sakai. 2003. An event-related fMRI study of explicit syntactic processing of normal/anomalous sentences in contrast to implicit syntactic processing. *Cerebral Cortex* 13: 517–526.

Talairach, Jean, and Pierre Tournoux. 1988. *Co-planar stereotaxic atlas of the human brain. 3-dimensional proportional system: An approach to cerebral imaging.* Stuttgart: Thieme.

Tatsuno, Yoshinori, and Kuniyoshi L. Sakai. 2005. Language-related activations in the left prefrontal regions are differentially modulated by age, proficiency, and task demands. *The Journal of Neuroscience* 25: 1637–1644.

Thompson, Cynthia K., Borna Bonakdarpour, Stepehn C. Fix, Henrike Blumenfeld, Todd B. Parrish, Darren R. Gitelman, and M.-Marsel Mesulam. 2007. Neural correlates of verb argument structure processing. *Journal of Cognitive Neuroscience* 19: 1753–1768.

Walton, Mark E., Joseph T. Devlin, and Matthew F. S. Rushworth. 2004. Interactions between decision making and performance monitoring within prefrontal cortex. *Nature Neuroscience* 7: 1259–1265.

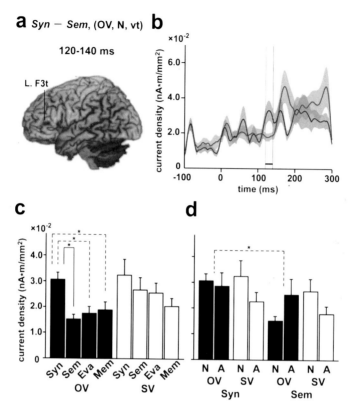

Plate 1 Selective responses to the Syn task. (a) The cortical responses to Syn and Sem were compared with a paired *t*-test under the normal OV sentence condition, and mapped on the transformed standard brain ($P_{corr} < 0.05$). Note the significant responses in the left (L.) F3t. (b) The averaged temporal changes of the current density for the left F3t. The red and blue lines correspond to the current density for Syn, (OV, N, vt) and Sem, (OV, N, vt), respectively. Their SEMs are shown as shaded bands ($n = 10$). The interval which resulted in significant differences is shown with a bar. (c) Histograms for the current density (mean ± SEM) under each normal sentence condition for the left F3t. (d) Histograms for the current density, including the anomalous sentences for Syn and Sem. Filled and open bars denote the current density under the OV and SV sentence conditions, respectively. The solid and dashed lines with asterisks above pairs of bars correspond to the significant contrasts used for the statistical parametric maps and other significant contrasts ($P < 0.05$, paired *t*-test), respectively.

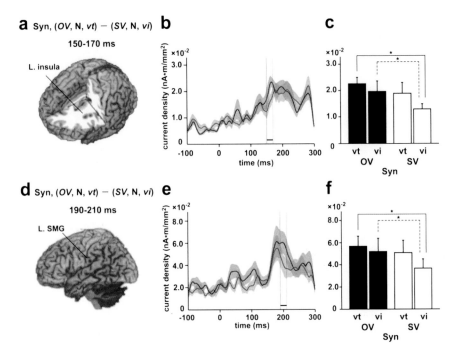

Plate 2 Cortical responses to sentence structure or verb transitivity. (a, d) The OV and SV sentence conditions were compared within the Syn task (Table 7.3). Note the significant responses in the left insula and left supramarginal gyrus (SMG). (b, e) The averaged temporal changes of the current density for the left insula and left SMG, respectively. The red and blue lines correspond to the current density for Syn, (OV, N, vt) and (SV, N, vi), respectively. (c, f) Histograms for the current density under each condition are shown for the left insula and the left SMG. Filled and open bars denote the current density under the OV and SV sentence conditions, respectively.

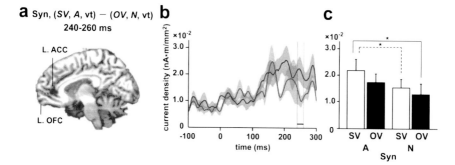

a Syn, (SV, A, vt) − (OV, N, vt)
240-260 ms

L. ACC

L. OFC

b

current density (nA·m/mm²) ×10⁻²
3.0
2.0
1.0
0

-100   0   100   200   300
time (ms)

c

×10⁻²
3.0
2.0
1.0
0

SV OV   SV OV
   A   N
        Syn

Plate 3 Cortical responses to syntactic anomaly or sentence structure. (a) The anomalous and normal sentence conditions were compared within the Syn task (Table 7.3). A parasagittal section ($x = -7$) is shown for the left anterior cingulate cortex (ACC) and left orbitofrontal cortex (OFC). (b) The averaged temporal changes of the current density for the left ACC. The red and blue lines correspond to the current density for Syn, (SV, A, vt) and (OV, N, vt), respectively. (c) Histograms for the current density under each condition are shown for the left ACC; the left OFC showed a similar tendency.

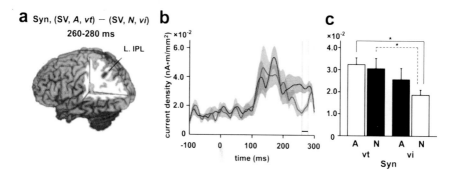

a Syn, (SV, A, vt) − (SV, N, vi)
260-280 ms

L. IPL

b

current density (nA·m/mm²) ×10⁻²
6.0
4.0
2.0
0

-100   0   100   200   300
time (ms)

c

×10⁻²
4.0
3.0
2.0
1.0
0

A   N   A   N
vt   vi
        Syn

Plate 4 Cortical responses to verb transitivity or syntactic anomaly. (a) The vt and vi sentence conditions were compared within the Syn task (Table 7.3). Note the significant responses in the left inferior parietal lobule (IPL). (b) The averaged temporal changes of the current density for the left IPL. The red and blue lines correspond to the current density for Syn, (SV, A, vt) and (SV, N, vi), respectively. (c) Histograms for the current density under each condition are shown for the left IPL.

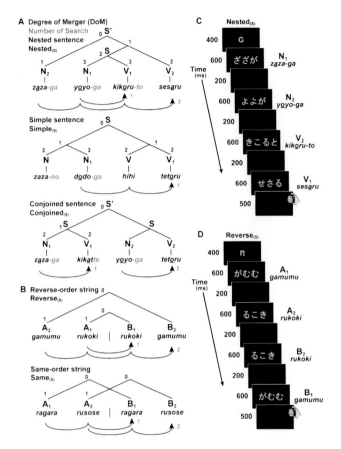

Plate 5 A paradigm for testing jabberwocky sentences and letter strings. Examples of short [(S) as a subscript] matching stimuli are shown here with the Romanization system, but actual stimuli were presented in hiragana without hyphen (see C and D). (A) Three sentence conditions with short stimuli: Nested(S), Simple(S), and Conjoined(S). Based on contemporary linguistics (O'Grady et al. 2010), each diagram represents a unique tree structure of each sentence (S and S') constructed from Ns and Vs. For the Nested(S), a sentence (S) at the lowest hierarchical level was nested into an entire sentence (S'), similar to "*Taro-ga Hanako-ga utau-to omou*" ("*Taro thinks that Hanako sings*"). For the Simple(S), a simple sentence was constructed by adding the same number of left/right branches to both Ns and Vs, similar to "*Taro-no ani-ga tabe hajimeru*" ("*Taro's brother starts eating*"). For the Conjoined(S), an entire sentence (S') was constructed by conjoining two sentences, similar to "*Taro-ga utatte Hanako-ga odoru*" ("*Taro sings, and Hanako dances*"). The digits shown in red and blue denote DoM for each node and "number of Search," respectively (see Table 8.1). The curved arrows denote the matching of sequentially presented stimuli. (B) Two string conditions with short stimuli: Reverse(S) and Same(S). Each letter string was formed by jumbling letters of either N or V. (C and D) Examples of stimulus presentation. Here, examples of matching stimuli are shown in hiragana for the Nested(S) and Reverse(S). Between the Nested(S) and Reverse(S), both of the symbol orders (the order of Ns, Vs, As, and Bs) and matching orders (denoted by subscripts) were identical.

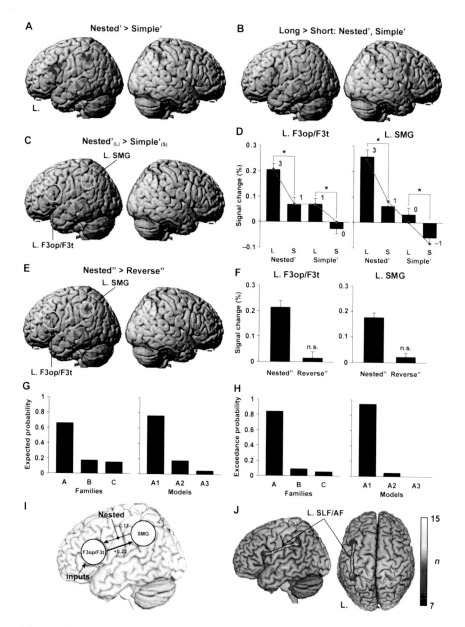

Plate 6 Functional and anatomical evidence of syntactic computation in language areas. For (A) and (B), we used a two-way ANCOVA with condition × length; for (C) and (E), a one-way ANCOVA was used. Activations were projected onto the left (L.) and right lateral surfaces of a standard brain. See Tables 8.3 and 8.4 for their stereotactic coordinates. (A) Regions identified by the main effect of condition, i.e., Nested' > Simple' (Nested' and Simple' denote [Nested – Conjoined] and [Simple – Conjoined], respectively).

(B) Regions identified by the main effect of length, i.e., Long > Short while combining Nested' and Simple'. (C) Regions identified by Nested'$_{(L)}$ > Simple'$_{(S)}$, which reflected both main effects. (D) Percent signal changes for Nested' and Simple', averaged across L. F3op/F3t and L. SMG in (C) (mean ± SEM). Overlaid red dots and lines denote the values fitted with the estimates (digits in red) for the best models: DoM for L. F3op/F3t and "DoM + number of Search" for L. SMG. (E) Regions identified by Nested" > Reverse" (Nested" and Reverse" denote [Nested – Simple] and [Reverse – Same], respectively). (F) Percent signal changes for Nested" and Reverse", averaged across the L. F3op/F3t and L. SMG in (E). (G–I) The results of DCM, testing effective connectivity between L. F3op/F3t and L. SMG (see Figure 8.S4). Bar graphs show expected probabilities (G) and exceedance probabilities (H) for each modulatory family and for the input models of the winning family A. The best model A1 (I) included a significant intrinsic connection (a thick line). (J) Anatomical connectivity between L. F3op/F3t and L. SMG revealed by DTI. The population probability map is shown on the left lateral and dorsal surfaces of a standard brain with maximum intensity projection. Blue spheres represent seed regions of L. F3op/F3t and L. SMG.

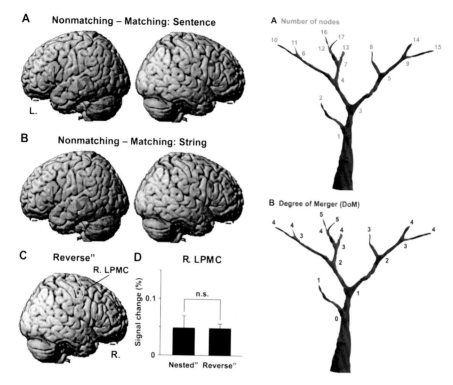

Plate 7a **left half.** Modulation of the right frontal activations by nonlinguistic factors. One-sample *t*-tests were used for the contrasts indicated. (A) Regions identified by [Nonmatching – Matching] under the sentence conditions, related to error-related factors. Note the right-dominant activation, especially in R. F3op/F3t. (B) Regions identified by [Nonmatching – Matching] under the string conditions. (C) Regions identified by Reverse". This contrast revealed the difference in matching orders (e.g., $A_2 A_1 B_1 B_2$ vs. $A_1 A_2 B_1 B_2$). Note the significant activation in R. LPMC. (D) The percent signal changes in R. LPMC, which was consistent with the equivalent estimates of memory span (see Table 8.2).

Plate 7b **right half.** Two models for measuring the complexity of tree structures. (A) "The number of nodes" counts the total number of nonterminal nodes (branching points) and terminal nodes of a tree structure. The number of nodes of the tree structure shown is 17. (B) "The Degree of Merger (DoM)" quantifies the maximum depth of merged subtrees, or the degree of branching. We increased the number one by one for each node, starting from the trunk (zero) to terminal nodes. The DoM of the tree structure shown is 5.

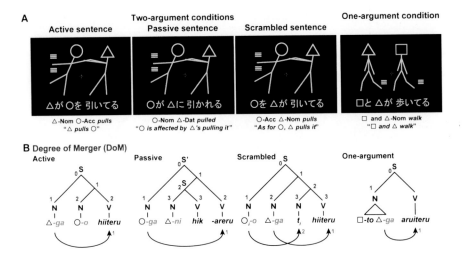

Plate 8 **upper half.** A picture-sentence matching paradigm in Kinno et al. (2008). (A) A picture-sentence matching task under either Two-argument conditions or a One-argument condition. Each stimulus consisted of one picture (top) and one sentence (bottom). Below each example, word-by-word and full translations in English are shown. An identical picture set was used under the Two-argument conditions, where we tested three sentence types: active sentences ("△-ga ○-o hiiteru"), passive sentences ("○-ga △-ni hik-areru"), and scrambled sentences ("○-o △-ga hiiteru"). Under the One-argument condition, we presented syntactically simpler active sentences ("□-to △-ga aruiteru"). (B) The syntactic structures of three sentence types. The digits shown in red and blue denote the DoM for each node and "number of Search," respectively.

Symbols used: S and S', sentence; N, noun phrase; V, verb phrase; Nom, nominative case; Acc, accusative case; Dat, dative case; -ga, nominative case marker; -o, accusative case marker; -ni, dative case marker; -to, coordinator; t, trace (subscripts denote the same entity).

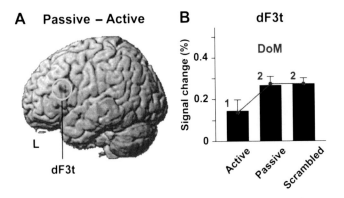

Plate 8 **lower half.** Activations in the L. dF3t modulated by the DoM. (A) A region identified by the Passive – Active contrast (see Plate 8 upper half). Activations were projected onto the left (L) lateral surface of a standard brain. (B) Percent signal changes for the active, passive, and scrambled sentence conditions in the L. dF3t, taking the One-argument condition as a reference. Overlaid red dots and lines denote the values fitted with the estimates (digits in red) for the model of the DoM.

8 Syntactic Computation in the Human Brain

The Degree of Merger as a Key Factor

With Shinri Ohta and Kuniyoshi L. Sakai

Abstract

Our goal of this study is to characterize the functions of language areas in most precise terms. Previous neuroimaging studies have reported that more complex sentences elicit larger activations in the left inferior frontal gyrus (L. F3op/F3t), although the most critical factor still remains to be identified. We hypothesize that pseudowords with grammatical particles and morpho-syntactic information alone impose a construction of syntactic structures, just like normal sentences, and that "the Degree of Merger" (DoM) in recursively merged sentences parametrically modulates neural activations. Using jabberwocky sentences with distinct constructions, we fitted various parametric models of syntactic, other linguistic, and nonlinguistic factors to activations measured with functional magnetic resonance imaging. We demonstrated that the models of DoM and "DoM + number of Search (searching syntactic features)" were the best to explain activations in the L. F3op/ F3t and supramarginal gyrus (L. SMG), respectively. We further introduced letter strings, which had neither lexical associations nor grammatical particles, but retained both matching orders and symbol orders of sentences. By directly contrasting jabberwocky sentences with letter strings, localized activations in L. F3op/F3t and L. SMG were indeed independent of matching orders and symbol orders. Moreover, by using dynamic causal modeling, we found that the model with an inhibitory modulatory effect for the bottom-up connectivity from L. SMG to L. F3op/F3t was the best one. For this best model, the top-down connection from L. F3op/F3t to L. SMG was significantly positive. By using diffusion-tensor imaging, we confirmed that the left dorsal pathway of the superior longitudinal and arcuate fasciculi consistently connected these regions. Lastly, we established that nonlinguistic order-related and error-related factors significantly activated the right (R.) lateral premotor cortex and R. F3op/F3t, respectively. These results indicate that the identified network of L. F3op/F3t and L. SMG subserves the calculation of DoM in recursively merged sentences.

Introduction

It is widely accepted that in human language, a sentence can be expressed by a unique tree structure with recursive branches (Hopcroft and Ullman 1979, O'Grady et al. 2010). Moreover, any sentence can be recursively combined within another sentence, as in e.g., "*I think that John believes that Mary assumes that . . .*," and there is in principle no upper bound for the length of sentences; this property is the so-called *discrete infinity* made possible by the computational power, or engine, of the human language faculty. One possible way to elucidate the neural basis of such computational properties is to examine how the brain responds to the modulation of specified syntactic factors. An early attempt with functional magnetic resonance imaging (fMRI) has reported that activations in the language areas were modulated by noncanonical/canonical word orders and the presence/absence of lexical contents (Röder et al. 2002), in which multiple factors, including memory-related and semantic factors, could account for these activations. Therefore, we should not be content with such a general cognitive phenomenon as so-called "syntactic complexity" or "syntactic working memory" that could involve both linguistic and nonlinguistic factors. We should instead identify which minimal factor *sufficiently* explains any activation changes obtained. In addition, the size of linguistic constituents may also modulate cortical activations. A recent fMRI study has reported that the left frontal activations increased with the number of words or terminal nodes (symbols) in a phrase (Pallier et al. 2011), but, as rightly pointed out by the authors, the precise phrase structures remained to be taken into account. Here we focus on different sentence constructions, and try to identify *minimal* syntactic factors associated with phrase structures, which parametrically modulate cortical responses measured with event-related fMRI.

Modern linguistics has accumulated mounting evidence that the construction of any grammatical phrases or sentences can be adequately and *minimally* explained by hierarchical syntactic structures with a set of relevant structural relations defined on such structures (Chomsky 1957, 1965), leading to the postulation of the fundamental linguistic operation of *Merge* (capitalized in linguistics to indicate formal operations), the structure-building operation, which combines two syntactic objects (words or phrases) to form a larger structure (Chomsky 1995). Besides Merge, we have proposed that *Search* (searching syntactic features) applies to a syntactic object already constructed by Merge, and that Search assigns relevant features to the syntactic object (Fukui and Sakai 2003). The total number of Merge and Search applications within an entire sentence are here simply denoted as "number of Merge" and "number of Search," respectively. To properly measure the depth of a tree structure with a formal property of Merge and *iterativity* (recursiveness) (Fukui 2011), we hypothesize that "the Degree of Merger (DoM)" is a key computational concept, which can

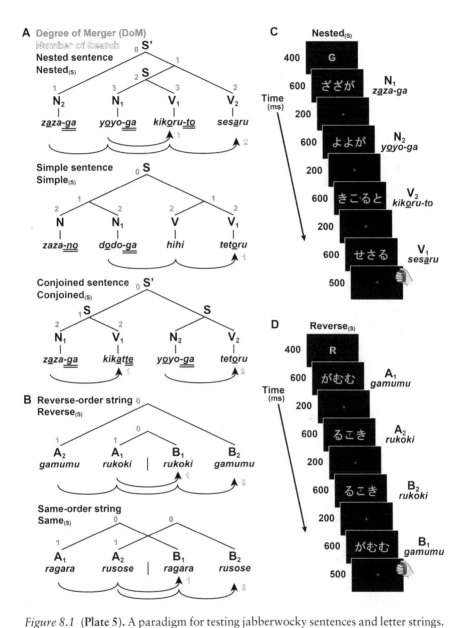

Figure 8.1 (**Plate 5**). A paradigm for testing jabberwocky sentences and letter strings.

Examples of short [(S) as a subscript] matching stimuli are shown here with the Romanization system, but actual stimuli were presented in hiragana without hyphen (see C and D). (A) Three sentence conditions with short stimuli: Nested(S), Simple(S), and Conjoined(S). Based on contemporary linguistics (O'Grady et al. 2010), each diagram represents a unique tree structure of each sentence (S and S') constructed

(Continued)

Figure 8.1 (Continued)

from Ns and Vs. For the Nested$_{(S)}$, a sentence (S) at the lowest hierarchical level was nested into an entire sentence (S'), similar to "*Taro-ga Hanako-ga utau-to omou*" ("*Taro thinks that Hanako sings*"). For the Simple$_{(S)}$, a simple sentence was constructed by adding the same number of left/right branches to both Ns and Vs, similar to "*Taro-no ani-ga tabe hajimeru*" ("*Taro's brother starts eating*"). For the Conjoined$_{(S)}$, an entire sentence (S') was constructed by conjoining two sentences, similar to "*Taro-ga utatte Hanako-ga odoru*" ("*Taro sings, and Hanako dances*"). The digits shown in gray and white denote DoM for each node and "number of Search," respectively (see Table 8.1). The curved arrows denote the matching of sequentially presented stimuli. (B) Two string conditions with short stimuli: Reverse$_{(S)}$ and Same$_{(S)}$. Each letter string was formed by jumbling letters of either N or V. (C and D) Examples of stimulus presentation. Here, examples of matching stimuli are shown in hiragana for the Nested$_{(S)}$ and Reverse$_{(S)}$. Between the Nested$_{(S)}$ and Reverse$_{(S)}$, both of the symbol orders (the order of Ns, Vs, As, and Bs) and matching orders (denoted by subscripts) were identical.

be defined as the *maximum depth* of merged subtrees (i.e., Mergers) within an entire sentence. Moreover, DoM can quantify and compare various syntactic phenomena, such as self-embedding, scrambling, *wh*-movement, etc. Furthermore, when Search applies to each syntactic object within hierarchical structures, the calculation of DoM plays a critical role. Indeed, from a nested sentence "[[*The boy*$_2$ [*we*$_3$ *like*$_3$]$_2$]$_1$ *sings*$_1$]$_0$" (subscripts denote DoM for each node, see Figure 8.1A), two sentences "[*The boy* . . .]$_1$ *sings*$_1$" and "*we*$_3$ *like*$_3$" are obtained, where relevant features (numbers and persons here) are searched and checked between the nodes with identical DoM. Because such analyses of hierarchical structures would produce specific loads in syntactic computation, we expect that DoM and associated "number of Search" modulate neural activations. Merge would be theoretically "costless" (Saito and Fukui 1998, Chomsky 2004), and thus "number of Merge" itself may not affect activations, which can be easily expected for *flat* structures (see Figure 8.1B).

In the present study, jabberwocky sentences that lacked lexical associations were prepared. Each sentence consisted of pseudonoun phrases (Ns) and pseudoverb phrases (Vs). We hypothesize that pseudowords with grammatical particles and morphosyntactic information alone impose a construction of syntactic structures, just like normal sentences (see **Materials and Methods**, Stimuli). Based on the nested (self-embedded), left/right-branching, and multiple-branching constructions (see Appendix S1), we introduced three basic types of sentence constructions: nested sentence (Nested), simple sentence (Simple), and conjoined sentence (Conjoined) (Figure 8.1A). When constructing syntactic structures like the ones shown in Figure 8.1A, the correspondence of each subject-verb pair is most crucial. To test that participants actually paid attention to this correspondence, we used a matching task, such that the vowel of a subject (N$_j$ as a sample stimulus) was matched with the last vowel of the corresponding verb root

(V_i as a comparison stimulus) (e.g., "*zaza-ga sesaru*," underlined vowels within pseudowords). These features of vowels were only *experimentally* introduced, and this matching involved a factor of encoding (i.e., memorization of features necessary for matching). Because Vs lacked grammatical (agreement) features (e.g., number, person, gender, etc.), as in the Japanese verbs, this property of matching did not mimic agreement itself, but involved a formal association between sample and comparison stimuli. It follows that the same syntactic structures were constructed from matching and nonmatching stimuli (Tables 8.S1 and 8.S2), which were both well-formed, i.e., *grammatical*, in Japanese. Matching strategy (counting, for example, first and fourth stimuli for matching) was useful in solving the task, but performing the task was *not* prerequisite for constructing syntactic structures. Our matching task is different from classification tasks for symbol orders (e.g., AABB vs. ABAB, where A and B are symbols representing certain sets of stimuli), which can be solved by counting the number of each set, A or B. We further examined whether cortical activations were modulated by the length of sentences: short (S as a subscript, four-phrase) and long (L as a subscript, six-phrase) sentences (Figure 8.2A).

We tested various parametric models of syntactic, other linguistic, and nonlinguistic factors (Table 8.1; see Appendix S1 for operational definitions), some of which were based on structure-based models (Figures 8.S1–8.S3). Given these factors with a limited number of experimental conditions, we wanted to narrow down the models as much as possible by adopting effective contrasts. For both short and long sentences, the estimates of "number of Merge," as well as those of "number of case markers (-*ga*/-*no*)" and "depth of postponed symbols," were identical among the three sentence conditions. By taking one of sentence conditions as a reference, these three factors could be eliminated from the analyses. Moreover, a reference condition should be chosen separately for each of short and long sentences, as we tested the short and long stimuli on separate days. The Conjoined condition was actually *simplest* among the three sentence conditions and thus served as an appropriate reference, because the Conjoined condition had same or less estimates than those under the Nested and Simple conditions for all factors except the numbers of Search and encoding. For brevity, a contrast with the Conjoined condition as a reference is denoted with a prime mark; e.g., [Nested$_{(S)}$ – Conjoined$_{(S)}$] and [Nested$_{(L)}$ – Conjoined$_{(L)}$] abbreviated as Nested'$_{(S)}$ and Nested'$_{(L)}$, respectively.

We further introduced letter strings, which had neither lexical associations nor grammatical particles, but retained both matching orders and symbol orders of sentences. There were two string conditions: reverse-order string (Reverse) and same-order string (Same) (Figures 8.1B, 8.2B, and Table 8.2). Like the sentence conditions, we used the same matching task under these string conditions, such that the first half of a string (A_i as a sample stimulus) was matched with the corresponding second half (B_i as a comparison stimulus) in the reverse or same order. These string conditions also controlled any

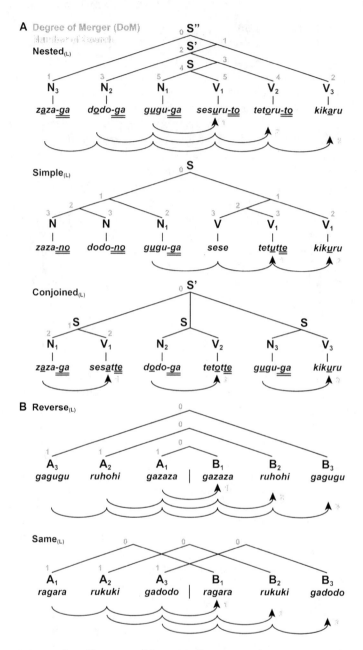

Figure 8.2 Examples of long matching stimuli.

(A) Three sentence conditions with long [(L) as a subscript] stimuli: Nested$_{(L)}$, Simple$_{(L)}$, and Conjoined$_{(L)}$. (B) Two string conditions with long stimuli: Reverse$_{(L)}$ and Same$_{(L)}$. See Appendix S2 for further explanation.

Table 8.1 Estimates of various factors to account for activations under the sentence conditions.

Syntactic factors	Factor	Nested(L)	Nested(S)	Simple(L)	Simple(S)	Conjoined(L)	Conjoined(S)
	Degree of Merger (DoM)	5	3	3	2	2	2
	No. of Search	3	2	2	1	3	2
	No. of Merge	5	3	5	3	5	3

		Nested'(L)	Nested'(S)	Simple'(L)	Simple'(S)
	DoM	3	1	1	0
	DoM + No. of Search	3	1	0	-1
	No. of Search	0	0	-1	-1
	No. of Merge	0	0	0	0

Other linguistic factors	Factor	Nested(L)	Nested(S)	Simple(L)	Simple(S)	Conjoined(L)	Conjoined(S)
	No. of case markers (-gal-no)	3	2	3	2	3	2
	No. of tense markers (-rul-ta)	3	2	1	1	1	1
	Degree of nesting	2	1	1	1	1	1
	Degree of self-embedding	2	1	1	0	1	0
	No. of nodes	11	7	11	7	10	7
	Depth of postponed symbols	3	2	3	2	3	2
	Integration costs	5	3	3	2	1	1
	Storage costs	3	2	2	2	1	1
	Syntactic interference	2	1	0	0	0	0
	Positional similarity	3	2	2	0	0	0

(Continued)

Table 8.1 (Continued)

	Nested'(L)	Nested'(S)	Simple'(L)	Simple'(S)	Conjoined(L)	Conjoined(S)
No. of case markers (-gal-no)	0	0	0	0		
No. of tense markers (-ru-ta)	2	1	0	0		
Degree of nesting	1	0	0	0		
Degree of self-embedding	1	1	0	0		
No. of nodes	1	0	1	0		
Depth of postponed symbols	0	0	0	0		
Integration costs	4	2	2	1		
Storage costs	2	1	1	1		
Syntactic interference	2	1	0	0		
Positional similarity	3	2	2	0		

Factor	Nested'(L)	Nested'(S)	Simple'(L)	Simple'(S)	Conjoined(L)	Conjoined(S)
Memory span	4	2	2	1	0	0
Counting	2	1	2	1	0	0
No. of encoding	6	4	3	2	6	4

Nonlinguistic factors	Nested'(L)	Nested'(S)	Simple'(L)	Simple'(S)
Memory span	4	2	2	1
Counting	2	1	2	1
No. of encoding	0	0	-3	-2
Memory span + counting	6	3	4	2
Memory span + No. of encoding	4	2	-1	-1

Table 8.1 (Continued)

We define the estimate of a factor as the largest value that the factor can variably take within an entire sentence. For each factor, its unit load should be invariable among all sentence conditions, making an independent subtraction between estimates of the *same* factor possible. Separately for long and short sentences, estimates under the Conjoined condition as a reference were subtracted from those under the other Nested and Simple conditions (e.g., the [Nested$_{(L)}$ – Conjoined$_{(L)}$] contrast abbreviated as Nested'$_{(L)}$; e.g., DoM for Nested'$_{(L)}$, $5 - 2 = 3$). Excluding "number of Merge," the estimates of which were null for all four contrasts, we regarded "DoM + number of Search" (i.e., adding the estimates of two factors) as an additional factor. Among the nonlinguistic factors, "memory span + counting" and "memory span + number of encoding" were regarded as additional factors, because they were temporal order-related and memory-related factors, respectively.

involvement of matching strategy stated earlier. Between the Nested ($N_2 N_1 V_1 V_2$ or $N_3 N_2 N_1 V_1 V_2 V_3$, where each subscript denotes a matching order) and Reverse ($A_2 A_1 B_1 B_2$ or $A_3 A_2 A_1 B_1 B_2 B_3$) conditions, the curved arrows shown in Figures 8.1 and 8.2 represent the *same* matching order of sequentially presented stimuli (e.g., for $N_2 N_1 V_1 V_2$, the inner symbol pair of N and V is matched first, and then the outer symbol pair is matched). The symbol order was also identical among the Nested, Simple, Reverse, and Same conditions in the form of $N^n V^n$ or $A^n B^n$. To control both matching orders and symbol orders, we directly compared the Nested with the Reverse, using the Simple and Same conditions as respective references (Table 8.2), i.e., (Nested – Simple) > (Reverse – Same). For brevity, the contrasts of [Nested – Simple] and [Reverse – Same] are denoted with a double prime mark, i.e., Nested" and Reverse", respectively. Our goal with such thorough controls was to demonstrate that *purely* syntactic factors of DoM and "number of Search" actually modulate neural activations.

It has been reported that more complex sentences elicit larger activations in the pars opercularis and pars triangularis of the left inferior frontal gyrus (L. F3op/F3t) (Stromswold et al. 1996, Dapretto and Bookheimer 1999, Embick et al. 2000, Hashimoto and Sakai 2002, Friederici et al. 2003, Musso et al. 2003, Suzuki and Sakai 2003, Kinno et al. 2008), suggesting that L. F3op/F3t is critical for syntactic processing as a grammar center (Sakai 2005). On the other hand, the left angular and supramarginal gyri (L. AG/SMG) have been suggested for vocabulary knowledge or lexical processing (Lee et al. 2007, Pattamadilok et al. 2010). To examine the functional specialization of any regions, including L. F3op/F3t and L. AG/SMG, in an unbiased manner, we adopted whole-brain analyses (Friston and Henson 2006). We also performed effective connectivity analyses by using dynamic causal modeling (DCM) (Friston et al. 2003) to examine the functional integration of identified regions. To provide empirical backup for the connection derived from DCM, we checked the anatomical plausibility of the network with diffusion-tensor imaging (DTI). According to recent DTI studies, there have been controversial issues as regards the functional roles of two different pathways for syntax, semantics, and phonology: dorsal tracts of the

Table 8.2 Estimates of nonlinguistic and syntactic factors to account for activations.

Nonlinguistic factors	Factor	Nested(L)	Nested(S)	Simple(L)	Simple(S)	Reverse(L)	Reverse(S)	Same(L)	Same(S)
	Memory span	4	2	2	2	4	2	2	1
	Counting	2	1	2	1	2	1	2	1
	No. of encoding	6	4	3	2	6	4	6	4
		Nested		Simple		Reverse		Same	
	Memory span	6		3		6		3	
	Counting	3		3		3		3	
	No. of encoding	10		5		10		10	
		Nested"				Reverse"			
	Memory span	3				3			
	Counting	0				0			
	No. of encoding	5				0			
Syntactic factors	Factor	Nested"				Reverse"			
	DoM	3				0			
	DoM + No. of Search	5				0			

For Nested, Simple, Reverse, and Same, the estimates for short and long stimuli were added together, because each factor's unit load would be invariable between short and long stimuli under each of the sentence and string conditions. Because the matching orders or symbol orders were identical between the Nested and Reverse conditions, the unit load of memory span or counting was invariable between the Nested and Reverse conditions, which was also invariable between the Reverse and Same conditions, thus invariable among the Nested, Simple, Reverse, and Same conditions. For brevity, the contrasts of [Nested – Simple] and [Reverse – Same] are denoted with a double prime mark, i.e., Nested" and Reverse", respectively. Note that the estimates of memory span in Nested" and Reverse" also became identical, and that the Reverse" contrast makes the listed estimates null, except memory span. The last two syntactic factors, whose models were best in Table 8.5, consistently accounted for the results of Figure 8.4F. All estimates of the other factors unlisted here were null in Reverse", which cannot account for the results of Figure 8.5C and 8.5D.

superior longitudinal and arcuate fasciculi (SLF/AF), as well as ventral tracts of the middle longitudinal fasciculus (MdLF) and extreme capsule (EmC); both pathways connect the inferior frontal and superior/middle temporal areas (Saur et al. 2008, Wilson et al. 2011, Wong et al. 2011, Griffiths et al. 2013). Our present study would elucidate the most crucial network and pathway for syntactic computation.

Materials and Methods

Participants

Eighteen native Japanese speakers (all males, aged 19–25 years), who had not majored in linguistics, participated in an fMRI experiment. Additional 15 participants (14 males, aged 19–40 years) were tested in a DTI experiment. All participants in the fMRI and DTI experiments were healthy and right-handed (laterality quotients: 11–100), according to the Edinburgh inventory (Oldfield 1971). Prior to participation in the study, written informed consent was obtained from each participant after the nature and possible consequences of the studies were explained. Approval for the experiments was obtained from the institutional review board of the University of Tokyo, Komaba.

Stimuli

Each visual stimulus consisted of two to five yellow letters in hiragana (Figure 8.1C and 8.1D). The stimuli were visually presented against a dark background through an eyeglass-like MRI-compatible display (resolution, 800 × 600; VisuaStim XGA; Resonance Technology Inc., Northridge, CA). The visual stimuli were always presented at the center of the monitor. At the initiation of every trial of the Nested, Simple, and Conjoined, the cue "G" (for grammar conditions with all grammatical sentences) was shown for 400 ms. The cue "R" (for reverse orders) was shown for the Reverse, and "M" (for memorizing orders) for the Same. Four (short) or six (long) stimuli were each sequentially presented to the participants for 600 ms, with an interstimulus interval of 200 ms, leading to 4.5 s and 6 s trials for the short and long stimuli, respectively. For fixation, a red cross was always displayed at the center of the monitor. During fMRI experiments, stimulus presentation, as well as acquisition of responses and reaction times (RTs), was controlled using the LabVIEW software and interface (National Instruments, Austin, TX).

Under the sentence conditions, jabberwocky sentences consisting of pseudonoun phrases and pseudoverb phrases alone were presented in a phrase-by-phrase manner to the participants. We made six pseudonouns by repeating the same syllables with voiced consonants and any one of /a/,

/u/, or /o/: *rara, zaza, mumu, gugu, yoyo,* and *dodo.* We also made four pseudoverb roots by repeating the same syllables with voiceless consonants and either /i/ or /e/: *kiki, hihi, sese,* and *tete.* The transitions between consecutive phrases or sentences were thoroughly randomized. Nonmatching stimuli included at least one odd vowel of V_i as a matching error (Tables 8. S1 and 8.S2). All matching and nonmatching stimuli were phonotactically legal, but lacked lexical associations in Japanese. There were 10 conditions (Figures 8.1 and 8.2); we prepared a set of 36 sentences for each of sentence conditions, and a set of 36 letter strings for each of string conditions. Each set consisted of 18 matching and 18 nonmatching stimuli. See Appendix S2 for detailed information about the stimuli.

We used only three kinds of grammatical particles, which represent *canonical* (i.e., in a prototypical use) case markings and syntactic information in Japanese: *-ga*, a nominative case marker; *-no*, a genitive case marker; and *-to*, a complementizer. In all jabberwocky sentences, the distinction between Ns and Vs was clear without memorizing pseudowords, because Ns, but not Vs, ended with either *-ga* or *-no*; only nouns and pronouns precede case markers in Japanese (e.g., "*momo-ga minoru*" and "*momo-no iro*": "*the peach ripens*" and "*the peach's color*"; real phrases will be translated hereafter). Moreover, Vs took a nonpast-tense form (*-ru*), past-tense form (*-ta*), or gerundive form (*-te*), following morphosyntactic and phonological features of Japanese verbs (Tsujimura 2007); Vs ended with *-to* and *-te* introduced *that*-clauses and *and*-conjunctives, respectively (see examples in Figure 8.1 legend). Including the first verb of a compound verb in an adverbial form (e.g., "*hihi*" and "*sese*"), all Ns and Vs with *-ga, -no, -to,* and *-te* endings (double underlined letters in Figures 8.1A and 8.2A) were associated with Merge applications to connect multiple nouns/verbs or sentences, amounting to "number of Merge."

Under the string conditions, stimuli were presented in the reverse order for the Reverse, whereas they were in the same order for the Same, as regards the first and second halves of a string (Figures 8.1B and 8.2B). Each letter string was formed by jumbling letters of either N or V, which had no lexical associations. For the Reverse and Same, there was actually no path connecting the nonterminal nodes of symbol pairs (e.g., $A_1 B_1$ and $A_2 B_2$), as there was *no* Merge application to connect the multiple pairs. The letter strings lacked *-ga, -no, -to,* or *-te* endings, and their flat constructions were determined by the cue of "R" or "M" alone. We estimated the syntactic factors for the letter strings, but all estimates of these factors were null in Reverse" (see Table 8.2).

Task

For each trial of a matching task under the sentence conditions or string conditions, the participants judged whether or not all pairs of the sample stimulus (N or A) and comparison stimulus (V or B) were matched, and responded by pressing one of two buttons (right for matching, and left for nonmatching) after the last stimulus appeared (Figure 8.1C and 8.1D). The accuracy and RTs were collected until 500 ms after the last stimulus disappeared. No feedback on each trial's performance was given to any participant. See Appendix S3 for task instructions and training procedures.

For the Nested, an entire sentence was constructed by nesting sentences in the form of $[N_2[N_1\ V_1]V_2]$ or $[N_3[N_2[N_1\ V_1]V_2]V_3]$, where $[N_i\ V_i]$ represents a subject-verb pair of a sentence (Figures 8.1A and 8.2A). In head-last languages, the key element (the "head") that determines the properties of a phrase is placed at the end of the phrase. Because Japanese is a head-last, and hence an SOV (verb-final) language, a main verb is placed after a subordinate clause. Therefore, Japanese sentences naturally yield nested structures of $N^n\ V^n$ without having to employ, as in English, object-relative clauses (e.g., "*The boy who$_i$ we like t_i sings*"), which require "movement" of an object (i.e., with more Merge applications) leaving behind a "trace" (t_i). For the Simple, a simple sentence was constructed by adding the same number of left/right branches to both Ns and Vs. The last noun (i.e., head) in the branches of Ns made a subject-verb pair with the last verb (i.e., head) of a compound verb. Each simple sentence thus took the form of $[(NN_1)\ (VV_1)]$, etc. For the Conjoined, an entire sentence was constructed by conjoining sentences in the form of $[N_1\ V_1][N_2\ V_2]$ or $[N_1\ V_1][N_2\ V_2][N_3\ V_3]$.

In a single run of 60 trials for the short stimuli, there were 10 trials each for the sentence conditions (the Nested$_{(S)}$, Simple$_{(S)}$, and Conjoined$_{(S)}$), and 15 trials each for the string conditions (the Reverse$_{(S)}$ and Same$_{(S)}$). Each trial was alternately a sentence condition and a string condition. If the sentence and string sequences were separated, the order of the Nested, Simple, and Conjoined was pseudo-randomized without repetition, and the order of the Reverse and Same was counterbalanced as Same-Reverse-Reverse-Same-. . . or Reverse-Same-Same-Reverse-. . . In a single run of 50 trials for the long stimuli, there were 10 trials each for the sentence conditions (the Nested$_{(L)}$, Simple$_{(L)}$, and Conjoined$_{(L)}$) and the string conditions (the Reverse$_{(L)}$ and Same$_{(L)}$), in the order of string-sentence-string-sentence-sentence-string-. . . With a maximum of nine runs, the same sentence stimulus appeared no more than three times for each participant.

MRI Data Acquisition

Depending on the time of experiments, the fMRI scans were conducted on a 1.5 T scanner (Stratis II, Premium; Hitachi Medical Corporation, Tokyo, Japan) with a bird-cage head coil, and the DTI scans were conducted on a 3.0 T scanner (Signa HDxt; GE Healthcare, Milwaukee, WI) with an 8-channel phased-array head coil. For the fMRI, we scanned 26 axial slices that were 3-mm thick with a 1-mm gap, covering from $z = -40$ to 63 mm from the anterior to posterior commissure (AC-PC) line, with a gradient-echo echo-planar imaging (EPI) sequence [repetition time (TR) = 3 s, echo time (TE) = 51 ms, flip angle (FA) = 90°, field of view (FOV) = 192 × 192 mm², resolution = 3 × 3 mm²]. In a single scanning run, we obtained 92 volumes for the short stimuli and 101 volumes for the long stimuli following three dummy images, which allowed for the rise of the MR signals. For each participant, five to nine runs for each of the short and long stimuli were tested, and four to nine runs without head movement were used for analyses. After completion of the fMRI session, high-resolution T1-weighted images of the whole brain (145 axial slices, 1 × 1 × 1 mm³) were acquired from all participants with a radio frequency spoiled steady-state acquisition with a rewound gradient echo sequence (TR = 30 ms, TE = 8 ms, FA = 60°, FOV = 256 × 256 mm²).

For the DTI, we scanned 50 axial slices that were 3-mm thick without gap, covering from $z = -60$ to 90 mm from the AC-PC line, with a diffusion-weighted spin-echo EPI sequence (b-value = 1,000 s/mm², TR = 15 s, TE = 87 ms, FOV = 256 × 256 mm², resolution = 2 × 2 mm², number of excitations = 2). A single image without diffusion-weighting (b0) was initially acquired, and then diffusion-weighting was isotropically distributed along 60 diffusion-encoding gradient directions. After completion of the DTI sessions, high-resolution T1-weighted images of the whole brain (192 axial slices, 1 × 1 × 1 mm³) were acquired from all participants with a fast spoiled gradient recalled acquisition in the steady state sequence (TR = 10 ms, TE = 4 ms, FA = 25°, FOV = 256 × 256 mm²). See Appendix S4 for MRI data analyses.

Results

Condition and Length Effects on the Accuracy/RTs

The accuracy data, as well as RTs measured from the onset of the last stimulus, are shown in Figure 8.3. The high accuracy under both sentence and string conditions indicated the participants' reliable and consistent judgments on the matching task. A two-way repeated-measures analysis of variance (rANOVA) with the condition [Nested, Simple, Conjoined, Reverse, Simple] × length [Long, Short] for the accuracy showed a significant main effect of condition [$F(4, 68) = 15$, $P < 0.0001$] and an interaction of condition by length [$F(4, 68) = 12$, $P < 0.0001$], but a main effect of length was not significant [$F(4, 68) = 3.8$, $P = 0.07$]. The RTs also showed a significant main effect of condition [$F(4, 68) = 43$, $P < 0.0001$] and an interaction of condition by length [$F(4, 68) = 13$, $P < 0.0001$], but a main effect of length was not significant [$F(4, 68) = 1.1$, $P = 0.30$]. Post-hoc paired t-tests among all conditions (significance level at $\alpha = 0.005$, Bonferroni corrected) showed that the accuracy for the Nested was significantly lower than that under the other conditions including the Reverse ($P < 0.0001$). This result indicates that the Nested was the most demanding condition, which cannot be explained by the *nonlinguistic* factors we examined (cf. the same estimates for the Nested and Reverse in Table 8.2, as well as its notes). On the other hand, post-hoc paired t-tests showed that the RTs under each sentence condition were significantly longer than those under each string condition ($P < 0.0001$). This difficulty was not in the task itself, but in vowel extraction; the sentence conditions, but not the string conditions, involved vowel extraction from the second syllable of V_1 presented in hiragana,

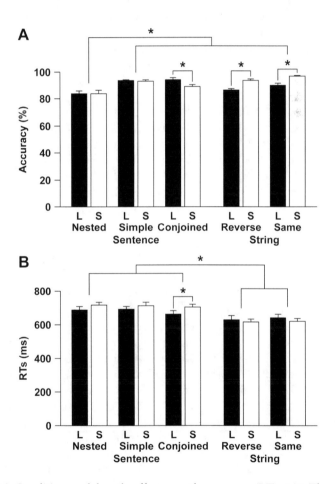

Figure 8.3 Condition and length effects on the accuracy/RTs. (A) The accuracy (mean ± SEM) for long (L) and short (S) stimuli, denoted by filled and open bars, respectively. Asterisks indicate the significance level at corrected $P < 0.05$ (paired t-tests). (B) RTs from the onset of the last stimulus.

especially for the last V_i that were directly linked with RTs (Figure 8.1C and 8.1D). The load of vowel extraction would also become larger for the *short* stimuli, as we tested the short and long stimuli on separate days in the order short, then long. Indeed, the accuracy for the Conjoined$_{(S)}$ was significantly lower than that for the Conjoined$_{(L)}$ [$t(17) = 3.1$, $P = 0.006$] (significance level at $\alpha = 0.01$, Bonferroni corrected), and the RTs for the Conjoined$_{(S)}$ were significantly longer than those for the Conjoined$_{(L)}$ [$t(17) = 2.8$, $P = 0.01$], probably reflecting associated effects for novices. For the Conjoined, length effects were apparently absent, and the estimates of both memory span and counting, which were associated with length effects, were indeed null for the Conjoined alone (Table 8.1). In the present study, we mainly analyzed activations that would show length effects (i.e., Long > Short), excluding the involvement of vowel extraction or effects for novices. Moreover, we used the Conjoined condition, which showed such effects most strongly, as a reference for both Nested and Simple conditions. Therefore, we can safely conclude that any elicited effects did not directly relate to the task.

Under the string conditions, the accuracy for the long stimuli was significantly lower than that for the short stimuli ($P < 0.001$), indicating length effects. For the Nested and Simple conditions, in contrast, the effects for novices and length would have been cancelled out, as neither the accuracy nor RTs differed significantly between the short and long stimuli ($P > 0.05$). Under the string conditions, the accuracy was more sensitive than the RTs.

Functional Evidence of Syntactic Computation in Language Areas

We examined brain activation under the sentence conditions, in particular focusing on selective activations for the most-demanding Nested condition. In a two-way analysis of covariance (ANCOVA) with the condition [Nested', Simple'] × length [Long, Short], the main effect of condition, i.e., Nested' > Simple' while combining Long and Short, resulted in left-dominant activation, especially in L. F3op/F3t, left lateral premotor cortex and F3op (L. LPMC/F3op), and L. SMG (Figure 8.4A and Table 8.3). Other significantly activated regions were the right (R.) F3op/F3t, R. LPMC, anterior cingulate cortex (ACC), and R. SMG. The main effect of length, i.e., Long > Short while combining Nested' and Simple', also showed significant activations in the same regions, while there were more significant voxels in the right hemisphere (Figure 8.4B). Therefore, length effects alone cannot account for the consistent activation in these regions. An interaction of condition by length did not show any significant activation.

To further narrow down candidate regions, we tested Nested'$_{(L)}$ > Simple'$_{(S)}$, which reflected both main effects, and found significant activation

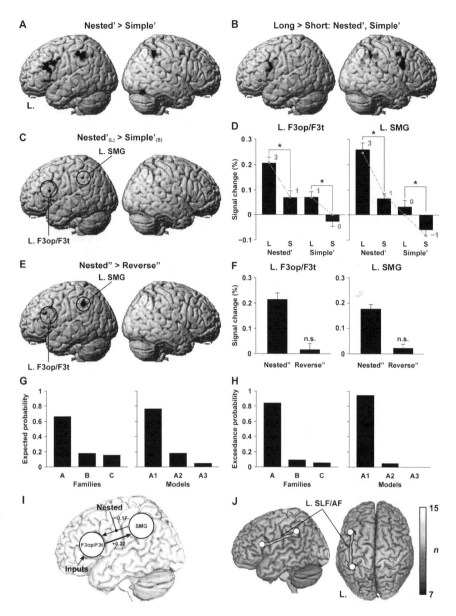

Figure 8.4 (**Plate 6**). Functional and anatomical evidence of syntactic computation in language areas. For (A) and (B), we used a two-way ANCOVA with condition × length; for (C) and (E), a one-way ANCOVA was used. Activations were projected onto the left (L.) and right lateral surfaces of a standard brain. See Tables 8.3 and 8.4 for their stereotactic coordinates. (A) Regions identified by the main effect of condition, i.e., Nested' > Simple' (Nested' and Simple' denote [Nested – Conjoined] and

(*Continued*)

Figure 8.4 (Continued)

[Simple – Conjoined], respectively). (B) Regions identified by the main effect of length, i.e., Long > Short while combining Nested' and Simple'. (C) Regions identified by Nested'$_{(L)}$ > Simple'$_{(S)}$, which reflected both main effects. (D) Percent signal changes for Nested' and Simple', averaged across L. F3op/F3t and L. SMG in (C) (mean ± SEM). Overlaid gray dots and lines denote the values fitted with the estimates (digits in gray) for the best models: DoM for L. F3op/F3t and "DoM + number of Search" for L. SMG. (E) Regions identified by Nested" > Reverse" (Nested" and Reverse" denote [Nested – Simple] and [Reverse – Same], respectively). (F) Percent signal changes for Nested" and Reverse", averaged across the L. F3op/F3t and L. SMG in (E). (G—I) The results of DCM, testing effective connectivity between L. F3op/F3t and L. SMG (see Figure 8.S4). Bar graphs show expected probabilities (G) and exceedance probabilities (H) for each modulatory family and for the input models of the winning family A. The best model *A1* (I) included a significant intrinsic connection (a thick line). (J) Anatomical connectivity between L. F3op/F3t and L. SMG revealed by DTI. The population probability map is shown on the left lateral and dorsal surfaces of a standard brain with maximum intensity projection. White spheres represent seed regions of L. F3op/F3t and L. SMG.

in L. F3op/F3t and L. SMG (Figure 8.4C and Table 8.4). The data used for selecting these regions and those for subsequent analyses were not independent, which might cause a selection bias (Kriegeskorte et al. 2009). Among the four contrasts, however, Nested'$_{(L)}$ and Simple'$_{(S)}$ yielded two extremes of the estimates of most factors, without apparent bias among the factors (see Table 8.1). In addition to both main effects, the percent signal changes in L. F3op/F3t and L. SMG (Figure 8.4D), averaged across significant voxels, showed a significant length effect within each of Nested' and Simple' (paired *t*-test, $P < 0.02$; significance level at $\alpha = 0.025$, Bonferroni corrected). Because we used appropriate references of the Conjoined$_{(L)}$ and Conjoined$_{(S)}$, we examined whether likewise *subtracted* estimates of each factor (e.g., DoM for Nested'$_{(L)}$; see Table 8.1) directly explained parametric modulation of activations in the four contrasts of Nested'$_{(L)}$, Nested'$_{(S)}$, Simple'$_{(L)}$, and Simple'$_{(S)}$. The signal changes in L. F3op/F3t and L. SMG indeed correlated exactly in a step-wise manner with the parametric models of DoM [3, 1, 1, 0] and "DoM + number of Search" [3, 1, 0, –1], respectively.

Next we examined how well activations in L. F3op/F3t and L. SMG correlated with DoM and other factors. All contrasts of Nested'$_{(L)}$, etc., predicted that activations should be exactly zero when a factor produced no effect or load relative to the Conjoined. We thus adopted a no-intercept model, in which percent signal changes of each region were fitted with a single (thus minimal) scale parameter to a model of each factor using its

Table 8.3 Regions related to the sentence conditions.

Contrast	Brain region	BA	Side	x	y	z	Z Value	Voxels
Main effect of condition, Nested' > Simple'	F3op/F3t	44/45	L	-51	27	24	5.6	109
	LPMC/F3op	6/44	L	-48	9	30	5.4	*
	F3op/F3t	44/45	R	54	15	36	4.9	2
	LPMC	6	R	33	3	51	5.3	12
	Insula	—	L	-30	24	-3	5.7	20
	ACC	6/8/32	M	-3	18	48	6.1	45
	SMG	40	L	-54	-33	48	5.3	101
				-39	-42	39	5.9	*
			R	42	-48	54	5.3	64
	AG/SMG	39/40	L	-30	-60	48	4.9	11
	Cerebellum, lobule VI	—	R	27	-69	-21	5.6	26
Main effect of length, Long > Short: Nested', Simple'	F3op/F3t	44/45	L	-48	12	18	5.9	63
	LPMC/F3op	6/44	L	-48	3	39	4.7	3
			R	48	6	30	6.0	129
	F3op/F3t	44/45	R	54	12	30	5.8	*
	LPMC	6	R	30	0	48	5.9	*
	ACC	6/8/32	M	0	27	39	4.9	9
	SMG	40	L	-57	-30	36	4.7	1
				-36	-45	39	5.3	26
	AG/SMG	39/40	R	42	-42	42	5.5	116
			R	33	-63	27	5.4	*

(Continued)

Table 8.3 (Continued)

Stereotactic coordinates (x, y, z) in the Montreal Neurological Institute (MNI) space (mm) are shown for each activation peak of Z values (corrected $P < 0.05$). BA, Brodmann's area; L, left hemisphere; R, right hemisphere; M, medial; F3op/F3t, pars opercularis and pars triangularis of the inferior frontal gyrus; LPMC, lateral premotor cortex; ACC, anterior cingulate cortex; SMG, supramarginal gyrus; AG, angular gyrus. The region with an asterisk is included within the same cluster shown one row above.

Table 8.4 Regions related to the sentence conditions and/or string conditions.

Contrast	Brain region	BA	Side	x	y	z	Z Value	Voxels
Nested'$_{(L)}$ > Simple'$_{(S)}$	F3op/F3t	44/45	L	−45	18	18	4.8	1
	SMG	40	L	−42	−45	42	4.8	2
Nested" > Reverse"	F3op/F3t	44/45	L	−51	24	24	5.8	5
	ACC	6/8/32	M	−3	18	45	5.2	1
	SMG	40	L	−39	−45	42	5.7	27
			R	39	−48	54	4.9	2
	Cerebellum, lobule VI	—	R	27	−69	−24	4.9	1
Nonmatching – Matching: Sentence	F3op/F3t	44/45	R	54	18	30	5.2	14
	LPMC/F3op	6/44	L	−45	9	30	4.8	1
	ACC	6/8/32	M	6	27	42	6.9	52
Nonmatching – Matching: String	F3op/F3t	44/45	R	54	18	30	5.3	21
			R	39	18	33	4.7	1
	SMG	40	R	42	−30	48	5.0	2
Reverse"	LPMC	6	R	27	−9	51	4.7	1

subtracted estimates. For the four contrasts, a least-squares method was used to minimize residual sum of squares (RSS) for the four fitted values (i.e., four estimates multiplied by the fitting scale) against corresponding signal changes averaged across participants (Table 8.5). Among a number of parametric models tested, the model of DoM for L. F3op/F3t, as well as that of "DoM + number of Search" for L. SMG, produced by far the least RSS (≤ 0.0020) and largest coefficient of determination (r^2) (≥ 0.97).

Table 8.5 Fittings and likelihood of various models tested.

L. F3op/F3t	Factor	RSS	r^2	P values for four contrasts	Log-likelihood	Likelihood ratio
	*DoM	0.0007	0.99	0.17, 0.92, 0.97, 0.99	65.0	1.0
	DoM + No. of Search	0.0065	0.88	0.0035, 0.064, 0.63, 0.88	59.2	3.1×10^{-3}
	No. of Search	0.052	<0.1	<0.0001, 0.018, 0.019, 0.031	33.4	2.0×10^{-14}
	No. of Merge	0.053	0	<0.0001, 0.0035, 0.018, 0.17	n/a	n/a
	No. of case markers (-gal-no)	0.053	0	<0.0001, 0.0035, 0.018, 0.17	n/a	n/a
	No. of tense markers (-ru/-ta)	0.0067	0.87	0.0035, 0.17, 0.32, 0.56	59.7	4.8×10^{-3}
	Degree of nesting	0.010	0.80	0.0035, 0.018, 0.17, >0.99	57.1	3.7×10^{-4}
	Degree of self-embedding	0.015	0.71	0.0035, 0.0075, 0.019, 0.17	53.3	8.7×10^{-6}
	No. of nodes	0.015	0.72	0.0050, 0.0082, 0.018, 0.17	53.7	1.2×10^{-5}
	Depth of postponed symbols	0.053	0	<0.0001, 0.0035, 0.018, 0.17	n/a	n/a
	Integration costs	0.0066	0.88	0.0017, 0.15, 0.48, 0.53	59.0	2.5×10^{-3}
	Storage costs	0.014	0.74	<0.0001, 0.024, 0.83, 0.85	53.8	1.3×10^{-5}
	Syntactic interference	0.0067	0.87	0.0035, 0.17, 0.32, 0.56	59.7	4.8×10^{-3}
	Positional similarity	0.0055	0.90	0.051, 0.12, 0.17, 0.19	60.1	7.8×10^{-3}
	Memory span	0.0066	0.88	0.0017, 0.15, 0.48, 0.53	59.0	2.5×10^{-3}
	Counting	0.017	0.67	0.0003, 0.0013, 0.035, 0.72	50.8	7.0×10^{-7}
	No. of encoding	0.051	<0.1	<0.0001, 0.014, 0.018, 0.12	32.9	1.2×10^{-14}
	Memory span + counting	0.0099	0.81	0.0007, 0.035, 0.15, 0.76	55.5	7.9×10^{-5}
	Memory span + No. of encoding	0.015	0.72	<0.0001, 0.10, 0.46, 0.59	52.5	3.6×10^{-6}

(Continued)

Table 8.5 (Continued)

L. SMG	Factor	RSS	r^2	P values for four contrasts	Log-likelihood	Likelihood ratio
	DoM	0.0063	0.92	0.013, 0.083, 0.44, 0.49	58.8	0.079
	*DoM + No. of Search	0.0020	0.97	0.22, 0.30, 0.42, 0.62	61.4	1.0
	No. of Search	0.075	<0.1	<0.0001, 0.0061, 0.045, 0.090	23.6	3.8×10^{-17}
	No. of Merge	0.076	0	<0.0001, 0.0061, 0.013, 0.22	n/a	n/a
	No. of case markers (-gal-no)	0.076	0	<0.0001, 0.0061, 0.013, 0.22	n/a	n/a
	No. of tense markers (-ru/-ta)	0.0079	0.90	0.013, 0.023, 0.22, 0.34	55.9	4.1×10^{-3}
	Degree of nesting	0.0088	0.88	0.0061, 0.013, 0.22, >0.99	55.5	2.8×10^{-3}
	Degree of self-embedding	0.023	0.69	0.0002, 0.0018, 0.013, 0.22	45.5	1.2×10^{-7}
	No. of nodes	0.033	0.56	0.0004, 0.0005, 0.0061, 0.013	40.1	6.0×10^{-10}
	Depth of postponed symbols	0.076	0	<0.0001, 0.0061, 0.013, 0.22	n/a	n/a
	Integration costs	0.021	0.72	0.0001, 0.014, 0.028, 0.18	46.3	2.7×10^{-7}
	Storage costs	0.032	0.58	<0.0001, 0.0014, 0.084, 0.49	40.3	7.1×10^{-10}
	Syntactic interference	0.0079	0.90	0.013, 0.023, 0.22, 0.34	55.9	4.1×10^{-3}
	Positional similarity	0.020	0.73	0.0039, 0.0052, 0.013, 0.029	47.6	1.0×10^{-6}
	Memory span	0.021	0.72	0.0001, 0.014, 0.028, 0.18	46.3	2.7×10^{-7}
	Counting	0.041	0.46	<0.0001, <0.0001, 0.0039, 0.77	35.6	6.2×10^{-12}
	No. of encoding	0.076	<0.1	<0.0001, 0.0061, 0.017, 0.16	22.5	1.4×10^{-17}
	Memory span + counting	0.028	0.63	<0.0001, 0.0018, 0.0086, 0.44	41.3	1.9×10^{-9}
	Memory span + No. of encoding	0.011	0.85	0.0034, 0.051, 0.13, 0.81	52.1	9.7×10^{-5}

Percent signal changes in L. F3op/F3t and L. SMG were fitted with a single scale parameter to a model of each factor using its subtracted estimates (Table 8.1) for the four contrasts of Nested', Nested', Simple', Simple' (L), and Simple' (S). The P values for the t-tests are shown in ascending order. Note that the models of DoM and "DoM + number of Search" (with an asterisk) resulted in the best fit for L. F3op/F3t and L. SMG, respectively, i.e., with the least residual sum of squares (RSS), largest coefficient of determination (r^2), and larger P values. The likelihood of models with all null estimates was incalculable (n/a). A likelihood ratio is the ratio of each model's likelihood to the best model's likelihood. The best models of DoM and "DoM + number of Search" for L. F3op/F3t and L. SMG, respectively, were by far more likely than the other models.

Goodness of fit was further evaluated for each model by using a one-sample *t*-test (significance level at $\alpha = 0.0125$, Bonferroni corrected) between the fitted value for each contrast and individual activations. The model of DoM for L. F3op/F3t, as well as that of "DoM + number of Search" for L. SMG, produced no significant deviation for the four contrasts (one-sample *t*-test, $P \geq 0.17$). For L. SMG, the second-best model was DoM (RSS = 0.0063, $r^2 = 0.92$, and its smallest $P = 0.013$ was marginal). To further take account of interindividual variability, we fitted "linear mixed-effects models" with individual activations (Table 8.5), and found that the models of DoM and "DoM + number of Search" were by far more likely for L. F3op/F3t and L. SMG, respectively.

Next, we examined whether the selective activation in these regions was replicated even after controlling both matching orders and symbol orders (e.g., $N_2 \, N_1 \, V_1 \, V_2$ and $A_2 \, A_1 \, B_1 \, B_2$) between the Nested and Reverse, i.e., in Nested" > Reverse" combining the short and long stimuli. This contrast indeed resulted in significant activation in L. F3op/F3t and L. SMG (Figure 8.4E and Table 8.4). In both regions, the signal changes in Reverse" were not significantly different from 0 (one-sample *t*-test, $P > 0.1$) (Figure 8.4F). Moreover, the models of DoM and "DoM + number of Search" were also consistent with the signal changes in both Nested" and Reverse" (Table 8.2). The number of encoding might explain the results of Figure 8.4F, but its estimates cannot consistently explain the results of Figure 8.4D.

Effective and Anatomical Connectivity between L. F3op/F3t and L. SMG

Based on these results, we modeled effective connectivity between L. F3op/F3t and L. SMG by using DCM. Our interest was to identify the direction of the connectivity modulated by the Nested condition with largest DoM among all conditions, and the models were grouped into three "modulatory families": families *A*, *B*, and *C*, corresponding to the modulation for the bottom-up connection from L. SMG to L. F3op/F3t, for the top-down connection from L. F3op/F3t to L. SMG, and for both connections, respectively. Here we assumed intrinsic, i.e., task-independent, bidirectional connections. Each family was composed of three "input models" as regards the regions receiving driving inputs (see Figure 8.S4 for all DCM models tested). Using a random-effects Bayesian model selection (BMS), we found that the family *A* was the most likely family (expected probability = 0.66, exceedance probability = 0.85) (Figure 8.4G and 8.4H). According to a second BMS for the input models within the family *A*, the model *A1*, in which L. F3op/F3t received driving inputs, was the best and highly probable model (expected probability = 0.77, exceedance probability = 0.95). For this particular model, we further tested whether the parameter estimates were significantly different from zero. The intrinsic connection from L. F3op/F3t to L. SMG was significantly positive [+0.22; one-sample *t*-test, $t(17) = 4.8$, $P < 0.0002$] (significance level at $\alpha = 0.025$, Bonferroni corrected within a parameter class of intrinsic connections) (Figure 8.4I), indicating that this top-down connection was consistent among the participants. The modulatory effect for the bottom-up connection was inhibitory [-0.17; $t(17) = 1.4$, $P = 0.17$], though it did not reach the significance level.

To further confirm the anatomical plausibility of the network between L. F3op/F3t and L. SMG revealed by DCM, we used DTI with a probabilistic tractography. Seed masks were set in the pair of L. F3op/F3t and L. SMG, both of which were significantly activated in Nested'$_{(L)}$ > Simple'$_{(S)}$. We identified a single continuous cluster of the left SLF/AF that connected these regions (cluster size, 3,189 mm^3), together with much smaller clusters or islands (Figure 8.4J). Moreover, the left SLF/AF was consistently observed in all participants.

Modulation of the Right Frontal Activations by Nonlinguistic Factors

We further examined the involvement of any error-related factors, which were residual factors that might induce cortical activation or deactivation. It should be noted that the factors listed in Tables 8.1 and 8.2 were equivalent to the matching and nonmatching stimuli. The [Nonmatching – Matching] contrast under either the sentence conditions (i.e., [Nested + Simple + Conjoined]) or the string conditions (i.e., [Reverse + Same]) consistently resulted in right-dominant activation, especially in R. F3op/F3t (Figure 8.5A and 8.5B), which was in accordance with the same demand of the matching task (Figure 8.1C and 8.1D). Other significantly activated regions were L. LPMC/F3op and ACC under the sentence conditions, as well as R. SMG under the string conditions (Table 8.4). As regards the [Matching – Nonmatching] contrast, no significant activation was seen under sentence or string conditions.

We also examined the activation in Reverse" for the effect of matching orders (e.g., A_2 A_1 B_1 B_2 vs. A_1 A_2 B_1 B_2; Figures 8.1B and 8.2B). The significant activation was observed only in R. LPMC (Figure 8.5C and Table 8.4), which suggested that activations could indeed be estimated by the one and only non-null factor of memory span in Reverse" (Table 8.2). In Nested", the signal changes in R. LPMC were also significant (one-sample *t*-test, $P < 0.05$), which were not significantly different between Nested" and Reverse" (paired *t*-test, $P = 0.98$) (Figure 8.5D). This result was consistent with the equivalent estimates of memory span between Nested" and Reverse". It should be noted that R. LPMC activation was also observed for the main effects of condition and length (Figure 8.4A and 8.4B), which probably reflected the factor of memory span.

Discussion

By employing a novel paradigm to directly contrast jabberwocky sentences (Nested, Simple, and Conjoined) with letter strings (Reverse and

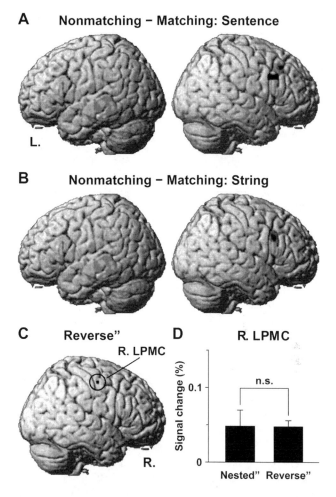

A   Nonmatching – Matching: Sentence

L.

B   Nonmatching – Matching: String

C   Reverse"
R. LPMC

R.

D   R. LPMC

Signal change (%)

n.s.

0.1

0

Nested" Reverse"

Figure 8.5 (**Plate 7 left half**). Modulation of the right frontal activations by nonlinguistic factors. One-sample t-tests were used for the contrasts indicated. (A) Regions identified by [Nonmatching – Matching] under the sentence conditions, related to error-related factors. Note the right-dominant activation, especially in R. F3op/F3t. (B) Regions identified by [Nonmatching – Matching] under the string conditions. (C) Regions identified by Reverse". This contrast revealed the difference in matching orders (e.g., $A_2 A_1 B_1 B_2$ vs. $A_1 A_2 B_1 B_2$). Note the significant activation in R. LPMC. (D) The percent signal changes in R. LPMC, which was consistent with the equivalent estimates of memory span (see Table 8.2).

Same) (Figures 8.1 and 8.2), we obtained four striking results. First, we found that DoM was indeed a key syntactic factor that could account for syntax-selective activations in L. F3op/F3t and L. SMG, localized by the Nested'$_{(L)}$ > Simple'$_{(S)}$ contrast (Figure 8.4C and 8.4D). By constructing a model of each syntactic, other linguistic, or nonlinguistic factor using its estimates (Table 8.1), we demonstrated that the models of DoM and "DoM + number of Search" were the best to explain L. F3op/F3t and L. SMG activations, respectively (Table 8.5). Secondly, by directly contrasting jabberwocky sentences with letter strings, i.e., Nested" > Reverse", we showed that the selective activation in L. F3op/F3t and L. SMG, which was consistent with the involvement of the syntactic factors demonstrated earlier, was replicated irrespective of identical matching orders and symbol orders (e.g., $N_2 N_1 V_1 V_2$ and $A_2 A_1 B_1 B_2$ for the Nested and Reverse, respectively) (Figure 8.4E and 8.4F). This point is particularly important, because temporal order-related or memory-related factors have often been confused with differences in structure or grammar type. Our results strongly support that syntactic structures are recursively constructed when well-formed sentences are given. Thirdly, by using DCM, we found that the model with an inhibitory modulatory effect for the bottom-up connectivity from L. SMG to L. F3op/F3t, and with driving inputs to L. F3op/F3t, was the best one (Figure 8.4G and 8.4H). For this best model, the top-down connection from L. F3op/F3t to L. SMG was significantly positive (Figure 8.4I). By using DTI, we also confirmed that the left dorsal pathway of SLF/AF consistently connected these two regions (Figure 8.4J). These results suggest that there is a transmission of information about DoM through this specific dorsal pathway. Lastly, we established that nonlinguistic order-related and error-related factors significantly activated mostly right frontal regions. The difference in memory span significantly modulated R. LPMC activation in Reverse", suggesting that this region plays a major role in tracking matching orders (Figure 8.5C and 8.5D), while error-related factors in [Nonmatching – Matching] consistently modulated R. F3op/F3t activation under both sentence and string conditions (Figure 8.5A and 8.5B). In summary, these results indicate that the identified network of L. F3op/F3t and L. SMG subserves the calculation of DoM in recursively merged sentences, and that R. LPMC monitors memory span to drive a memory-maintenance system. If multiple factors, such as the number of nodes, memory span, etc., are equally plausible to explain activations, then a superordinate concept, such as "syntactic complexity," can be a more useful factor than individual factors. However, in the present experiment, the minimal factor of DoM *sufficiently* explained the activation pattern observed, while other factors were by far less likely (see Table 8.5). Therefore, syntactic complexity was restricted and replaced by DoM as a more fundamental concept, just like the historical development from "gene" to DNA.

It remains a central issue in cognitive sciences whether or not the faculty of language is also shared by animals. Animals have been thus tested with regular symbolic sequences such as $A^n B^n$ ($n \geq 2$; i.e., AABB, AAABBB, . . .) and $(AB)^n$ ($n \geq 2$; i.e., ABAB, ABABAB, . . .), which differ in *symbol order*. In an animal study, songbirds were trained to discriminate patterns of $A^n B^n$ and $(AB)^n$ in more than ten thousand trials (Gentner et al. 2006). However, this learning can be achieved by a counting strategy alone (Corballis 2007). There is also a recent report that songbirds seemed to discriminate strings with or without nesting (Abe and Watanabe 2011), but this learning can be achieved by simply remembering partial strings (Beckers et al. 2012). Along the line of contrasting $A^n B^n$ and $(AB)^n$, fMRI studies have tested participants with different symbolic sequences, such as $A_2 A_1 B_1 B_2$ versus $A_1 B_1 A_2 B_2$, which also differ in *matching order* (Bahlmann et al. 2008). However, the difference in activation patterns can be simply explained by differences in any factors associated with matching orders and symbol orders, i.e., temporal order-related factors. It was thus necessary to completely control these general factors when extracting any syntactic factors from a number of cognitive factors involved in actual symbol processing.

Our finding that L. F3op/F3t subserves the syntactic computation further extends the functional specialization of this region reported previously (Embick et al. 2000, Musso et al. 2003, Sakai 2005, Kinno et al. 2008). Some previous fMRI studies have interpreted L. F3op/F3t activation as reflecting temporal order-related or memory-related factors (Bahlmann et al. 2007, Santi and Grodzinsky 2010). However, these previous studies contrasted hierarchically complex sentences with simpler sentences, while it is clear that syntactic factors, including DoM, were also involved. Moreover, the previously reported modulation of the L. F3op/F3t activation by scrambling word orders (Röder et al. 2002) can be consistently explained by DoM, because scrambling requires "movements" of NPs to higher nodes by applying more Merge operations, thus increasing DoM. The size of linguistic constituents also correlates with DoM, especially when the number of left/right branches was increased as in the case of Pallier et al. (2011). In the present study, we characterized the neural substrates of syntactic computation by segregating a number of possible factors, and demonstrated that the exact activations in L. F3op/F3t can be used to calculate DoM. Indeed, each structure of our jabberwocky sentences was uniquely represented by DoM, together with the numbers of Merge and Search (see Table 8.1).

A previous fMRI study involving the implicit learning of an artificial regular grammar has reported that the "ungrammatical – grammatical" contrast for symbol sequences activated L. F3op/F3t, suggesting that such activation was due to artificial syntactic violations among any error-related factors (Petersson et al. 2004). However, this result may not depend on the presence of errors themselves, but on other rule-related processes associated with error-correction, etc. In contrast, we have previously demonstrated that an explicit syntactic decision enhanced L. F3op/F3t activation under *both* grammatical and ungrammatical conditions (Suzuki and Sakai 2003). On the other hand, a recent fMRI study has compared nested and branching constructions, suggesting that activation in the bilateral posterior superior temporal cortex reflects an integration of lexico-semantic and syntactic information (Friederici et al. 2009). However, as regards this previous result, the effects of semantic factors were inevitably confounded with any structural processing, because real German sentences were used as stimuli in that study. Furthermore, according to our paradigm, the temporal cortex in neither of the hemispheres showed any significant activation for the Nested (Figure 8.4). It was thus quite important to verify that activation in L. F3op/F3t, but not in the temporal cortex, is indeed crucial for syntactic processing.

In the present study, we found that L. SMG activations were modulated by "DoM + number of Search." Consistent with the suggested role of L. AG/SMG for vocabulary knowledge or lexical processing (Lee et al. 2007, Pattamadilok et al. 2010), the number of Search is likely to induce such a modulation, in the sense that Search assigns a specific feature that can be linked with morphosyntactic changes. The Japanese language happens to lack the agreement of grammatical features, but it is nevertheless equipped with the general Search procedure attested for various phenomena in the language (Fukui and Sakai 2003). Our results suggest that Search actually applied to a subject-verb pair of a jabberwocky sentence in the present paradigm, where the relevant features (vowels here) are experimentally "inserted." It should also be noted in this connection that the Japanese language exhibits a phenomenon called "honorification" (the case of an honored person and the form of honorifics on verbs optionally match) (Gunji 1987, Ivana and Sakai 2007), in which Search assigns such features as honorifics. Our previous fMRI study using an honorification judgment task reported activation in L. F3op/F3t and L. LPMC, as well as in the L. inferior parietal gyrus and L. AG (Momo et al. 2008), which is consistent with activation in L. AG/SMG in the present study (Tables 8.3 and 8.4).

Our DCM and DTI results further indicate that L. SMG activations reflecting DoM mirrored a top-down influence from L. F3op/F3t through the left dorsal pathway of SLF/AF. A recent DCM study with a picture-sentence matching task has suggested that L. F3op/F3t received driving inputs (den Ouden et al. 2012), which was consistent with our DCM results. Moreover, our previous studies revealed that the functional connectivity between L. F3t/F3O (pars orbitalis) and L. AG/SMG was selectively enhanced during sentence processing (Homae et al. 2003), and that L. AG/SMG was also activated during the identification of correct past-tense forms of verbs, probably reflecting an integration of syntactic and vocabulary knowledge

(Tatsuno and Sakai 2005). Considering the role of L. AG/SMG in lexical processing, the Search operation based on DoM would be essential in assigning relevant features to the syntactic objects derived from lexical items.

In [Nonmatching – Matching], R. F3op/F3t was consistently activated under both sentence and string conditions (Figure 8.5A and 8.5B), whereas L. LPMC/F3op, ACC, or R. SMG were activated under either condition. These four regions were also activated in Nested' > Simple', and in Long > Short while combining Nested' and Simple'; the ACC and R. SMG were activated in Nested" > Reverse" as well. It appears likely that a part of the activation in these four regions reflects error-related factors including the detection and correction of errors, which would be more demanding with the Nested, as well as in the Long > Short contrast. Because L. LPMC has been known to selectively subserve syntactic processing (Indefrey et al. 2001b, Hashimoto and Sakai 2002, Kinno et al. 2008), a weak activation in L. LPMC/F3op only under the sentence conditions may reflect the confirmation of sentence constructions when confronted with nonmatching stimuli. On the other hand, it has been suggested that the dorsal ACC plays a major role during conflict monitoring during a highly demanding task, e.g., a Stroop task (Botvinick et al. 2004). Our recent magnetoencephalography study also suggested that the anterior portion of the ACC is a candidate region for monitoring syntactically anomalous sentences (Iijima et al. 2009). Moreover, previous studies on a response inhibition, typically tested with a No-go task, suggested that R. F3op/F3t, ACC, and R. SMG were also involved in monitoring anomalous stimuli (Chikazoe et al. 2007). In contrast to these factors that activated mostly right and medial regions, it is noteworthy that the syntactic factors clearly activated the left frontal and parietal regions.

Any factors associated with matching orders and symbol orders might influence activation in the language areas, but we clearly showed that R. LPMC was activated in Reverse" (Figure 8.5C) for the effect of memory span related to matching orders. The study of real German sentences also reported activation in the right dorsal premotor area for the contrast of nested vs. branching constructions (Friederici et al. 2009), but the right dorsal premotor area was not the same region as R. LPMC in the present study. In this German study, memory span was controlled by the insertion of some words, while matching orders and symbol orders still differed, and thus factors other than memory span were inevitably introduced to interpret the right dorsal premotor activation. The identification of critical factors in language processing thus inevitably depends on an experimental design that involves an effective contrast of conditions. One promising direction of research is to further clarify activations modulated by other linguistic and nonlinguistic factors, which may eventually make possible the elucidation of all aspects of linguistic information in the human brain.

Supporting Information

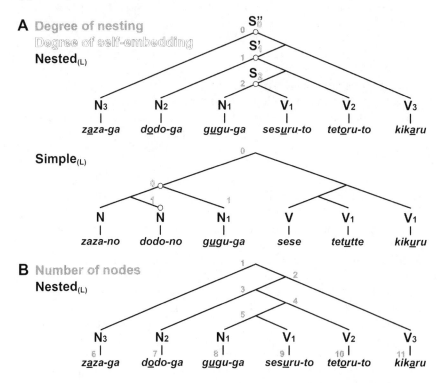

Figure 8.S1 Application of other structure-based models to sentences with complex structures, I. (A) The digits shown in gray and white denote "degree of nesting" and "degree of self-embedding," respectively. Nested and self-embedded constructions occur within sentences (Ss). Note that each shortest "zigzag path" counts one for the degree of nesting or self-embedding. For the Nested(L), S_1 dominates [N_2 S_2 V_2], and S_0 in turn dominates [N_3 S_1 V_3], i.e., [N_3[N_2 S_2 V_2]V_3]; the degree of nesting or self-embedding is thus two (the number of white dots minus one). For the Simple(L), both of (NN)N_1 and N(NN$_1$) yield the same maximum degree of nesting or self-embedding for an entire sentence. (B) The digits shown in gray denote "number of nodes."

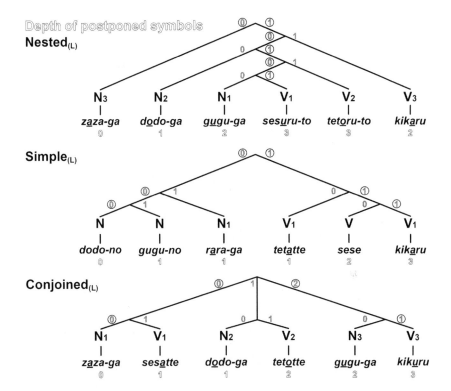

Figure 8.S2 Application of other structure-based models to sentences with complex structures, II. The digits shown in gray and white denote the number of branches from each node and "depth of postponed symbols" (Yngve 1960), respectively. The largest estimate can be obtained by adding together the digits shown in gray with circles. For the Simple$_{(L)}$, the largest estimate of "depth of postponed symbols" is obtained, when Vs take a right-branching construction of $V_1(VV_1)$. For the Conjoined$_{(L)}$, the depth of postponed symbols is increased by two to reach the rightmost branches, when conjoining three sentences at a multiple-branching node.

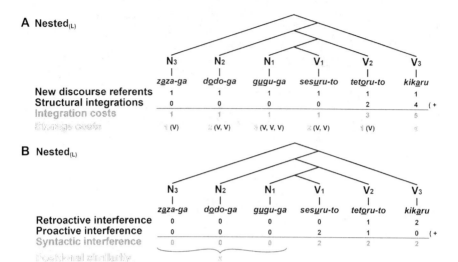

A Nested(L)

	N₃	N₂	N₁	V₁	V₂	V₃
	zaza-ga	dodo-ga	gugu-ga	sesuru-to	tetoru-to	kikaru
New discourse referents	1	1	1	1	1	1
Structural integrations	0	0	0	0	2	4 (+
Integration costs	1	1	1	1	3	5
Storage costs	1 (V)	2 (V, V)	3 (V, V, V)	2 (V, V)	1 (V)	0

B Nested(L)

	N₃	N₂	N₁	V₁	V₂	V₃
	zaza-ga	dodo-ga	gugu-ga	sesuru-to	tetoru-to	kikaru
Retroactive interference	0	0	0	0	1	2
Proactive interference	0	0	0	2	1	0 (+
Syntactic interference	0	0	0	2	2	2
Positional similarity		3				

Figure 8.S3 Application of other structure-based models to sentences with complex structures, III. (A) The digits shown in gray and white denote "integration costs" and "storage costs" (Gibson 2000), respectively. Integration costs are estimated at every stimulus by adding together "new discourse referents" and "structural integrations." For example, at V_2 of the Nested(L), N_1 and V_1 intervene while making [N_2[N_1 V_1] V_2] (structural integrations = 2), and one verb completes the input with *-to* or *-te* (storage cost = 1). Note that the estimate of maximum structural integrations in a sentence matches with that of memory span in our paradigm. (B) The digits shown in gray and white denote "syntactic interference" and "positional similarity" (Lewis and Nakayama 2002), respectively. Syntactic interference is estimated at every stimulus by adding together "retroactive interference" and "proactive interference." For example, at V_2 of the Nested(L), the attachment of V_2 to N_2 suffers from one unit of retroactive interference from N_1, and from one unit of proactive interference from N_3 (syntactic interference = 2). There are three adjacent nominative NPs in this sentence (positional similarity = 3).

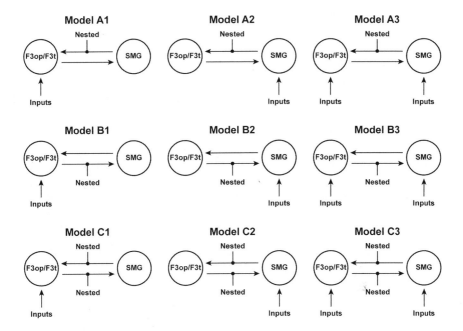

Figure 8.S4 The DCM models tested. We assumed bidirectional connectivity between L. F3op/F3t and L. SMG. The models were grouped into three modulatory families based on the modulations of the connections under the Nested condition: Family *A* (*A1—A3*), in which the connection from L. SMG to L. F3op/F3t was modulated, Family *B* (*B1—B3*), in which the connection from L. F3op/F3t to L. SMG was modulated, and Family *C* (*C1—C3*), in which both connections were modulated. Each family was composed of three "input models" as regards the regions receiving driving inputs.

Table 8.S1 Examples of short nonmatching stimuli.

Condition	Error type	Stimulus example
Nested sentence, short	$[N_2[N_1 \ V_1]V_2{}^*]$	*mumu-ga rara-ga tetaru-to hih<u>o</u>ru*
(Nested$_{(S)}$)	$[N_2[N_1 \ V_1{}^*]V_2{}^*]$	*dodo-ga gugu-ga tet<u>o</u>ru-to kik<u>a</u>ru*
	$[N_2[N_1 \ V_1{}^*]V_2]$	*rara-ga mumu-ga ses<u>o</u>tta-to kikatta*
Simple sentence, short (Simple$_{(S)}$)	$[(NN_1) \ (VV_1{}^*)]$	*rara-no gugu-ga tete ses<u>a</u>tta*
Conjoined sentence, short	$[N_1 \ V_1][N_2 \ V_2{}^*]$	*rara-ga hihatte gugu-ga tet<u>o</u>ru*
(Conjoined$_{(S)}$)	$[N_1 \ V_1{}^*][N_2 \ V_2{}^*]$	*yoyo-ga hih<u>u</u>tte rara-ga ses<u>o</u>tta*
	$[N_1 \ V_1{}^*][N_2 \ V_2]$	*gugu-ga tet<u>o</u>tte zaza-ga hiharu*
Reverse-order string, short	$A_2 \ A_1 \ B_1 \ B_2{}^*$	*nododo rukiku rukiku <u>donodo</u>*
(Reverse$_{(S)}$)	$A_2 \ A_1 \ B_1{}^* \ B_2{}^*$	*gayoyo settasa <u>sasseta gadodo</u>*
	$A_2 \ A_1 \ B_1{}^* \ B_2$	*mugamu sessota <u>kittako</u> mugamu*
Same-order string, short (Same$_{(S)}$)	$A_1 \ A_2 \ B_1 \ B_2{}^*$	*ruteta gugagu ruteta <u>yogayo</u>*
	$A_1 \ A_2 \ B_1{}^* \ B_2{}^*$	*yonoyo rusesu <u>donodo rususe</u>*
	$A_1 \ A_2 \ B_1{}^* \ B_2$	*norara kuruki <u>noyoyo</u> kuruki*

For each condition, nonmatching stimuli with errors in different positions are listed in descending order of frequency. Under the sentence conditions, Vs with asterisks represent matching errors (underlined vowels in stimulus examples here; no underline in the real stimuli). Under the string conditions, Bs with asterisks represent matching errors (underlined letter strings in stimulus examples here; no underline in the real stimuli).

Table 8.S2 Examples of long nonmatching stimuli.

Condition	Error type	Stimulus example
Nested$_{(L)}$	$[N_3[N_2[N_1\ V_1]V_2]V_3{}^*]$	*mumu-ga zaza-ga yoyo-ga kikotta-to hihatta-to tetatta*
	$[N_3[N_2[N_1\ V_1]V_2{}^*]V_3]$	*dodo-ga rara-ga mumu-ga hihuru-to teturu-to kikoru*
	$[N_3[N_2[N_1\ V_1]V_2{}^*]V_3{}^*]$	*dodo-ga mumu-ga zaza-ga tetaru-to sesoru-to hihuru*
	$[N_3[N_2[N_1\ V_1{}^*]V_2]V_3{}^*]$	*rara-ga mumu-ga yoyo-ga hiharu-to teturu-to sesoru*
Simple$_{(L)}$	$[((NN)N_1)\ ((VV_1)V_1{}^*)]$	*rara-no gugu-no yoyo-ga kiki sesotte teturu*
	$[((NN)N_1)\ ((VV_1{}^*)V_1)]$	*gugu-no zaza-no dodo-ga kiki tetatte sesoru*
	$[((NN)N_1)\ ((VV_1{}^*)V_1{}^*)]$	*yoyo-no rara-no mumu-ga tete hihotte kikotta*
Conjoined$_{(L)}$	$[N_1\ V_1][N_2\ V_2][N_3\ V_3{}^*]$	*dodo-ga tetotte mumu-ga sesutte zaza-ga hihoru*
	$[N_1\ V_1][N_2\ V_2{}^*][N_3\ V_3]$	*gugu-ga kikutte zaza-ga tetotte dodo-ga sesoru*
	$[N_1\ V_1][N_2\ V_2{}^*][N_3\ V_3{}^*]$	*zaza-ga sesatte yoyo-ga kikutte gugu-ga tetotta*
	$[N_1\ V_1{}^*][N_2\ V_2][N_3\ V_3{}^*]$	*mumu-ga sesotte rara-ga kikatte dodo-ga hihutta*
Reverse$_{(L)}$	$A_3\ A_2\ A_1\ B_1\ B_2\ B_3{}^*$	*gazaza rusose gunogu gunogu rusose nozaza*
	$A_3\ A_2\ A_1\ B_1\ B_2{}^*\ B_3{}^*$	*ragara hiruhu gayoyo gayoyo huruhi gazaza*
	$A_3\ A_2\ A_1\ B_1\ B_2{}^*\ B_3$	*serusa gugagu hohiru hohiru nogugu serusa*
	$A_3\ A_2\ A_1\ B_1{}^*\ B_2\ B_3{}^*$	*gunogu ruteta nododo noyoyo ruteta gugagu*
Same$_{(L)}$	$A_1\ A_2\ A_3\ B_1\ B_2\ B_3{}^*$	*hiruho gunogu haruhi hiruho gunogu hahiru*
	$A_1\ A_2\ A_3\ B_1\ B_2{}^*\ B_3{}^*$	*dogado rutetu zagaza dogado suruse zanoza*
	$A_1\ A_2\ A_3\ B_1\ B_2{}^*\ B_3$	*kattaki yonoyo tutetta kattaki nododo tutetta*
	$A_1\ A_2\ A_3\ B_1{}^*\ B_2\ B_3{}^*$	*noyoyo tahihha munomu nododo tahihha mugamu*

For the Simple$_{(L)}$, there were also other error types, i.e., $V_1{}^*(VV_1{}^*)$, $V_1(VV_1{}^*)$, and $V_1{}^*(VV_1)$. For the Nested$_{(L)}$ and Conjoined$_{(L)}$, we included nonmatching stimuli with a maximum variety of vowels in Vs, as shown here; for the Simple$_{(L)}$, we included nonmatching stimuli with a least variety of vowels in Vs. Therefore, the strategy of noting the variety of vowels was not effective. Under all conditions, there were more variations in error for the long than short stimuli.

Acknowledgments

This chapter is dedicated to the memory of S.-Y. Kuroda, who was a truly distinguished linguist and a great mentor for all of us in the field. We would like to thank A. Sakurai and A. Morita for their help in earlier experiments, H. Miyashita, K. Iijima, and T. Inubushi for their comments on the earlier manuscript, N. Komoro and N. Saeki for their technical assistance, and H. Matsuda and S. Matsukura for their administrative assistance.

References

Abe, Kentaro, and Dai Watanabe. 2011. Songbirds possess the spontaneous ability to discriminate syntactic rules. *Nature Neuroscience* 14: 1067–1074.

Bahlmann, Jörg, Antoni Rodriguez-Fornells, Michael Rotte, and Thomas F. Münte. 2007. An fMRI study of canonical and noncanonical word order in German. *Human Brain Mapping* 28: 940–949.

Bahlmann, Jörg, Ricarda I. Schubotz, and Angela D. Friederici. 2008. Hierarchical artificial grammar processing engages Broca's area. *NeuroImage* 42: 525–534.

Beckers, Gabriël J. L., Johan J. Bolhuis, Kazuo Okanoya, and Robert C. Berwick. 2012. Birdsong neurolinguistics: Songbird context-free grammar claim is premature. *NeuroReport* 23: 139–145.

Botvinick, Matthew M., Jonathan D. Cohen, Cameron S. Carter. 2004. Conflict monitoring and anterior cingulate cortex: An update. *Trends in Cognitive Science* 8: 539–546.

Chikazoe, Junichi, Seiki Konishi, Tomoki Asari, Koji Jimura, and Yasushi Miyashita. 2007. Activation of right inferior frontal gyrus during response inhibition across response modalities. *Journal of Cognitive Neuroscience* 19: 69–80.

Chomsky, Noam. 1957. *Syntactic structures*. The Hague: Mouton. 2nd edition, Mouton de Gruyter, 2002.

Chomsky, Noam. 1965. *Aspects of the theory of syntax*. Cambridge, MA: MIT Press.

Chomsky, Noam. 1995. *The minimalist program*. Cambridge, MA: MIT Press.

Chomsky, Noam. 2004. Beyond explanatory adequacy. In *Structures and beyond: The cartography of syntactic structures*, volume 3, ed. Adriana Belletti, 104–131. Oxford: Oxford University Press.

Corballis, Michael C. 2007. Recursion, language, and starlings. *Cognive Science* 31: 697–704.

Dapretto, Mirella, and Susan Y. Bookheimer. 1999. Form and content: Dissociating syntax and semantics in sentence comprehension. *Neuron* 24: 427–432.

den Ouden, Dirk-Bart, Dorothee Saur, Wolfgang Mader, Björn Schelter, Sladjana Lukic, Eisha Wali, Jens Timmer, and Cynthia K. Thompson. 2012. Network modulation during complex syntactic processing. *NeuroImage* 59: 815–823.

Embick, David, Alec Marantz, Yasushi Miyashita, Wayne O'Neil, and Kuniyoshi L. Sakai. 2000. A syntactic specialization for Broca's area. *Proceedings of the National Academy of Sciences of the United States of America* 97: 6150–6154.

Friederici, Angela D., Michiru Makuuchi, and Jörg Bahlmann. 2009. The role of the posterior superior temporal cortex in sentence comprehension. *NeuroReport* 20: 563–568.

Friederici, Angela D., Shirley-Ann Rüschemeyer, Anja Hahne, and Christian J. Fiebach. 2003. The role of left inferior frontal and superior temporal cortex in sentence comprehension: Localizing syntactic and semantic processes. *Cerebral Cortex* 13: 170–177.

Friston, Karl J., Lee Harrison, and Will Penny. 2003. Dynamic causal modelling. *NeuroImage* 19: 1273–1302.

Friston, Karl J., and Richard N. Henson. 2006. Commentary on: Divide and conquer; a defence of functional localisers. *NeuroImage* 30: 1097–1099.

Fukui, Naoki. 2011. Merge and bare phrase structure. In *The Oxford handbook of linguistic minimalism*, ed. Cedric Boeckx, 73–95. Oxford: Oxford University Press. [Chapter 1, this volume.]

Fukui, Naoki, and Hiromu Sakai. 2003. The visibility guideline for functional categories: Verb raising in Japanese and related issues. *Lingua* 113 (4–6): 321–375. [Reprinted in *Theoretical comparative syntax: Studies in macroparameters*, Naoki Fukui, 289–336. London: Routledge. (2006).]

Gentner, Timothy Q., Kimberly M. Fenn, Daniel Margoliash, and Howard C. Nusbaum. 2006. Recursive syntactic pattern learning by songbirds. *Nature* 440: 1204–1207.

Gibson, Edward. 2000. The dependency locality theory: A distance-based theory of linguistic complexity. In *Image, language, brain: Papers from the First Mind Articulation Project Symposium*, ed. Alec Marantz, Yasushi Miyashita, and Wayne O'Neil, 95–126. Cambridge, MA: MIT Press.

Griffiths, John D., William D. Marslen-Wilson, Emmanuel A. Stamatakis, and Lorraine K. Tyler. 2013. Functional organization of the neural language system: Dorsal and ventral pathways are critical for syntax. *Cerebral Cortex* 23: 139–147.

Gunji, Takao. 1987. *Japanese phrase structure grammar: A unification-based approach*. Dordrecht: D. Reidel Publishing Company.

Hashimoto, Ryuichiro, and Kuniyoshi L. Sakai. 2002. Specialization in the left prefrontal cortex for sentence comprehension. *Neuron* 35: 589–597.

Homae, Fumitaka, Noriaki Yahata, and Kuniyoshi L. Sakai. 2003. Selective enhancement of functional connectivity in the left prefrontal cortex during sentence processing. *NeuroImage* 20: 578–586.

Hopcroft, John E., and Jeffrey D. Ullman. 1979. *Introduction to automata theory, languages, and computation*. Reading, MA: Addison-Wesley.

Iijima, Kazuki, Naoki Fukui, and Kuniyoshi L. Sakai. 2009. The cortical dynamics in building syntactic structures of sentences: An MEG study in a minimal-pair paradigm. *NeuroImage* 44: 1387–1396. [Chapter 7, this volume.]

Indefrey, Peter, Peter Hagoort, Hans Herzog, Rüdiger J. Seitz, Colin M. Brown. 2001b. Syntactic processing in left prefrontal cortex is independent of lexical meaning. *NeuroImage* 14: 546–555.

Ivana, Adrian, and Hiromu Sakai. 2007. Honorification and light verbs in Japanese. *Journal of East Asian Linguistics* 16: 171–191.

Kinno, Ryuta, Mitsuru Kawamura, Seiji Shioda, and Kuniyoshi L. Sakai. 2008. Neural correlates of noncanonical syntactic processing revealed by a picture-sentence matching task. *Human Brain Mapping* 29: 1015–1027.

Kriegeskorte, Nikolaus, W. Kyle Simmons, Patrick S. F. Bellgowan, Chris I. Baker. 2009. Circular analysis in systems neuroscience: The dangers of double dipping. *Nature Neuroscience* 12: 535–540.

Lee, HweeLing, Joseph T. Devlin, Clare Shakeshaft, Lauren H. Stewart, Amanda Brennan, Jen Glensman, Katherine Pitcher, Jenny Crinion, Andrea Mechelli, Richard S. J. Frackowiak, David W. Green, and Cathy J. Price. 2007. Anatomical traces of vocabulary acquisition in the adolescent brain. *The Journal of Neuroscience* 27: 1184–1189.

Lewis, Richard, and Mineharu Nakayama. 2002. Syntactic and positional similarity effects in the processing of Japanese embeddings. In *Sentence processing in East Asian languages*, ed. Mineharu Nakayama, 85–111. Stanford: CSLI Publications.

Momo, Kanako, Hiromu Sakai, and Kuniyoshi L. Sakai. 2008. Syntax in a native language still continues to develop in adults: Honorification judgment in Japanese. *Brain and Language* 107: 81–89.

Musso, Mariacristina, Andrea Moro, Volkmar Glauche, Michel Rijntjes, Jürgen Reichenbach, Christian Büchel, and Cornelius Weiller. 2003. Broca's area and the language instinct. *Nature Neuroscience* 6: 774–781.

O'Grady, William, John Archibald, Mark Aronoff, and Janie Rees-Miller. 2010. *Contemporary linguistics: An introduction*, 6th edition. Boston: Bedford/St. Martin's.

Oldfield, Richard Charles. 1971. The assessment and analysis of handedness: The Edinburgh Inventory. *Neuropsychologia* 9: 97–113.

Pallier, Christophe, Anne-Dominique Devauchelle, and Stanislas Dehaene. 2011. Cortical representation of the constituent structure of sentences. *Proceedings of the National Academy of Sciences of the United States of America* 108: 2522–2527.

Pattamadilok, Chotiga, Iris N. Knierim, Keith J. Kawabata Duncan, and Joseph T. Devlin. 2010. How does learning to read affect speech perception? *The Journal of Neuroscience* 30: 8435–8444.

Petersson, Karl Magnus, Christian Forkstam, and Martin Ingvar. 2004. Artificial syntactic violations activate Broca's region. *Cognitive Science* 28: 383–407.

Röder, Brigitte, Oliver Stock, Helen Neville, Siegfried Bien, and Frank Rösler. 2002. Brain activation modulated by the comprehension of normal and pseudo-word sentences of different processing demands: A functional magnetic resonance imaging study. *NeuroImage* 15: 1003–1014.

Saito, Mamoru, and Naoki Fukui. 1998. Order in phrase structure and movement. *Linguistic Inquiry* 29: 439–474. [Reprinted in *Theoretical comparative syntax: Studies in macroparameters*, Naoki Fukui, 179–208. London: Routledge. (2006).]

Sakai, Kuniyoshi L. 2005. Language acquisition and brain development. *Science* 310: 815–819.

Santi, Andrea, and Yosef Grodzinsky. 2010. fMRI adaptation dissociates syntactic complexity dimensions. *NeuroImage* 51: 1285–1293.

Saur, Dorothee, Björn W. Kreher, Susanne Schnell, Dorothee Kümmerer, Philipp Kellmeyer, Magnus-Sebastian Vry, Rosa Umarova, Mariacristina Musso, Volkmar Glauche, Stefanie Abel, Walter Huber, Michel Rijntjes, Jürgen Hennig, and Cornelius Weiller. 2008. Ventral and dorsal pathways for language. *Proceedings of the National Academy of Sciences of the United States of America* 105: 18035–18040.

Stromswold, Karin, David Caplan, Nathaniel Alpert, and Scott Rauch. 1996. Localization of syntactic comprehension by positron emission tomography. *Brain and Language* 52: 452–473.

Suzuki, Kei, and Kuniyoshi L. Sakai. 2003. An event-related fMRI study of explicit syntactic processing of normal/anomalous sentences in contrast to implicit syntactic processing. *Cerebral Cortex* 13: 517–526.

Tatsuno, Yoshinori, and Kuniyoshi L. Sakai. 2005. Language-related activations in the left prefrontal regions are differentially modulated by age, proficiency, and task demands. *The Journal of Neuroscience* 25: 1637–1644.

Tsujimura, Natsuko. 2007. *An introduction to Japanese linguistics*, 2nd edition. Malden, MA: Blackwell.

Wilson, Stephen M., Sebastiano Galantucci, Maria Carmela Tartaglia, Kindle Rising, Dianne K. Patterson, Maya L. Henry, Jennifer M. Ogar, Jessica DeLeon,

Bruce L. Miller, and Maria Luisa Gorno-Tempini. 2011. Syntactic processing depends on dorsal language tracts. *Neuron* 72: 397–403.

Wong, Francis C. K., Bharath Chandrasekaran, Kyla Garibaldi, and Patrick C. M. Wong. 2011. White matter anisotropy in the ventral language pathway predicts sound-to-word learning success. *The Journal of Neuroscience* 31: 8780–8785.

Yngve, Victor H. 1960. A model and an hypothesis for language structure. *Proceedings of the American Philosophical Society* 104: 444–466.

Appendix S1 Theoretical issues

Theoretical Background

Sentences with different constructions have been previously discussed in terms of the acceptability of sentences (cf. Chomsky 1965: 12).

(i)   nested constructions
(ii)   self-embedded constructions
(iii) multiple-branching constructions
(iv)   left-branching constructions
(v)   right-branching constructions

The nested constructions are created by *centrally* embedding a phrase within another phrase (with some non-null element to its left and some non-null element to its right), and the self-embedded constructions are the special case of nested constructions when nesting occurs within the *same* type of phrases (e.g., noun phrases). The multiple-branching constructions are made by conjoining phrases at the same hierarchical level, and the left/right-branching constructions are yielded by merging a phrase in the leftmost or rightmost phrase. The degrees of nesting and self-embedding have been already proposed to model the understanding of sentences (Miller and Chomsky 1963). By generalizing this attractive idea to include any constructions with merged phrases, we introduced DoM as a key computational concept.

We have proposed that various other "miscellaneous" operations that have been employed in the linguistics literature, such as Agree, Scope determination, Copy, etc., are in fact different manifestations of one and the same, i.e., more generalized, operation of Search (Fukui and Sakai 2003). Thus, Agree, which has been assumed to be an operation mainly responsible for the agreement of grammatical features, is actually not an operation specific to agreement, but rather is just an instance of the basic operation Search, when it assigns specific features. Human language, therefore, should minimally contain only two universal operations, Merge and Search.

As regards the formal symbol sequences beyond the bounds of finite state languages, three specific types of language have been discussed in the linguistic literature: (i) "counter language," (ii) "mirror-image language," and (iii) "copying language" (cf. Chomsky 1957: 21).

(i) *ab, aabb, aaabbb,* . . ., and in general, all sentences consisting of *n* occurrences of *a* followed by *n* occurrences of *b* and only these;

(ii) *aa, bb, abba, baab, aaaa, bbbb, aabbaa, abbbba,* . . ., and in general, all sentences consisting of a string *X* followed by the "mirror image" of *X* (i.e., *X* in reverse), and only these;

(iii) *aa, bb, abab, baba, aaaa, bbbb, aabaab, abbabb,* . . ., and in general, all sentences consisting of a string *X* of *a*'s and *b*'s followed by the identical string *X*, and only these.

The counter language can be handled by a counting mechanism to match the number of each symbol, whereas the mirror-image language contains a mirror-image dependency, requiring more than a mere counter. If the number of symbols is not fixed (i.e., infinite), both of these languages are to be generated by context-free (simple) phrase structure grammars, while the copying language with a cross-serial dependency clearly goes beyond the bounds of context-free phrase structure grammars, requiring a more powerful device, viz., context-sensitive phrase structure grammars or transformational grammars (Chomsky 1959, Hopcroft and Ullman 1979). In the present study, the Reverse and Same under the string conditions took the above type (i) of A^n B^n. As regards the matching orders, the Reverse took the type (ii) of A_2 A_1 B_1 B_2 or A_3 A_2 A_1 B_1 B_2 B_3, while the Same took the type (iii) of A_1 A_2 B_1 B_2 or A_1 A_2 A_3 B_1 B_2 B_3.

Because the number of symbols is inevitably fixed (i.e., finite) in any actual experiments, it should be noted that any symbol sequences can be expressed by a regular (finite state) grammar, i.e., the least powerful grammar in the so-called Chomsky hierarchy. Therefore, one cannot claim in principle that individual grammars (e.g., context-free phrase structure vs. regular grammars) are differentially represented in the brain, and the neural representation of individual grammars was *not* within the scope of the present study. Besides various models examined, other nonstructural and nonsymbolic models with simple recurrent networks have been proposed to process some examples of even context-free and context-sensitive phrase structure languages, generalizing to some degree to longer strings than the training set (Rodriguez 2001). However, these models do not account for any parametric modulation of activations in the present study, except the length of sentences.

Operational Definitions of All Factors Examined

We operationally defined syntactic factors within an entire sentence (see Table 8.1) as follows. If a tree structure [a Phrase-marker (P-marker) associated with a linguistic expression] contains as its subtree a domain in which a node *N* immediately dominates *n* elements ($n > 1$), then we can say that the domain constitutes a *merged* structure. Note that under the binary

Merge hypothesis, n equals 2, except for relatively rare "multiple branching" structures (see Appendix S2). In the present study, we abstract away from the noun/verb (N/V or N'/V' vs. noun phrase/verb phrase (NP/VP) distinction, as well as the sentence (S) vs. complementizer phrase (CP or S') distinction. The operational definitions of syntactic factors examined here are as follows (see Figures 8.1A and 8.2A). "Number of Merge" is the total number of binary branches. "Number of Search" is the total number of correspondences between sample and comparison stimuli. DoM is the largest integer m meeting the following condition: there is a continuous path passing through $m + 1$ nodes $N_0, \ldots, N_m$, where each N_i ($i \geq 1$) is *merged* in the subtree dominated by N_{i-1}.

From both theoretical and experimental points of view, we also examined in detail the validity of other structure-based models, here categorized as "other linguistic factors." If a merged structure is surrounded by non-null elements on both sides, we get a "nested" structure. If a nesting structure occurs within the *same* type of elements, the structure is called a "self-embedded" structure. "Degree of nesting" (or "degree of self-embedding") is the largest integer m meeting the following condition (Figure 8.S1A): there is a continuous path passing through $m + 1$ nodes $N_0, \ldots, N_m$, where each N_i ($i \geq 1$) is nested (or fully self-embedded) in the subtree dominated by N_{i-1} (Miller and Chomsky 1963). "Number of nodes" is the total number of nonterminal nodes and terminal nodes (Figure 8.S1B).

As regards "depth of postponed symbols," its original definition was for *producing* a given output sequence (Yngve 1960). As we tested stimuli for *understanding* a given input sequence, we reversed the numbering for the listener/reader as follows. "Depth of postponed symbols" is the amount of temporary storage needed for parsing a given input sequence, which can be calculated in the following way: first, number the branches of each node from 0 to $n - 1$ (Figure 8.S2, the digits shown in gray), where n is the number of branches from that node. Start numbering from the left. Then, compute the depth d of each terminal node by adding together the numbers written along all branches leading to that terminal node, starting from the leftmost branch (i.e., the first input for the listener/reader).

According to the dependency locality theory (Gibson 2000), two components of sentence parsing that consume computational resources have been proposed: "integration costs," which are connecting words into the structure for the input thus far, and "storage costs," which are the minimum number of words required to complete the current input as a grammatical sentence (Figure 8.S3A). By adding together "new discourse referents" (Ns and Vs in our paradigm) and "structural integrations" (the number of discourse referents in the intervening region), "integration costs" are obtained. According to the similarity-based interference theory (Lewis and Nakayama 2002), there are combined effects of "retroactive interference" (the number of nominative NPs between the subject-verb pair, when a verb is processed) and "proactive interference" (the number of nominative NPs, which are prior to the subject and still active in the parse) on syntactic attachments (Figure 8.S3B). By adding both interference effects together, "syntactic interference" is obtained. Another source of interference is "positional similarity," which is the number of adjacent syntactically similar NPs (i.e., marked with similar case markers).

Nonlinguistic factors may also variably contribute to the processing load of sentences with different constructions. At least three basic nonlinguistic factors may be involved in our experiment: memory span, counting, and "number of encoding." The operational definitions of these nonlinguistic factors are as follows. Memory span is the maximum cost needed to maintain an item for matching against intervening or skipped stimuli (e.g., zero for $N_1 V_1$ in the Conjoined$_{(S)}$, and one for $N_1 VV_1$ in the Simple$_{(S)}$), and its operational definition is the maximum number of cusps in the curved arrows (Figures 8.1 and 8.2). Counting is an operation needed to track symbol repetition, and its operational definition is the maximum number of consecutively repeated symbols (e.g., zero for NVNV or NVNVNV, one for NNVV, and two for NNNVVV). Encoding is memorization of features necessary for matching, and "number of encoding" is the total number of sample and comparison stimuli. Memory span and counting were considered temporal order-related factors in our experiment; memory span was related to matching orders, while counting was related to symbol orders. On the other hand, memory span and "number of encoding" were memory-related factors.

References

Chomsky, Noam. 1957. *Syntactic structures*. The Hague: Mouton. 2nd edition, Mouton de Gruyter, 2002.

Chomsky, Noam. 1959. On certain formal properties of grammars. *Information and Control* 2: 137–167.

Chomsky, Noam. 1965. *Aspects of the theory of syntax*. Cambridge, MA: MIT Press.

Fukui, Naoki, and Hiromu Sakai. 2003. The visibility guideline for functional categories: Verb raising in Japanese and related issues. *Lingua* 113 (4–6): 321–375. [Reprinted in *Theoretical comparative syntax: Studies in macroparameters*, Naoki Fukui, 289–336. London: Routledge. (2006).]

Gibson, Edward. 2000. The dependency locality theory: A distance-based theory of linguistic complexity. In *Image, language, brain: Papers from the First Mind Articulation Project Symposium*, ed. Alec Marantz, Yasushi Miyashita, and Wayne O'Neil, 95–126. Cambridge, MA: MIT Press.

Hopcroft, John E., and Jeffrey D. Ullman. 1979. *Introduction to automata theory, languages, and computation*. Reading, MA: Addison-Wesley.

Lewis, Richard, and Mineharu Nakayama. 2002. Syntactic and positional similarity effects in the processing of Japanese embeddings. In *Sentence processing in East Asian languages*, ed. Mineharu Nakayama, 85–111. Stanford: CSLI Publications.

Miller, George A, and Noam Chomsky. 1963. Finitary models of language users. In *Handbook of mathematical psychology*, volume II, ed. R. Duncan Luce, Robert R. Bush, and Eugene Galanter, 419–491. New York: John Wiley and Sons.

Rodriguez, Paul. 2001. Simple recurrent networks learn context-free and context-sensitive languages by counting. *Neural Computation* 13: 2093–2118.

Yngve, Victor H. 1960. A model and an hypothesis for language structure. *Proceedings of the American Philosophical Society* 104: 444–466.

Appendix S2 Detailed Information about the Stimuli

In the Japanese language, all regular verbs are either of *ichidan* (one-tier) or *godan* (five-tier) conjugation (Shibatani 1990). In our experiments, Vs took a nonpast-tense form (*-ru*), past-tense form (*-ta*), or gerundive form (*-te*) (e.g., "*teteru,*" "*teteta,*" and "*tetete*"), inflecting like normal *ichidan* verbs (e.g., "*tateru,*" "*tateta,*" and "*tatete*": "*build,*" "*built,*" and "*building*"). In a subordinate clause, Vs took tense markers (*-ru*/*-ta*) just before *-to*. The last V in an entire sentence always ended with tense markers. As the tense of verbs can be independently marked in a Japanese nested sentence (e.g., "*Taro-ga Hanako-ga utau-to omotta*": "*Taro thought that Hanako would sing*"), we regarded "number of tense markers (*-ru*/*-ta*)" as one of other linguistic factors (Table 8.1).

In Japanese, there are a number of morphologically/semantically related pairs of transitive and intransitive verbs with vowel changes (e.g., "*kakeru*" and "*kakaru*": "*hang up*" and "*hang down*") (Tsujimura 2007). Not only such vowel dissimilation, but vowel assimilation, i.e., *vowel harmony*, is commonly observed in natural languages (Nevins 2010). Vowel harmony is possible between adjacent or distant vowels within a word (Mailhot and Reiss 2007). Indeed, the presence of vowel harmony has been indicated in the history of the Japanese language (Shibatani 1990). In the present study, vowel harmony was adopted to change the last, i.e., second, vowel of the verb root, so that this vowel harmonized with the vowel (i.e., /a/, /u/, or /o/) of the corresponding subject (e.g., "*rara-ga tetaru*" and "*rara-ga tetatta*" from "*teteru*" and "*teteta,*" respectively). This property of vowel harmony made each V_i inflect like a normal *godan* verb, which root always ends in a consonant, and this change made V_i distinct from the original form of *ichidan* verbs. It should be noted that V_i of nonmatching stimuli also inflected like normal *godan* verbs (Tables 8.S1 and 8.S2). When a *godan* verb root ends in *r*, *t*, or *w*, an euphonic change of a geminated consonant *t* occurs before *-ta* or *-te* (e.g., "*kakatta*" from "*kakari-ta*": "*hung down*"). Each V_i with *-ta* or *-te* (e.g., "*tetatta*") was consistent with its adverbial form *ri* ("*tetari-ta*"), *ti* ("*tetati-ta*"), or (*w*)*i* ("*tetai-ta*"). On the other hand, the first verb of a compound verb remained an *ichidan* verb in an adverbial form (e.g., "*tete*").

There are some grammatical, but noncanonical (i.e., in a special use), usages of -*ga* or -*no*: parallel subjects marked with -*ga* (e.g., "*Taro-ga yuujin-ga sorezore utatta*": "*Taro and his friend each sang*"), an object marked with -*ga* (e.g., "*Taro-ga yuujin-ga suki-da*": "*Taro likes his friend*"), an external possessor marked with -*ga* (e.g., "*Taro-ga yuujin-ga sinsetu-da*": "*Taro's friend is kind*"), and a subject marked with -*no* (e.g., "*Taro-no suki-na yuujin*": "*the friend Taro likes*"). Considering such canonicity, we regarded "number of case markers (-*ga*/-*no*)" as one of other linguistic factors (Table 8.1). However, these noncanonical case markings are rare in both comprehension and production, as shown by previous behavioral experiments (Miyamoto 2002, Uehara and Bradley 2002). We assured the participants that case markings for our stimuli were always canonical (see Appendix S3). Actual usage of canonical case markings was fully guaranteed by the high accuracy under the sentence conditions (Figure 8.3A), as the matching task could not be performed correctly if such noncanonical case markings were employed.

We imposed three following constraints for the letter strings. First, for the first half of a string (As), letter strings derived from Ns and Vs (denoted here as $\mathcal{N}s$ and $\mathcal{V}s$, respectively) were in the order of $\mathcal{N}\mathcal{V}$ or $\mathcal{V}\mathcal{N}$ for the short stimuli, and $\mathcal{N}\mathcal{V}\mathcal{N}$ or $\mathcal{V}\mathcal{N}\mathcal{V}$ for the long stimuli. Secondly, we avoided endings with -*ga*/-*no* for $\mathcal{N}s$, but some $\mathcal{V}s$ with -*ru*/-*ta* endings were used as stimuli. Lastly, neither $\mathcal{V}s$ with -*to*/-*te* endings nor Vs in the adverbial form were used for making $\mathcal{V}s$.

Examples of long sentences are shown in Figure 8.2A. For the Nested$_{(L)}$, a sentence at the lowest hierarchical level (S) was self-embedded twice into an entire sentence (S"). For the Simple$_{(L)}$, we tested both stimuli of $(VV_1)V_1$ and $V_1(VV_1)$, where two verbs, i.e., VV_1 (a compound verb) and V_1, were conjoined. As regards the Ns in the Simple$_{(L)}$, branching constructions were ambiguous between $(NN)N_1$ and $N(NN_1)$, like "*Japanese history teacher*" ([[*Japanese history*] *teacher*] and [*Japanese* [*history teacher*]], respectively), both of which yielded the same DoM. For Japanese relative clauses, as well as for noun phrases with a genitive case marker -*no*, left-branching constructions predominate (cf. Miller and Chomsky 1963: 471–472). For the Conjoined$_{(L)}$, DoM for a node was increased by one from the highest nodes of an entire sentence (S') to the same hierarchical level of conjoined sentences (Ss). Since all the conjoined sentences were equivalent with respect to their status in the multiple branching, two Merge applications involved here were assumed to follow, as a marked (i.e., "exceptional") option, the associative law (i.e., $[[a \# b] \# c] = [a \# [b \# c]]$, where # represents Merge). This type of associative Merge (which yields n-ary structures by applying $n - 1$ times) has been argued to be permissible for a certain class of marked constructions in human language (Fukui 2011). In this way, the number of Merge in a sentence becomes always one less than the number of terminal nodes, *irrespective of sentence structures*.

References

Fukui, Naoki. 2011. Merge and bare phrase structure. In *The Oxford handbook of linguistic minimalism*, ed. Cedric Boeckx, 73–95. Oxford: Oxford University Press. [Chapter 1, this volume.]

Mailhot, Frédéric, and Charles Reiss. 2007. Computing long-distance dependencies in vowel harmony. *Biolinguistics* 1: 28–48.

Miller, George A., and Noam Chomsky. 1963. Finitary models of language users. In *Handbook of mathematical psychology*, Volume II, ed. R. Duncan Luce, Robert R. Bush, and Eugene Galanter, 419–491. New York: John Wiley and Sons.

Miyamoto, Edison T. 2002. Case markers as clause boundary inducers in Japanese. *Journal of Psycholinguistic Research* 31: 307–347.

Nevins, Andrew. 2010. *Locality in vowel harmony*. Cambridge, MA: MIT Press.

Shibatani, Masayoshi. 1990. *The languages of Japan*. Cambridge: Cambridge University Press.

Tsujimura, Natsuko. 2007. *An introduction to Japanese linguistics*, 2nd edition. Malden, MA: Blackwell.

Uehara, Keiko, and Dianne C. Bradley. 2002. Center-embedding problem and the contribution of nominative case repetition. In *Sentence processing in East Asian languages*, ed. Mineharu Nakayama, 257–287. Stanford: CSLI Publications.

Appendix S3 Task Instructions and Training Procedures

Task Instructions

Before the experiments, all participants were fully informed about the stimuli and task. We instructed and trained the sentence conditions in the order of Simple$_{(S)}$, Conjoined$_{(S)}$, Nested$_{(S)}$, Simple$_{(L)}$, Conjoined$_{(L)}$, and Nested$_{(L)}$, as the number of vowel extraction increased in this order. The following is a translation of task instructions in Japanese.

[Day 1 Instructions]

Words Used in a Task

Special pseudowords and letter strings will be used in a task. **You don't have to remember the following words.**

Pseudowords used as nouns (six kinds) are: "*rara*," "*zaza*," "*mumu*," "*gugu*," "*yoyo*," and "*dodo*."

Grammatical particles attached to the noun (two kinds) are: "*-ga*," which marks a subject, and "*-no*," which marks a modifier (e.g., "*zaza-ga*," "*mumu-no*," etc.).

Pseudowords used as verbs (four kinds) are: "*hihi*," "*kiki*," "*sese*," and "*tete*."

Verb endings (five kinds) and verb conjugation patterns are:

1. Verb endings: "*-ru*" (present tense), "*-tta*" (past tense), "*-tte*" (e.g., "*utatte*"), "*-ru-to*" (e.g., "*odoru-to*"), and "*-tta-to*" (e.g., "*odotta-to*"); and
2. Verb conjugation: **When a subject corresponds to a verb within a sentence,** *the latter vowel* (second syllable) *of the verb root will change in order to match the vowel of the corresponding subject.* You don't have to recall the root form of the verb.

Correct examples:

"*rara-ga hiharu*" (conjugation of "*hihi*")
"*mumu-ga kikutta*" (conjugation of "*kiki*")
"*dodo-ga sesoru*" (conjugation of "*sese*")
"*rara-ga tetatta*" (conjugation of "*tete*")

Wrong examples:

"*zaza-ga hihoru*"
"*gugu-ga kikotta*"
"*yoyo-ga sesuru*"
"*zaza-ga tetoru*"

Other letter strings are: "*ragara*," "*nogugu*," "*huhhita*," "*kottaki*," etc.

Types of Conditions

1) Grammar (G) conditions, 2) Memory (M) condition, and 3) Reverse (R) condition.

You will perform a task under three types of conditions during scanning of your head images inside the MRI scanner. At the beginning of each trial, a cue ("G," "M," or "R") denoting a condition will appear. By noting these cues, please judge which condition will be presented. During the task, a small red cross remains at the center of the monitor. Fixate this red cross as much as you can, but you may blink. *Please do not speak or read aloud during the task.*

During the task, please respond by pressing a button. Hold a switch box by both hands, with a red button to your right. When you press one, use your right thumb without looking at the buttons. Please note the following crucial points:

- Press a button only once, when necessary.
- *Please press the button as fast as you can, while the stimuli are presented.*

- Every stimulus is consisted of a cue denoting a condition and of four or six phrases or strings.
- *Do not press a button before the last stimulus.*

1. Grammar Conditions

There are six patterns under the Grammar conditions. The task is to judge whether or not the vowel of a subject is matched with the last vowel of the corresponding verb root. At the beginning of each trial, the cue "G" denoting a condition will appear. Do not overlook this cue, so that you can answer correctly. For every pattern shown in the following section, "G" will appear.

1.1 PATTERN 1 (SIMPLE(s))

Pattern 1 is similar to *"Taro-no ani-ga sinobi aruita"* (*"Taro's brother sneaked around"*). The subject is *"ani,"* and the verb is *"aruita."* Please judge whether or not the vowel of the *second* phrase (subject) is matched with that of the *fourth* phrase (corresponding verb). Please press *the rightmost button* if correct, and press *the second one from the right* if wrong. Press the button quickly with your right thumb, while the fourth stimulus is presented.

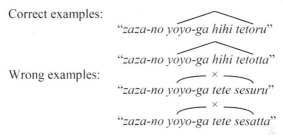

Correct examples:
"*zaza-no yoyo-ga hihi tetoru*"

"*zaza-no yoyo-ga hihi tetotta*"

Wrong examples:
"*zaza-no yoyo-ga tete sesuru*"

"*zaza-no yoyo-ga tete sesatta*"

1.2 PATTERN 2 (CONJOINED(s))

Pattern 2 is similar to *"Taro-ga utatte Hanako-ga odoru"* (*"Taro sings, and Hanako dances"*). Please judge whether or not the vowel of the *first* phrase is matched with that of the *second* phrase, and the vowel of the *third* phrase with that of the *fourth* phrase.

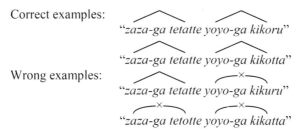

Correct examples:
"*zaza-ga tetatte yoyo-ga kikoru*"

"*zaza-ga tetatte yoyo-ga kikotta*"

Wrong examples:
"*zaza-ga tetatte yoyo-ga kikuru*"

"*zaza-ga tetotte yoyo-ga kikatta*"

1.3 PATTERN 3 (NESTED(s))

Pattern 3 is similar to *"Taro-ga Hanako-ga utau-to omotta"* (*"Taro thought that Hanako would sing"*). Please judge whether or not the vowel of the *first* phrase is matched with that of the *fourth* phrase, and the vowel of the *second* phrase with that of the *third* phrase.

Correct examples:

"zaza-ga yoyo-ga tetoru-to kikaru"

"zaza-ga yoyo-ga tetotta-to kikatta"

Wrong examples:

"zaza-ga yoyo-ga tetoru-to kikoru"

"zaza-ga yoyo-ga tetatta-to kikutta"

TIPS

1   Please do not forget the first noun.
2   There are sentences that have multiple errors; *please check them up to the last phrase.*
3   Please press the button *as fast as you can, while the last phrase is presented.*
4   *When the last phrase disappears, please quit the button press, and concentrate on the next trial.*

2. Memory Condition (Same(s))

The task is to memorize the presented letter strings. At the beginning of each trial, the cue "M" denoting a condition will appear. Do not overlook this cue, so that you can answer correctly.

Four strings will appear one by one on the monitor. Please memorize these four strings, and judge whether or not the *first* and *third* strings, and the *second* and *fourth* ones, are exactly the same.

Correct examples:

"yogayo tarute yogayo tarute"
"hiruhu garara hiruhu garara"

Wrong examples:

"yonoyo tettata yonoyo tatetta"
"hihhata nogugu settaso gunogu"

3. Reverse Condition (Reverse*(S)*)

The task is to memorize the presented letter strings. At the beginning of each trial, the cue "R" denoting a condition will appear. Do not overlook this cue, so that you can answer correctly.

Four strings will appear one by one on the monitor. Please memorize these four strings, and judge whether or not the *first* and *fourth* strings, and the *second* and *third* ones, are exactly the same.

Correct examples:

"*yogayo tarute tarute yogayo*"
"*hiruhu garara garara hiruhu*"

Wrong examples:

"*yonoyo tettata tatetta yonoyo*"
"*hihhata nogugu nogugu settaso*"

[Day 2 Instructions]

1. Grammar Conditions

1.1 PATTERN 4 (SIMPLE*(L)*)

Pattern 4 is similar to "*Taro-no ani-no yujin-ga hasiri mawatte utatta*" ("*Taro's brother's friend run around and sang*"). The subject is "*yujin,*" and the verbs are "*mawatte*" and "*utatta.*" Please judge whether or not the vowel of the *third* phrase is matched with that of the *fourth* or *fifth* phrase, and the vowel of the *third* phrase with that of the *sixth* phrase. Please press *the rightmost button* if correct, and press *the second one from the right* if wrong. Press the button quickly with your right thumb, while the sixth stimulus is presented.

Correct examples:

"*zaza-no yoyo-no mumu-ga tete kikutte hihuru*"

"*zaza-no yoyo-no mumu-ga tetutte kiki hihutta*"

Wrong examples:

"*zaza-no yoyo-no mumu-ga tetutte kiki hiharu*"

"*zaza-no yoyo-no mumu-ga tete kikatte hihotta*"

1.2 PATTERN 5 (CONJOINED*(L)*)

Pattern 5 is similar to "*Taro-ga odotte Hanako-ga utatte Jiro-ga asobu*" ("*Taro dances, Hanako sings, and Jiro plays*"). Please judge whether or not the vowel of the *first* phrase is matched with that of the *second* phrase, the vowel of the *third* phrase with that of the *fourth* phrase, and the vowel of the *fifth* phrase with that of the *sixth* phrase.

Correct examples:

"*zaza-ga tetatte yoyo-ga kikotte mumu-ga hihuru*"

"*zaza-ga tetatte yoyo-ga kikotte mumu-ga hihutta*"

Wrong examples:

"*zaza-ga tetatte yoyo-ga kikotte mumu-ga hiharu*"

"*zaza-ga tetutte yoyo-ga kikotte mumu-ga hihatta*"

1.3 PATTERN 6 (NESTED$_{LL}$)

Pattern 6 is similar to "*Taro-ga Hanako-ga Jiro-ga utau-to omou-to kangaeta*" ("*Taro supposed that Hanako would think that Jiro would sing*"). Please judge whether or not the vowel of the *first* phrase is matched with that of the *sixth* phrase, the vowel of the *second* phrase with that of the *fifth* phrase, and the vowel of the *third* phrase with that of the *fourth* phrase.

Correct examples:

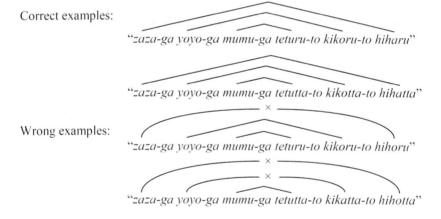

"*zaza-ga yoyo-ga mumu-ga teturu-to kikoru-to hiharu*"

"*zaza-ga yoyo-ga mumu-ga tetutta-to kikotta-to hihatta*"

Wrong examples:

"*zaza-ga yoyo-ga mumu-ga teturu-to kikoru-to hihoru*"

"*zaza-ga yoyo-ga mumu-ga tetutta-to kikatta-to hihotta*"

2. *Memory Condition (Same$_{LL}$)*

Six strings will appear one by one on the monitor. Please memorize these six strings, and judge whether or not the *first* and *fourth* strings, the *second* and *fifth* ones, and the *third* and *sixth* ones, are exactly the same.

Correct examples:

"*yogayo teruta gagugu yogayo teruta gagugu*"
"*huruhi garara ruseso huruhi garara ruseso*"

Wrong examples:

"*noyoyo tattate gunogu noyoyo tattate munomu*"
"*huttahi ranora sottase hihhuta ranora tattate*"

3. Reverse Condition (Reverse$_{(L)}$)

Six strings will appear one by one on the monitor. Please memorize these six strings, and judge whether or not the *first* and *sixth* strings, the *second* and *fifth* ones, and the *third* and *fourth* ones, are exactly the same.

Correct examples:

"yogayo teruta gagugu gagugu teruta yogayo"
"huruhi garara ruseso ruseso garara huruhi"

Wrong examples:

"noyoyo tattate gunogu munomu tattate noyoyo"
"huttahi ranora sottase tattate ranora hihhuta"

Training Procedures

Experiments with short or long stimuli were performed on separate days in the order short, then long. Before scanning, the participants were trained until they scored 80% at each of the following stages. Each of the Simple, Conjoined, and Nested were separately tested with self-paced reading in 10 to 30 trials with this order. Only one participant took 50 trials for the Nested$_{(L)}$. When these conditions were randomized, all participants took additional 20 or 40 trials. The Reverse and Same were much easier to perform, and so required only 10 or 20 trials for a randomized sequence from the beginning. When all of these conditions were mixed, participants additionally took 20 or 40 trials. Finally, participants were tested on a sequence of all conditions at the regular rate of presentation (see Figure 8.1C and 8.1D) in 40 and 20 trials for the short and long stimuli, respectively. Only three participants required 60 or 80 trials for the short stimuli. Due to technical problems, four participants were retested with short or long stimuli on another day; two participants received 20 trials for the mixed conditions with self-paced reading, and all received 20–60 trials for the final stage.

Appendix S4 MRI Data Analyses

fMRI Data Analyses

Data analyses with fMRI were performed using SPM5 statistical parametric mapping software (Wellcome Department of Cognitive Neurology, London, UK; http://www.fil.ion.ucl.ac.uk/spm/) (Friston et al. 1995) on MATLAB software (Math Works, Natick, MA). The acquisition timing of each slice was corrected using the middle slice as a reference for the EPI data. We realigned the EPI data in multiple runs to the first volume in multiple runs, and removed runs that included data with a translation of >2 mm in one of the three directions and with a rotation of >1.4° around one of the three axes. Each participant's T1-weighted image was coregistered to the mean image of its own EPI data, followed by the segmentation of the T1-weighted image into gray- and white-matter probability maps. With this latter step, each individual brain was spatially normalized to the standard brain space as defined by Montreal Neurological Institute (MNI). Resampling was performed every 3 mm using seventh-degree B-spline interpolation, and images were smoothed with an isotropic Gaussian kernel of 9 mm full width at half maximum (FWHM).

Using these preprocessed data, low-frequency noise and global changes in activity were further removed (cut-off period: 128 s). Hemodynamic responses induced by the trials were modeled with a box-car function with a duration of 3.5 s (short stimuli) or 5.1 s (long stimuli), i.e., from the onset of the first stimulus (N or A) to 500 ms after the disappearance of the last stimulus (Figure 8.1C and 8.1D), and the box-car function was convolved with a hemodynamic function that peaked at 6 s. These functions were used as run-specific covariates for matching or nonmatching stimuli for each condition in a general linear model (GLM). Only event-related responses to correct trials were analyzed.

For random effects analyses using either an analysis of covariance (AN-COVA) with t-statistics or a one-sample t-test, contrast images were generated for each participant and used for intersubject comparisons. For all fMRI data analyses, the statistical threshold was set to $P < 0.05$ for the voxel level, corrected for multiple comparisons [family-wise error (FWE) correction] across the whole brain. To exclude any general cognitive factors related to task difficulty from the evaluation of cortical activation, the accuracy was used as a nuisance variable for each contrast of random effects analyses. If a subtraction between conditions served as a reference, an exclusive mask (uncorrected $P < 0.01$) was applied to reduce the contribution of deactivation. For example, in Nested' > Simple', an exclusive mask of the [Conjoined – Simple] contrast was applied to reduce the contribution of deactivation in Simple'.

We used a factorial design for a two-way ANCOVA with condition [Nested', Simple'] × length [Long, Short], where activations in Nested' or Simple' for long or short sentences were estimated for each participant, and then the main contrast (as denoted by a greater-than symbol) was calculated for intersubject comparisons. A one-way ANCOVA was used for a direct comparison of Nested'$_{(L)}$ > Simple'$_{(S)}$, and for Nested" > Reverse" contrasting the sentence and string conditions. To ensure an independent statistical test in the latter contrast, the inclusive mask of Nested' > Simple' (corrected $P < 0.05$) was iteratively applied to the contrast image of each participant, thereby leaving out that participant from the calculation of the mask, i.e., the "leave-one-subject-out cross-validation" approach (Esterman et al. 2010). A one-sample t-test was used for [Nonmatching – Matching] separately under the sentence and string conditions, and for Reverse".

For the anatomical identification of activated regions, we basically used the Anatomical Automatic Labeling method (Tzourio-Mazoyer et al. 2002).

The percent signal changes averaged across the voxels in each activated region were extracted using the MarsBaR-toolbox (http://marsbar.sourceforge. net/). To fit a model of each factor to activations, a fitting scale and residual sum of squares (RSS) were calculated with MATLAB, and the fitted values were obtained by multiplying the estimates by the fitting scale. For a no-intercept model, the coefficient of determination (r^2) should be calculated as $r^2 = 1 - \Sigma(y - \hat{y})^2 / \Sigma y^2$, where $\hat{y}$ and y denote the fitted values and the signal changes for each contrast, respectively (Kvålseth 1985). For this calculation, we used R software (http://www.r-project.org/). By using a restricted maximum-likelihood method, we further fitted "linear mixed-effects models" with individual activations as dependent variables, the estimates of each factor as a regressor, and the participants as random effects. For this calculation, we used an nlme (linear and nonlinear mixed-effects models) package (http://cran.r-project.org/web/packages/nlme/) on R software.

DCM Data Analyses

Data analyses with DCM were performed using DCM10 on SPM 8 (Friston et al. 2003). For DCM analyses, we concatenated the scans from the separate runs, and reanalyzed the preprocessed data with GLM, which contained regressors representing the Nested, Simple, Reverse, and Same (correct trials alone; see Table 8.2), as well as a regressor representing all conditions (correct trials alone including Conjoined). In addition, the effects of transition between runs were taken into account by adding regressors for each run.

We imposed following functional and anatomical constraints for selecting ROIs (regions of interest) in L. F3op/F3t or L. SMG for each participant with the individually preprocessed data (Stephan et al. 2007). The individual local maxima should be significant in Nested" – Reverse" estimated for each participant (uncorrected $P < 0.05$), nearest to the group local maxima of Nested" > Reverse" within twice the FWHM of the smoothing kernel, and obviously in L. F3op/F3t or L. SMG. The averaged MNI coordinates of these individual local maxima were (–50, 26, 25) and (–39, –45, 43) for L. F3op/F3t and L. SMG, respectively. With the volume-of-interest (VOI) tool on SPM8, the time series was extracted by taking the first eigenvariate across all suprathreshold voxels within 6 mm of the individual local maxima.

We specified nine models with systematic variations in a modulatory effect and driving inputs (Figure 8.S4). The regressor representing the Nested was used for a modulatory effect, whereas that representing all conditions was used for driving inputs. After estimating all models for each participant, we identified the most likely model by using random-effects Bayesian model selection (BMS) on DCM10. Inferences from BMS can be based on the expected probability, i.e., the expected likelihood of obtaining the model for any randomly selected participants, or on the exceedance probability, i.e., the probability that the model is a better fit to the data than any other models tested. We adopted the family inference method (Penny et al. 2010), in which three modulatory families were compared first, and then the input models within the winning family were further compared. After determining the best model, the parameter estimates of this particular model were evaluated by a one-sample *t*-test (Stephan et al. 2010).

DTI Data Analyses

Data analyses with DTI were performed using FSL [Oxford Centre for Functional MRI of the Brain's (FMRIB) Software Library 4.1.7; http://fsl.fmrib.ox.ac.uk/fsl/fslwiki/] and FDT (FMRIB's Diffusion Toolbox 2.0) (Smith et al. 2004). Diffusion-weighted images were first resliced to an isotropic voxel of 1 mm³, and then eddy current distortions and motion artifacts were corrected using affine registration to the b0 image. We then extracted the brain shape from the b0 image, and created the binary mask image (i.e., zero for the outside of the brain) for each participant. Markov Chain Monte Carlo sampling was performed to build up distributions on diffusion parameters at each voxel, which allowed for an estimation of the most probable pathway by Bayesian estimation (number of fibers modeled per voxel = 2) (Behrens et al. 2007). The implicit modeling of noise in a probabilistic model made a fiber tracking near gray matter possible.

By using FLIRT (FMRIB's Linear Image Registration Tool) on FSL, the b0 image was first coregistered to the individual T1-weighted image for each participant, and the T1-weighted image was spatially normalized to the MNI space by using both affine and nonlinear transformations with FLIRT and FNIRT (FMRIB's Nonlinear Image Registration Tool). With the transformation matrices and estimated deformation fields, the peak MNI coordinates of each local maximum were transformed to the individual b0 images, and a sphere of 6-mm radius centered at the new coordinates was defined as a seed mask for the probabilistic tractography. All fiber tracking was conducted in an individual DTI space. In order to find the connections between these regions, we employed a two-ROI approach with two seed masks, which repeatedly sampled tracts from one seed mask, and retained only those tracts that passed through the other seed mask. Probabilistic fiber tracking was initiated from all voxels within the seed masks to generate 10,000 streamline samples, with a step length of 0.5 mm, a maximum number of steps of 2,000, a curvature threshold of 0.2 (±78.5°), and a loopcheck option.

In the connectivity distributions obtained, each voxel value represented the total number of the streamline samples passing through that voxel. The connectivity probability maps were then created for each participant by dividing the connectivity distributions with a sum of waytotal values, i.e., the total number of generated tracts from one seed mask that have reached the other seed mask. This normalization approach allowed for a comparison of connectivity probability values across participants; note that the pattern of connectivity did not change by this scaling. To remove any spurious connections, pathways in individual participants were thresholded to include only voxels that had at least 1% connectivity probability values (Flöel et al. 2009). Thresholded pathways in each participant were then normalized as noted earlier and binarized using "fslmaths" on FSL. The binarized pathways were overlaid across participants to produce population probability maps for each pathway, in which voxel values represent the number of participants with a pathway through that voxel. These population probability maps with thresholding (at least seven out of 15 participants) were smoothed and shown using MRIcroN software (http://www.mccauslandcenter.sc.edu/mricro/mricron/).

References

Behrens, Timothy E. J., Heidi Johansen Berg, Saad Jbabdi, Matthew F. S. Rushworth, and Mark W. Woolrich. 2007. Probabilistic diffusion tractography with multiple fibre orientations: What can we gain? *NeuroImage* 34: 144–155.

Esterman, Michael, Benjamin J. Tamber-Rosenau, Yu-Chin Chiu, and Steven Yantis. 2010. Avoiding non-independence in fMRI data analysis: Leave one subject out. *NeuroImage* 50: 572–576.

Flöel, Agnes, Meinou H. de Vries, Jan Scholz, Caterina Breitenstein, and Heidi Johansen-Berg. 2009. White matter integrity in the vicinity of Broca's area predicts grammar learning success. *NeuroImage* 47: 1974–1981.

Friston, Karl J., Lee Harrison, and Will Penny. 2003. Dynamic causal modelling. *NeuroImage* 19: 1273–1302.

Friston, Karl J., Andrew P. Holmes, Keith J. Worsley, Jean-Baptiste Poline, Christopher D. Frith, and Richard S. J. Frackowiak. 1995. Statistical parametric maps in functional imaging: A general linear approach. *Human Brain Mapping* 2: 189–210.

Kvålseth, Tarald O. 1985. Cautionary note about R^2. *The American Statistician* 39: 279–285.

Penny, Will D., Klaas E. Stephan, Jean Daunizeau, Maria J. Rosa, Karl J. Friston, Thomas M. Schofield, and Alex P. Leff. 2010. Comparing families of dynamic causal models. *PLoS Computational Biololy* 6 (3): 1–14.

Smith, Stephen M., Mark Jenkinson, Mark W. Woolrich, Christian F. Beckmann, Timothy E. J. Behrens, Heidi Johansen-Berg, Peter R. Bannister, Marilena De Luca, Ivana Drobnjak, David E. Flitney, Rami K. Niazy, James Saunders, John Vickers, Yongyue Zhang, Nicola De Stefano, J. Michael Brady, and Paul M. Matthews. 2004. Advances in functional and structural MR image analysis and implementation as FSL. *NeuroImage* 23: S208–S219.

Stephan, Klaas E., John C. Marshall, Will D. Penny, Karl J. Friston, and Gereon R. Fink. 2007. Interhemispheric integration of visual processing during task-driven lateralization. *The Journal of Neuroscience* 27: 3512–3522.

Stephan, Klaas E., Will D. Penny, Rosalyn J. Moran, Hanneke E. M. den Ouden, Jean Daunizeau and Karl J. Friston. 2010. Ten simple rules for dynamic causal modeling. *NeuroImage* 49: 3099–3109.

Tzourio-Mazoyer, Nathalie, Brigitte. Landeau, Dimitri Papathanassiou, Fabrice Crivello, Olivier Etard, Nicolas Delcroix, Bernard Mazoyer, and Marc Joliot. 2002. Automated anatomical labeling of activations in SPM using a macroscopic anatomical parcellation of the MNI MRI single-subject brain. *NeuroImage* 15: 273–289.

9 Computational Principles of Syntax in the Regions Specialized for Language

Integrating Theoretical Linguistics and Functional Neuroimaging

With Shinri Ohta and Kuniyoshi L. Sakai

Abstract

The nature of computational principles of syntax remains to be elucidated. One promising approach to this problem would be to construct formal and abstract linguistic models that parametrically predict the activation modulations in the regions specialized for linguistic processes. In this chapter, we review recent advances in theoretical linguistics and functional neuroimaging in the following respects. First, we introduce the two fundamental linguistic operations: Merge (which combines two words or phrases to form a larger structure) and Search (which searches and establishes a syntactic relation of two words or phrases). We also illustrate certain universal properties of human language, and present hypotheses regarding how sentence structures are processed in the brain. Hypothesis I is that the Degree of Merger (DoM), i.e., the maximum depth of merged subtrees within a given domain, is a key computational concept to properly measure the complexity of tree structures. Hypothesis II is that the basic frame of the syntactic structure of a given linguistic expression is determined essentially by functional elements, which trigger Merge and Search. We then present our recent functional magnetic resonance imaging experiment, demonstrating that the DoM is indeed a key syntactic factor that accounts for syntax-selective activations in the left inferior frontal gyrus and supramarginal gyrus. Hypothesis III is that the DoM domain changes dynamically in accordance with iterative Merge applications, the Search distances, and/or task requirements. We confirm that the DoM accounts for activations in various sentence types. Hypothesis III successfully explains activation differences between object- and subject-relative clauses, as well as activations during explicit syntactic judgment tasks. A future research on the computational principles of syntax will further deepen our understanding of uniquely human mental faculties.

Keywords: syntax, universal grammar, recursive computation, inferior frontal gyrus, supramarginal gyrus, fMRI

Introduction

Tree structures are one of the most ubiquitous structures in nature, appearing in the branchings of rivers, lightning, snowflakes, trees, blood vessels, nervous systems, etc., and can be simulated in part by fractal geometry (Mandelbrot 1977). To properly quantify the complexity of such tree structures, various models have been proposed. The number of nodes would be one of the simplest models; this approach consists of simply counting the total number of nonterminal nodes (branching points) and terminal nodes of a tree structure (Figure 9.1A). This model obviously cannot capture hierarchical levels within the tree (sister relations in linguistic terms). To properly measure the hierarchical levels of a tree structure, we have proposed the Degree of Merger (DoM) as a key computational concept (Figure 9.1B) (Ohta et al. 2013). The DoM is defined as the *maximum depth* of merged subtrees (called Mergers) within a given domain. With this model, the same numbers are assigned to the nodes with an identical hierarchical level. The DoM corresponds to the number of iterations for generating fractal figures, when the tree structures are self-similar.

In this chapter, we first explain certain universal properties of human language discovered in modern linguistics, and we present hypotheses regarding how sentence structures are processed in the brain. We then introduce our recent functional magnetic resonance imaging (fMRI) study, which demonstrated that the DoM is indeed a key syntactic factor that accounts for syntax-selective activations in the regions specialized for language (Ohta et al. 2013). We also show that the top-down connectivity from the left inferior frontal gyrus to the left supramarginal gyrus is critical for the syntactic processing. Next, we clarify that the DoM can account for activation modulations in the frontal region, depending on different sentence structures. Finally, we hypothesize that the DoM domain changes dynamically in accordance with iterative Merge applications, the distance required for Search operations (or simply the "Search distance"), and/or task requirements. This hypothesis accounts for activation differences between subject-relative and object-relative clauses, as well as for activations during explicit syntactic judgment tasks.

1 Universal Properties of Human Language

1.1 Theoretical Background

Modern linguistics has clarified universal properties of human language, which, directly or indirectly, reflect the computational power, or engine, of the human language faculty. A sentence is not a mere string of words, but is made of phrase structure (called constituent structure). Moreover, a single phrase contains the key element (i.e., the "head") that determines the basic properties of the phrase. Furthermore, a sentence can be recursively embedded within other sentences, as in e.g., "*I think that John believes that Mary*

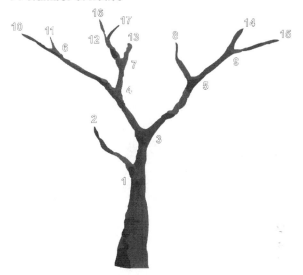

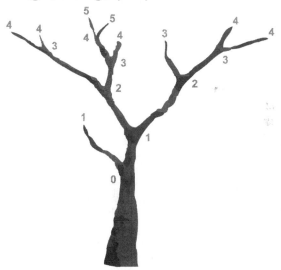

Figure 9.1 (**Plate 7 right half**). Two models for measuring the complexity of tree structures. (**A**) "The number of nodes" counts the total number of non-terminal nodes (branching points) and terminal nodes of a tree structure. The number of nodes of the tree structure shown is 17. (**B**) "The Degree of Merger (DoM)" quantifies the maximum depth of merged subtrees, or the degree of branching. We increased the number one by one for each node, starting from the trunk (zero) to terminal nodes. The DoM of the tree structure shown is 5.

assumes that . . .," and there is in principle no upper bound for the length of sentences. These universal properties can be adequately and minimally expressed by hierarchical tree structures with a set of relevant structural relations defined on such structures (Chomsky 1957, Chomsky 1965).

To construct hierarchical tree structures, modern linguistics has proposed the fundamental linguistic operation of *Merge* (capitalized in linguistics to indicate a formal operation). Merge is a structure-building operation that combines two syntactic objects (words or phrases) to form a larger structure (Chomsky 1995). Merge would be theoretically "costless," requiring no driving force for its application (Saito and Fukui 1998, Chomsky 2004, Fukui 2011). Besides Merge, we have proposed *Search* operation of searching syntactic features, which applies to a syntactic object already constructed by Merge, where Search couples and connects two distinct parts of the same structure, thereby assigning relevant features from one to the other part (Fukui and Sakai 2003). Various other "miscellaneous" operations that have been employed in the linguistics literature, such as Agree, Scope determination, Copy, etc., are in fact different manifestations of one and the same, i.e., more generalized, operation of Search (Fukui and Sakai 2003). Human language, therefore, should minimally contain two universal operations, Merge and Search. The total number of Merge and Search applications within an entire sentence are here simply denoted as "number of Merge" and "number of Search," respectively. The number of Merge in a sentence becomes always one less than the number of terminal nodes, *irrespective of sentence structures* (see Appendix S2 of Ohta et al. 2013).

1.2 Symbol Sequences and Formal Languages

In regard to formal symbol sequences beyond the bounds of finite state languages, three specific types of language have been discussed in the linguistics literature: (i) "counter language," (ii) "mirror-image language," and (iii) "copying language" (cf. Chomsky 1957: 21).

(i) *ab, aabb, aaabbb,* . . ., and in general, all sentences consisting of *n* occurrences of *a* followed by *n* occurrences of *b* and only these;
(ii) *aa, bb, abba, baab, aaaa, bbbb, aabbaa, abbbba,* . . ., and in general, all sentences consisting of a string *X* followed by the "mirror image" of *X* (i.e., *X* in reverse), and only these;
(iii) *aa, bb, abab, baba, aaaa, bbbb, aabaab, abbabb,* . . ., and in general, all sentences consisting of a string *X* of *a*'s and *b*'s followed by the identical string *X*, and only these.

The counter language can be handled by a counting mechanism to match the number of each symbol, whereas the mirror-image language contains a mirror-image dependency, requiring more than a mere counter. If the number of symbols is not fixed (i.e., infinite), both of these languages are beyond the bounds of finite-state grammars, and are to be generated by context-free (simple) phrase structure grammars, while the copying language with a cross-serial dependency clearly goes beyond the bounds of even context-free phrase structure grammars, requiring a more powerful device, viz., context-sensitive phrase structure grammars or transformational grammars (Chomsky 1959, Hopcroft and Ullman 1979).

It remains a central issue in cognitive sciences whether or not the faculty of language is also shared by animals. Animals have thus been tested with regular symbol sequences such as $A^n B^n$ ($n \geq 2$; i.e., AABB, AAABBB, ...) and $(AB)^n$ ($n \geq 2$; i.e., ABAB, ABABAB, ...), which differ in *symbol order*. In an animal study, songbirds were trained to discriminate patterns of $A^n B^n$ and $(AB)^n$ in more than ten thousand trials (Gentner et al. 2006). However, this learning can be achieved by tracking symbol repetition or counting strategy alone (Corballis 2007). There is also a recent report that songbirds seemed to discriminate strings with or without nesting (Abe and Watanabe 2011), but this learning can be achieved by simply remembering partial strings (Beckers et al. 2012). Along the lines of contrasting $A^n B^n$ and $(AB)^n$, fMRI studies have tested participants with different symbol sequences, such as $A_2 A_1 B_1 B_2$ versus $A_1 B_1 A_2 B_2$ (each subscript denotes a matching order), which also differ in matching order (Bahlmann et al. 2008). The difference in activation patterns can be simply explained by differences in any factor associated with matching orders and symbol orders, i.e., temporal order-related factors. It is thus necessary to completely control these general factors when extracting any syntactic factor from a number of cognitive factors involved in actual symbol processing.

Since the number of symbols is inevitably fixed (i.e., finite) in any actual experiment, it should be noted that any symbol sequence can be expressed by a regular (finite state) grammar, i.e., the least powerful grammar in the so-called Chomsky hierarchy. Therefore, one cannot, in principle, claim from the experiments that individual grammars (e.g., context-free phrase structure grammars vs. regular grammars) are differentially represented in the brain. Thus, the neural representation of individual grammars was *not* within the scope of Ohta et al. (2013). In addition to the various models examined, other nonstructural and nonsymbolic models with simple recurrent networks have been proposed to process some examples of even context-free and context-sensitive phrase structure languages, generalizing to some degree to longer strings than the training set (Rodriguez 2001). However, these models do not account for any parametric modulation of the activations reported in Ohta et al. (2013), except the length of sentences.

In the previous experiment, we introduced letter strings, which had no lexical associations but had both symbol orders (e.g., AABB and ABAB) and matching orders (e.g., $A_2 A_1 B_1 B_2$). There were two basic types of strings: reverse-order strings (Reverse) and same-order strings (Same). In the Reverse strings, the first and second halves of a string were presented in the reverse order, while in the Same strings the halves were presented in the same order

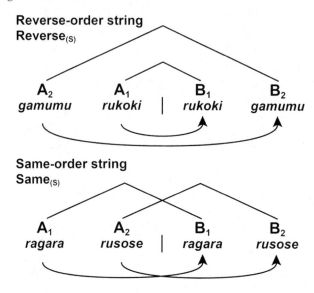

Figure 9.2 Two basic types of letter strings related to formal languages. We tested two string conditions with short [(S) as a subscript] stimuli: Reverse$_{(S)}$ and Same$_{(S)}$. Each letter string was formed by jumbling letters of either a pseudonoun or pseudoverb (see Figure 9.4). We also tested the long stimuli with six items (see Figure 8.2B). Each curved arrow with an arrowhead denotes a Search operation, as in the following figures. See also Plate 5B.

Symbols used: A, sample stimulus; B, comparison stimulus.

(Figure 9.2). Under these conditions, there was actually no path connecting the nonterminal nodes of symbol pairs (e.g., A_1 B_1 and A_2 B_2), as there was *no* Merge application to connect the multiple pairs. In regard to the symbol orders, both the Reverse and Same strings took the above type (i) of A^n B^n. In regard to the matching orders, the Reverse string took the type (ii) of A_2 A_1 B_1 B_2 or A_3 A_2 A_1 B_1 B_2 B_3, while the Same string took the type (iii) of A_1 A_2 B_1 B_2 or A_1 A_2 A_3 B_1 B_2 B_3.

1.3 Hypothesis I

Given a tree structure with a formal property of Merge and *iterativity* (recursiveness) (Fukui 2011), we propose the following hypothesis (Hypothesis I):

(1) The DoM, which can be defined as the *maximum depth* of merged subtrees within a given domain, is a key computational concept to properly measure the complexity of tree structures.

The DoM can quantify and compare various syntactic phenomena, such as self-embedding, scrambling, *wh*-movement, etc. Furthermore, when Search applies to each syntactic object with its hierarchical structure, the calculation of the DoM plays a critical role. Indeed, from a nested sentence "$[[$*The boy*$_2$ $[we_3$ $like_3]_2]_1$ $sings_1]_0$" (subscripts denote the DoM for each node), two sentences "$[$*The boy* . . .$]_1$ $sings_1$" and "we_3 $like_3$" are obtained, where relevant features (numbers and persons here) are searched and matched between the nodes with the identical DoM. Since such analyses of hierarchical structures would produce specific loads in syntactic computation, we expect that the DoM and associated "number of Search" would affect performances and cortical activations.

Sentences with various constructions have been previously discussed in terms of the acceptability of sentences (cf. Chomsky 1965: 12).

(i)   nested constructions
(ii)   self-embedded constructions
(iii) multiple-branching constructions
(iv)   left-branching constructions
(v)   right-branching constructions

The nested constructions are created by *centrally* embedding a phrase within another phrase (with some non-null element to its left and some non-null element to its right), and the self-embedded constructions are the special case of nested constructions when nesting occurs within the *same* type of phrases (e.g., noun phrases). The multiple-branching constructions are made by conjoining phrases at the same hierarchical level, and the left/right-branching constructions are yielded by merging a phrase in the leftmost or rightmost phrase. The degrees of nesting and self-embedding have already been proposed to model the understanding of sentences (Miller and Chomsky 1963). By generalizing this attractive idea in such a way as to include any construction with merged phrases, we introduced the DoM as a key computational concept.

Based on the nested (self-embedded), left/right-branching, and multiple-branching constructions, three basic types of sentences can be distinguished: the nested sentence (Nested), simple sentence (Simple), and conjoined sentence (Conjoined), respectively. The sentences shown in Figure 9.3 are some examples in Japanese. Given syntactic structures like the ones shown, the correspondence of each subject-verb pair becomes fixed. Here N and V denote a noun phrase and a verb phrase, respectively. For the sentence shown in Figure 9.3A, an entire sentence is constructed by nesting sentences in the form of $[N_2[N_1 \ V_1]V_2]$, where $[N_i \ V_i]$ represents a subject-verb pair of a sentence. Since Japanese is a head-last, and hence an SOV (verb-final) language, a main verb is placed after a subordinate clause. Therefore, Japanese sentences naturally yield nested structures without having to employ, as in English, object-relative clauses (e.g., "*The boy who$_i$ we like t$_i$ sings*"), which require "movement" of an object (i.e., with more Merge applications) and thus leave behind a "trace" (t_i, subscripts denote the same entity). For the sentence shown in Figure 9.3B, a simple sentence is constructed by adding

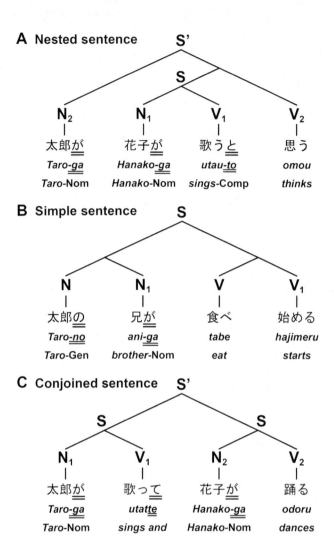

Figure 9.3 Japanese sentences with three major constructions. The figure shows three basic types of sentences in Japanese: the nested sentence, simple sentence, and conjoined sentence. Based on contemporary linguistics, each diagram represents a unique tree structure of each sentence constructed from nouns and verbs. Following each example, word-by-word translations in English are shown. (**A**) A sentence (S) at the lowest hierarchical level was nested into an entire sentence (S') ("*Taro-ga Hanako-ga utau-to omou*," "*Taro thinks that Hanako sings*"). (**B**) A simple sentence was constructed by adding the same number of left/right branches to both nouns and verbs ("*Taro-no ani-ga tabe hajimeru*," "*Taro's brother starts eating*"). (**C**) An entire sentence (S') was constructed by conjoining two sentences ("*Taro-ga utatte Hanako-ga odoru*," "*Taro sings, and Hanako dances*").

Symbols used: S and S', sentence; N, noun phrase; V, verb phrase; -*ga*, nominative case marker; -*no*, genitive case marker; -*to*, complementizer; -*te*, gerundive form; Nom, nominative case; Gen, genitive case; Comp, complementizer.

the same number of left/right branches to both Ns and Vs. The last noun (i.e., head) in the branches of Ns made a subject-verb pair with the last verb (i.e., head) of a compound verb. Each simple sentence thus takes the form of $[(NN_1)(VV_1)]$. For the sentence shown in Figure 9.3C, an entire sentence is constructed by conjoining sentences in the form of $[N_1 V_1][N_2 V_2]$. When considering longer sentences like $N_3 N_2 N_1 V_1 V_2 V_3$, these constructions have distinct values for DoM.

1.4 Hypothesis II

In any sentence, functional elements, such as inflections, auxiliary verbs, and grammatical particles, serve an essentially grammatical function without descriptive content. In regard to the fundamental role of these functional elements, we propose the following hypothesis (Hypothesis II):

(2) The basic frame of the syntactic structure of a given linguistic expression (e.g., sentence) is determined essentially by functional elements, which trigger Merge and Search operations.

In the nonsense poem "Jabberwocky" by Lewis Carroll, e.g., "*'Twas* ('*It was*') *brillig, and the slithy toves did* . . .," the basic frames of syntactic structures are indeed determined by the functional elements of "*'Twas,*" "*and,*" "*the,*" "*-s,*" and "*did.*" In the Japanese language, grammatical particles and morphosyntactic inflections are functional elements. The sentences shown in Figure 9.3 actually contain only three kinds of grammatical particles, which represent *canonical* (i.e., in a prototypical use) case markings and syntactic information in Japanese: *-ga*, a nominative case marker; *-no*, a genitive case marker; and *-to*, a complementizer. It should be noted that both the nested and simple sentences have the same symbol order of $N^n V^n$, but they have different grammatical particles and syntactic structures. In contrast, both the simple and conjoined sentences have the same tree structures as a result, but they have different symbol orders of $N^n V^n$ or $(NV)^n$ ($n \geq 2$). It is the grammatical particles and morphosyntactic inflections, but not symbol orders or matching orders themselves, that determine the basic frame of syntactic structures of a sentence.

Following morphosyntactic and phonological features of Japanese verbs (Tsujimura 2007), Vs take a nonpast-tense form (*-ru*), past-tense form (*-ta*), or gerundive form (*-te*); Vs ending with *-to* and *-te* introduce *that*-clauses and *and*-conjunctives, respectively. The gerundive form can be used not only in *and*-conjunctives, but in compound verbs (e.g., "*tabete-simau,*" "*to finish eating*"; actual Japanese words will be translated hereafter), much as gerunds can in English. The *-ga*, *-no*, *-to*, and *-te* endings (*double underlined* letters in Figures 9.3 and 9.4), together with the first verb of a compound verb in an adverbial form (e.g., "*tabe*"), are associated with Merge applications to connect multiple nouns/verbs or sentences, amounting to "number of Merge." The Japanese language lacks the "agreement features" (i.e., number, person, gender, etc.), but it is nevertheless equipped with the general Search procedure that is employed in agreement phenomena in other languages. This Search mechanism is in fact attested for various other phenomena in Japanese (see Fukui and Sakai 2003 for further discussion). For example, the Japanese language exhibits a phenomenon called "honorification," where a noun phrase denoting an honored person and the form of honorifics in verbs are to be matched (Gunji 1987, Ivana and Sakai 2007).

In this section, we provided some theoretical discussions based on modern linguistics, focusing on the two fundamental linguistic operations of Merge and Search. We hypothesized that the DoM is a key computational concept to properly quantify the complexity of tree structures, and that the basic frame of the syntactic structure of a given linguistic expression is determined essentially by grammatical particles and morphosyntactic inflections, which trigger Merge and Search operations.

2 The DoM as a Key Syntactic Factor Elucidated by an fMRI Experiment

One possible way to elucidate the neural basis of computational properties of natural language is to examine how the brain responds to the modulation of specified syntactic factors. We should not be content with such a general cognitive factor as so-called "syntactic complexity" or "syntactic working memory," which could involve both linguistic and nonlinguistic factors. We should instead identify minimal factors that *sufficiently* explain any activation change obtained. In our recent study, we focused on different sentence constructions, and found that the DoM and "number of Search" were the *minimal* syntactic factors associated with phrase structures, which parametrically modulate cortical responses measured with event-related fMRI (Ohta et al. 2013). In this section, we will present the basic paradigm and results of this work.

2.1 A Paradigm to Test Hypotheses I and II

We used jabberwocky sentences, which consist of pseudonoun phrases (Ns) and pseudoverb phrases (Vs) that lack lexical associations, but have grammatical particles and morphosyntactic inflections (Figure 9.4). According to Hypothesis II stated earlier, these jabberwocky sentences had the same syntactic structures as normal sentences. Under the sentence conditions of Nested, Simple, and Conjoined with the same structures shown in Figure 9.3, the jabberwocky sentences were visually presented in a phrase-by-phrase manner to the participants. We made six pseudonouns by repeating the same syllables with voiced consonants and any one of /a/, /u/, or /o/: *rara*, *zaza*, *mumu*, *gugu*, *yoyo*, and *dodo*. We also made four pseudoverb

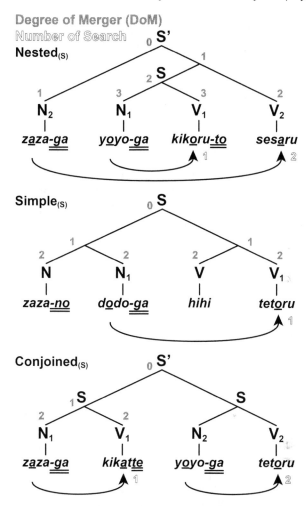

Figure 9.4 A paradigm for testing various sentence structures. We tested three sentence conditions with short [(S) as a subscript] jabberwocky sentences: Nested$_{(S)}$, Simple$_{(S)}$, and Conjoined$_{(S)}$. Note the syntactic structures of these jabberwocky sentences are same as those of real sentences in Figure 9.3. The digits shown in gray and white denote the DoM for each node and "number of Search," respectively. We also tested the long stimuli with six words (see Figure 8.2A). See also Plate 5A.

roots by repeating the same syllables with voiceless consonants and either /i/ or /e/: *kiki*, *hihi*, *sese*, and *tete*. Here, vowel harmony was adopted to change the last, i.e., the second, vowel of the verb root, so that this vowel harmonized with the vowel (i.e., /a/, /u/, or /o/) of the corresponding subject (e.g., "*rara-ga tetaru*" from "*teteru*," underlined vowels within pseudowords).

248 Merge in the Brain

These features of vowels were only *experimentally* introduced, and these pseudoverbs lacked grammatical features, as in the Japanese verbs. In all jabberwocky sentences, the distinction between Ns and Vs was clear without memorizing pseudowords, because Ns, but not Vs, ended with either -*ga* or -*no*, i.e., case markers in Japanese such as -*ga* and -*no* can be generally attached only to nominal phrases.

To test whether participants actually paid attention to the correspondence of each subject-verb pair, we used a matching task, such that the vowel of a subject (N_i as a sample stimulus) was matched with the last vowel of the corresponding verb root (V_i as a comparison stimulus), probing the goal with the same vowel as explained earlier. It follows that the same syntactic structures were constructed from matching stimuli and nonmatching stimuli (e.g., "*rara-ga teturu*"), which were both well-formed, i.e., *grammatical*, in Japanese. A matching strategy (counting, for example, the first and the fourth stimuli for matching) was useful in solving the task, but performing the task was *not* prerequisite for constructing syntactic structures. Our matching task is different from classification tasks for symbol orders (e.g., AABB vs. ABAB, where A and B are symbols representing certain sets of stimuli), which can be solved by counting the maximum number of consecutively repeated symbols. The order of the Nested, Simple, and Conjoined was pseudo-randomized without repetition. We further examined whether cortical activations were modulated by the length of sentences: short (S as a subscript, e.g., Conjoined$_{(S)}$; four-word) and long (L as a subscript, e.g., Conjoined$_{(L)}$; six-word) sentences, where the DoM domain spanned four and six relevant words, respectively.

We also used the same matching task under the string conditions of Reverse and Same (Figure 9.2), such that the first half of a string (A_i as a sample stimulus) was matched with the corresponding second half (B_i as a comparison stimulus) in the reverse or same order. These string conditions also controlled any involvement of the matching strategy stated earlier. Between the Nested (N_2 N_1 V_1 V_2) and Reverse (A_2 A_1 B_1 B_2) conditions, the curved arrows shown in Figures 9.2 and 9.4 represent the *same* matching order of sequentially presented stimuli. The symbol order was also identical among the Nested, Simple, Reverse, and Same conditions in the form of N^n V^n or A^n B^n. Combining these multiple conditions, we were able to properly examine whether different structures were actually constructed between sentences and strings. The spatial and temporal resolution of fMRI, as well as its sensitivity, has been proven to be high enough to confirm various hypotheses about human cognitive functions like ours.

2.2 Syntax-Selective Activations Modulated by the DoM and the Number of Search

To control both matching orders and symbol orders, we directly compared the Nested with the Reverse condition, using the Simple and Same conditions

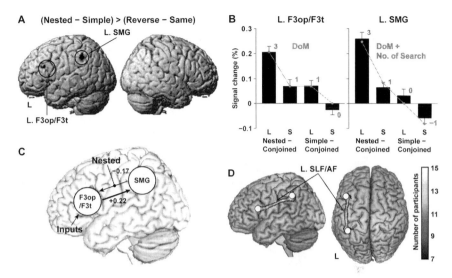

Figure 9.5 Functional and anatomical evidence of a syntax-related network. (**A**) Regions identified by the (Nested − Simple) > (Reverse − Same) contrast (see Figure 9.4). Activations were projected onto the left (L) and right lateral surfaces of a standard brain. (**B**) Percent signal changes for Nested − Conjoined and Simple − Conjoined in the L. F3op/F3t and L. SMG. Overlaid gray dots and lines denote the values fitted with the estimates (digits in gray) for the best models: DoM for the L. F3op/F3t and "DoM + number of Search" for the L. SMG. (**C**) The results of DCM, testing effective connectivity between the L. F3op/F3t and L. SMG. The best model included a significant top-down connection from the L. F3op/F3t to L. SMG (a thick line). (**D**) Anatomical connectivity between the L. F3op/F3t and L. SMG revealed by DTI. The population probability map is shown on the left lateral and dorsal surfaces of a standard brain with maximum intensity projection. White spheres represent seed regions of the L. F3op/F3t and L. SMG. See also Plate 6D, 6E, 6I, and 6J.

Symbols used: L, long sentences; S, short sentences.

as respective references, i.e., (Nested − Simple) > (Reverse − Same), where we combined the short and long stimuli. This contrast further controlled various linguistic and nonlinguistic factors, such as the number of Merge, number of case markers, number of nodes, memory span, and counting. This point is particularly important, because temporal order-related or memory-related factors have often been confused with differences in structure or grammar type. Significant activation was elicited by this contrast in the pars opercularis and pars triangularis of the left inferior frontal gyrus (L. F3op/F3t) [local maximum: $(x, y, z) = (-51, 24, 24)$, $Z = 5.8$], and the left supramarginal gyrus (L. SMG) [$(-39, -45, 42)$, $Z = 5.7$] (Figure 9.5A). Our results are best explained by the linguistic factors associated with the Nested

Table 9.1 Estimates of various factors to account for activations in Ohta et al. (2013).

Factor	Nested(L)	Nested(S)	Simple(L)	Simple(S)	Conjoined(L)	Conjoined(S)
Degree of Merger (DoM)	5	3	3	2	2	2
No. of Search	3	2	2	1	3	2
No. of nodes	11	7	11	7	10	7

	Nested(L)—Conjoined(L)	Nested(S)—Conjoined(S)	Simple(L)—Conjoined(L)	Simple(S)—Conjoined(S)
DoM	3	1	1	0
DoM + No. of Search	3	1	0	−1
No. of Search	0	0	−1	−1
No. of nodes	1	0	1	0

Estimates under the Conjoined condition were subtracted from those under the other Nested and Simple conditions [e.g., DoM for Nested(L) – Conjoined(L), 5 – 2 = 3], separately for long and short sentences. We regarded "DoM + number of Search" (i.e., adding the estimates of two factors) as an additional factor.

condition, supporting our second hypothesis that basic syntactic structures are constructed when well-formed sentences are given even without lexical meanings.

For these two critical regions, we examined the percent signal changes under the Nested and Simple conditions by subtracting those under the Conjoined condition, which had the simplest tree structures (Figure 9.4 and Table 9.1), separately for long and short sentences. Since we used the Conjoined(L) and Conjoined(S) as appropriate references, we examined whether likewise *subtracted* estimates of each factor (e.g., DoM for Nested(L) – Conjoined(L); see Table 9.1) directly explained the parametric modulation of activations in the four contrasts of Nested(L) – Conjoined(L), Nested(S) – Conjoined(S), Simple(L) – Conjoined(L), and Simple(S) – Conjoined(S). The percent signal changes in the L. F3op/F3t and L. SMG, averaged across significant voxels, indeed correlated exactly in a step-wise manner with the parametric models of the DoM [3, 1, 1, 0] and "DoM + number of Search" [3, 1, 0, –1], respectively (Figure 9.5B). By generalizing

Table 9.2 Fittings and likelihood of various models tested in Ohta et al. (2013).

L. F3op/F3t	Factor	RSS	r^2	P-values for four contrasts	Log-likelihood	Likelihood ratio
	*DoM	0.0007	0.99	0.17, 0.92, 0.97, 0.99	65.0	1.0
	DoM + No. of Search	0.0065	0.88	0.0035, 0.064, 0.63, 0.88	59.2	3.1×10^{-3}
	No. of Search	0.052	<0.1	<0.0001, 0.018, 0.019, 0.031	33.4	2.0×10^{-14}
	No. of nodes	0.015	0.72	0.0050, 0.0082, 0.018, 0.17	53.7	1.2×10^{-5}
L. SMG	Factor	RSS	r^2	P-values for four contrasts	Log-likelihood	Likelihood ratio
	DoM	0.0063	0.92	0.013, 0.083, 0.44, 0.49	58.8	0.079
	*DoM + No. of Search	0.0020	0.97	0.22, 0.30, 0.42, 0.62	61.4	1.0
	No. of Search	0.075	<0.1	<0.0001, 0.0061, 0.045, 0.090	23.6	3.8×10^{-17}
	No. of nodes	0.033	0.56	0.0004, 0.0005, 0.0061, 0.013	40.1	6.0×10^{-10}

Percent signal changes in the L. F3op/F3t and L. SMG were fitted with a single scale parameter to a model of each factor using its subtracted estimates (Table 9.1) for the four contrasts of Nested$_{(L)}$ – Conjoined$_{(L)}$, Nested$_{(S)}$ – Conjoined$_{(S)}$, Simple$_{(L)}$ – Conjoined$_{(L)}$, and Simple$_{(S)}$ – Conjoined$_{(S)}$. The P-values for the t-tests are shown in ascending order. The models with an asterisk resulted in the best fit of 19 models tested (four models are shown here) for explaining activations in the L. F3op/F3t or L. SMG, i.e., with the least residual sum of squares (RSS), largest coefficient of determination (r^2), and larger P-values. The likelihood ratio was taken as the ratio of each model's likelihood to the best model's likelihood. The best models were by far more likely than the other models.

the role of Search, we assumed that Search applied to a subject-verb pair, where the relevant features (vowels here) are experimentally "inserted" (Ohta et al. 2013).

We further examined 19 models proposed in theoretical linguistics, psycholinguistics, and natural language processing to verify that the models of the DoM and "DoM + number of Search" best explained the cortical activations (Ohta et al. 2013). All contrasts of Nested$_{(L)}$ – Conjoined$_{(L)}$, etc., predicted that the activations should be exactly zero when a factor produced no effect or load relative to the Conjoined. We thus adopted a no-intercept model, in which percent signal changes of each region were fitted with a single (thus minimal) scale parameter to a model of each factor using its subtracted estimates. For the four contrasts, a least-squares method was used to minimize the residual sum of squares (RSS) for the four fitted values (i.e., four estimates multiplied by a fitting scale) against the corresponding signal changes averaged across participants (Table 9.2).

The model of the DoM for the L. F3op/F3t, as well as that of "DoM + number of Search" for the L. SMG, indeed produced by far the least RSS (≤ 0.0020) and largest coefficient of determination (r^2) (≥ 0.97). Goodness of fit was further evaluated for each model by using a one-sample t-test (significance level at $\alpha = 0.0125$, Bonferroni corrected) between the fitted value for each contrast and individual activations. The model of the DoM for the L. F3op/F3t, as well as that of "DoM + number of Search" for the L. SMG, produced no significant deviation for the four contrasts ($P \geq 0.17$). To further take account of interindividual variability, we fitted "linear mixed-effects models" with individual activations, and found that the models of the DoM and "DoM + number of Search" were by far more likely for the L. F3op/F3t and L. SMG, respectively. Even if we took the Simple condition as a reference for subtracted estimates, we obtained the same results of best models. These results directly support Hypotheses I and II, such that the basic frame of syntactic structures are determined essentially by functional elements, whereas the DoM, together with the number of Search, is a key factor to properly quantify the complexity of the syntactic structures.

2.3 The Significance of the Connectivity between the L. F3op/F3t and L. SMG

It has been reported that the L. F3op/F3t is specialized for syntactic processing (Stromswold et al. 1996, Dapretto and Bookheimer 1999, Embick et al. 2000, Hashimoto and Sakai 2002, Friederici et al. 2003, Musso et al. 2003, Suzuki and Sakai 2003, Kinno et al. 2008), suggesting that this region subserves a grammar center (Sakai 2005). On the other hand, the left angular gyrus and SMG (L. AG/SMG) have been suggested to be important for vocabulary knowledge or lexical processing (Lee et al. 2007,

Pattamadilok et al. 2010). To elucidate the relationships between the L. F3op/F3t and L. SMG, we modeled the effective connectivity between these two regions by using dynamic causal modeling (DCM). Our interest was to identify the direction of the connectivity modulated by the Nested condition, which has the largest DoM of all conditions. First, we assumed intrinsic, i.e., task-independent, bi-directional connections, and the models were grouped into three "modulatory families": families with modulation for the bottom-up connection from the L. SMG to L. F3op/F3t, for the top-down connection from the L. F3op/F3t to L. SMG, and for both connections. Each family was composed of three "input models" as regards the regions receiving driving inputs. We found that the model with the modulation for the bottom-up connection, in which the L. F3op/F3t received driving inputs, was the best and most probable model (Figure 9.5C). We further confirmed that the intrinsic top-down connectivity was significantly positive (+0.22; $P < 0.0002$), while the bottom-up connectivity was negatively modulated.

A recent DCM study with a picture-sentence matching task has suggested that the L. F3op/F3t received driving inputs (den Ouden et al. 2012), which was consistent with our DCM results. Moreover, our previous studies revealed that the functional connectivity between the L. F3t/F3O (pars orbitalis) and L. AG/SMG was selectively enhanced during sentence processing (Homae et al. 2003), and that the L. AG/SMG was also activated during the identification of correct past-tense forms of verbs, probably reflecting an integration of syntactic and vocabulary knowledge (Tatsuno and Sakai 2005). Considering the role of the L. AG/SMG in lexical processing, the Search operation based on the DoM would be essential in assigning relevant features to the syntactic objects derived from lexical items.

To further confirm the anatomical plausibility of the network between the L. F3op/F3t and L. SMG revealed by DCM, we used diffusion-tensor imaging (DTI) with a probabilistic tractography. We observed that a single continuous cluster of the left superior longitudinal and arcuate fasciculi (SLF/AF) connected these regions (cluster size, 3,189 mm^3), together with much smaller clusters or islands (Figure 9.5D). Moreover, the left SLF/AF was consistently observed in all participants.

The findings of recent DTI studies have been controversial regarding the functional roles of two different pathways in language processes: the dorsal tracts of the SLF/AF, and the ventral tracts of the middle longitudinal fasciculus (MdLF) and extreme capsule (EmC). Both pathways connect the inferior frontal and superior/middle temporal areas (Saur et al. 2008, Wilson et al. 2011, Wong et al. 2011, Griffiths et al. 2013). Our DCM and DTI results indicate that the L. SMG activations reflecting the DoM mirrored a top-down influence from the L. F3op/F3t through the left dorsal pathway of the SLF/AF, revealing the most crucial network and pathway for syntactic computation.

3 Further Confirmation of Hypotheses I and II

3.1 *A Picture-Sentence Matching Paradigm*

We further examined whether our hypotheses hold for various cases discussed in previous studies. In our fMRI study (Kinno et al. 2008), we used a picture-sentence matching task with three sentence types in Japanese: active, passive, and scrambled sentences (Figure 9.6A). In the picture-sentence matching task, the participants read a sentence covertly and judged whether or not the action depicted in a picture matched the meaning of the sentence. Each sentence had two noun phrases called *arguments*, each of which assumes a different grammatical relation ("subject, direct object, or indirect object" in linguistic terms) and a semantic role ("agent, experiencer, or patient" in linguistic terms, i.e., an agent who performs the action, and an experiencer/patient who is affected by it); these three conditions were thus called Two-argument conditions. More specifically,

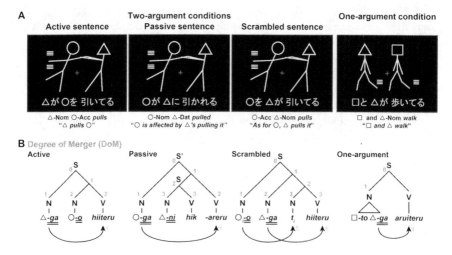

Figure 9.6 (**Plate 8 upper half**). A picture-sentence matching paradigm in Kinno et al. (2008). (**A**) A picture-sentence matching task under either Two-argument conditions or a One-argument condition. Each stimulus consisted of one picture (top) and one sentence (bottom). Below each example, word-by-word and full translations in English are shown. An identical picture set was used under the Two-argument conditions, where we tested three sentence types: active sentences ("△-ga ○-o hiiteru"), passive sentences ("○-ga △-ni hik-areru"), and scrambled sentences ("○-o △-ga hiiteru"). Under the One-argument condition, we presented syntactically simpler active sentences ("□-to △-ga aruiteru"). (**B**) The syntactic structures of three sentence types. The digits shown in gray and white denote the DoM for each node and "number of Search," respectively.

Symbols used: S and S', sentence; N, noun phrase; V, verb phrase; Nom, nominative case; Acc, accusative case; Dat, dative case; *-ga*, nominative case marker; *-o*, accusative case marker; *-ni*, dative case marker; *-to*, coordinator; t, trace (subscripts denote the same entity).

the active, passive, and scrambled sentences corresponded to "agent and patient" (subject and direct object), "experiencer and agent" (subject and indirect object), and "patient and agent" (direct object and subject) types, respectively. Pictures consisted of two stick figures, each of which was distinguished by a "head" symbol: a circle (○), square (□), or triangle (△). These sentences excluded the involvement of pragmatic information about word use (e.g., "*An officer chases a thief*" is more acceptable than "*A thief chases an officer*"). To minimize the effect of general memory demands, a whole sentence of a minimal length was visually presented for a longer time than was needed to respond.

In Japanese syntax, the grammatical relations are first marked by grammatical particles (nominative, dative, or accusative), which in turn allow the assignment of semantic roles. In the active sentences we used, a noun phrase with the nominative case marker *-ga* (*double underlined* letters in Figures 9.6) is associated with an agent, and the one with the accusative case marker *-o* is associated with a patient. For the passive sentences we used, however, a noun phrase with the nominative case marker *-ga* is associated with an experiencer (a person experiencing a situation), whereas a passive bound verb "*-(r)areru*" marks passiveness, making a subject-verb pair with the experiencer. In contrast, a noun phrase with the dative marker *-ni* is associated with an agent, whereas an action verb (e.g., "*hik(u)*," "*pull*") makes a subject-verb pair with the agent, forming a subordinate clause within the main clause "○-*ga* . . . -*(r)areru*." Note that there exist similar causative structures in both Japanese and English: "*Hanako-ga kare-ni hik-aseta*," "*Hanako made him pull*." Actually, there are two types of passivization in Japanese: *ni* passive (e.g., "*Hanako-ga Taro-ni hik-areru*," "*Hanako is affected by Taro's pulling her*") and *ni yotte* passive (e.g., "*Hanako-ga Taro-ni yotte hik-areru*," "*Hanako is pulled by Taro*"). According to Kuroda (1992), the *ni* passive involves no noun-phrase movement, while the *ni yotte* passive involves a movement similar to the case in English. For the scrambled sentences, an object moves from its canonical position to higher nodes by undergoing another Merge operation. This type of constructions is perfectly normal, not only in Japanese but in German, Finnish, and other languages. We also tested the One-argument condition, under which each sentence was presented with an intransitive verb and double agents. This condition did not involve two-argument relationships, and was thus syntactically simpler than any of the Two-argument conditions.

3.2 Hypothesis III

Here we present the following hypothesis (Hypothesis III):

(3) The DoM domain changes dynamically in accordance with iterative Merge applications, the Search distances, and/or task requirements.

Since Merge combines two syntactic objects to form a larger structure, Merge always produces a one-level higher node. When Merge applies iteratively to an existing phrase or sentence, the DoM domain becomes thus larger in accordance with the number of Merge applications. The Search distance is the structural distance between two distinct parts to which the Search operation applies, regardless of the nodes that are irrelevant to the Search operation. As observed from Figure 9.4, the DoM domain changes in accordance with the Search distance. On the other hand, for every sentence stimulus in the study of Ohta et al. (2013), the construction of syntactic structures was ensured by task requirements, in which three sentence types had to be distinguished while they were completely mixed. Task requirements include not only certain constraints required by experimental tasks, but detailed parsing naturally required to understand a part of phrases or sentences (e.g., subject-verb relationships and noun-pronoun (coreference) relationships).

In the aforementioned paradigm (Kinno et al. 2008), the four task conditions (three sentence types under the Two-argument conditions, as well as one type under the One-argument condition) were completely mixed (see Figure 9.6A). With such task requirements, the DoM domain spanned three relevant words for all sentence types under the Two-argument conditions. Under the One-argument condition, the action of two stick figures was always identical, and thus a subject (a triangle just below N in Figure 9.6B) is regarded as a unit. Under these four task conditions, participants were required to check at least one of the argument-verb relationships, demanding Search at least once. For the scrambled sentences alone, an additional Search operation should match the identical indices of the moved object and its trace. For the active, passive, and scrambled sentences, the estimates of DoM were 2, 3, and 3, respectively, while those of the DoM was 1 under the One-argument condition.

3.3 Applying the DoM to Various Sentence Types

In the study of Kinno et al. (2008), we directly contrasted passive and active sentence conditions to identify a cortical region that is activated by purely syntactic processes. This stringent contrast resulted in significant activation in the left dorsal F3t (L. dF3t) alone [(−48, 24, 21), $Z = 3.8$] (Figure 9.7A), which was very close to the L. F3op/F3t activation in the study of Ohta et al. (2013). The L. dF3t activation was significantly enhanced under both the passive and scrambled sentence conditions compared to that under the active sentence condition ($P \leq 0.033$) (Figure 9.7B), whereas there was no significant difference between the passive and scrambled sentence conditions ($P = 0.15$). Taking the One-argument condition as a reference for subtracted estimates, the signal changes in the L. dF3t were precisely correlated in a step-wise manner with the parametric model of the DoM [1, 2, 2], producing the RSS of 0.0001 and r^2 of 0.99, without significant deviation for the three

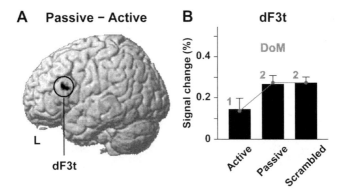

Figure 9.7 (**Plate 8 lower half**). Activations in the L. dF3t modulated by the DoM. (**A**) A region identified by the Passive – Active contrast (see Figure 9.6). Activations were projected onto the left (L) lateral surface of a standard brain. (**B**) Percent signal changes for the active, passive, and scrambled sentence conditions in the L. dF3t, taking the One-argument condition as a reference. Overlaid gray dots and lines denote the values fitted with the estimates (digits in gray) for the model of the DoM.

contrasts ($P \geq 0.87$). The model of the DoM thus *sufficiently* explains the L. dF3t activations. It should be noted that the parametric model of "the number of nodes" [2, 4, 4] also yielded the same fitting results in this case. The design of experimental paradigms limits the separation of multiple factors.

In a recent fMRI study, only right-branching constructions were examined, and activations in the L. F3t were modulated by the size of constituents (i.e., number of terminal nodes) (Pallier et al. 2011). Since the estimates of the DoM were identical to those of "the number of Merge" or "the number of nonterminal nodes" in this case, it was not possible to separate these factors. Taking the simplest condition (lists of unrelated words) as an appropriate reference, the model of the DoM actually showed a comparable or better goodness of fit for activations in the L. F3t, when compared with their log-fitting models.

4 Further Confirmation of Hypothesis III

4.1 The Effect of the Search Distances on the DoM

Neuroimaging and psycholinguistic studies have reported that English sentences with object-relative clauses have higher processing loads than those with subject-relative clauses (Just et al. 1996, Stromswold et al. 1996, Gibson 2000). To properly parse the relative clauses, the relative pronoun and its antecedent are coindexed; "*who$_i$*" and "*the boy$_i$*," respectively, in the example shown in Figure 9.8. In a subject-relative clause, a relative pronoun

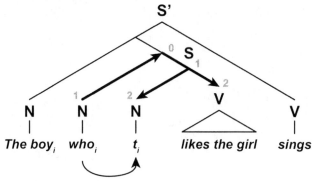

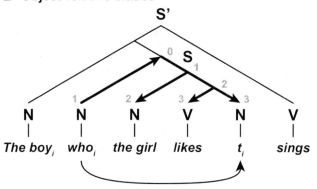

Figure 9.8 The DoM domains varied with the Search distances. (**A**) A sentence with a subject-relative clause. (**B**) A sentence with an object-relative clause. In these relative clauses, a relative pronoun *who*ᵢ is displaced from its subject or object position denoted by a trace *t*ᵢ. A set of thick straight arrows corresponds to the DoM domains. The digits shown in gray denote the DoM for each node within the domain.

Symbols used: S and S', sentence; N, noun phrase; V, verb phrase; *t*ᵢ, trace (subscripts denote the same entity).

"*who*ᵢ" was displaced from the *subject* position denoted by a trace *t*ᵢ (originally, "*the boy*ᵢ *likes the girl*"), while in an object-relative clause, a relative pronoun was displaced from the *object* position (originally, "*the girl likes the boy*ᵢ"). Following the proposal by Hawkins (1999), we assume that the relative pronoun searches the corresponding trace within tree structures of a sentence (see curved arrows in Figure 9.8). In a subject-relative clause, Search ends at the initiation of the verb phrase, while in an object-relative clause, Search ends *after* a verb appears within a subordinate clause. In accordance with the Search distances for these examples, the DoM would become one unit larger for the object-relative clause than the subject-relative one. Higher processing loads observed with object-relative clauses are consistent with this inference.

4.2 The Effect of Task Requirements on the DoM

If Hypothesis III is correct, then the L.F3op/F3t activations can be different in accordance with task requirements, even when the same sentences are presented. In our previous fMRI study, we compared three explicit linguistic tasks with the same set of normal two-word sentences: syntactic decision, semantic decision, and phonological decision tasks (Suzuki and Sakai 2003). In the syntactic decision task, the participants judged whether or not the presented sentence was syntactically correct, and this judgment required syntactic knowledge about the distinction between transitive and intransitive verbs (e.g., normal sentence, *"yuki-ga tumoru," "snow lies (on the ground)"*; anomalous sentence, *"yuki-o tumoru," "(something) lies snow"*). In the semantic decision task, lexico-semantic knowledge about selectional restrictions was indispensable. In the phonological decision task, phonological knowledge about accent patterns was required. Neither the semantic decision task nor the phonological decision task, both with *implicit* syntactic processing, elicited significant activations in the L. F3op/F3t (−57, 9, 6), which was significantly activated during *explicit* syntactic processing, even by a direct comparison between the syntactic decision task and the other tasks. These results suggest the presence of the DoM domain in accordance with the task requirements of explicit syntactic processing.

4.3 The Mixed Effects of the Search Distances and Task Requirements on the DoM

In another fMRI study, we directly compared syntactic decision and short-term memory tasks (Hashimoto and Sakai 2002). In this unique paradigm, we visually presented nested sentences that included two proper nouns, two verbs, and one pronoun, in which either verb or pronoun was underlined. After presenting one complete sentence in a phrase-by-phrase manner, paired phrases including an underlined phrase were shown. In one syntactic decision task (SYN-1), participants were required to judge whether the subject of an underlined verb corresponded to the person in paired phrases (Figure 9.9A). In this case, the Search distance was the structural distance between the subject and verb of the same clause. In the other syntactic decision task (SYN-2), the participants were required to judge whether an underlined pronoun was able to refer to the person in paired phrases (Figure 9.9B). In this case, the Search distance was the structural distance between the coindexed noun and pronoun. In these syntactic decision tasks, the Search distance, and consequently the DoM domain, changed dynamically in accordance with the different task requirements, even when the same sentences were presented.

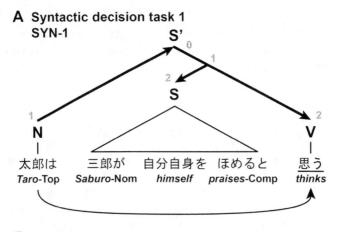

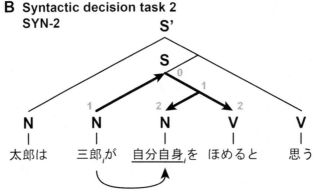

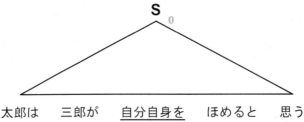

Figure 9.9 The DoM domains varied with the Search distances and task require-
ments. In this task, participants read Japanese nested sentences
("*Taro-wa Saburo-ga jibunjishin-o homeru-to omou*," "*Taro thinks that
Saburo praises himself*"), in which phrases were sequentially presented.
(**A**) A syntactic decision task 1, in which participants judged subject-
verb relationships. A set of thick straight arrows corresponds to the
DoM domains. The digits shown in gray denote the DoM for each node
within the domain. (**B**) A syntactic decision task 2, in which participants
judged noun-pronoun (coreference) relationships (subscripts denote the
same entity). (**C**) A short-term memory task with a sentence, in which
participants judged the temporal order of the phrases.

Symbols used: S and S', sentence; N, noun phrase; V, verb phrase; Top, topic; Nom, nominative
case; Comp, complementizer.

The estimate of the resultant DoM was 2 for both cases. In a short-term memory task with a sentence, the participants memorized the linear order of the phrases, and judged whether the left-hand phrase preceded the right-hand one in the original sequence (Figure 9.9C). With such a task requirement, the factor of DoM would become less effective. Indeed, we found that activations in the L. F3op/F3t were equally enhanced in both syntactic decision tasks when compared with the short-term memory task.

Conclusions

In this chapter, we reviewed recent advances in theoretical linguistics and functional neuroimaging in the following respects. First, we provided theoretical discussions about the hierarchical tree structures of sentences, and introduced the two fundamental linguistic operations of Merge and Search. We also presented our hypotheses that the DoM is a key computational concept to properly measure the complexity of tree structures (Hypothesis I), and that the basic frame of the syntactic structure of a given linguistic expression is determined essentially by functional elements, which trigger Merge and Search operations (Hypothesis II). Second, we presented our recent fMRI studies, which have demonstrated that the DoM, together with the number of Search, is indeed a key syntactic factor that accounts for syntax-selective activations in the L. F3op/F3t and L. SMG (Ohta et al. 2013). Moreover, based on the DCM and DTI results, we revealed the significance of the top-down connection from the L. F3op/F3t to L. SMG, suggesting that information about the DoM is transmitted through this specific dorsal pathway. Third, we further hypothesized that the DoM domain changes dynamically in accordance with iterative Merge applications, the Search distances, and/ or task requirements (Hypothesis III). We showed that the DoM sufficiently explains activation modulations due to different structures reported in previous fMRI studies (Kinno et al. 2008, Pallier et al. 2011). Finally, we confirmed that Hypothesis III accounts for higher processing loads observed with object-relative clauses, as well as activations in the L. F3op/F3t during explicit syntactic decision tasks, reported in the previous neuroimaging and psycholinguistic studies (Just et al. 1996, Stromswold et al. 1996, Gibson 2000, Hashimoto and Sakai 2002, Suzuki and Sakai 2003). It is likely that the DoM serves as a key computational principle for other human-specific cognitive capacities, such as mathematics and music, both of which can be expressed by hierarchical tree structures. A future investigation into the computational principles of syntax will further deepen our understanding of uniquely human mental faculties.

Conflict of Interest Statements

The authors declare that the research was conducted in the absence of any commercial or financial relationships that could be construed as a potential conflict of interest.

Acknowledgments

We would like to thank R. Kinno, H. Miyashita, K. Iijima, and T. Inubushi for their helpful discussions, N. Komoro for her technical assistance, and H. Matsuda for her administrative assistance. This research was supported by a Core Research for Evolutional Science and Technology (CREST) grant from the Japan Science and Technology Agency (JST), by Grants-in-Aid for Scientific Research (S) (Nos. 20220005) from the Ministry of Education, Culture, Sports, Science and Technology, and by a Grant-in-Aid for Japan Society for the Promotion of Science (JSPS) Fellows (No. 24·8931).

References

Abe, Kentaro, and Dai Watanabe. 2011. Songbirds possess the spontaneous ability to discriminate syntactic rules. *Nature Neuroscience* 14: 1067–1074.

Bahlmann, Jörg, Ricarda I. Schubotz, and Angela D. Friederici. 2008. Hierarchical artificial grammar processing engages Broca's area. *NeuroImage* 42: 525–534.

Beckers, Gabriël J. L., Johan J. Bolhuis, Kazuo Okanoya, and Robert C. Berwick. 2012. Birdsong neurolinguistics: Songbird context-free grammar claim is premature. *NeuroReport* 23: 139–145.

Chomsky, Noam. 1957. *Syntactic structures*. The Hague: Mouton. 2nd edition, Mouton de Gruyter, 2002.

Chomsky, Noam. 1959. On certain formal properties of grammars. *Information and Control* 2: 137–167.

Chomsky, Noam. 1965. *Aspects of the theory of syntax*. Cambridge, MA: MIT Press.

Chomsky, Noam. 1995. *The minimalist program*. Cambridge, MA: MIT Press.

Chomsky, Noam. 2004. Beyond explanatory adequacy. In *Structures and beyond: The cartography of syntactic structures*, volume 3, ed. Adriana Belletti, 104–131. Oxford: Oxford University Press.

Corballis, Michael C. 2007. Recursion, language, and starlings. *Cognive Science* 31: 697–704.

Dapretto, Mirella, and Susan Y. Bookheimer. 1999. Form and content: Dissociating syntax and semantics in sentence comprehension. *Neuron* 24: 427–432.

den Ouden, Dirk-Bart, Dorothee Saur, Wolfgang Mader, Björn Schelter, Sladjana Lukic, Eisha Wali, Jens Timmer, and Cynthia K. Thompson. 2012. Network modulation during complex syntactic processing. *NeuroImage* 59: 815–823.

Embick, David, Alec Marantz, Yasushi Miyashita, Wayne O'Neil, and Kuniyoshi L. Sakai. 2000. A syntactic specialization for Broca's area. *Proceedings of the National Academy of Sciences of the United States of America* 97: 6150–6154.

Friederici, Angela D., Shirley-Ann Rüschemeyer, Anja Hahne, and Christian J. Fiebach. 2003. The role of left inferior frontal and superior temporal cortex in sentence comprehension: Localizing syntactic and semantic processes. *Cerebral Cortex* 13: 170–177.

Fukui, Naoki. 2011. Merge and bare phrase structure. In *The Oxford handbook of linguistic minimalism*, ed. Cedric Boeckx, 73–95. Oxford: Oxford University Press. [Chapter 1, this volume.]

Fukui, Naoki, and Hiromu Sakai. 2003. The visibility guideline for functional categories: Verb raising in Japanese and related issues. *Lingua* 113 (4–6): 321–375.

[Reprinted in *Theoretical comparative syntax: Studies in macroparameters*, Naoki Fukui, 289–336. London: Routledge. (2006).]

Gentner, Timothy Q., Kimberly M. Fenn, Daniel Margoliash, and Howard C. Nusbaum. 2006. Recursive syntactic pattern learning by songbirds. *Nature* 440: 1204–1207.

Gibson, Edward. 2000. The dependency locality theory: A distance-based theory of linguistic complexity. In *Image, language, brain: Papers from the First Mind Articulation Project Symposium*, ed. Alec Marantz, Yasushi Miyashita, and Wayne O'Neil, 95–126. Cambridge, MA: MIT Press.

Griffiths, John D., William D. Marslen-Wilson, Emmanuel A. Stamatakis, and Lorraine K. Tyler. 2013. Functional organization of the neural language system: Dorsal and ventral pathways are critical for syntax. *Cerebral Cortex* 23: 139–147.

Gunji, Takao. 1987. *Japanese phrase structure grammar: A unification-based approach*. Dordrecht: D. Reidel Publishing Company.

Hashimoto, Ryuichiro, and Kuniyoshi L. Sakai. 2002. Specialization in the left prefrontal cortex for sentence comprehension. *Neuron* 35: 589–597.

Hawkins, John A. 1999. Processing complexity and filler-gap dependencies across grammars. *Language* 75: 244–285.

Homae, Fumitaka, Noriaki Yahata, and Kuniyoshi L. Sakai. 2003. Selective enhancement of functional connectivity in the left prefrontal cortex during sentence processing. *NeuroImage* 20: 578–586.

Hopcroft, John E., and Jeffrey D. Ullman. 1979. *Introduction to automata theory, languages, and computation*. Reading, MA: Addison-Wesley.

Ivana, Adrian, and Hiromu Sakai. 2007. Honorification and light verbs in Japanese. *Journal of East Asian Linguistics* 16: 171–191.

Just, Marcel Adam, Patricia A. Carpenter, Timothy A. Keller, William F. Eddy, and Keith R. Thulborn. 1996. Brain activation modulated by sentence comprehension. *Science* 274: 114–116.

Kinno, Ryuta, Mitsuru Kawamura, Seiji Shioda, and Kuniyoshi L. Sakai. 2008. Neural correlates of noncanonical syntactic processing revealed by a picture-sentence matching task. *Human Brain Mapping* 29: 1015–1027.

Kuroda, S. Y. 1992. On Japanese passives. In *Japanese syntax and semantics: Collected papers*, 183–221. Dordrecht: Kluwer.

Lee, HweeLing, Joseph T. Devlin, Clare Shakeshaft, Lauren H. Stewart, Amanda Brennan, Jen Glensman, Katherine Pitcher, Jenny Crinion, Andrea Mechelli, Richard S. J. Frackowiak, David W. Green, and Cathy J. Price. 2007. Anatomical traces of vocabulary acquisition in the adolescent brain. *The Journal of Neuroscience* 27: 1184–1189.

Mandelbrot, Benoit B. 1977. *The fractal geometry of nature*. New York: W. H. Freeman and Company.

Miller, George A., and Noam Chomsky. 1963. Finitary models of language users. In *Handbook of mathematical psychology*, volume II, ed. R. Duncan Luce, Robert R. Bush, and Eugene Galanter, 419–491. New York: John Wiley and Sons.

Musso, Mariacristina, Andrea Moro, Volkmar Glauche, Michel Rijntjes, Jürgen Reichenbach, Christian Büchel, and Cornelius Weiller. 2003. Broca's area and the language instinct. *Nature Neuroscience* 6: 774–781.

Ohta, Shinri, Naoki Fukui, and Kuniyoshi L. Sakai. 2013. Syntactic computation in the human brain: The degree of merger as a key factor. *PLoS One* 8 (2): 1–16. [Chapter 8, this volume.]

Pallier, Christophe, Anne-Dominique Devauchelle, and Stanislas Dehaene. 2011. Cortical representation of the constituent structure of sentences. *Proceedings of the National Academy of Sciences of the United States of America* 108: 2522–2527.

Pattamadilok, Chotiga, Iris N. Knierim, Keith J. Kawabata Duncan, and Joseph T. Devlin. 2010. How does learning to read affect speech perception? *The Journal of Neuroscience* 30: 8435–8444.

Rodriguez, Paul. 2001. Simple recurrent networks learn context-free and context-sensitive languages by counting. *Neural Computation* 13: 2093–2118.

Saito, Mamoru, and Naoki Fukui. 1998. Order in phrase structure and movement. *Linguistic Inquiry* 29: 439–474. [Reprinted in *Theoretical comparative syntax: Studies in macroparameters*, Naoki Fukui, 179–208. London: Routledge. (2006).]

Sakai, Kuniyoshi L. 2005. Language acquisition and brain development. *Science* 310: 815–819.

Saur, Dorothee, Björn W. Kreher, Susanne Schnell, Dorothee Kümmerer, Philipp Kellmeyer, Magnus-Sebastian Vry, Rosa Umarova, Mariacristina Musso, Volkmar Glauche, Stefanie Abel, Walter Huber, Michel Rijntjes, Jürgen Hennig, and Cornelius Weiller. 2008. Ventral and dorsal pathways for language. *Proceedings of the National Academy of Sciences of the United States of America* 105: 18035–18040.

Stromswold, Karin, David Caplan, Nathaniel Alpert, and Scott Rauch. 1996. Localization of syntactic comprehension by positron emission tomography. *Brain and Language* 52: 452–473.

Suzuki, Kei, and Kuniyoshi L. Sakai. 2003. An event-related fMRI study of explicit syntactic processing of normal/anomalous sentences in contrast to implicit syntactic processing. *Cerebral Cortex* 13: 517–526.

Tatsuno, Yoshinori, and Kuniyoshi L. Sakai. 2005. Language-related activations in the left prefrontal regions are differentially modulated by age, proficiency, and task demands. *The Journal of Neuroscience* 25: 1637–1644.

Tsujimura, Natsuko. 2007. *An introduction to Japanese linguistics*, 2nd edition. Malden, MA: Blackwell.

Wilson, Stephen M., Sebastiano Galantucci, Maria Carmela Tartaglia, Kindle Rising, Dianne K. Patterson, Maya L. Henry, Jennifer M. Ogar, Jessica DeLeon, Bruce L. Miller, and Maria Luisa Gorno-Tempini. 2011. Syntactic processing depends on dorsal language tracts. *Neuron* 72: 397–403.

Wong, Francis C. K., Bharath Chandrasekaran, Kyla Garibaldi, and Patrick C. M. Wong. 2011. White matter anisotropy in the ventral language pathway predicts sound-to-word learning success. *The Journal of Neuroscience* 31: 8780–8785.

Bibliography

Abe, Kentaro, and Dai Watanabe. 2011. Songbirds possess the spontaneous ability to discriminate syntactic rules. *Nature Neuroscience* 14: 1067–1074.

Abney, Steven Paul. 1987. The English noun phrase in its sentential aspect. Doctoral dissertation, MIT.

Bahlmann, Jörg, Antoni Rodriguez-Fornells, Michael Rotte, and Thomas F. Münte. 2007. An fMRI study of canonical and noncanonical word order in German. *Human Brain Mapping* 28: 940–949.

Bahlmann, Jörg, Ricarda I. Schubotz, and Angela D. Friederici. 2008. Hierarchical artificial grammar processing engages Broca's area. *NeuroImage* 42: 525–534.

Baker, Mark. 2008. *The syntax of agreement and concord*. Cambridge: Cambridge University Press.

Beckers, Gabriël J. L., Johan J. Bolhuis, Kazuo Okanoya, and Robert C. Berwick. 2012. Birdsong neurolinguistics: Songbird context-free grammar claim is premature. *NeuroReport* 23: 139–145.

Behrens, Timothy E. J., Heidi Johansen Berg, Saad Jbabdi, Matthew F. S. Rushworth, and Mark W. Woolrich. 2007. Probabilistic diffusion tractography with multiple fibre orientations: What can we gain? *NeuroImage* 34: 144–155.

Ben-Shachar, Michal, Dafna Palti, and Yosef Grodzinsky. 2004. Neural correlates of syntactic movement: Converging evidence from two fMRI experiments. *NeuroImage* 21: 1320–1336.

Berwick, Robert. 2011. All you need is Merge: Biology, computation, and language from the bottom up. In *The biolinguistic enterprise: New perspectives on the evolution and nature of the human language faculty*, ed. Anna Maria Di Sciullo and Cedric Boeckx, 461–491. Oxford: Oxford University Press.

Bittner, Maria, and Ken Hale. 1996. The structural determination of Case and agreement. *Linguistic Inquiry* 27: 1–68.

Bloomfield, Leonard. 1933. *Language*. New York: Holt, Rinehart & Winston.

Boeckx, Cedric. 2008. *Bare syntax*. Oxford: Oxford University Press.

Boeckx, Cedric. 2009. On the locus of asymmetry in UG. *Catalan Journal of Linguistics* 8: 41–53.

Boeckx, Cedric. 2014. *Elementary syntactic structures*. Cambridge: Cambridge University Press.

Boeckx, Cedric, and Sandra Stjepanović. 2001. Head-ing toward PF. *Linguistic Inquiry* 32: 345–355.

Bornkessel, Ina, Stefan Zysset, Angela D. Friederici, D. Yves von Cramon, and Matthias Schlesewsky. 2005. Who did what to whom? The neural basis of argument hierarchies during language comprehension. *NeuroImage* 26: 221–233.

Bošković, Željko. 2007. On the locality and motivation of Move and Agree: An even more minimal theory. *Linguistic Inquiry* 38: 589–644.

Bošković, Željko, and Daiko Takahashi. 1998. Scrambling and last resort. *Linguistic Inquiry* 29: 347–366.

Botvinick, Mattew M., Jonathan D. Cohen, and Cameron S. Carter. 2004. Conflict monitoring and anterior cingulate cortex: An update. *Trends in Cognitive Science* 8: 539–546.

Brame, Michael. 1981. The general theory of binding and fusion. *Linguistic Analysis* 7 (3): 277–325.

Brame, Michael. 1982. The head-selector theory of lexical specifications and the nonexistence of coarse categories. *Linguistic Analysis* 10 (4): 321–325.

Brody, Michael. 1999. Relating syntactic elements: Remarks on Norbert Hornstein's "Movement and chains." *Syntax* 2: 210–226.

Brody, Michael. 2002. One more time. *Syntax* 4: 126–138.

Bruening, Benjamin. 2014. Defects of defective intervention. *Linguistic Inquiry* 45: 707–719.

Bush, George, Phan Luu, and Michael I. Posner. 2000. Cognitive and emotional influences in anterior cingulate cortex. *Trends in Cognitive Science* 4: 215–222.

Cable, Seth. 2010. *The grammar of Q: Q-particles, _wh_-movement, and pied-piping.* Oxford: Oxford University Press.

Chikazoe, Junichi, Seiki Konishi, Tomoki Asari, Koji Jimura, and Yasushi Miyashita. 2007. Activation of right inferior frontal gyrus during response inhibition across response modalities. *Journal of Cognitive Neuroscience* 19: 69–80.

Chomsky, Noam. 1955/1975. The logical structure of linguistic theory. Ms., Harvard University, 1955. Published in part in 1975, New York: Plenum.

Chomsky, Noam. 1956. Three models for the description of language. *IRE Transactions on Information Theory* IT-2: 113–124. [Reprinted, with corrections, in *Readings in mathematical psychology*, volume 2, ed. R. Duncan Luce, Robert R. Bush, and Eugene Galanter. New York: Wiley. (1965).]

Chomsky, Noam. 1957. *Syntactic structures.* The Hague: Mouton. 2nd edition, Mouton de Gruyter, 2002.

Chomsky, Noam. 1959. On certain formal properties of grammars. *Information and Control* 2: 137–167.

Chomsky, Noam. 1963. Formal properties of grammars. In *Handbook of mathematical psychology*, volume II, ed. R. Duncan Luce, Robert R. Bush, and Eugene Galanter, 323–418. New York: John Wiley & Sons.

Chomsky, Noam. 1965. *Aspects of the theory of syntax.* Cambridge, MA: MIT Press.

Chomsky, Noam. 1970. Remarks on nominalization. In *Readings in English transformational grammar*, ed. Roderick A. Jacobs and Peter S. Rosenbaum, 184–221. Waltham, MA: Ginn.

Chomsky, Noam. 1975. *Reflections on language.* New York: Pantheon Books.

Chomsky, Noam. 1980. *Rules and representations.* New York: Columbia University Press.

Chomsky, Noam. 1981. *Lectures on government and binding: The Pisa lectures.* Dordrecht: Foris.

Chomsky, Noam. 1986a. *Barriers.* Cambridge, MA: MIT Press.

Chomsky, Noam. 1986b. *Knowledge of language: Its nature, origin, and use.* New York: Praeger.

Chomsky, Noam. 1993. A minimalist program for linguistic theory. In *The view from Building 20: Essays in linguistics in honor of Sylvain Bromberger*, ed. Ken Hale and Samuel J. Keyser, 1–52. Cambridge, MA: MIT Press.

Chomsky, Noam. 1995a. Bare phrase structure. In *Evolution and revolution in linguistic theory: Essays in honor of Carlos Otero*, ed. Héctor Ramiro Campos and Paula Marie Kempchinsky, 51–109. Washington, DC: Georgetown University Press.

Chomsky, Noam. 1995b. *The minimalist program*. Cambridge, MA: MIT Press.

Chomsky, Noam. 2000. Minimalist inquiries: The framework. In *Step by step: Minimalist essays in honor of Howard Lasnik*, ed. Roger Martin, David Michaels, and Juan Uriagereka, 89–155. Cambridge, MA: MIT Press.

Chomsky, Noam. 2001. Derivation by phase. In *Ken Hale: A life in language*, ed. Michael Kenstowicz, 1–52. Cambridge, MA: MIT Press.

Chomsky, Noam. 2004a. Beyond explanatory adequacy. In *Structures and beyond: The cartography of syntactic structures*, volume 3, ed. Adriana Belletti, 104–131. Oxford: Oxford University Press.

Chomsky, Noam. 2004b. *The generative enterprise revisited: A conversation with Riny Huybregts, Henk van Riemsdijk, Naoki Fukui, and Mihoko Zushi*. Berlin: Mouton de Gruyter.

Chomsky, Noam. 2005. Three factors in language design. *Linguistic Inquiry* 36: 1–22.

Chomsky, Noam. 2007. Approaching UG from below. In *Interfaces + recursion = language? Chomsky's minimalism and the view from syntax-semantics*, ed. Uli Sauerland and Hans-Martin Gärtner, 1–29. Berlin: Mouton de Gruyter.

Chomsky, Noam. 2008. On phases. In *Foundational issues in linguistic theory: Essays in honor of Jean-Roger Vergnaud*, ed. Robert Freidin, Carlos P. Otero, and Maria Luisa Zubizarreta, 133–166. Cambridge, MA: MIT Press.

Chomsky, Noam. 2012a. Introduction. In *Gengokisoronsyu* [*Foundations of biolinguistics: Selected writings*], ed. and trans. Naoki Fukui, 17–26. Tokyo: Iwanami Shoten.

Chomsky, Noam. 2012b. *Chomsky's linguistics*, ed. Peter Graff and Coppe van Urk. Cambridge, MA: MIT Working Papers in Linguistics.

Chomsky, Noam. 2013. Problems of projection. *Lingua* 130: 33–49.

Chomsky, Noam. 2015a. Problems of projection: Extensions. In *Structures, strategies and beyond: Studies in honour of Adriana Belletti*, ed. Elisa Di Domenico, Cornelia Hamann, and Simona Matteini, 3–16. Amsterdam and Philadelphia: John Benjamins.

Chomsky, Noam. 2015b. A discussion with Naoki Fukui and Mihoko Zushi (March 4, 2014). In *The Sophia Lectures* (*Sophia Linguistica* 64), 69–97. Tokyo: Sophia Linguistic Institute for International Communication, Sophia University.

Chomsky, Noam, and Marcel Paul Schützenberger. 1963. The algebraic theory of context-free languages. In *Computer programming and formal systems*, ed. Paul Braffort and David Hirschberg, 118–161. Amsterdam: North-Holland.

Cinque, Guglielmo. 1999. *Adverbs and functional heads: A cross-linguistic perspective*. Oxford: Oxford University Press.

Cinque, Guglielmo. 2002. *Functional structure in DP and IP: The cartography of syntactic structures*, volume 1. Oxford: Oxford University Press.

Citko, Barbara. 2008. Missing labels. *Lingua* 118: 907–944.

Citko, Barbara. 2011. *Symmetry in syntax: Merge, Move, and labels.* Cambridge: Cambridge University Press.

Cleeremans, Axel, and James L. McClelland. 1991. Learning the structure of event sequences. *Journal of Experimental Psychology* 120: 235–253.

Collins, Chris. 1997. *Local economy.* Cambridge, MA: MIT Press.

Collins, Chris. 2002. Eliminating labels. In *Derivation and explanation in the minimalist program,* ed. Samuel David Epstein and T. Daniel Seely, 42–64. Oxford: Blackwell.

Collins, Chris, and Edward Stabler. 2011. A formalization of minimalist syntax. Ms., New York University and University of California, Los Angeles.

Corballis, Michael C. 2007. Recursion, language, and starlings. *Cognive Science* 31: 697–704.

Corina, David P., Erin K. Gibson, Richard Martin, Andrew Poliakov, James Brinkley, and George A. Ojemann. 2005. Dissociation of action and object naming: Evidence from cortical stimulation mapping. *Human Brain Mapping* 24: 1–10.

Dale, Anders M., and Martin I. Sereno. 1993. Improved localization of cortical activity by combining EEG and MEG with MRI cortical surface reconstruction: A linear approach. *Journal of Cognitive Neuroscience* 5: 162–176.

Dapretto, Mirella, and Susan Y. Bookheimer. 1999. Form and content: Dissociating syntax and semantics in sentence comprehension. *Neuron* 24: 427–432.

den Ouden, Dirk-Bart, Dorothee Saur, Wolfgang Mader, Björn Schelter, Sladjana Lukic, Eisha Wali, Jens Timmer, and Cynthia K. Thompson. 2012. Network modulation during complex syntactic processing. *NeuroImage* 59: 815–823.

Elman, Jeffrey L. 1991. Distributed representations, simple recurrent networks, and grammatical structure. *Machine Learning* 7: 195–225.

Embick, David, Alec Marantz, Yasushi Miyashita, Wayne O'Neil, and Kuniyoshi L. Sakai. 2000. A syntactic specialization for Broca's area. *Proceedings of the National Academy of Sciences of the United States of America* 97: 6150–6154.

Epstein, Samuel David, Erich M. Groat, Ruriko Kawashima, and Hisatsugu Kitahara. 1998. *A derivational approach to syntactic relations.* Oxford: Oxford University Press.

Epstein, Samuel David, Hisatsugu Kitahara, and T. Daniel Seely. 2010. Uninterpretable features: What are they and what do they do? In *Exploring crash-proof grammars,* ed. Michael Putnam, 124–142. Amsterdam: John Benjamins.

Epstein, Samuel David, Hisatsugu Kitahara, and T. Daniel Seely. 2012. Structure building that can't be! In *Ways of structure building,* ed. Myriam Uribe-Etxebarria and Vidal Valmala, 253–270. Oxford: Oxford University Press.

Esterman, Michael, Benjamin J. Tamber-Rosenau, Yu-Chin Chiu, and Steven Yantis. 2010. Avoiding non-independence in fMRI data analysis: Leave one subject out. *NeuroImage* 50: 572–576.

Everaert, Martin, and Riny Huybregts. 2013. The design principles of natural language. In *Birdsong, speech, and language: Exploring the evolution of mind and brain,* ed. Johan J. Bolhuis and Martin Everaert, 3–26. Cambridge, MA: MIT Press.

Fitch, W. Tecumseh, Marc D. Hauser, and Noam Chomsky. 2005. The evolution of the language faculty: Clarifications and implications. *Cognition* 97: 179–210.

Flöel, Agnes, Meinou H. de Vries, Jan Scholz, Caterina Breitenstein, and Heidi Johansen-Berg. 2009. White matter integrity in the vicinity of Broca's area predicts grammar learning success. *NeuroImage* 47: 1974–1981.

Friederici, Angela D., Christian J. Fiebach, Matthias Schlesewsky, Ina D. Bornkessel, and D. Yves von Cramon. 2006. Processing linguistic complexity and grammaticality in the left frontal cortex. *Cerebral Cortex* 16: 1709–1717.

Friederici, Angela D., Michiru Makuuchi, and Jörg Bahlmann. 2009. The role of the posterior superior temporal cortex in sentence comprehension. *NeuroReport* 20: 563–568.

Friederici, Angela D., Bertram Opitz, and D. Yves von Cramon. 2000a. Segregating semantic and syntactic aspects of processing in the human brain: An fMRI investigation of different word types. *Cerebral Cortex* 10: 698–705.

Friederici, Angela D., Erdmut Pfeifer, and Anja Hahne. 1993. Event-related brain potentials during natural speech processing: Effects of semantic, morphological and syntactic violations. *Cognitive Brain Research* 1: 183–192.

Friederici, Angela D., Shirley-Ann Rüschemeyer, Anja Hahne, and Christian J. Fiebach. 2003. The role of left inferior frontal and superior temporal cortex in sentence comprehension: Localizing syntactic and semantic processes. *Cerebral Cortex* 13: 170–177.

Friederici, Angela D., Yunhua Wang, Christoph S. Herrmann, Burkhard Maess, and Ulrich Oertel. 2000b. Localization of early syntactic processes in frontal and temporal cortical areas: A magnetoencephalographic study. *Human Brain Mapping* 11: 1–11.

Friston, Karl J., Lee Harrison, and Will Penny. 2003. Dynamic causal modelling. *NeuroImage* 19: 1273–1302.

Friston, Karl J., and Richard N. Henson. 2006. Commentary on: Divide and conquer; a defence of functional localisers. *NeuroImage* 30: 1097–1099.

Friston, Karl J., Andrew P. Holmes, Keith J. Worsley, Jean-Baptiste Poline, Christopher D. Frith, and Richard S.J. Frackowiak. 1995. Statistical parametric maps in functional imaging: A general linear approach. *Human Brain Mapping* 2: 189–210.

Fujita, Koji. 2007. Kaiki-sei kara mieru bunpou-no hattatu to sinka [The development and evolution of grammar in light of recursion]. *Gengo* 36 (11): 16–24.

Fujita, Koji. 2009. A prospect for evolutionary adequacy: Merge and the evolution and development of human language. *Biolinguistics* 3: 128–153.

Fujita, Koji. 2012. Toogoenzan-nooryoku to gengo-nooryoku no sinka [The evolution of the capacity for syntactic operations and linguistic competence]. In *Sinkagengogaku no kootiku: Atarasii ningenkagaku o mezasite* [*Constructing evolutionary linguistics: Toward a new human science*], ed. Koji Fujita and Kazuo Okanoya, 55–75. Tokyo: Hituzi Syobo.

Fujita, Koji. 2013. Evolutionary problems of projection. Paper read at Tokyo Workshop on Biolinguistics, Sophia University, Tokyo.

Fukui, Naoki. 1986/1995. A theory of category projection and its applications. Doctoral dissertation, MIT. Published in 1995 with revisions as *Theory of projection in syntax*, Tokyo: Kurosio Publishers and Stanford: CSLI publications.

Fukui, Naoki. 1988. Deriving the differences between English and Japanese: A case study in parametric syntax. *English Linguistics* 5: 249–270.

Fukui, Naoki. 1993. Parameters and optionality. *Linguistic Inquiry* 24: 399–420. [Reprinted in Fukui (2006).]

Fukui, Naoki. 1995. The principles-and-parameters approach: A comparative syntax of English and Japanese. In *Approaches to language typology*, ed.

Masayoshi Shibatani and Theodora Bynon, 327–372. Oxford: Oxford University Press. [Reprinted in Fukui (2006).]

Fukui, Naoki. 1998. Kyokusyoo-moderu-no tenkai: Gengo-no setumei-riron-o mezasite [The development of a minimalist program: Toward a truly explanatory theory of language]. In *Seisei bunpo* [*Generative grammar*], ed. Yukinori Takubo, Toshiaki Inada, Shigeo Tonoike, Heizo Nakajima, and Naoki Fukui, 161–210. Tokyo: Iwanami Shoten.

Fukui, Naoki. 1999. UG and parametric theory: A plenary lecture at the 118th annual meeting of the Linguistic Society of Japan, Tokyo Metropolitan University. An abridged version was published in 1999 as "Gengo no fuhensei to tayoosei" [Universals and diversity of human language]. *Gengo* 28 (12): 36–43. [Reprinted in Fukui (2012).]

Fukui, Naoki. 2001. Phrase structure. In *The handbook of contemporary syntactic theory*, ed. Mark Baltin and Chris Collins, 374–406. Oxford: Blackwell. [Reprinted in Fukui (2006).]

Fukui, Naoki, ed. 2003. Formal Japanese syntax and universal grammar: The past 20 years. *Lingua Special Issue* 113 (4–6): 315–320.

Fukui, Naoki. 2004. Broca's aphasics: A generative approach. Paper presented at the Sophia International Workshop on Speech Pathology, Sophia University, Tokyo.

Fukui, Naoki. 2005. Embed. Paper presented at the Third International Conference on Formal Linguistics, Hunan University, Changsha.

Fukui, Naoki. 2006. *Theoretical comparative syntax: Studies in macroparameters.* London and New York: Routledge.

Fukui, Naoki. 2008. Gengo no kihon enzan-o meguru oboegaki [Some notes on the basic operations of human language]. In *Gengo kenkyu no genzai: Keisiki to imi no intaafeisu* [*The state of the art in linguistic research: The interface of form and meaning*], ed. Yoshiaki Kaneko, Akira Kikuchi, Daiko Takahashi, Yoshiki Ogawa, and Etsuro Shima, 1–21. Tokyo: Kaitakusha. [Reprinted in Fukui (2012).]

Fukui, Naoki. 2011. Merge and bare phrase structure. In *The Oxford handbook of linguistic minimalism*, ed. Cedric Boeckx, 73–95. Oxford: Oxford University Press. [Chapter 1, this volume.]

Fukui, Naoki. 2012. *Sin sizen kagaku to site no gengogaku: Seisei bunpoo towa nanika* [*A new and expanded edition of linguistics as a natural science: What is generative grammar?*]. Tokyo: Chikumasyoboo.

Fukui, Naoki, and Hiroki Narita. 2012. Merge and (a)symmetry. Paper presented at the Kyoto Conference on Biolinguistics, Kyoto University, March 12, 2012. [Revised and expanded version published as Chapter 2 of this volume.]

Fukui, Naoki, and Hiromu Sakai. 2003. The visibility guideline for functional categories: Verb raising in Japanese and related issues. *Lingua* 113 (4–6): 321–375. [Reprinted in Fukui (2006).]

Fukui, Naoki, and Magaret Speas. 1986. Specifiers and projection. *MIT Working Papers in Linguistics* 8: 128–172. [Reprinted in Fukui (2006).]

Fukui, Naoki, and Yuji Takano. 1998. Symmetry in syntax: Merge and Demerge. *Journal of East Asian Linguistics* 7: 27–86. [Reprinted in Fukui (2006).]

Fukui, Naoki, and Mihoko Zushi. 2003. Yakusya-niyoru zyosetu [Translator's introduction]. In *Seiseibunpou no kuwadate* [*The generative enterprise revisited*], ed. Noam Chomsky and trans. Naoki Fukui and Mihoko Zushi, 1–34. Tokyo: Iwanami Shoten.

Fukui, Naoki, and Mihoko Zushi. 2004. Introduction. [Abridged English translation of Fukui and Zushi 2003.] In *The generative enterprise revisited: A conversation with Riny Huybregts, Henk van Riemsdijk, Naoki Fukui, and Mihoko Zushi*, ed. Noam Chomsky, 1–25. Berlin: Mouton de Gruyter.

Gallego, Ángel J. 2010. *Phase theory*. Amsterdam: John Benjamins.

Gallego, Ángel J., ed. 2012. *Phases: Developing the framework*. Berlin: Mouton de Gruyter.

Gell-Mann, Murray, and Merritt Ruhlen. 2011. The origin and evolution of word order. *Proceedings of the National Academy of Sciences* 108 (42): 17290–17295.

Gentner, Timothy Q., Kimberly M. Fenn, Daniel Margoliash, and Howard C. Nusbaum. 2006. Recursive syntactic pattern learning by songbirds. *Nature* 440: 1204–1207.

George, Leland M. 1980. Analogical generalization in natural language syntax. Doctoral dissertation, MIT.

George, Leland M., and Jaklin Kornfilt. 1981. Finiteness and boundedness in Turkish. In *Binding and filtering*, ed. Frank Heny, 105–127. London: Croom Helm; Cambridge, MA: MIT Press.

Gibson, Edward. 2000. The dependency locality theory: A distance-based theory of linguistic complexity. In *Image, language, brain: Papers from the First Mind Articulation Project Symposium*, ed. Alec Marantz, Yasushi Miyashita, and Wayne O'Neil, 95–126. Cambridge, MA: MIT Press.

Grewe, Tanja, Ina Bornkessel, Stefan Zysset, Richard Wiese, D. Yves von Cramon, Matthias Schlesewsky. 2006. Linguistic prominence and Broca's area: The influence of animacy as a linearization principle. *NeuroImage* 32: 1395–1402.

Griffiths, John D., William D. Marslen-Wilson, Emmanuel A. Stamatakis, and Lorraine K. Tyler. 2013. Functional organization of the neural language system: Dorsal and ventral pathways are critical for syntax. *Cerebral Cortex* 23: 139–147.

Grimshaw, Jane. 2005. Extended projection. In *Words and structure*, ed. Jane Grimshaw, 1–73. Stanford: CSLI.

Gunji, Takao. 1987. *Japanese phrase structure grammar: A unification-based approach*. Dordrecht: D. Reidel Publishing Company.

Hahne, Anja, and Angela D. Friederici. 1999. Electrophysiological evidence for two steps in syntactic analysis: Early automatic and late controlled processes. *Journal of Cognitive Neuroscience* 11: 194–205.

Halle, Morris, and Alec Marantz. 1993. Distributed morphology and the pieces of inflection. In *The view from Building 20*, ed. Kenneth Hale and Samuel Jay Keyser, 111–176. Cambridge, MA: MIT Press.

Hämäläinen, Matti, Riitta Hari, Risto J. Ilmoniemi, Jukka Knuutila, and Olli V. Lounasmaa. 1993. Magnetoencephalography: Theory, instrumentation, and applications to noninvasive studies of the working human brain. *Reviews of Modern Physics* 65: 413–497.

Harris, Zellig S. 1951. *Methods in structural linguistics*. Chicago: University of Chicago Press.

Harris, Zellig S. 1957. Co-occurrence and transformation in linguistic structure. *Language* 33: 283–340. [Reprinted in *The structure of language: Readings in the philosophy of language*, ed. Jerry A. Fodor and Jerrold J. Katz, 155–210. Englewood Cliffs, NJ: Prentice Hall. (1964).]

Harris, Zellig S. 1965. Transformational theory. *Language* 41 (3): 363–401.

Hashimoto, Ryuichiro, and Kuniyoshi L. Sakai. 2002. Specialization in the left prefrontal cortex for sentence comprehension. *Neuron* 35: 589–597.

Hauser, Marc D., Noam Chomsky, and W. Tecumseh Fitch. 2002. The faculty of language: What is it, who has it, and how did it evolve? *Science* 298 (5598): 1569–1579.

Hawkins, John A. 1999. Processing complexity and filler-gap dependencies across grammars. *Language* 75: 244–285.

Helenius, Päivi, Riitta Salmelin, Elisabet Service, and John F. Connolly. 1998. Distinct time courses of word and context comprehension in the left temporal cortex. *Brain* 121: 1133–1142.

Hinzen, Wolfram. 2006. *Mind design and minimal syntax*. Oxford: Oxford University Press.

Hoji, Hajime. 2009. A foundation of generative grammar as an empirical science. Ms., University of Southern California.

Homae, Fumitaka, Ryuichiro Hashimoto, Kyoichi Nakajima, Yasushi Miyashita, and Kuniyoshi L. Sakai. 2002. From perception to sentence comprehension: The convergence of auditory and visual information of language in the left inferior frontal cortex. *NeuroImage* 16: 883–900.

Homae, Fumitaka, Noriaki Yahata, and Kuniyoshi L. Sakai. 2003. Selective enhancement of functional connectivity in the left prefrontal cortex during sentence processing. *NeuroImage* 20: 578–586.

Hopcroft, John E., and Jeffrey D. Ullman. 1979. *Introduction to automata theory, languages, and computation*. Reading, MA: Addison-Wesley.

Hornstein, Norbert. 1998. Movement and chains. *Syntax* 1: 99–127.

Hornstein, Nobert. 2009. *A theory of syntax: Minimal operations and universal grammar*. Cambridge: Cambridge University Press.

Hornstein, Nobert, Jairo Nukes, and Kleanthes K. Grohmann. 2005. *Understanding minimalism*. Cambridge: Cambridge University Press.

Iijima, Kazuki, Naoki Fukui, and Kuniyoshi L. Sakai. 2009. The cortical dynamics in building syntactic structures of sentences: An MEG study in a minimal-pair paradigm. *NeuroImage* 44: 1387–1396. [Chapter 7, this volume.]

Indefrey, Peter, Colin M. Brown, Frauke Hellwig, Katrin Amunts, Hans Herzog, Rüdiger J. Seitz, and Peter Hagoort. 2001a. A neural correlate of syntactic encoding during speech production. *Proceedings of the National Academy of Sciences of the United States of America* 98: 5933–5936.

Indefrey, Peter, Peter Hagoort, Hans Herzog, Rüdiger J. Seitz, and Colin M. Brown. 2001b. Syntactic processing in left prefrontal cortex is independent of lexical meaning. *NeuroImage* 14: 546–555.

Ishii, Toru. 1997. An asymmetry in the composition of phrase structure and its consequences. Doctoral dissertation, University of California, Irvine.

Ivana, Adrian, and Hiromu Sakai. 2007. Honorification and light verbs in Japanese. *Journal of East Asian Linguistics* 16: 171–191.

Jackendoff, Ray. 1977. *X'-syntax: A study of phrase structure*. Cambridge, MA: MIT Press.

Jaeggli, Osvaldo. 1981. *Topics in Romance syntax*. Dordrecht: Foris.

Joshi, Aravind. 1985. How much context-sensitivity is necessary for characterizing structural descriptions. In *Natural language processing: Theoretical, computational and psychological perspectives*, ed. David Dowty, Lauri Karttunen, and Arnold Zwicky, 206–250. New York: Cambridge University Press.

Just, Marcel Adam, Patricia A. Carpenter, Timothy A. Keller, William F. Eddy, and Keith R. Thulborn. 1996. Brain activation modulated by sentence comprehension. *Science* 274: 114–116.

Kang, A. Min, R. Todd Constable, John C. Gore, and Sergey Avrutin. 1999. An event-related fMRI study of implicit phrase-level syntactic and semantic processing. *NeuroImage* 10: 555–561.

Karniski, Walt, R. Clifford Blair, and Arthur David Snider. 1994. An exact statistical method for comparing topographic maps, with any number of subjects and electrodes. *Brain Topography* 6: 203–210.

Kato, Kazuya. 2009. *Fermat-no saisyuuteiri, Sato-Tate yosoo kaiketu-eno miti* [Fermat's last theorem and the paths towards the proof of the Sato-Tate conjecture]. Tokyo: Iwanami Shoten.

Kato, Takaomi. 2006. Symmetries in coordination. Doctoral dissertation, Harvard University.

Kato, Takaomi, Masakazu Kuno, Hiroki Narita, Mihoko Zushi, and Naoki Fukui. 2014. Generalized Search and cyclic derivation by phase: A preliminary study. *Sophia Linguistica* 61: 203–222. Tokyo: Sophia Linguistic Institute for International Communication, Sophia University. [Chapter 3, this volume.]

Kato, Takaomi, Hiroki Narita, Hironobu Kasai, Mihoko Zushi, and Naoki Fukui. 2016. On the primitive operations of syntax. In *Advances in biolinguistics: The human language faculty and its biological basis*, ed. Koji Fujita and Cedric Boeckx, 29–45. London and New York: Routledge.

Kayne, Richard S. 1981. Unambiguous paths. In *Levels of syntactic representation*, ed. Robert May and Jan Koster, 143–183. Dordrecht: Foris.

Kayne, Richard S. 1994. *The antisymmetry of syntax*. Cambridge, MA: MIT Press.

Kayne, Richard S. 2009. Antisymmetry and the lexicon. *Linguistic Variation Yearbook* 8: 1–31. [Reprinted in *The biolinguistic enterprise: New perspectives on the evolution and nature of the human language faculty*. ed. Anna Maria Di Sciullo and Cedric Boeckx, 329–353. Oxford: Oxford University Press. (2011).]

Kayne, Richard S. 2011. Why are there no directionality parameters? In *Proceedings of the 28th West Coast Conference on Formal Linguistics*, ed. Mary Byram Washburn, Katherine McKinney-Bock, Erika Varis, Ann Sawyer, and Barbara Tomaszewicz, 1–23. Somerville, MA: Cascadilla Proceedings Project.

Kinno, Ryuta, Mitsuru Kawamura, Seiji Shioda, and Kuniyoshi L. Sakai. 2008. Neural correlates of noncanonical syntactic processing revealed by a picture-sentence matching task. *Human Brain Mapping* 29: 1015–1027.

Ko, Heejeong. 2005. Syntax of *why-in-situ*: Merge into [Spec, CP] in the overt syntax. *Natural Language and Linguistic Theory* 23: 867–916.

Kriegeskorte, Nikolaus, and Rainer Goebel. 2001. An efficient algorithm for topologically correct segmentation of the cortical sheet in anatomical MR volumes. *NeuroImage* 14: 329–346.

Kriegeskorte, Nikolaus, W. Kyle Simmons, Patrick S. F. Bellgowan, Chris I. Baker. 2009. Circular analysis in systems neuroscience: The dangers of double dipping. *Nature Neuroscience* 12: 535–540.

Kuno, Susumu. 1973. *The structure of the Japanese language*. Cambridge, MA: MIT Press.

Kuroda, S.-Y. 1965. Generative grammatical studies in the Japanese language. Doctoral dissertation, MIT.

Kuroda, S.-Y. 1976. A topological study of phrase-structure languages. *Information and Control* 30: 307–379.

Kuroda, S.-Y. 1988. Whether we agree or not: A comparative syntax of English and Japanese. *Linguisticae Investigationes* 12: 1–47. [Reprinted in Kuroda (1992a).]

Kuroda, S.-Y. 1992a. *Japanese syntax and semantics: Collected papers.* Dordrecht: Kluwer.

Kuroda, S.-Y. 1992b. On Japanese passives. In *Japanese syntax and semantics: Collected papers*, 183–221. Dordrecht: Kluwer.

Kuroda, S.-Y. 2008. Suugaku to seiseibunpoo: Setumeiteki datoosei-no kanatani sosite gengo-no suugakuteki zituzairon [Mathematics and generative grammar: Beyond explanatory adequacy and mathematical realism of language] (with an extended English summary). *Sophia Linguistica* 56: 1–36.

Kvålseth, Tarald O. 1985. Cautionary note about R^2. *The American Statistician* 39: 279–285.

Lasnik, Howard. 1999. Chains of arguments. In *Working minimalism*, ed. Samuel D. Epstein and Norbert Hornstein, 189–215. Cambridge, MA: MIT Press.

Lebeaux, David. 1991. Relative clauses, licensing, and the nature of the derivation. In *Perspectives on phrase structure: Heads and licensing*, ed. Susan Rothstein, 209–239. New York: Academic Press.

Lechner, Winfried. 2006. An interpretive effect of head movement. In *Phases of interpretation*, ed. Mara Frascarelli, 45–70. Berlin: Mouton de Gruyter.

Lee, Hwee Ling, Joseph T. Devlin, Clare Shakeshaft, Lauren H. Stewart, Amanda Brennan, Jen Glensman, Katherine Pitcher, Jenny Crinion, Andrea Mechelli, Richard S.J. Frackowiak, David W. Green, and Cathy J. Price. 2007. Anatomical traces of vocabulary acquisition in the adolescent brain. *The Journal of Neuroscience* 27: 1184–1189.

Lewis, Richard, and Mineharu Nakayama. 2002. Syntactic and positional similarity effects in the processing of Japanese embeddings. In *Sentence processing in East Asian languages*, ed. Mineharu Nakayama, 85–111. Stanford: CSLI Publications.

Lohndal, Terje. 2012. Without specifiers: Phrase structure and events. Doctoral dissertation, University of Maryland, College Park.

Lyons, John. 1968. *Introduction to theoretical linguistics.* Cambridge: Cambridge University Press.

Mailhot, Frédéric, and Charles Reiss. 2007. Computing long-distance dependencies in vowel harmony. *Biolinguistics* 1: 28–48.

Mandelbrot, Benoit B. 1977. *The fractal geometry of nature.* New York: W.H. Freeman and Company.

Marantz, Alec. 1984. *On the nature of grammatical relations.* Cambridge, MA: MIT Press.

Matushansky, Ora. 2006. Head movement in linguistic theory. *Linguistic Inquiry* 37: 69–109.

Miller, George A., and Noam Chomsky. 1963. Finitary models of language users. In *Handbook of mathematical psychology*, volume II, ed. R. Duncan Luce, Robert R. Bush, and Eugene Galanter, 419–491. New York: John Wiley and Sons.

Miyagawa, Shigeru, and Mamoru Saito, ed. 2008. *The handbook of Japanese linguistics.* Oxford: Oxford University Press.

Miyamoto, Edison T. 2002. Case markers as clause boundary inducers in Japanese. *Journal of Psycholinguistic Research* 31: 307–347.

Momo, Kanako, Hiromu Sakai, and Kuniyoshi L. Sakai. 2008. Syntax in a native language still continues to develop in adults: Honorification judgment in Japanese. *Brain and Language* 107: 81–89.

Moro, Andrea. 2000. *Dynamic antisymmetry*. Cambridge, MA: MIT Press.

Musso, Mariacristina, Andrea Moro, Volkmar Glauche, Michel Rijntjes, Jürgen Reichenbach, Christian Büchel, and Cornelius Weiller. 2003. Broca's area and the language instinct. *Nature Neuroscience* 6: 774–781.

Muysken, Pieter. 1982. Parametrizing the notion 'head'. *Journal of Linguistic Research* 2: 57–75.

Narita, Hiroki. 2009a. Full interpretation of optimal labeling. *Biolinguistics* 3: 213–254.

Narita, Hiroki. 2009b. Multiple transfer in service of recursive Merge. Paper presented at the 32nd GLOW Colloquium. Abstract published in *GLOW Newsletter* 62: 89–91.

Narita, Hiroki. 2010a. Phase cycles in service of projection-free syntax. Ms., Harvard University.

Narita, Hiroki. 2010b. The tension between explanatory and biological adequacy: Review of Fukui (2006). *Lingua* 120: 1313–1323.

Narita, Hiroki. 2011. Phasing in full interpretation. Doctoral dissertation, Harvard University (Downloadable at http://ling.auf.net/lingBuzz/001304).

Narita, Hiroki. 2012a. Remarks on the nature of headedness and compositionality in bare phrase structure. *Proceedings of Sophia University Linguistic Society* 26: 81–126.

Narita, Hiroki. 2012b. Phase cycles in service of projection-free syntax. In *Phases: Developing the framework*, ed. Ángel J. Gallego, 125–172. Berlin: Mouton de Gruyter.

Narita, Hiroki. 2014. *Endocentric structuring of projection-free syntax*. Amsterdam: John Benjamins.

Narita, Hiroki, and Koji Fujita. 2010. A naturalist reconstruction of minimalist and evolutionary biolinguistics. *Biolinguistics* 4: 356–376.

Narita, Hiroki, and Naoki Fukui. 2016. Feature-equilibria in syntax. In *Advances in biolinguistics: The human language faculty and its biological basis*, ed. Koji Fujita and Cedric Boeckx, 9–28. London and New York: Routledge.

Narita, Hiroki, and Naoki Fukui. forthcoming. *Symmetry-driven syntax*. London and New York: Routledge.

Nevins, Andrew. 2010. *Locality in vowel harmony*. Cambridge, MA: MIT Press.

Newman, Sharlene D., Marcel Adam Just, Timothy A. Keller, Jennifer Roth, and Patricia A. Carpenter. 2003. Differential effects of syntactic and semantic processing on the subregions of Broca's area. *Cognitive Brain Ressearch* 16: 297–307.

Nichols, Thomas E., and Andrew P. Holmes. 2002. Nonparametric permutation tests for functional neuroimaging: A primer with examples. *Human Brain Mapping* 15: 1–25.

O'Doherty, John, Morten L. Kringelbach, Edmund T. Rolls, Julia Hornak, and Caroline Andrews. 2001. Abstract reward and punishment representations in the human orbitofrontal cortex. *Nature Neuroscience* 4: 95–102.

O'Grady, William, John Archibald, Mark Aronoff, and Janie Rees-Miller. 2010. *Contemporary linguistics: An introduction*, 6th edition. Boston: Bedford/St. Martin's.

Ohta, Shinri, Naoki Fukui, and Kuniyoshi L. Sakai. 2013a. Syntactic computation in the human brain: The degree of merger as a key factor. *PLoS One* 8 (2): 1–16. [Chapter 8, this volume.]

Ohta, Shinri, Naoki Fukui, and Kuniyoshi L. Sakai. 2013b. Computational principles of syntax in the regions specialized for language: Integrating theoretical linguistics and functional neuroimaging. *Frontiers in Behavioral Neuroscience* 7 (204): 1–13. [Chapter 9, this volume.]

Ohta, Shinri, Masatomi Iizawa, Kazuki Iijima, Tomoya Nakai, Naoki Fukui, Mihoko Zushi, Hiroki Narita, and Kuniyoshi L. Sakai. 2014. An on-going research: The experimental design. Paper presented at the CREST Workshop with Noam Chomsky, The University of Tokyo.

Oka, Toshifusa. 1993. Shallowness. *MIT Working Papers in Linguistics* 19: 255–320.

Oldfield, Richard Charles. 1971. The assessment and analysis of handedness: The Edinburgh inventory. *Neuropsychologia* 9: 97–113.

Ott, Dennis. 2012. *Local instability.* Berlin and New York: Walter de Gruyter.

Pallier, Christophe, Anne-Dominique Devauchelle, and Stanislas Dehaene. 2011. Cortical representation of the constituent structure of sentences. *Proceedings of the National Academy of Sciences of the United States of America* 108: 2522–2527.

Pantazis, Dimitrios, Thomas E. Nichols, Sylvain Baillet, and Richard M. Leahy. 2005. A comparison of random field theory and permutation methods for the statistical analysis of MEG data. *NeuroImage* 25: 383–394.

Pattamadilok, Chotiga, Iris N. Knierim, Keith J. Kawabata Duncan, and Joseph T. Devlin. 2010. How does learning to read affect speech perception? *The Journal of Neuroscience* 30: 8435–8444.

Penny, Will D., Klaas E. Stephan, Jean Daunizeau, Maria J. Rosa, Karl J. Friston, Thomas M. Schofield, and Alex P. Leff. 2010. Comparing families of dynamic causal models. *PLoS Computational Biololy* 6 (3): 1–14.

Petersson, Karl Magnus, Christian Forkstam, and Martin Ingvar. 2004. Artificial syntactic violations activate Broca's region. *Cognitive Science* 28: 383–407.

Pesetsky, David. 1982. Paths and categories. Doctoral dissertation, MIT.

Pesetsky, David, and Esther Torrego. 2001. T-to-C movement: Causes and consequences. In *Ken Hale: A life in language*, ed. Michael Kenstowicz, 355–426. Cambridge, MA: MIT Press.

Pesetsky, David, and Esther Torrego. 2004. Tense, case, and the nature of syntactic categories. In *The syntax of time*, ed. Jacqueline Gueron and Jacqueline Lecarme, 495–538. Cambridge, MA: MIT Press.

Post, Emil L. 1943. Formal deductions of the general combinatorial decision problem. *American Journal of Mathematics* 65 (2): 197–215.

Pylkkänen, Liina, and Alec Marantz. 2003. Tracking the time course of word recognition with MEG. *Trends in Cognitive Science* 7: 187–189.

Quine, Willard V.O. 1940. *Mathematical logic.* Cambridge, MA: Harvard University Press.

Reinhart, Tanya. 1976. Syntactic domain of anaphora. Doctoral dissertation, MIT.

Reinhart, Tanya. 1983. *Anaphora and semantic interpretation.* London: Croom Helm.

Reinhart, Tanya. 1987. Specifier and operator binding. In *The representation of (in) definiteness*, ed. Eric J. Reuland and Alice G. B. ter Meulen, 130–167. Cambridge, MA: MIT Press.

Richards, Marc D. 2004. Object shift, scrambling, and symmetrical syntax. Doctoral dissertation, University of Cambridge.

Richards, Marc D. 2007a. Dynamic linearization and the shape of phases. *Linguistic Analysis* 33: 209–237.

Richards, Marc D. 2007b. On feature inheritance: An argument from the phase impenetrability condition. *Linguistic Inquiry* 38: 563–572.

Richards, Norvin. 2001. *Movement in language: Interactions and architectures.* Oxford: Oxford University Press.

Rizzi, Luigi. 1990. *Relativized minimality.* Cambridge, MA: MIT Press.

Rizzi, Luigi. 1997. The fine structure of the left periphery. In *Elements of grammar: Handbook of generative syntax*, ed. Liliane Haegeman, 281–337. Dordrecht: Kluwer.

Rizzi, Luigi, ed. 2004. *The structure of CP and IP: The cartography of syntactic structures*, volume 2. Oxford: Oxford University Press.

Rizzi, Luigi. 2006. On the form of chains: Criterial positions and ECP effects. In *Wh-movement: Moving on*, ed. Lisa Lai-Shen Cheng and Norbert Corver, 97–133. Cambridge, MA: MIT Press.

Roberts, Ian. 2010. *Agreement and head movement: Clitics, incorporation, and defective goals.* Cambridge, MA: MIT Press.

Röder, Brigitte, Oliver Stock, Helen Neville, Siegfried Bien, and Frank Rösler. 2002. Brain activation modulated by the comprehension of normal and pseudo-word sentences of different processing demands: A functional magnetic resonance imaging study. *NeuroImage* 15: 1003–1014.

Rodriguez, Paul. 2001. Simple recurrent networks learn context-free and context-sensitive languages by counting. *Neural Computation* 13: 2093–2118.

Rooryck, Johan, and Guido Vanden Wyngaerd. 2011. *Dissolving binding theory.* Oxford and New York: Oxford University Press.

Saito, Mamoru, and Naoki Fukui. 1998. Order in phrase structure and movement. *Linguistic Inquiry* 29: 439–474. [Reprinted in Fukui (2006).]

Sakai, Kuniyoshi L. 2005. Language acquisition and brain development. *Science* 310: 815–819.

Sakai, Kuniyoshi L., Yasuki Noguchi, Tatsuya Takeuchi, and Eiju Watanabe. 2002. Selective priming of syntactic processing by event-related transcranial magnetic stimulation of Broca's area. *Neuron* 35: 1177–1182.

Samuels, Bridget. 2011. *Phonological architecture: A biolinguistic approach.* Oxford: Oxford University Press.

Santi, Andrea, and Yosef Grodzinsky. 2010. fMRI adaptation dissociates syntactic complexity dimensions. *NeuroImage* 51: 1285–1293.

Saur, Dorothee, Björn W. Kreher, Susanne Schnell, Dorothee Kümmerer, Philipp Kellmeyer, Magnus-Sebastian Vry, Rosa Umarova, Mariacristina Musso, Volkmar Glauche, Stefanie Abel, Walter Huber, Michel Rijntjes, Jürgen Hennig, and Cornelius Weiller. 2008. Ventral and dorsal pathways for language. *Proceedings of the National Academy of Sciences of the United States of America* 105: 18035–18040.

Seely, T. Daniel. 2006. Merge, derivational c-command, and subcategorization in a label-free syntax. In *Minimalist essays*, ed. Cedric Boeckx, 182–217. Amsterdam: John Benjamins.

Shibatani, Masayoshi. 1990. *The languages of Japan*. Cambridge: Cambridge University Press.

Shlonsky, Ur, and Gabriela Soare. 2011. Where's 'why'? *Linguistic Inquiry* 42: 651–669.

Smith, Stephen M., Mark Jenkinson, Mark W. Woolrich, Christian F. Beckmann, Timothy E. J. Behrens, Heidi Johansen-Berg, Peter R. Bannister, Marilena De Luca, Ivana Drobnjak, David E. Flitney, Rami K. Niazy, James Saunders, John Vickers, Yongyue Zhang, Nicola De Stefano, J. Michael Brady, and Paul M. Matthews. 2004. Advances in functional and structural MR image analysis and implementation as FSL. *NeuroImage* 23: S208–S219.

Speas, Margaret J. 1986. Adjunctions and projections in syntax. Doctoral dissertation, MIT.

Speas, Margaret J. 1990. *Phrase structure in natural language*. Dordrecht: Kluwer.

Stabler, Edward. 2004. Varieties of crossing dependencies: Structure dependence and mild context sensitivity. *Cognitive Science* 28: 699–720.

Stabler, Edward. 2010. Computational perspectives on minimalism. In *The Oxford handbook of linguistic minimalism*, ed. Cedric Boeckx, 617–641. Oxford: Oxford University Press.

Starke, Michal. 2004. On the inexistence of specifiers and the nature of heads. In *Structures and beyond: The cartography of syntactic structures*, volume 3, ed. Adriana Belletti, 252–268. Oxford: Oxford University Press.

Stephan, Klaas E., John C. Marshall, Will D. Penny, Karl J. Friston, and Gereon R. Fink. 2007. Interhemispheric integration of visual processing during task-driven lateralization. *The Journal of Neuroscience* 27: 3512–3522.

Stowell, Tim. 1981. Origins of phrase structure. Doctoral dissertation, MIT.

Stromswold, Karin, David Caplan, Nathaniel Alpert, and Scott Rauch. 1996. Localization of syntactic comprehension by positron emission tomography. *Brain and Language* 52: 452–473.

Suzuki, Kei, and Kuniyoshi L. Sakai. 2003. An event-related fMRI study of explicit syntactic processing of normal/anomalous sentences in contrast to implicit syntactic processing. *Cerebral Cortex* 13: 517–526.

Svenonius, Peter. 2003. Limits on P: Filling in holes vs. falling in holes. *Nordlyd* 31 (2): 431–445.

Svenonius, Peter. 2010. Spatial P in English. In *Mapping spatial PPs: The cartography of syntactic structures*, volume 6, ed. Guglielmo Cinque and Luigi Rizzi, 127–161. Oxford: Oxford University Press.

Szabolcsi, Anna. 1984. The possessor that ran away from home. *The Linguistic Review* 3: 89–102.

Takano, Yuji. 1996. Movement and parametric variation in syntax. Doctoral dissertation, University of California, Irvine.

Talairach, Jean, and Pierre Tournoux. 1988. *Co-planar stereotaxic atlas of the human brain. 3-dimensional proportional system: An approach to cerebral imaging*. Stuttgart: Thieme.

Tatsuno, Yoshinori, and Kuniyoshi L. Sakai. 2005. Language-related activations in the left prefrontal regions are differentially modulated by age, proficiency, and task demands. *The Journal of Neuroscience* 25: 1637–1644.

Thompson, Cynthia K., Borna Bonakdarpour, Stepehn C. Fix, Henrike Blumenfeld, Todd B. Parrish, Darren R. Gitelman, and M.-Marsel Mesulam. 2007. Neural correlates of verb argument structure processing. *Journal of Cognitive Neuroscience* 19: 1753–1768.

Tsujimura, Natsuko. 2007. *An introduction to Japanese linguistics*, 2nd edition. Malden, MA: Blackwell.

Tzourio-Mazoyer, Nathalie, Brigitte. Landeau, Dimitri Papathanassiou, Fabrice Crivello, Olivier Etard, Nicolas Delcroix, Bernard Mazoyer, and Marc Joliot. 2002. Automated anatomical labeling of activations in SPM using a macroscopic anatomical parcellation of the MNI MRI single-subject brain. *NeuroImage* 15: 273–289.

Uehara, Keiko, and Dianne C. Bradley. 2002. Center-embedding problem and the contribution of nominative case repetition. In *Sentence processing in East Asian languages*, ed. Mineharu Nakayama, 257–287. Stanford: CSLI Publications.

Ura, Hiroyuki. 1994a. Superraising in Japanese. *MIT Working papers in Linguistics* 24: 355–374.

Ura, Hiroyuki. 1994b. Hyper-raising and the theory of *pro*. *MIT Working Papers in Linguistics* 23: 297–316.

Ura, Hiroyuki. 1996. Multiple feature checking: A theory of grammatical function splitting. Doctoral dissertation, MIT.

Uriagereka, Juan. 1999. Multiple spell-out. In *Working minimalism*, ed. Samuel David Epstein and Norbert Hornstein, 251–282. Cambridge, MA: MIT Press.

Uriagereka, Juan. 2002. *Derivations*. London: Routledge.

van Riemsdijk, Henk. 1998a. Categorial feature magnetism: The endocentricity and distribution of projections. *Journal of Comparative Germanic Linguistics* 2: 1–48.

van Riemsdijk, Henk. 1998b. Head movement and adjacency. *Natural Language and Linguistic Theory* 16: 633–678.

Vergnaud, Jean-Roger. 1977/2008. Letter to Noam Chomsky and Howard Lasnik on "Filters and Control," April 17, 1977. Reprinted in *Foundational issues in linguistic theory*, ed. Robert Freidin, Carlos Otero, and Maria Luisa Zubizarreta, 3–15. Cambridge, MA: MIT Press.

Walton, Mark E., Joseph T. Devlin, and Matthew F. S. Rushworth. 2004. Interactions between decision making and performance monitoring within prefrontal cortex. *Nature Neuroscience* 7: 1259–1265.

Weil, André. 1949. Numbers of solutions of equations in finite fields. *Bulletin of the American Mathematical Society* 55: 497–508. [Reprinted in *Oeuvres scientifiques: Collected papers*, volume 1, 399–410. New York: Springer. (1979).]

Wells, Rulon S. 1947. Immediate constituents. *Language* 23: 81–117. [Reprinted in *Readings in linguistics: The development of descriptive linguistics since 1925*, ed. Martin Joos, 186–207. Washington, DC: American Council of Learned Societies (1957).]

Wilson, Stephen M., Sebastiano Galantucci, Maria Carmela Tartaglia, Kindle Rising, Dianne K. Patterson, Maya L. Henry, Jennifer M. Ogar, Jessica DeLeon, Bruce L. Miller, and Maria Luisa Gorno-Tempini. 2011. Syntactic processing depends on dorsal language tracts. *Neuron* 72: 397–403.

Wong, Francis C. K., Bharath Chandrasekaran, Kyla Garibaldi, and Patrick C. M. Wong. 2011. White matter anisotropy in the ventral language pathway predicts sound-to-word learning success. *The Journal of Neuroscience* 31: 8780–8785.

Yngve, Victor H. 1960. A model and an hypothesis for language structure. *Proceedings of the American Philosophical Society* 104: 444–466.

Author Index

Subject Index